NO MAN'S LAND 1 · THE WAR OF THE WORDS

NO MAN'S LAND

The Place of the Woman Writer
in the Twentieth Century

Volume 1 • The War of the Words

SANDRA M. GILBERT AND SUSAN GUBAR

Yale University Press • New Haven and London

The authors gratefully acknowledge permission to reprint material from the following sources: From "The Walls Do Not Fall" by H. D., from *H. D. Collected Poems, 1912–1944*, copyright © 1982 by the Estate of Hilda Doolittle. Reprinted by permission of New Directions Publishing Corporation. From "The Sisters" by Amy Lowell, in *The Complete Poetical Works of Amy Lowell*, copyright © 1955 by Houghton Mifflin Company; copyright © 1983 renewed by Houghton Mifflin Company, Brinton P. Roberts, Esquire, and G. D'Andelot Belin, Esquire. Reprinted by permission of Houghton Mifflin Company. From the following articles by Sandra M. Gilbert and Susan Gubar: "Tradition and the Female Talent," *Literary History: Theory and Practice*, volume 2 of the *Proceedings of the Center for Literary Studies*. Reprinted by permission of the Center for Literary Studies, Department of English, Northeastern University; " 'Forward Into the Past': The Complex Female Affiliation Complex," copyright © 1985, Jerome McGann, ed. *Historical Studies and Literary Criticism* (Madison: The University of Wisconsin Press); "Ceremonies of the Alphabet: Female Grandmatologies and the Female Authorgraph," *New York Literary Forum*, 13–14; "Sexual Linguistics," *New Literary History*, volume XVI (Spring 1985, No. 3). From Sandra M. Gilbert, "Woman's Sentencing, Man's Sentence," from *Virginia Woolf and Bloomsbury*, Jane Marcus, ed. copyright © 1984. Reprinted by permission of Indiana University Press. The drawings from "The War Between Men and Women" in *Men, Women and Dogs* by James Thurber in *Vintage Thurber*, copyright © Hamish Hamilton 1963, are reproduced by permission.

Set in Baskerville type by David E. Seham Associates. Printed in the United States of America by Vail-Ballou Press, Binghamton, N.Y.

Library of Congress Cataloging-in-Publication Data

Gilbert, Sandra M.
   No man's land.
   Includes index.
   Contents: v. 1. The war of the words.
   1. English literature—Women authors—History and
criticism.   2. English literature—20th century—History and
criticism.   3. American literature—Women authors—History and
criticism.   4. American literature—20th century—History and
criticism.   5. Women and literature—Great Britain.   6. Women and
literature—United States.   7. Feminism and literature—Great
Britain.   8. Feminism and literature—United States.   I. Gubar, Susan,
1944–   II. Title.
PR116.G5   1987   820'.9'9287   87–10560
ISBN 0–300–04005–9 (v. 1 : cloth)
      0–300–04587–5 (pbk.)

The paper in this book meets the guidelines for permanence and durability of the Committee on Production Guidelines for Book Longevity of the Council on Library Resources.

10   9   8   7   6   5

In memory of
Alexis J. Mortola and Frank W. David

The woman had been set free. . . . One had but to pass a week in Florida, or on any of a hundred huge ocean steamers, or walk through the Place Vendome, or join a party of Cook's tourists to Jerusalem, to see that the woman had been set free. . . . Behind them, in every city, town and farmhouse, were myriads of new types,—or type-writers,— telephone and telegraph-girls, shopclerks, factory hands, running into millions on millions, and, as classes, unknown to themselves as to historians. . . . all these new women had been created since 1840; all were to show their meaning before 1940.

—Henry Adams, *The Education of Henry Adams*

The history of men's opposition to women's emancipation is more interesting perhaps than the story of that emancipation itself. An amusing book might be made of it if some young student at Girton or Newnham would collect examples and deduce a theory—but she would need thick gloves on her hands, and bars to protect her of solid gold.

—Virginia Woolf, *A Room of One's Own*

Perhaps the greatest revolution of modern times is the emancipation of women; and perhaps the deepest fight for two thousand years and more, has been the fight for woman's independence, or freedom, call it what you will. The fight was deeply bitter and, it seems to me, it is won. It is even going beyond, and becoming a tyranny of woman, of the individual woman in the house, and of the feminine ideas and ideals in the world.

—D. H. Lawrence, *"The Real Thing"*

Some people think that women are the cause of modernism, whatever that is.

—*New York Evening Sun,* February 13, 1917

Contents

Preface

This book is intended as the first part of a three-volume sequel to *The Madwoman in the Attic,* our study of the woman writer and the nineteenth-century literary imagination. When, in 1979, we embarked on the project, we were naively certain that we could produce a volume comparable in length to *The Madwoman,* and that we could do so in just a few years. Despite comical colleagues who insisted that it would be hard to construct "Daughter of Madwoman" or "Madwoman Meets Abbott and Costello" (or even "Madwoman Meets the Lost Generation"), we forged ahead, only to discover that we had to confront a host of problems: what exactly *is* the canon of twentieth-century literature by women, given that increasing numbers of women have entered the literary marketplace in the last one hundred years and that so many reputations are still in flux? how can we disentangle ourselves from a history in which we ourselves are enmeshed? and finally, considering that at last it is, and has for some time been, evident that women do have a literary tradition, what have been the diverse effects of that tradition on both female and male talents?

As we explored these issues, we saw with some alarm that our enterprise had significantly expanded. We had, now, to discuss not just literary history but social history; we had, also, to examine not just the writings of women in the twentieth century but the texts and contexts associated with those men who have long been considered the most canonical modernists. In fact, we had to rethink everything we had ever been taught about twentieth-century literature. Consequently, what had been planned as a single volume split itself, in a kind of surprising intellectual mitosis, into three books:

the one published here and two others that are intended as parts of the same whole.

More specifically, in this volume—*The War of the Words*—we offer an overview of social, literary, and linguistic interactions between men and women from the middle of the nineteenth century to the present, and in doing so we attempt to theorize about the ways in which modernism, because of the distinctive social and cultural changes to which it responds, is differently inflected for male and female writers. Indeed, we will argue here that, especially in the twentieth century, both women and men engendered words and works which continually sought to come to terms with, and find terms for, an ongoing battle of the sexes that was set in motion by the late nineteenth-century rise of feminism and the fall of Victorian concepts of "femininity."

In particular, we will suggest that the literary phenomenon ordinarily called "modernism" is itself—though no doubt overdetermined—for men as much as for women a product of the sexual battle that we are describing here, as are the linguistic experiments usually attributed to the revolutionary poetics of the so-called avant-garde. We should note, however, that because this introductory volume deals with such a mass of material, and because the forthcoming books will devote entire chapters to key figures, our readings here must often be brief. Rather than analyzing major texts in detail, we have frequently chosen to focus on stories and poems whose configurations allow us to lay the groundwork for the fuller interpretations to come later. We should mention, too, that because of the complexity of the issues we are exploring here, we have departed from our usual mode of composition: instead of drafting chapters separately and then exchanging and revising them, we have written all five chapters collaboratively.

The next two of the three books that we have planned will be entitled, respectively, *Sexchanges* and *Letters from the Front*. In *Sexchanges*, through readings of Rider Haggard, Olive Schreiner, Charlotte Perkins Gilman, Kate Chopin, Willa Cather, Edith Wharton, and a number of writers associated either with the Great War or with the emergence of a lesbian literary tradition, we will trace in greater detail than we do here literary responses to the social and cultural metamorphoses that created the phenomenon known as modernism. Then, in *Letters from the Front,* we will study the flowering of feminist modernism in the works of such writers as Virginia Woolf, Zora Neale Hurston, Edna St. Vincent Millay, Marianne Moore, and H. D., as well as the move beyond modernism that was made by Sylvia Plath and a number of other daughters of the early twentieth century's aesthetic regiment of women. Taken together, all three books will, we hope, help to illuminate the radical transformations of culture that we must all continue to face, transformations that have made not just the territory of literature but the institutions of marriage and the family, of education and the professions, into a no man's land—a vexed terrain—in which scattered armies of men and women all too often clash by day and by night.

That we continue to inhabit such a no man's land means that the subject matter of this book may be as emotionally charged for our readers as it has sometimes been for us. Because the sex antagonisms dramatized in late nineteenth- and twentieth-century literature in England and America are often disturbingly bitter, it is tempting to want to reproach authorial or fictive combatants on one side or another for their respectively misogynistic or misandric stances. Yet, in doing this work, we have concluded that, no matter what a militant writer's position may be, it is precisely his or her belligerent passion that generates texts marked by compelling intensity—often, indeed, by aesthetic excellence. To be sure, doctrinaire politics can, as we all know, deform creativity, yet the productions of most of the writers we discuss in this volume—masculinist as well as feminist—prove to us that ideology must be disentangled from evaluation. What some feminists now call "positive role models" don't always make for great literature, and effective works of art don't always say what readers think they should. As critics who are describing the frequently controversial texts discussed here, therefore, we are, we should stress, *de*scribing, not *pre*scibing, for our ultimate goal is to record and analyze the history that has made all of us who we are.

We should explain here, then, that the account of sexual battle we will be offering in all three volumes of *No Man's Land* is based on two assumptions: first, that there is a knowable history and, second, that texts are authored by people whose lives and minds are affected by the material conditions of that history. Both these assumptions have lately been challenged, of course: on the one hand by thinkers who claim that all accounts of history are arbitrary fictions, and on the other hand by theorists who deny the reality of the author while assigning ultimate authority to the text and its reader. In our view, both these challenges to history and authorship, radically antipatriarchal as they may seem, ultimately erase the reality of gendered human experience. For if all history is fictive, how can we trace the changing dynamics of the relationship between the sexes in patriarchal culture? And if the author is also a fiction, how can we define the ways in which texts are as marked by the maker's gender as they are by the historical moment in which they were produced or by the generic conventions to which they adhere?

After all, even before such thinkers as Hayden White, Roland Barthes, and Jacques Derrida sought to deconstruct naïve concepts of history and authorship, a number of literary critics dealt with texts as if they were autonomous and universal monuments of un-aging intellect, and it was precisely that practice which often distorted their understanding of the period about which we are writing in this book. Privileging certain turn-of-the-century and twentieth-century works as purely aesthetic or philosophic objects and repressing significant aspects of the history in which the authors of these works were engaged, many readers and teachers failed to perceive the sexual struggle that, as we shall claim, influences much of the literature written between the mid-nineteenth century and the present. Once we reimagine the author as a gendered human being whose text reflects key cultural conditions, we can conflate and collate individual literary narratives, so that they constitute one possible metastory, a story of stories about gender strife in this period. In our view, the history of sexual battle that we shall relate here is one of the major tales that begins to emerge from the apparent chaos of history, and it is a tale told differently over time and formulated differently by men and women.

In spite of—or, indeed, in the midst of—this battle, our work has been enriched and enlivened by the advice and counsel of many friends, both male and female. Specifically, our thinking in this volume has profited from extensive comments on the whole manuscript by Carolyn Heilbrun and Garrett Stewart, as well as from comments on individual chapters by Joanne Feit Diehl, Donald Gray, James

Kincaid, Lawrence Lipking, and Elaine Showalter. In addition, we are grateful for both suggestions and support from Elyse Blankley, Harold Bloom, Ralph Cohen, Natalie Davis, Mary Davidson, Geoffrey Hartman, A. Walton Litz, Mary Jo Weaver, and many others whom we thank in our notes. Without the skeptical and energetic intervention of our students—in a 1981 NEH Summer Seminar, at the School of Criticism and Theory in 1984, at Indiana University, at the University of California at Davis, at Princeton University, and at the Johns Hopkins University—the project would have been less exciting. And without support from the National Endowment for the Humanities, the Rockefeller and Guggenheim Foundations, and the Indiana Commission for the Humanities, it simply could not have been pursued. Further, as collaborators who must travel in order to write together, we are especially grateful to many institutions that have offered us hospitality, in particular, to Barnard College, to the University of Delaware, to Georgetown University, to the University of Kansas, to the University of Notre Dame, and to Smith College. Similarly, our work would have been made much more difficult without essential financial help from the University of California, Davis, from Indiana University, from Tufts University, and from Princeton University.

Equally to the point, we must acknowledge with thanks the contributions of our exemplary research assistants, Alice Falk (at Indiana), Marjorie Howes (at Princeton), and Helen Sword (at Princeton), as well as the dedicated labors of our excellent manuscript editor, Judith Calvert, and the continuing encouragement of both Tina Weiner and John Ryden at Yale University Press. Most important here, Ellen Graham, our longstanding editor at the Press, has never failed to be a patient, affectionate, and inspiring presence in our lives as we struggled to bring this volume to completion. Finally, as we pursued this project, we learned a great deal from our husbands: Elliot L. Gilbert nobly contributed ideas, references, and interpretations while also being consistently supportive throughout all the minor crises of daily life that marked the writing process; Edward Gubar methodically and patiently guided us through all the intricacies of word processing, in particular helping to make our two systems compatible; both continually forced us to confront the implications of our ideas. In addition, as we worked, we were constantly heartened by the resilience, optimism, and generosity of our children, Roger, Katherine, and Susanna Gilbert; Molly and Simone Gubar. We are grateful, also, for the acts of attention our mothers—Angela Mortola and Luise David—continue to bestow upon us, and for the fierce survival instincts they have bequeathed us. But to the memory of our fathers—Alexis J. Mortola and Frank W. David—two men who lived through some of the most painful years that we will be describing in these volumes, and the two men who first taught us to love men, we dedicate this book.

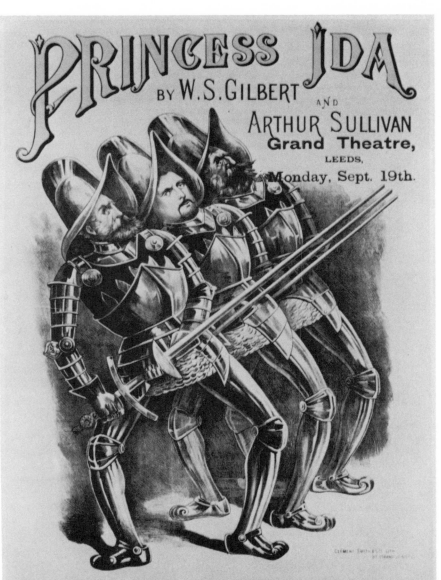

PRINCESS IDA

BY W.S. GILBERT

AND ARTHUR SULLIVAN

Grand Theatre,

LEEDS,

Monday, Sept. 19th.

D·OYLY·CARTE'S·OPERA·COMPANY·

Illustration on preceding page: *Princess Ida*. Poster for the production by D'Oyly Carte's Opera Company. Courtesy of the Pierpont Morgan Library. The Gilbert and Sullivan Collection.

1 The Battle of the Sexes: The Men's Case

Fight for your life, men. Fight your wife out of her own self-conscious preoccupation with herself. Batter her out of it till she's stunned.
—D. H. Lawrence

No age can ever have been as stridently sex-conscious as our own; those innumerable books by men about women in the British Museum are a proof of it. The Suffrage campaign was no doubt to blame. It must have aroused in men an extraordinary desire for self-assertion; it must have made them lay an emphasis upon their own sex and its characteristics which they would not have troubled to think about had they not been challenged. And when one is challenged, even by a few women in black bonnets, one retaliates, if one has never been challenged before, rather excessively.
—Virginia Woolf

No relationship between a man and a woman can survive if they don't know how to fight. This means each has to be fierce. In our culture, it is usually the woman who is willing to be fierce and not the man. The man now has to learn how to be fierce.
—Robert Bly

Is a pen a metaphorical pistol? Are words weapons with which the sexes have fought over territory and authority? As if to imply such notions, Ted Hughes, now the poet laureate of England, published in *Crow* (1971) a poem ironically entitled "Lovesong," in which western culture's traditional, Petrarchan song of love, with its narrative of male/female romance, becomes a sardonic song of hate:

His words were occupying armies
Her laughs were an assassin's attempts

3

His looks were bullets daggers of revenge
Her glances were ghosts in the corner with horrible secrets
His whispers were whips and jackboots
Her kisses were lawyers steadily writing[.][1]

Hughes's military metaphors—(male) words as armies, (female) laughs as assassin's attempts—seem to dramatize a sexual conflict in which one would not expect so official a representative of literary culture as a poet laureate ever to have been a combatant, even if he were, like Hughes, the onetime husband of such a dauntingly competitive female artist as Sylvia Plath. Making the best of a bad personal bargain, Hughes might merely have been crowing over his defeat of a woman whose "love tricks were the grinding of locks." But, in fact, his poem is just one of a number of texts which focus on a dialectic that has for the last century or so impelled, imperiled, and, paradoxically enough, even empowered writers of both sexes. Reflecting a crucial shift in mid-nineteenth-century Anglo-American society, this sexual struggle became a key theme in late Victorian literature and ultimately a shaping element in modernist and post-modernist literature. Indeed, to many late nineteenth- and early twentieth-century men, women seemed to be agents of an alien world that evoked anger and anguish, while to women in those years men appeared as aggrieved defenders of an indefensible order. Thus both male and female writers increasingly represented women's unprecedented invasion of the public sphere as a battle of the sexes, a battle over a zone that could only be defined as a no man's land.

Ultimately, though neither sex could definitively imagine either victory or defeat—the twentieth century has not produced a monolithic "story" about the conquest of one sex by the other—different periods can be said to have resolved the plot of sexual struggle in distinctive ways. Mid-Victorian writers of both sexes tended to dramatize a defeat of the female, while turn-of-the-century authors began to envision the possibility of women's triumph. Interestingly, that possibility appears to have filled men with such dread that they had to produce especially ferocious fantasies about female defeat even though women did not elaborate fantasies about their own victory with any special confidence. At the height of the modernist era, however, both sexes by and large agreed that women were winning, while postmodernist male and female writers, working in the 1940s and 1950s, reimagined masculine victory. Finally, contemporary artists, influenced by the second wave of feminism, began again to conceive of feminine triumph. Whichever side they championed, though, all these writers evinced a militant urgency that made their texts especially compelling.

The plot of sexual battle is of course as old as literature itself. From the legendary Lilith, who resists Adam's (and God's) wish to control both her body and her language, to the rebellious women of Aristophanes' *Lysistrata* and the mythical Amazons who secede from, and war upon, patriarchal culture, women have often been depicted as militants and frequently as warriors fighting men who would subordinate them. Throughout literary history, however, such conflicts have often been either tropes for erotic duelling—almost forms of foreplay—or dramatizations of the viciousness of unleashed female desire and the virtue of female chastity. A long poem by the fourth-century Greek poet Quintus Smyrnaeus gives a characteristic account of the defeat of the Amazon Penthesilea by the heroic Achilles: though in life Penthesilea boasted that she was "insatiate of the battle-cry" because "my might is more than any man's," in death she becomes seductive, "as fair and sweet" as the wives of Greek soldiers seem when "laid on the bed of love." Again, in Tasso's *Gerusalemme Liberata* (1580) the Christian hero Tancred unknowingly fights and kills Clorinda, an Islamic woman whom he loves. Their struggle functions like a seduction, with the revelation of the woman's identity and her subsequent death in the arms of her antagonist figuring as a sexual consummation comparable to a climactic "little death."[2]

In just the years when the Italian poet was erotically fetishizing the dead woman warrior, moreover, an English artist was using a living Amazon as a monitory figure to inveigh against female eroticism. Spenser's lustful Radigund in *The Faerie Queene* (1596) defeats the "Elfin knight" Artegall, forcing him to dress as a woman, and she herself can only be defeated by the chaste and righteous woman warrior Britomart, who reinstates male rule and repeals "the liberty of women . . . which they [the lustful Amazons] had long usurpt."[3]

Even more dramatically, Heinrich von Kleist's *Penthesilea* (1808) revises Greek accounts of the battle between Achilles and Penthesilea
to show that the Amazon's desire to combat Achilles arises from
uncontrollable, even cannibalistic, sexual passion; arriving with dogs
and elephants to engage in what the hero had thought would be a
mock duel, Penthesilea falls upon Achilles, tearing and biting at him
"in ghastly rivalry" with her hounds, exclaiming "Kissing—biting—
/ Where is the difference?" But when she realizes that he is now
nothing more than a mangled corpse, she kills herself, consumed
by "the hot, biting venom of remorse."[4] Thus, whether the female
will-to-battle, manifested by characters as diverse as Clorinda, Radigund, and Penthesilea, arises from sexual recalcitrance or sensual
eagerness, it is historically rooted in male ideas about female sexuality, specifically in the male notion that dead women are desirable
and live women should not desire.

   In fact, it is not really until the moment in the mid-nineteenth
century when female resistance becomes feminist rebellion that the
battle of the sexes emerges as a trope for struggle over political as
well as personal power. At this point, Tennyson—himself on the
verge of becoming, as poet laureate, an official spokesman for his
society—records a tale of sexual battle whose contours of hostility
interestingly prefigure the antagonisms at the center of Hughes's
"Lovesong." *The Princess: A Medley* (1847–51) tells the story of Prince
Hilarion's efforts to woo and win Princess Ida, a protofeminist who
has withdrawn from her father's court with a retinue of other ladies,
"All wild to found an University."[5] Refusing to see men—over her
gate she has placed a Dantesque inscription warning "LET NO MAN
ENTER IN ON PAIN OF DEATH" (II.178)—she writes, according to her
bewildered father, "awful odes . . . and rhymes / And dismal lyrics,
prophesying change / Beyond all reason" (I.137–42). Accompanied
by his two friends Cyril and Florian, Hilarion dresses as a woman
and penetrates Ida's citadel, but the true identities of the interlopers
are revealed when Cyril drinks too much wine and begins "To troll
a careless, careless tavern-catch . . . Unmeet for ladies" (IV.139–41).
Although shortly after this episode Hilarion saves Ida from drowning when she falls into a river while fleeing him, she has him and
his companions arrested. Then, when his father threatens that he
will "pluck [her] palace down . . . unless you send us back / Our son,

on the instant, whole" (IV.395–97), she declares that if necessary she will "Unfurl the maiden banner of our rights, / And clad in iron burst the ranks of war, / Or, falling protomartyr of our cause, / Die" (IV.482–85).

In the ensuing battle (into which the prince only reluctantly enters), he, along with Cyril and Florian, is vanquished by Ida's brother Arac and Arac's men, who descend upon Hilarion like "a pillar of electric cloud" (V.513), while the princess herself, standing "Between a cymball'd Miriam and a Jael," watches, "No saint—inexorable— no tenderness— / Too hard, too cruel" (V.500, 504–05). Later, however, after exulting "Our enemies have fallen, have fallen," Ida decides that "We will be liberal since our rights are won" and agrees to nurse her former foes. Thus her "sanctuary" is "violated" by the presence of men, her "fair college turn'd to hospital" (VI.17, 52; VII.1–2).[6] Worse still, as the prince lingers on the threshold of death, she discovers that she has a womanly heart, she is divested of her former pretensions—"Her false self slipt from her like a robe" (VII.146)—and, in the nakedness of a reborn femininity, she submits to the prince's courtship. But now, in response to her explanation that "She still were loth to yield herself to one / That wholly scorn'd to help their equal rights / Against the sons of men and barbarous laws" (VII.217–19), the prince assures her that "Henceforth thou hast a helper, me, that know / The woman's cause is man's" (VII.242–43). Though she must renounce her dream of equality— "This proud watchword rest / Of equal; seeing either sex alone / Is half itself, and in true marriage lies / Nor equal nor unequal"—he will teach her to become an "Interpreter between the gods and men" like the mother whom he adored, and she will help him "accomplish" his "manhood" (VII.303, 344).

As should be clear from this summary, the outcome of the battle Tennyson describes is on the surface indeterminate, since the defeated prince has made the woman's cause his own at the same time that the presumably victorious princess has yielded up her cherished autonomy and abandoned her dream of a female intellectual community. It is no wonder that early critics of the poem were confounded as to Tennyson's intentions and that even now some readers (generally male) see the work as feminist, others (usually female) as misogynist.[7] Indeed, as if anticipating such reactions, Tennyson himself built a gender-specific interpretive disagreement into the frame narrative which surrounds Hilarion's and Ida's story. The tale of *The Princess* is told by seven college men at a summer festival that a large landowner has given for friends, neighbors, and villagers, while the interpolated lyrics are sung by women listeners "To give [the men] breathing-space" (Prol. 236). More specifically, the theme of the tale is a response to one young woman's exclamation " 'O, I wish / That I were some great princess, I would build / Far off from men a college like a man's, / And I would teach them all that men are taught; / We are twice as quick!' " (Prol. 133–37) Inevitably, then, the women have one view of the story, the men another: the women wish the narrator to produce a text celebrating "A gallant fight, a noble princess—Why / Not make her true-heroic, true-sublime?" but the men "required that I should give throughout / [A] sort of mock-heroic gigantesque." Ultimately, torn by a feud "Betwixt the mockers and the realists," the author-surrogate, like the author himself, moves "as in a strange diagonal" (Concl. 19–20, 10–11, 24, 27).

The direction of Tennyson's strange diagonal, however, is at least covertly revealed by a number of elements in his "medley" which directly or indirectly subvert the prince's espousal of the princess's cause. For one thing, from part I to part VI, we are insistently reminded that Hilarion's masculinity is in some sense problematic. Introducing himself as "fair in face . . . with lengths of yellow ringlets like a girl," he confides that all his life he has suffered from "weird seizures" in which "I seem'd to move among a world of ghosts, / And feel myself a shadow of a dream" (I.1–3; 14–18).[8] Dazed and insubstantial, he is threatened with hallucinations that would deprive him of his potency, so that his transvestite dress becomes as much a sign of victimized unmanliness as it is a strategy for victimizing conquest, a point actually made by one of Ida's brothers when he taunts Hilarion with the claim that "The woman's garment hid the woman's heart" (V.295). Then, after having been wounded by "the pillar of electric cloud" that is the phallic Arac—Ida's older brother, who is not only a member of her family but acts as a quasisexual "member" for Ida—Hilarion languishes like an invalid lady on his sickbed, "well-nigh close to death / For weakness," staring helplessly at walls "wherein were wrought / Two grand designs . . . on one side arose / The women up in wild revolt, and storm'd / At the Oppian law. Titanic shapes, they cramm'd / The forum, and half-crush'd among the rest / A dwarf-like Cato cower'd. On the other side / Hortensia spoke against the tax; behind / A train of dames" (VII.104–13).

That the prince is tormented by visions of Titanic women and dwarfed men makes sense, however, in terms of another element in his story, an element which reveals again the direction of Tennyson's strange diagonal. Although Ida's students and tutors speak with loving reverence of such notable women as Socrates's teacher Diotima and the Biblical Vashti, they themselves are often described as either physically or morally monstrous. Ida, for instance, sitting on her throne with a single jewel on her brow burning like a "prophet of storm," and "a handmaid on each side . . . combing out her long black hair," is attended by "Eight daughters of the plough, stronger than men, / Huge, blowzed with health, and wind, and rain, / And labor. Each was like a Druid rock" (IV.252–61). And it is this monstrous regiment who evict him and his friends from the princess's palace as unceremoniously as any nightclub bouncer. Equally monstrous, though, is Ida's advisor and sometime governess Lady Blanche, a would-be philosopher queen whose quasi-erudition is a mask for naked ambition, and whose fierce rivalry with the princess's friend Lady Psyche demonstrates the divisiveness that, Tennyson implies, would split apart even the most apparently pacific community of women. Significantly, too, Blanche's ascendency over the princess was achieved because of the failure of patriarchal authority: Ida's father, Gama, is shown to be "swamp'd in lazy tolerance," a tolerance that, according to the prince's father, King Hildebrand, leads to social chaos, for "When the man wants weight, the woman takes it up, / And topples down the scales" (V.433–35).

King Hildebrand's judgment is confirmed by the vision of French misrule which is incorporated into the conclusion of the poem. Looking at "the skirts of France" from the point of view of an England associated with "duty," "faith," "reverence for the laws," and "civic manhood firm against the crowd," one of Tennyson's speakers shudderingly connects the monstrosities of social unrest and political revolution with Ida's feminist restlessness and naive idealism. Inhabited by a scared king, cowardly soldiers, and irrational citizens,

France is a kingdom that "topples over with a shriek," the prey to "revolts, republics, revolutions" that are as mad as the dreams of "our wild Princess" so that, gazing at the channel, this young man blesses "the narrow sea which keeps her off" (Concl. 51–69). Even before this point is made, however, Tennyson's strange diagonal has dramatized another cultural disruption threatened by the monstrosity of female self-will. Lady Psyche, one of the few purely "good" women at the college, is the widowed mother of a two-year-old daughter from whom Ida vindictively separates her after Psyche fails to reveal the masculinity of the three disguised interlopers. In the context of Victorian pieties, this action implies that Tennyson regards female intellectual aspiration as having the potential to sunder even the most sacred bond, the bond between mother and child.

It is not irrelevant, therefore, that Ida's redemption from feminism is brought about at least in part when she tries to wean the child from its mother and paradoxically learns the joys of motherhood as well as when she resolves to conform to Hilarion's idealized vision of his dead mother. As one critic remarked in 1884, "Psyche's baby is the conquering heroine of the epic"; in fact, waxing eloquent, he exclaimed, "O fatal babe! more fatal to the hopes of woman than the doomful horse to the proud towers of Ilion; for through thee the walls of pride are breached, and all the conquering affections flock in."[9] But finally, too, by learning to love Psyche's child and striving to emulate not only Psyche's maternal benevolence but also Hilarion's mother's goodness, Ida comes to repudiate purely intellectual education. In the end her loving submissiveness cures the prince of his seizures and creates his so far uncreated masculinity, a consummation which suggests that, for Tennyson, maleness ultimately requires a primacy based on female secondariness.

Interestingly, even when *The Princess* is read as one of Tennyson's statements about art, the aesthetic its author is celebrating and certifying seems to involve a differentiation of an implicitly masculine and responsible Victorian authority from an explicitly feminine and irresponsibly passive Romantic creativity. As Jerome Buckley argues, Princess Ida's initial frigidity echoes the "cold aestheticism"—and, we might add, the *spätromantische* solipsism—of the female soul who anxiously inhabits "The Palace of Art."[10] Learning to love Hilarion, the poet Ida is taught to reject the isolation of the Romantic imagination symbolized by her proud self-will and, by acquiescing in her proper role as Hilarion's helpmate, to join in a community based on the Carlylean imperative to "Work while it is called Today; for the Night cometh, wherein no man can work."[11] Reflecting Tennyson's own sense of ambivalent belatedness toward his great Romantic precursors, Ida, like the soul in the Palace of Art, shows the way in which mid-nineteenth-century male anxiety about paternal influence may have been sexualized. Implicitly redefining the Romantic poet not only as an effeminate but as a female figure, Tennyson hints that his male precursor is curiously comparable to a selfish woman who needs direction from the revitalized man of action, the proto-Victorian sage.

How did Tennyson's filial worries happen to merge with sexual ones? Biographical answers might of course abound, but more general historical replies are ultimately more useful. Surely it is not merely coincidental that 1847, the year of *The Princess*'s first publication, saw also the appearance of Charlotte Brontë's Byronically feminist *Jane Eyre*, whose heroine stalks apart in joyless revery, proclaiming that

> Women are supposed to be very calm generally: but women feel just as men feel; they need exercise for their faculties and a field for their efforts as much as their brothers do; they suffer from too rigid a restraint, too abstract a stagnation, precisely as men would suffer; and it is narrow-minded in their more privileged fellow-creatures to say that they ought to confine themselves to making puddings and knitting stockings, to playing on the piano and embroidering bags. It is thoughtless to condemn them, or laugh at them, if they seek to do more or learn more than custom has pronounced necessary for their sex. [ch. 12]

Jane's protest articulated the dissatisfactions of an era that had been marked by the French Revolution (1789), the publication of Mary Wollstonecraft's *A Vindication of the Rights of Woman* (1792), Percy Bysshe Shelley's *Prometheus Unbound* (1820), Caroline Norton's *The Natural Right of a Mother to the Custody of her Child* (1837), and Margaret Fuller's *Woman in the Nineteenth Century* (1845). Indeed, as John Killham has argued, *The Princess* "is closely connected with the sacrifice of her fair fame by one woman—the Hon. Mrs. Caroline Norton" (who became notorious for her unexpectedly vigorous custody battle with her estranged husband) and with the appearance at Tennyson's Cambridge and elsewhere in early Victorian England of a number of tracts that were beginning to debate the pros and cons of what was later to be called "the woman question."[12]

A year after the first publication of *The Princess*, moreover, Elizabeth Cady Stanton and Susan B. Anthony were to summon the first women's rights convention at Seneca Falls, New York, an event to which an 1855 critic of the poem would allude in the *Edinburgh Review*, remarking that the work was full of "noise about 'women's rights,' which even now ceases to make itself heard anywhere but in the refuge of exploded European absurdities beyond the Atlantic."[13] In fact, despite the sangfroid of this writer, the "European absurdities" associated with the struggle for women's rights were only to gain in intensity after the publication of Tennyson's poem. And that both aesthetic Romanticism and political revolution should have been implicitly or explicitly linked by Tennyson's narrator to Ida's rebellion was perhaps inevitable. The Romantic movement, with its concerns about imaginative autonomy, sexual freedom, and political revolution, had plainly fostered an atmosphere in which long-standing feminist demands could be articulated with new fervor. In addition, as Leslie Fiedler has observed, the Romantic emphasis on Wordsworthian "wise passiveness" and mysterious natural origins fueled a resurrection of "matriarchal" ideals and thus an implicit redefinition of female power that might well have been inspiring to women, whose femininity had almost always before been imagined as a negative rather than a positive force, an absence rather than a presence.[14]

Certainly, within a few years of the appearance of *The Princess*, early feminists like Barbara Bodichon and Emily Davies had confirmed its author's sense that women would soon plan a battle for equal rights which would involve an invasion of male bastions of higher education. Just when Tennyson was writing *The Princess*, the founders of the Governesses' Benevolent Institution were initiating a series of "Lectures to Ladies" which would rapidly evolve into

Queens College for Women in London. In addition, throughout
the mid-century, while various groups of women were agitating for
colleges of their own at Cambridge and Oxford (with similar groups
working to start women's colleges in the United States), Florence
Nightingale was establishing nurse's training institutions; the Englishwomen Sophia Jex-Blake and Elizabeth Garrett were following
the American pioneer Elizabeth Blackwell into medical schools;
Harriet Taylor and John Stuart Mill were attacking "the subjection
of women"; and Barbara Bodichon was helping to organize committees and journals to seek women's suffrage. But even in the 1840s,
Charles Kingsley, who would later praise *The Princess* for its censorious depiction of a woman taking "her stand on the false masculine ground of intellect," was lecturing at Queens College "because
he believed in the higher education of women" while at the same
time Elizabeth Barrett Browning was celebrating the achievements
of the rebellious French novelist George Sand and publishing
learned essays on the Greek Christian poets.[15] By 1870, Girton College had been established at Cambridge, followed by Newnham
College and, at Oxford, Somerville and Lady Margaret Hall; by
1884, women had the right to do degree-level work at both major
British universities (though they were not yet granted degrees). As
early as 1870, moreover, the Victorian moralist Nicholas Francis
Cooke warned, as if in response to these developments, that "if carried out in actual practice, this matter of 'Woman's Rights' " will
cause woman to "become rapidly unsexed and degraded. . . ; she
will cease to be the gentle mother, and become the Amazonian
brawler."[16]

   It seems fitting, therefore, that in 1884 a "respectful Operatic
Perversion of Tennyson's *Princess*" opened at the Savoy Theatre in
London.[17] Gilbert and Sullivan's *Princess Ida*, a revision of Gilbert's
1870 dramatization of *The Princess*, rewrites Tennyson to eliminate
the strange diagonal through which the laureate had mediated between feminism and misogyny, between his female and his male
readers. In fact, coming down strongly on the side of the "mockers"
rather than the "realists," the famous collaborators produced hilarious parodies of all of Tennyson's characters while transforming his
plot so as to leave the inhabitants of the princess's college—here
sardonically called Castle Adamant—with no illusions of female

freedom. From the first, too, Gilbert links Ida's feminism with madness and misrule.[18] Swearing that "woman . . . shall conquer Man," she commands her acolytes to "Let all your things misfit, and you yourselves / At inconvenient moments come undone."[19] But her comic philosophy of costume ("Let hairpins lose their virtue: let the hook / Disdain the fascination of the eye—") leads, as she herself declares, to a general advocacy of social disorder: "Let old associations all dissolve . . . let Chaos come again!" That the projects of her school are presented from a neo-Swiftian perspective as bizarre, even impossible, reinforces the idea that female intellectual autonomy contradicts the natural order of things. Among other endeavors, the ladies "in this College / [Of] useful knowledge" forswear fashion in order to concentrate on "send[ing] a wire / To the moon," "set[ting] the Thames on fire," and "squar[ing] the circle." Even more grotesquely, "the little pigs they're teaching / For to fly . . . And the niggers they'll be bleaching, / By and by"—all jobs, Gilbert implies, as impossible as their major plan to "repudiate the Tyrant / Known as man" (267).

Equally bizarre from Gilbert and Sullivan's point of view is this female community's concept of man himself. Lady Psyche, who is here revised so that instead of being a "good" woman she is a half-cracked Professor of Humanities, articulates with pseudo-Popeian solemnity the lunatic misandry that presumably motivates the school's feminist separatism. Proclaiming that "Man's a ribald—Man's a rake, / Man is Nature's sole mistake!," Psyche goes on to retell the story of Genesis with decidedly female complacency, using Darwin as a stick to beat her male antagonists with. Her myth of origin involves a lady of high lineage and an unsightly ape; about their failed relationship, she concludes that

> . . . the Maiden fair, whom the monkey crav'd,
>   Was a radiant Being,
>   With a brain far-seeing—
> While Darwinian Man
>   Though well-behaved,
> At best is only a monkey shaved!   [273]

As for her counterpart, Lady Blanche, who is here a Professor of Abstract Science, she broods ineffectually throughout the operetta on "the five Subjunctive Possibilities— / The May, the Might, the

Would, the Could, the Should" (293–4) while cattily singing "hoity, toity" about her rivalrous feelings toward Psyche.

The atmosphere created by these women inevitably unmans *Princess Ida*'s men throughout most of the action. After Hilarion, Cyril, and Florian engage in a burlesque turn as maidens "pure and simple," Ida's moronic brother Arac prepares for battle by doing a kind of military striptease in which he flings off his helmet, his cuirass, his brassets, and some leg pieces about which he confesses "I quite forget their name." As he makes himself increasingly vulnerable to the accompaniment of an ironically Handelian melody, the chorus enthusiastically assents to his decisions: "Yes, yes, yes, / So off goes that cuirass" (292–93). But of course Arac's foolishness reflects his relationship to his sister, a woman who is ultimately shown to be as weak as he.

Indeed, where Tennyson's Arac was a "pillar of electric cloud" who manifested Ida's threatening potency and defeated Hilarion in combat, Gilbert and Sullivan's Arac loses the battle of the sexes for Ida in the operetta's most significant swerve from its source text. Hilarion's concluding speech summarizes the implications of the princess's defeat: "Madam, you placed your trust in woman—well, / Woman has failed you utterly—try Man" (294). At the same time, the prince's father makes a speech which explains another crucial Gilbert and Sullivan revision of Tennyson. Where *The Princess* had had as its hopeful "heroine" Psyche's "fatal babe," the women of Castle Adamant have no children and seem to have forgotten about the need to reproduce their community. "If you enlist all women in your cause, / And make them all abjure tyrannic Man," observes the king, "The obvious question then arises, How / Is [your] Posterity to be provided?" (294). Female intellectual pretension, Gilbert and Sullivan imply, leads to biological sterility, even to a form of race suicide, and only the proper—that is, traditionally hierarchical— love between the sexes makes the world go round and on.

The contrast between Tennyson's strange diagonal, on the one hand, and Gilbert and Sullivan's straightforward mockery, on the other, can no doubt be explained not only by Gilbert's well-known conservatism but also by male worry about the increasingly intense feminist activity that marked the years between 1847 and 1884. What Tennyson had felt might be imminent was experienced by the Savoyards as actual, as an Amazonian movement from the private to the public sphere that had to be met with defensive jeers and aggressive insults. Gilbert and Sullivan had always, of course, chosen timely targets, ranging from Parliament to the navy, the aesthetic movement, and the late nineteenth-century fad for "all one sees / That's Japanese."[20] Their selection of women's demand for, and entrance into, higher education as an issue to satirize, therefore, underlines the centrality of the so-called "woman question" in the last quarter of the nineteenth century. That Gilbert was conscious of the unprecedented existence of college-educated women is revealed by his creation in *Utopia Ltd.* (1893) of a princess who has been educated at Girton, where, as she explains to one of her suitors, "all is wheat, and idle chaff is never heard within its walls" (542). But such a transformation of Tennyson's fantasy into a reality must have been unnerving and certainly may have impelled the author of *Princess Ida* to substitute for the laureate's claim that "The woman's cause is man's" the anxious (and mendacious) assertion that Hilarion implicitly directs to female audiences as well as to the ladies of Castle Adamant: "Woman has failed you utterly. . . ."

To make matters worse, women's educational advances were clearly matched by gains on other fronts, a fact that was symbolized in the year of *Utopia Ltd.*'s premiere by the opening of the Woman's Building at the World's Columbian Exposition in Chicago.[21] The first public edifice entirely administered, designed, and decorated by women, this real-life version of Castle Adamant recorded and celebrated women's entrance into the arts and professions, science and industry. Among works by visual artists, the building included Mary Cassatt's mural depicting women plucking the fruits of knowledge, Adelaide McFayden Johnson's busts of the "Founding Mothers," and Anna Whitney's memorial sculpture of Harriet Beecher Stowe. In addition, the building held a kind of feminist-critical library—the first American collection of women's books to have been assembled by women—as well as a British Nurses' Exhibit, a model kitchen, an ethnographic display, and an Invention Room memorializing Josephine Cochran's dishwashing machine, Harriet Ruth Tracey's sewing machine, and Maria Mitchell's discovery of a new comet in 1847, precisely the year when Tennyson published *The Princess*. Finally, this museum of female achievement offered a few items of interest which were slightly more exotic or eccentric than most of its intensely serious holdings—for instance, a photograph of the Grand Canyon taken by a woman suspended from a rope, and a memoir by Kate Marsden entitled *By Sleigh and Horseback to Outcast Siberian Lepers.* The entrance of the "gentler sex" into unknown territory, these objects demonstrated, was not only figurative but literal, so that a world that had previously been a male empire might now become a no man's land, a disputed domain.

It was in 1893, the year when both *Utopia Ltd.* and the Woman's Building opened, that the niece of the same Charles Kingsley who had deplored the "false masculinity" of Tennyson's heroine made a dramatic decision: Mary Kingsley seriously committed herself to a career of exploration and scientific research in West Africa.[22] And unlike those of such earlier, splendid eccentrics as Mary Wortley Montague, her travels were paradigmatic rather than privileged, representative rather than idiosyncratic. Her nineteenth-century predecessors included Marie Pardis, who climbed Mont Blanc in 1808 and then opened a refreshment stand near the foot of the mountain; Mrs. Cole, who published *A Lady's Tour Round Mont Rosa* in 1858 to encourage other women to undertake similar journeys; Isabella Bird, who traveled on horseback across the Rockies in 1873; and May French Sheldon, who studied native crafts during her four journeys around the world, in spite of the fact that people "boldly denounced [her] as *mad.*"[23] As defensive as Gilbert and Sullivan, the Royal Geographic Society was less than enthusiastic about welcoming such madwomen into its ranks:

A lady explorer? A traveler in skirts?
The notion's just a trifle too seraphic;
Let them stay and mind the babies or hem our ragged shirts;
But they mustn't, they can't, and shan't be geographic.[24]

Yet the subtext of the female territorial imperative was brought to the surface by one Fanny Bullock Workman when in 1912 she had herself photographed on a Himalayan pass in the Karakoran with a "Votes for Women" placard.

For of course women's invasion of new fields and lands was directly associated with the most ferocious literal battle between the sexes: the suffrage struggle. Occupying the attention of thinkers on both sides of the Atlantic between 1847 and 1920, this conflict, as amply documented by historians, was always intensely heated and often became brutally physical.[25] Slashing the Rokeby Venus, burning letters in letterboxes, flinging themselves in front of racehorses, requiring to be force-fed, smashing the windows of government buildings with bricks, and—most important—meeting and marching by the thousands, women demanded social and political rights not only in militant rhetoric but also through physical militancy. "English women were much criticized for using force in the battle for the franchise," remembered Virginia Woolf in *Three Guineas* (1938), noting that

> When in 1910 Mr. Birrell had his hat "reduced to pulp" and his shins kicked by suffragettes, Sir Almeric Fitzroy commented, "an attack of this character upon a defenseless old man by an organized band of 'janissaries' will, it is hoped, convince many people of the insane and anarchical spirit actuating the movement." [148]

Nevertheless, from stories of the hatchet-wielding Carrie Nation who led the quasi-feminist Temperance Movement in America to tales of British suffragists taunting and tormenting Lloyd George, examples of female militancy could probably be multiplied indefinitely.

Ultimately, although these militants were represented as battle axes in popular magazines and newspapers (figure, p. 19), their crusades for "the Cause" had not only a political but a deep social— that is, aesthetic, familial, economic—impact. Perhaps most obviously, the intensity of the suffrage struggle was reflected in popular culture through the proliferation of male-authored dystopias and female-authored utopias about sexual battle and female rule. As Katherine Stern has shown in a fine essay on this subject, in the years 1882–90 and 1905–10, "periods which saw the first mobilisation and the radical crisis of the British women's suffrage movement . . . the number of popular novels . . . with titles such as *The War of the Sexes, The Sex Triumphant, When Women Reign* . . . suggests the degree to which, at the turn of the century, women"—or at least the problems raised by women—"*were* the future."[26]

Such a phenomenon, however, was one that a range of proto-feminist male thinkers in both England and America had already anticipated. As early as 1859, Emily Dickinson's famous "mentor,"

·LIFE·

Militants

AS THEY ARE

AS THEY THINK THEY ARE

Rodney Thomson
with apologies to
Orson Lowell

AS THEY APPEAR TO THE POLICE AND SHOPKEEPERS

Rodney Thomson. *Militants*. Cartoon. *Life Magazine*, volume 61, no. 1587, March 27, 1913.

Thomas Wentworth Higginson, produced a pioneering essay entitled "Ought Women to Learn the Alphabet?" in which he observed, "There can be no question that the present epoch is initiating an empire of the higher reason, of arts, affections, aspirations; and for that epoch the genius of woman has been reserved." Yet, he added, though "Everybody sees that the times are altering the whole material position of woman . . . most people do not appear to see the inevitable social and moral changes which are also involved."[27] Ten years later, John Stuart Mill made a comparable point. Calling for women's legal and political rights in *The Subjection of Women* (1869), he nonetheless noted that "the feelings connected with this subject [are] the most intense and most deeply-rooted of all those which gather round and protect old institutions and customs."[28]

Within a decade, George Meredith, recreating Caroline Norton as a feminist heroine in *Diana of the Crossways* (1885) and parodying patriarchal pretensions to authority in *The Egoist* (1879), had documented a significant change in "old institutions and customs." By the turn of the century, the American historian Henry Adams was able to be more specific about social transformations that, in his view, had already occurred, though he too understood their impact to be both deep and deeply problematic. "The woman had been set free," wrote Adams in 1903 in a passage we have used as an epigraph for this volume, adding that

> One had but to pass a week in Florida, or on any of a hundred huge ocean steamers, or walk through the Place Vendome, or join a party of Cook's tourists to Jerusalem, to see that the woman had been set free. . . . At Washington, one saw other swarms as grave gatherings of Dames or Daughters, taking themselves seriously. . . . Behind them, in every city, town and farmhouse, were myriads of new types,—or type-writers,— telephone and telegraph-girls, shop-clerks, factory hands, running into millions on millions, and, as classes, unknown to themselves as to historians. . . . All these new women had been created since 1840; all were to show their meaning before 1940.[29]

But of course the suffrage battle was itself one of the "meanings" implicit in the "new women" whose entrance into public history Adams, along with such other turn-of-the-century male thinkers as

Samuel Butler and George Bernard Shaw, had commented on with interest.

Yet despite the clarity and the often vigorous sympathy with which these earlier observers had meditated on the changing dynamics of sex relations, few recent historians have grasped the profundity of the social metamorphoses brought about by "new women" and, in particular, by their struggle for the vote. Instead, historians and literary critics have traditionally associated the problems of so-called "modernity" with "the long withdrawing roar" of "the Sea of Faith," with Darwinian visions of "Nature, red in tooth and claw," with the discontents fostered by an industrial civilization, with the enemies within the self that were defined by Freud, and ultimately with the no man's land of the Great War. But while all these phenomena did, of course, shape the twentieth century as an age of anxiety, their meaning is notably altered when they are juxtaposed with what Samuel Hynes has called "the vast change that took place in the relations between the sexes and in the place of women in English [and, we would add, American] society in the years before the War."[30] That these intellectual and social crises should be related to such change, and more specifically to the sexual battle it fostered, is a point implicitly made by one of the few contemporary thinkers besides Hynes who has acknowledged the importance of the woman problem.

In a classic essay, "The Hard and the Soft: The Force of Feminism in Modern Times," Theodore Roszak observes that

> by the late nineteenth century . . . this supposedly marginal curiosity called the "woman problem" had become one of the most earth-shaking debates in the Western world, fully as ex-plosive an issue as the class or national conflicts of the day. Here, after all, was the world's largest oppressed "minority" threatening mutiny: something no man could ignore. And none did. . . . The "woman problem" was argued about, shouted about, raved about, agonized about, endlessly, endlessly. By the final decades of the century, it permeated everything.[31]

But to the extent that the " 'woman problem' . . . permeated every-thing," it must have seemed like part of the shredding fabric of patriarchal authority, for by the turn of the century "the Sea of Faith" had withdrawn when God the *Father* disappeared, and Darwin had shown that man is not a lord of the universe but a "monkey shav'd." In addition, during the first two decades of the twentieth century, the Captains of Industry were being threatened by rebellious troops of laborers, Freud was claiming that sons secretly resented and feared fathers, and eventually a generation of sons was destroyed in battle.

Even in the first decade of the century, in such radical texts as Otto Weininger's widely read and influential *Sex and Character* (1904; trans. 1906) and in such extremist movements as protofascist Italian Futurism—a movement whose masculinism Roszak documents—we can see the connection between the disintegration of traditional patriarchal assumptions and the apparently marginal "woman problem." We would argue that Weininger's claim—"Women have no existence and no essence; they are not, they are nothing. . . . Woman has no share in ontological reality"—attained what Ford Madox Ford contemptuously called an "epidemic" popularity among "Young Liberals" because it solved, by repressing, the problem that was woman, and thereby proved to "Liberals" what, despite their ostensible politics, they secretly wanted to believe: that, in Ford's ironic phrase, "Miss Pankhurst was a very naughty girl indeed."[32] We would argue, further, that Filippo Marinetti's 1909 "Futurist Manifesto" interested such crucial twentieth-century artists as Wyndham Lewis and D. H. Lawrence not only because it proposes avant-garde certitudes in a world whose center would no longer hold but also because it captures the aggressiveness with which many men in England and America responded to feminist incursions by refusing to see "the woman's cause [as] man's," instead insisting, with Gilbert and Sullivan's prince, that "Woman has failed you utterly—try Man." Ostensibly celebrating patriotic vigor, Marinetti tellingly links male militarism with misogyny:

> We are out to glorify war:
> The only health-giver of the world!
> Militarism! Patriotism!
> The Destructive Arm of the Anarchist!
> Ideas that kill!
> Contempt for women![33]

The militarist impulse that impelled the Futurists' glorification of war did not just help fuel a war that would occur in the near future;

it also indirectly enacted and reflected the war between the sexes that was already being waged.

———————

"Ideas that kill!" Although in one way or another such nineteenth-century men of letters as Higginson, Mill, Meredith, and Adams made the woman's cause their own because they saw feminist proposals as socially restorative ideas, many British and American literary men regarded feminism as in some sense deadly, and they fantasized about "killing" its proponents in order to save the life of male tradition. In Rider Haggard's *She* (1883)—a bestselling turn-of-the-century text that we will discuss in more detail in our next volume—three male explorers come upon a matriarchal society ruled by the apparently omnipotent She-who-must-be-obeyed, a society whose subjugated men periodically rise up in righteous revolution and kill the monstrous regiment of women who rule them: "We worship [women]," a native guide explains, "till at last they grow unbearable" and then "we rise, and kill the old ones as an example to the young ones, and to show them that we are the strongest."[34] But long before Haggard composed this work, the overt sexual hostility it dramatizes had been provisionally articulated in a number of texts.

Nathaniel Hawthorne's "The Christmas Banquet" (1844), for example, describes a gathering of "ten of the most miserable persons that could be found" at which was present "a woman of unemployed energy, who found herself in the world with nothing to achieve, nothing to enjoy, and nothing even to suffer. She had, therefore, driven herself to the verge of madness by dark broodings over the wrongs of her sex, and its exclusion from a proper field of action."[35] The ideas that seem to have plunged this rebel toward madness are comparable to the ambitious plans and polemics of Zenobia, the exotic advocate of women's rights who reigns over *The Blithedale Romance* (1852). Thus, the ferocity with which Hawthorne punishes Zenobia, who was at least in part modeled on Margaret Fuller, suggests the fate he and a number of his contemporaries would have liked to inflict not only on the quasi feminist of "The Christmas Banquet" but on all self-willed, intellectual women.

Central to *The Blithedale Romance* is a debate about women's rights which is carried on by Coverdale, Hollingsworth, and Zenobia for the benefit of the wide-eyed, decorous Priscilla. Declares Coverdale, the effete bachelor who narrates the novel, "I should love dearly—for the next thousand years, at least—to have all government devolve into the hands of women." "In denying us our rights," Zenobia adds, "[man] betrays even more blindness to his own interests than profligate disregard to ours!"[36] Both are expressing the kind of visionary feminism that Tennyson's prince had claimed to advocate a few years earlier. But the denouement of the book hints that the novelist's sympathies may be with the masculinist Hollingsworth, who makes a statement that predicts the hostility with which Hawthorne's literary descendants would battle Margaret Fuller's political heirs.

> All the separate action of woman is, and ever has been, and always shall be, false, foolish, vain, destructive of her own best and holiest qualities, void of every good effect, and productive of intolerable mischiefs! Man is a wretch without woman; but woman is a monster—and, thank Heaven an almost impossible and hitherto imaginary monster—without man, as her acknowledged principal! As true as I had once a mother, whom I loved, were there any possible prospect of woman's taking the social stand which some of them—poor, miserable, abortive creatures who only dream of such things because they have missed woman's peculiar happiness, or because Nature made them really neither man nor woman!—if there were a chance of their attaining the end which these petticoated monstrosities have in view, I would call upon my own sex to use its physical force, that unmistakeable evidence of sovereignty, to scourge them back within their proper bounds! [122–23]

Perhaps because Zenobia's love for Hollingsworth implies that she is capable of at least partly acquiescing in his ideas, it never becomes necessary for him to use actual "physical force" against her living body. But when he chooses Priscilla rather than her, she intuits the meaning of his decision: "Tell him he has murdered me!" she cries to Coverdale (226).

After Zenobia drowns herself, moreover, Hollingsworth does literally wound her, tearing open her breast with the grappling hook that he has used to fish her body from the stream. In addition, Hawthorne's description of the drowned woman's corpse acts as a "scourge" not only against her but also against her prototype, Margaret Fuller. Coldly observing that drowning is "the ugliest" mode of death, Coverdale shudders at Zenobia's "terrible inflexibility" and in particular at her hands, which "were clenched in immitigable defiance" (235). What makes matters worse, the narrator sardonically implies, is that this egotistical woman's "Arcadian affectation" had probably led her to believe that in her death she would appear picturesque. The ugliness of her corpse now functions, however, as a comment on the ugliness of her inflexible self-will. Even more ferociously, it functions as a comment on the death of her feminist prototype, Margaret Fuller, who two years before the composition of *The Blithedale Romance* had drowned when her ship was wrecked off the coast of New York. Although Coverdale's disdain for and disgust at the "unseemly aspect" of actual rather than poetical drowning might well have struck countless informed readers as itself unseemly, it is possible that the novelist was here at least covertly crowing over the death of the author of *Woman in the Nineteenth Century*.

In 1886, two years after *Princess Ida* opened at the Savoy, Hawthorne's admirer Henry James produced a revision of *The Blithedale Romance* whose hero was even more contemptuous of feminist "ideas that kill" than Hawthorne's Hollingsworth had been. Basil Ransom, the impoverished southerner who speaks for masculine values in *The Bostonians*, characterizes the age of women over which Olive Chancellor presides as "a feminine, a nervous, hysterical, chattering, canting age."[37] His actions speak even louder than his words, however. After he falls in love with the feminist Olive Chancellor's protegée Verena Tarrant—a newly enlisted platform speaker for women's rights—he mounts a campaign not only to win Verena for his wife but also to defeat Olive by destroying her influence over the girl. In her passionate ambition for her sex, as well as in her learning, the domineering Olive is of course comparable to Hawthorne's Zenobia, while the submissive Verena (as a number of critics have pointed out) may have been directly modeled on Hawthorne's Priscilla: just as Priscilla is hypnotized to perform in public as "The Veiled Lady," "a phenomenon in the mesmeric line" (57), Verena is mesmerized by her father to speak on public issues before she is entranced by Olive to speak on feminist questions.[38]

Striking as the similarities are between *The Blithedale Romance* and *The Bostonians*, however, the later novel makes several crucial changes in Hawthorne's plot, all of which suggest that the relationship between the two works is not unlike the relationship between *Princess Ida* and *The Princess*. First, James's Olive rules over a community of women whose separatist impulses and bluestocking proclivities are far more pronounced than those of Zenobia, who lives in a utopian commune that includes men working in the fields and women who work in the kitchen. Second, Olive is pale, frail, morbid, neurasthenic, while Zenobia is described as "an admirable figure of a woman," full of "bloom, health, and vigor, which she possessed in such overflow that a man might well have fallen in love with her for their sake only" (15–16). Finally, unlike Zenobia, who kills herself because of her love for Hollingsworth, Olive feels little but contempt for men in general and for Basil Ransom in particular. In fact, James revises Hawthorne's love triangle so that instead of two women struggling for the affection of one man, a man and a woman must battle each other for the love of a woman. At least covertly, moreover, James shows Olive's passion for Verena to be vampirically lesbian—the "spells" she casts on the younger woman are as erotic as they are political and as needy as they are manipulative—and therefore he suggests that her desire is a threat to the heterosexual order, an order which is never really questioned in *The Blithedale Romance*.

Like Gilbert and Sullivan, then, James depicted the escalation in the battle of the sexes that marked the progress of the nineteenth century. For although Basil Ransom's chivalric conservatism about the protection and domestication of Verena cannot necessarily be identified with his creator's personal thinking about women, there is considerable evidence, as we shall argue in our third chapter, that the author of *The Bostonians* himself felt weakened and assaulted by what he saw as the feminization of American culture in his own period. Thus, it is arguable that Basil's aesthetic is an essentially Jamesian one, a belief that the man of letters must set himself against "an age of hollow phrases and false delicacy . . . which, if we don't soon look out, will usher in the reign of mediocrity" (318); that Basil's male bonding with the fallen Union dead memorialized in the Harvard library reflects James's own fellowship with lost New England forefathers; and that Basil's rescue of Verena from the diseased clutches of Olive and her band of fanatical acolytes reflects James's desire to tell women that "Woman has failed you utterly—try Man." Finally, in spite of what some critics have seen as James's identification with the feminine,[39] his plot shows that the man who is determined to become Verena's husband and to find "a way to strike her dumb" (306) will inevitably, by virtue of his "muscular force," succeed in wrenching his bride not only from her perverse patroness but also from the unruly feminist movement which that patroness represents. Equivocal as the figure of the triumphant Basil, "palpitating with . . . victory" (426), may seem to many readers, the conclusion of *The Bostonians* implies James's sense that even in a society where heterosexuality has been undermined, the norms of traditional marriage will inevitably reassert themselves.

But, of course, James's suspicion that Olive's lesbianism is a symptom of social disorder which requires that woman "try Man" was not anomalous. The author of *The Bostonians* was living, after all, in a "nervous, chattering, canting age" in which works by such poets of decadence as Baudelaire and Swinburne were widely read. Thus Olive as lesbian vampire resembles not only the palpitating females of Baudelaire's *Les Lesbiennes* (the original title of *Les Fleurs du Mal* [1857]) but also such *belles dames sans merci* as LeFanu's eponymous Carmilla (1871–72) as well as Swinburne's Sappho, Faustine, and Dolores, and Oscar Wilde's Salome. Praising the "rapture of that cruelty which yet is love," Carmilla sinks her "long, thin, pointed" tooth—a tooth "like an awl, like a needle"—into the breast of her female beloved.[40] In the same mode, parasitically wooing Anactoria ("Oh that I / Durst crush thee out of life with love, and die"), Swinburne's Sappho had already made explicit in 1866, two decades before the appearance of *The Bostonians,* the cruel female self-will implicit in Olive's behavior.[41] Even more horribly, Swinburne's Faustine is seen to exult in the destruction of men:

> She loved the games men played with death,
>   Where death must win;
> As though the slain man's blood and breath
>   Revived Faustine.   [110]

Similarly, Swinburne's "mystic and sombre" Dolores, who is not only "splendid" but also "sterile," attacks and destroys heterosexual "Love." Addressing her, the poet cries, "Thou shalt blind his bright eyes though he wrestle, / Thou shalt chain his light limbs though he strive" (141, 143, 147). Finally, Wilde's Salome declares "I tell thee, there are not dead men enough."[42] Although the overt sadism of these femmes fatales, particularly those created by Swinburne, may often be a projection of the writer's own psychopathology, it is also representative of a fairly widespread Victorian fetishizing of (male) bondage and (female) discipline that has been studied by such figures as Mario Praz, Stephen Marcus, Nina Auerbach, and Bram Dijkstra.[43] Yet Swinburne's masochistic delight in female ferocity is countered by the faintly gloating tone of his speaker in "Sapphics," a poem about the defeat of Sappho's Lesbians which notes that these primordial "Sapphists" inhabit a "barren" land, "Full of fruitless women . . . Unbeloved . . . Ghosts of outcast women" (185) who should, like Zenobia and Olive, have renounced their passion for self-determination and tried Man.

———————

In 1913, one Walter Heape, M. A., F. R. S.—a reader in zoology at Cambridge—produced a book entitled *Sex Antagonism* in which he summarized the increasing fervor with which the battle of the sexes was being waged as the suffrage campaign intensified during the first two decades of the twentieth century. Reviewing many of the same social transformations that, say, Henry Adams summarized, he cogently described the escalated hostilities to which those trans-formations led:

> To most of us a sex war appears to be an entirely new expe-rience. For fifty years we may have noted the gradual growth of opinions which have led to a more or less indefinite alteration in the tone of the sexes to each other; for the last twenty-five years we may have recognized just cause for that alteration and some of the advantages to be derived from it; but of late we have been face to face with strife as selfish, as brutal, as bitter, and as unrestrained as that shown in any class war between men alone, and man's opinion of woman has been definitely modified—his attitude toward her as an integral component of society can never be the same again.[44]

Later in the book, Heape elaborated and clarified this point, de-claring that "the present woman's movement has its origin in sex antagonism" and that regardless of its avowed goals the movement's "driving force is engendered by desire to alter the laws which regulate the relations, and therefore the relative power, of the sexes" (205).

Heape's view of the matter was one shared by many contemporary literary men, though relatively few of them spoke so plainly about the connection between the suffrage battle and sex antagonism. In the same year that Heape's book appeared, for instance, Ford Madox Ford began to write his classic, *The Good Soldier: A Tale of Passion* (1915). Though this book is usually read as an epistemological analysis of a moral maze in which its unreliable narrator is hopelessly trapped, it is significant that this moral maze is a labyrinth of sex antagonisms and that its author's characterizations of women seem to controvert his own frequently expressed feminist leanings.[45] Leonora, the anti-heroine who is married to Edward Ashburnham, the "good soldier" of the book's ironic title, fights "a long, silent duel with invisible weapons" against her husband because she sees "Life as a perpetual sex-battle between husbands who desire to be unfaithful to their wives, and wives who desire to recapture their husbands in the end."[46] As for the woman Edward desires, propelled by what the narrator defines as "the sex instinct that makes women be intolerably cruel to the beloved person" (245), she joins with Leonora to give

> him an unimaginable hell. Those two women pursued that poor devil and flayed the skin off him as if they had done it with whips. I tell you his mind bled almost visibly. I seem to see him stand, naked to the waist, his forearms shielding his eyes, and flesh hanging from him in rags. I tell you that is no exaggeration of what I feel. It was as if Leonora and Nancy banded themselves together to do execution, for the sake of humanity, upon the body of a man who was at their disposal. They were like a couple of Sioux who had got hold of an Apache and had him well tied to a stake. I tell you there was no end to the tortures they inflicted upon him.[47]

That the "finest French novel in the English language" (xx), as Ford liked to report his book had been characterized, dramatizes moral and epistemological problems through a sex antagonism that is infiltrated by Swinburnean (and Flaubertian) imagery of flagel-

lation suggests the ways in which the "brutal," "bitter" strife Walter
Heape describes became crucial in even the most apparently rarefied
modernist aesthetic experiments. More openly than Ford, for instance, such figures as T. S. Eliot and D. H. Lawrence often concentrate with virtually sadistic fervor on the war between the sexes,
a war that they frequently imagine as being waged with Swinburnean
eroticism. Like Quintus's Achilles or Kleist's Penthesilea, their protagonists fetishize dead bodies with necrophiliac intensity or savor
sadistic bites as if they were kisses. But where the mythic Amazons
of earlier texts were allegorized as private sexual threats to a public
social order that was perceived as ultimately changeless, the modernists' Amazonian New Women represented a female sexual autonomy that was a sign of radical social change, a kind of social
change that only partially surfaced in Swinburne's work but whose
implications Walter Heape has analyzed and protested.

To be sure, Eliot's early unpublished "The Love Song of St. Sebastian" seems to be entirely under the sado-masochistic influence
of Swinburne in its depiction of the battle between men and women,
and this text may seem shocking, coming as it does from the classical,
royalist, Anglican Nobel prizewinner who produced such orthodox
works as "Ash Wednesday" and *Murder in the Cathedral.* Yet in a
sense the poem simply dramatizes the most "brutal" implications of
sexual hostilities that are also embedded in other texts by Eliot, including the far more subdued "Love Song of J. Alfred Prufrock."
Swearing deadly loyalty to his mistress, the self-flagellating speaker
of "St. Sebastian" openly associates desire with destruction, sex with
violence, for he promises first to flog himself in order to demonstrate
his erotic passion and then to strangle and disfigure his beloved so
that she will no longer be beautiful to anyone but him.[48] Indeed,
the rhetoric of this extraordinary "Love Song" virtually replicates
a passage in Swinburne's *Lesbia Brandon* (written ca. 1864–70; published 1952) about one of the novel's men in love, a character who
seems to represent many of Swinburne's enamoured personae when
he fantasizes about his beloved that

> Deeply he desired to die by her, if that could be; and more
> deeply, if this could be, to destroy her: scourge her with
> swooning and absorb the blood with kisses; caress and lacerate
> her loveliness, alleviate and heighten her pains; to feel her foot

upon his throat, and wound her own with his teeth; submit his body and soul for a little to her lightest will, and satiate upon hers the desperate caprice of his immeasurable desire; to inflict careful torture on limbs too tender to embrace, suck the tears off her laden eyelids, bite through her sweet and shuddering lips.[49]

It is significant that, beyond its Swinburnean overtones, "St. Sebastian" points to a consciousness of sex warfare that permeates much of Eliot's work because several other texts written in the same period specifically associate such struggle with the demands of the New Woman. "Petit Epître," a Laforguian verse in French from the same manuscript in which "St. Sebastian" appears, mockingly takes a stand against votes for women, while "Cousin Nancy" (1917) frankly satirizes the specious modernity of the liberated Miss Nancy Ellicott, who not only "smoked / And danced all the modern dances" but also, as if to destroy the earth itself, "Strode across the hills and *broke* them" (emphasis ours).[50] Even the poem's allusive conclusion implicitly censures this aggressive protoflapper:

> Upon the glazen shelves kept watch
> Matthew and Waldo, guardians of the faith,
> The army of unalterable law. [22]

Though Eliot presents Matthew (Arnold) and Waldo (Emerson) ironically, as fragile "guardians of the faith," the fact that they are identified with the "army of unalterable law" which defeats "Prince Lucifer" in Meredith's "Lucifer in Starlight" suggests that Eliot sees the rebellious Nancy as a diabolical upstart whose breaking of nature (the hills) also threatens to break the grounds of culture.

But if Nancy Ellicott is characterized through metaphor and allusion as a problematic figure, the unnatural culture she epitomizes is more graphically explored in "Prufrock Among the Women," a draft of "The Love Song of J. Alfred Prufrock" (1917) in which Eliot's famously balding, modern anti-Hamlet wanders woefully through what is clearly a red-light district, a sinister city of women that is even sleazier than the city of women from which James's Ransom rescues his Verena in *The Bostonians*.[51] And the published text of "Prufrock" also emphasizes the ways in which the absurdly self-conscious modern male intellectual is rendered impotent by, and in, the company of women. Pinned to the wall by "eyes that fix you in a formulated phrase" (5) and that make it impossible for him to formulate his own phrases, Prufrock becomes a helpless object of the deadly female gaze. Yet his escapist encounters with "sea-girls wreathed with seaweed red and brown" (7) are equally fatal. Nature, contaminated by female sexuality, drowns the male subject while culture, polluted by women who "come and go / Talking of Michelangelo" (3), denies or derides him.

Oddly enough, Prufrock's obsession with the fact that women *could* freely come and go, not only "talking of" but also gazing at and metaphorically possessing the paintings and sculptures of Michelangelo, foreshadows a reference to the Renaissance artist in a later, and very dissimilar, poem by another modernist writer, and a conflation of the two texts illuminates twentieth-century men's heightened anxiety about women's invasion of culture. Yeats's "Under Ben Bulben," praising "measurement," notes that

> Michael Angelo left a proof
> On the Sistine Chapel roof,
> Where but half-awakened Adam
> Can disturb globe-trotting Madam
> Till her bowels are in heat. . . .[52]

Both the travels and the sexuality of Yeats's heated, "globe-trotting Madam" help reveal the problems of Eliot and his contemporaries, problems that Yeats, like Eliot, probably at least at first associated with the suffrage movement. Just as Eliot indicated his opposition to votes for women in "Petit Epître," Yeats had expressed in "In Memory of Eva Gore-Booth and Con Markiewicz" his antagonism toward feminism, noting of the suffrage partisan Gore-Booth that she "dreams— / Some vague Utopia—and she seems, / When withered old and skeleton-gaunt, / An image of such politics" (229).

But Madam's travels and her sexuality also symbolize a modernist transformation of the turn-of-the-century world inhabited by Princess Ida that was as drastic as the change reflected in the shift from Tennyson's text to Gilbert and Sullivan's operetta. Where fin-de-siècle lady travelers explored the globe, early twentieth-century women began to colonize it, creating not only intellectual communities—colleges and professional societies—where women might "come and go / Talking of Michelangelo," but also artistic circles and avant-garde salons where they might, and did, experiment with new aesthetic as well as erotic styles. As Winifred Holtby observed in the first major study of Virginia Woolf (1932),

> When she wrote of women, [Virginia Woolf] wrote of a generation as adventurous in its exploration of experience as the Elizabethan men had been in their exploration of the globe. The women whom Mrs. Woolf knew were exploring the professional world, the political world, the world of business, discovering that they themselves had legs as well as wombs, brains as well as nerves, reason as well as sensibility; their Americas lay within themselves, and altered the map as profoundly as any added by Cabot or Columbus. Like Raleigh, they founded their new colonies; like Drake, they combined national service with privateering.[53]

What Holtby intuited has, of course, long since been statistically documented. According to the historian William Chafe, the first two decades of the twentieth century witnessed, in America, a "1000 per cent" increase of women's enrollment in public colleges and a "482 per cent" increase of female enrollment in private schools; if the figures for England were not quite so striking, they were almost equally impressive to contemporary observers, so much so that an advertisement for Abdulla cigarettes, which appeared in Oxford's *Isis* magazine, comically articulated the defensive bravado with which male undergraduates greeted their female classmates:

> Pretty Phyllis with a vote
> And a Varsity degree,
> Greek and Latin you may quote
> But you can't bamboozle me!
> Brilliant, up-to-date and smart,
> You're a savage squaw at heart. . . .
>
> Phyllis, when I come to woo,
> Disregarding sneer and snub
> I shall act as cave-men do—
> Knock you senseless with a club!
> Courtships of a higher grade
> Simply bore a savage maid.[54]

Besides educational advances, the years between 1914 and 1918 saw the entrance of massive numbers of women into the work force, an event necessitated by the exigencies of World War I; as we shall demonstrate in our next volume, when formerly male-occupied places in industry were taken by women, men often felt as assaulted on the home front as they were on the military front itself. Finally, the end of the second decade of the century witnessed what seemed at the time the ultimate female victory: the winning of the vote by English and American women like *Isis*'s "pretty Phyllis" after almost a century-long battle.

But the crisis caused by male dispossession and female self-possession would also have been intensified by the dramatic achievements of a growing number of notable women. From the spiritualists Madame Blavatsky and Annie Besant, founders of the Theosophical Society, and the anthropologists Jane Harrison, Jessie Weston, Ruth Benedict, Margaret Mead, and Zora Neale Hurston to such dancers, painters, and musicians as Isadora Duncan, Martha Graham, Mary Cassatt, and Ethel Smyth, such birth-control advocates as Margaret Sanger and Marie Stopes, and such psychologists as Helene Deutsch, Karen Horney, and Melanie Klein, women established themselves in positions of increasing intellectual centrality. In addition, from Renée Vivien and Natalie Barney to Vita Sackville-West, Gertrude Stein, Edna St. Vincent Millay, and Elinor Wylie, female writers flouted Victorian conventions as they flaunted their sexuality through well-publicized lesbian affairs or equally well-publicized heterosexual promiscuity.

Clearly the new liberation of these literary women, like the awakened desire of Yeats's "globe-trotting Madam," reflected a radical alteration in the very conception of female sexuality, an alteration that began with the proselytizings of Free Love advocates like Victoria Woodhull and Emma Goldman and was further implemented by the obviously influential works of the sexologists Edward Carpenter and Havelock Ellis and, even more obviously, by the writings of Sigmund Freud. Though Freud in particular may have had— and may have meant to have—a negative impact on feminism because, among other things, of his theory that woman had to accept the "fact" of her "castration," the general effect of his studies and others was a reimagining of female desire.[55] Where most Victorian theorists had hypothesized an essential and appropriate female "passionlessness," modernist thinkers assumed an essential and somewhat alarming female passion.[56] They knew, too, that women were now freer than ever before to act on that passion, for the dissemination of birth-control information and equipment in the 1910s and 1920s disengaged reproduction from sexuality, removing one major impediment to female erotic freedom.[57]

Inevitably, then, such a feminist theorist as Dora Russell supported Yeats's suspicion about his Madam's "bowels" by claiming in her 1925 *Hypatia* that, for women, "sex, even without children and without marriage is . . . a thing of dignity, beauty, and delight."[58] Perhaps just as inevitably, male thinkers were daunted by women's new-found libidinous energy, and literary men tended to reenvision the battle of the sexes as an erotically charged sexual struggle. Where both *The Princess* and *Princess Ida* had set masses of women, represented by male champions, against platoons of men in a publicly enacted military contest, modernist texts describe explicitly sexual duels between characters who tend to incarnate female voracity and male impotence. "A feature of modern life," mused Dora Russell in *Hypatia,* "is that matrimonial quarrels, like modern war, are carried on on a large scale, involving not individuals, nor even small groups of individuals, but both sexes and whole classes of society" (1). That Russell's female contemporaries felt they would win that modern war is evident from the title of their polemical journal, *Time and Tide,* with its allusion to a feminist victory which will "wait for no man."[59]

But that men feared they were losing such contests is plain even in a number of texts which do not explicitly deal with sexual battles. Images of impotence recur with unnerving frequency in the most canonical male modernist novels and poems. Of course, a number of Victorian literary men also deal with threats to masculine authority. As early as 1852, for example, Charles Dickens created a character whose name, Nemo, as much as his enthrallment to the sinister Lady Deadlock, implied that a no man lingers and sickens at the heart of *Bleak House,* while Tennyson presented both his King Arthur and his Prince Hilarion as feminized and, in the case of Arthur, cuckolded.[60] But from the betrayed and passive narrator of Ford's *Good Soldier* to cuckolded Leopold Bloom in Joyce's *Ulysses* and the wounded Fisher King in Eliot's *The Waste Land* to the eunuch Jake Barnes in Hemingway's *The Sun Also Rises,* the paralyzed Clifford Chatterley in Lawrence's *Lady Chatterley's Lover,* and the gelded Benjy in Faulkner's *The Sound and the Fury* as well as the castrated Joe Christmas in *Light in August,* maimed, unmanned, victimized characters are obsessively created by early twentieth-century literary men.[61] Because until recently the texts in which these characters appear have been privileged as documents in a history of cultural crises, the sexual anxieties they articulate have been seen mainly as metaphors of metaphysical angst. But though they do, of course, express angst, it is significant that these modernist formulations of societal breakdown consistently employed imagery of male impotence and female potency.

Not only in letters but in life, moreover, a number of modernist authors record, if not their own, their contemporaries' sexual anxiety. William Carlos Williams, for instance, recalls in his *Autobiography* that a member of the French Chamber of Deputies, during a visit to Natalie Barney's Paris salon, had responded to the sight of women "dancing gaily together on all sides" by undoing "his pants buttons, [taking] out his tool and, shaking it right and left, yell[ing] out in a rage, 'Have you never seen one of these?' "[62] Similarly, Hemingway remembers in *A Moveable Feast* how, in his role as "Papa," he had allayed F. Scott Fitzgerald's fears about penile inadequacy not only by explaining that "It is not basically the size in repose . . . It is the size that it becomes. It is also a question of angle" but also by taking the author of *The Great Gatsby* to the Louvre—which they viewed as a veritable penile colony—where the anxious Fitzgerald could compare his own equipment with that attached to Greek statues.[63]

Given such nightmarish intimations of no-manhood, the virulence with which many of these writers struck out against the women whom they saw as both the sources and the witnesses of their emasculation was perhaps understandable. Again, the author of *Sex Antagonism* describes the situation, recording the link between male discontent and masculinist backlash. "Perhaps the most remarkable fact in connection with the modern woman's revolt is not the activity of the dissatisfied woman so much as the complacency of the dissatisfied man," Walter Heape observes, but he then goes on to warn that the oppressed man will "act with all the more force when the proper time comes for action" (214). As if to illustrate his point, modernist men of letters sought to define appropriately virile reactions. Whether they imagined male characters defeating or defeated in the sexual combats and marital quarrels which Dora Russell associated with a world embroiled in gender warfare, their side of the war of the words was motivated by murderous intensity.

Even T. S. Eliot, his theories about the "extinction of personality" in poetry notwithstanding, responded to the threats posed by women who "come and go / Talking of Michelangelo" with fantasies of femicide. In life, the creator of Prufrock was fascinated by—and once attended a party costumed as—the wife-murderer Dr. Crippen.[61] And in the fragmentary drama *Sweeney Agonistes* (1927), a work whose title obviously alludes to Milton's *Samson Agonistes*, Eliot's protagonist, who may well be modeled on murderous Sweeney Todd, "the demon barber of Fleet Street," first threatens the floozy Doris by promising to take her to a "cannibal isle" and convert her into "a nice little, white little, missionary stew" and then tells the sinister story of a man who "once did a girl in," explaining that

> Any man might do a girl in
> Any man has to, needs to, wants to
> Once in a lifetime, do a girl in.   [122]

In *The Family Reunion* (1939), moreover, Eliot dramatized the tale of a man who may have killed (and certainly believes he has killed) a hard-drinking, New Womanly, Delilahesque wife of whom his mother remarks that "She never wanted to fit herself to Harry, / But only to bring Harry down to her own level" because she was no more than "A restless shivering painted shadow."[65] That in reality the author of *The Family Reunion* had abandoned his own wife a few years before his composition of this play suggests the subjective intensity that shaped the "objective correlative" he constructed here.[66]

As many critics have observed, such intensity also permeates the work of D. H. Lawrence, the male contemporary whom Eliot so savagely attacked in his 1934 *After Strange Gods*. Expatriates in different directions, D. H. Lawrence and T. S. Eliot would seem to have been diametrically opposed both in class allegiances and in theological theories. Yet even while the philosophical quarrels that characterized their careers made them into aesthetic opposites, their sexual anxieties made them into mirror images of each other—indeed, to use one of Lawrence's favorite terms, into blood brothers. Lawrence's short story "Samson and Delilah," for instance, alludes, as did *Sweeney Agonistes*, to the Biblical and Miltonic account of *Samson Agonistes* but imagines female defeat by male sexuality rather than by male murderousness. The tale begins by describing an Amazonian woman who, with the help of some soldiers, inflicts bondage and discipline on her estranged husband while questioning and ridiculing his manhood ("Do you call yourself a *man?*"), but it concludes with his insistence on his sexual authority: as "his hand insinuate[s] itself between her breasts," he blandly remarks that "a bit of a fight for a how-de-do pleases me, that it do. But that doesn't mean that you're going to deny as you're my missis."[67]

Elsewhere, lamenting a world occupied by "cocksure women" and "hensure men," Lawrence finds it harder to envision male victory.[68] In the poem "Figs," for instance, he brings to the surface the sexual tensions that haunt Eliotian texts from "The Love Song of St. Sebastian" to "The Love Song of J. Alfred Prufrock" and *Sweeney Agonistes*, complaining that "the year of our women has fallen overripe"; for, demanding an equal place in the sun, "our women" have horrifyingly "bursten into self-assertion."[69] But nowhere is the *Blütbruderschaft* of that odd couple Eliot and Lawrence more vividly revealed than in Lawrence's ironically titled *Women in Love* (1920). Although this novel, like its precursor *The Rainbow*, frequently adopts a female perspective in order both to celebrate the sensitivity and receptivity of one of its heroines—Ursula Brangwen—and, in the case of *Women in Love*, to critique the priggish "Salvator Mundi" quality of its hero, Rupert Birkin, the book also records the corrosiveness of female desire in order to repudiate " 'Cybele—curse her! the accursed Syria Dea!' "[70]

With varying degrees of intensity, three couples in this work engage in metaphysical and physical struggles for primacy which seem to replicate the Swinburnean struggles Eliot records and to dramatize the implications of the more superficially civilized struggles enacted in *The Bostonians*, *The Blithedale Romance*, *Princess Ida*, and *The Princess*. In the chapter called "Breadalby," for instance, Birkin's sometime mistress Hermione experiences "a terrible voluptuous thrill" (78) in her arms as she approaches the moment of "perfect, unutterable consummation" (78) when she will smash a ball of lapis lazuli on her lover's head. Her arms tingling with what seems like Zenobia's "terrible inflexibility" and with what Lawrence describes as "never-ending hostility," she knows that "It was coming!" (78)—a consummation of agonistic desire not unlike the sexual fury Eliot and Swinburne transcribe. Again, in the chapter called "Water Party," a woman assaults a man. Gerald's sister Diana is not content to drown alone the way Zenobia does; having fallen overboard from a miniature steamer like the one that plies the squire's lake at the opening of *The Princess*, this young girl, who is tellingly nicknamed "Di," dies with "her arms tight round the neck" of the young doctor who tried to save her; and " 'She killed him,' said Gerald" (181). But finally, of course, the most radical combat in the book is between Gerald and Gudrun, two characters whose profoundly sexual struggle is central to *Women in Love*.

Modeled in part on Katherine Mansfield, Gudrun is an archetypal New Woman whose feelings for Gerald are even more ambivalent than those of Hermione for Birkin. But while the famous "Rabbit" chapter reveals the perverse sadism she and her lover share, their struggle in the snow at the end of the novel epitomizes the sexual hostility which engendered so much literary violence in the modernist period. High in the glittering Alps, after the relationship between the pair has begun seriously to disintegrate, Gerald feels a sudden desire to murder Gudrun: "He thought, what a perfect voluptuous fulfillment it would be to kill her . . . to strangle her, to strangle every spark of life out of her, till she lay completely inert, soft, relaxed for ever, a soft heap lying dead between his hands, utterly dead. Then he would have had her finally and for ever; there would be such a perfect voluptuous finality" (452). As if he were reworking Robert Browning's "Porphyria's Lover" with little of Browning's distance, Lawrence transcribes Gerald's femicidal desire without irony. Yet what happens on the slopes is that Gudrun, unlike the seductively passive Porphyria, raises "her clenched hand high, and [brings] it down, with a great downward stroke on to the face and on to the breast of Gerald" (463), and it is only at this point that he decides to "take the apple of his desire" and, like Eliot's Saint Sebastian, strangle his mistress. "What bliss! Oh what bliss, at last, what satisfaction, at last!" he thinks while—as if echoing Hawthorne's

Coverdale—he observes the horror of her "swollen face" and notices "How ugly she was!" (463) When his own murderous desire fails, however, and he climbs an icy ridge, lit by "a small bright moon" (464)—a moon reminiscent of "the accursed Syria Dea" Birkin tries to shatter—her deadly will at least figuratively triumphs, for he understands, as he ascends toward death, that "Somebody was going to murder him" (465).

Not insignificantly, the triumph of Gudrun's New Womanly determination at the end of *Women in Love* is facilitated by the intervention of a New Man, the terrifying no-man named (after Wagner's Loge) Loerke, a dwarfish and, says Birkin, probably Jewish industrial artist whose arrogance and cynicism utterly undermine the plans of the Siegfried-like hero that Gerald ought to have been. Discussing him earlier, Gerald and Birkin have mused on his inexplicable attractiveness to women. In response to Gerald's quasi-Freudian query "What *do* women want, at the bottom?," Birkin has speculated that it is "Some satisfaction in basic repulsion, it seems to me. They seem to creep down some ghastly tunnel of darkness, and will never be satisfied till they've come to the end. . . . They want to explore the sewers, and [Loerke] is the wizard rat that swims ahead" (418–19). It is therefore fitting that during the battle in the snow Loerke's intervention arrests Gerald's murderous will to throttle Gudrun. "Monsieur," says the little sculptor sardonically in a French which represents the sinister country that had threatened Tennyson's college men, "Quand vous aurez fini—" (464), and it is this phrase which inspires in Gerald "a decay of strength . . . a fearful weakness" that causes him to abandon his femicidal project and "drift" up the mountainside toward annihilation. In a world inhabited by murderous women who seek "satisfaction in basic repulsion," Gerald must die because there are "no more *men*, there [are] only creatures, little, ultimate *creatures* like Loerke" (443).[71]

Such a no man's land of mad women and unmanned or maddened men appears with striking frequency throughout the works of a number of Lawrence's and Eliot's contemporaries. Booth Tarkington, Ernest Hemingway, William Faulkner, and Nathanael West, for instance, record their horror at a battle they fear men are losing. In Tarkington's fantasy "The Veiled Feminists of Atlantis" (1926), women's rebellion against male rule takes the form of wanting not just equality but superiority, and specifically a superiority which depends on their gaining access to the educational mysteries once solely known to men even while they retain the erotic mystery conferred by the female veil. Because the men "had accepted equality" but "they could not accept the new inequality" which placed them at a "disadvantage," the two sexes go to war, using "mountain ranges and thunder and lightning as familiar weapons," until "the ocean came over the land in waves thousands of feet tall" and both sexes perish in the fabled sinking of Atlantis.[72] Less apocalyptically but just as catastrophically, in "The Short Happy Life of Francis Macomber" (1936) Hemingway describes a married couple, the Macombers, on safari with their white hunter, Robert Wilson; Wilson's belief that Mrs. Macomber is "simply enamelled in that American female cruelty" is corroborated, first, when she responds to her husband's cowardice on a lion hunt by sleeping with Wilson and then when she reacts to her husband's courageous confrontation with a buffalo by accidentally-on-purpose shooting him, while ostensibly firing at the wounded beast. "Why didn't you poison him? That's what they do in England," Wilson scathingly remarks, for, though Wilson may be in some ways a problematic character, Hemingway's tale implies that Macomber is trapped in a dire double bind: whether he is cowardly or courageous, unmanned or manly, his wife is determined to betray him.[73]

Even more disturbing depictions of female sexuality and aggression occur in Faulkner's *Light in August* (1932) and West's *Miss Lonelyhearts* (1933). Joanna Burden, the mannish spinster of *Light in August*, is shown to want and to deserve the phallic retribution exacted by her black lover Joe Christmas, who first despoils her virginity, then arouses her desire, and finally murders her after a long sexual struggle. Perhaps because she is unnatural—she has the "strength and fortitude of a man" and "man-trained muscles and . . . man-trained habit[s] of thinking"—Joe experiences intercourse with her as combat, musing that "It was as if he struggled physically with another man." Yet when she is erotically unmanned, Joanna becomes even more unnatural: yielding to nymphomania, she reveals a "rotten richness ready to flow into putrefaction at a touch, like something

growing in a swamp."[74] Finally, therefore, her unnatural toxicity
leads to Joe's own unmanning, for after he murders her he is castrated and killed by a vengeful white man. And as Joyce Carol Oates
observes, "the dead woman at the center of the novel is judged [by
Faulkner] as rightly dead, and her murderer is 'innocently' guilty
in the service of a complex of passions that dramatize the tragic
relations between white and black *men*."[75]

Similarly, although all the characters in West's *Miss Lonelyhearts*
are grotesque, the final unmanning of the man called "Miss Lonelyhearts" is a direct result of his sexual victimization by, and struggle
against, the monstrous Mrs. Doyle. Looking "like a police captain,"
with "legs like Indian clubs" and "massive hams . . . like two enormous grindstones,"[76] this insatiable lady seduces the columnist at
their first meeting, then a few days later sends her crippled husband
to invite him to dinner. The meal is bizarrely marked by her skir-
mishes with both men: as Miss Lonelyhearts enters her house, she
"goose[s] him and laugh[s]" (47); then she "roll[s] a newspaper into
a club and [strikes] her husband on the mouth with it." At this Doyle
unaccountably tears open Miss Lonelyhearts' fly as the gigantic
woman kicks the cripple.

Finally, after her mate has left to buy some gin, Mrs. Doyle tries
again to seduce Miss Lonelyhearts in what becomes virtually a rape
scene. Although he tries to fend her off,

> she opened the neck of her dress and tried to force his head
> between her breasts [and] he parted his knees with a quick jerk
> that slipped her to the floor. She tried to pull him down on
> top of her. He struck out blindly and hit her in the face. She
> screamed and he hit her again and again. He kept hitting her
> until she stopped trying to hold him, then he ran out of the
> house. [50]

When at the end of the novel Miss Lonelyhearts rushes downstairs
to greet the crippled Mr. Doyle in a Christlike effort to restore him
to wholeness, the explosion of Doyle's gun functions at least covertly
as an assertion of Mrs. Doyle's will (not unlike Loerke's assertion of
Gudrun's will in *Women in Love*). Thus when the columnist dies,
locked in the deadly embrace of a dwarfish no-man, West implies
that, like so many other male characters created by modernist men

of letters, he is not only a prisoner of sex but a prisoner of the female sex.

That West's *Miss Lonelyhearts*, as a casualty in the sex war, has to assume a female pseudonym reemphasizes the fear of emasculation that characterized so much modernist literature, a fear that was often associated by men of letters with a moral and spiritual as well as a psychological fall. As Henry Miller declared not long after the publication of West's novel, "the loss of sex polarity is part and parcel of the larger disintegration, the reflex of the soul's death, and coincident with the disappearance of great men, great causes, great wars."[77] No doubt at least in part as a response to such feelings of disintegration, many literary men, from the 1940s through the 1970s, sought to reintegrate themselves through fervent and often feverish reimaginings of male potency. To be sure, the theme of gender strife continued, often parodically, to mark the works of male artists, appearing quite explicitly, for instance, in James Thurber's hilarious cartoon sequence "The War Between Men and Women" (1945), in which male and female combatants "battle on the stairs," "fight in the grocery," take each other hostage, experience a "zero hour" in Connecticut, snipe at each other, and struggle at a climactic "Gettysburg" (figures, pp. 44, 45).[78] In films, moreover, such sexual battling was dramatized by movies from, say, *Adam's Rib* (1949) to *Prizzi's Honor* (1985). But the sexualization of this combat began as early as 1928, when D. H. Lawrence constructed a theology of the phallus in *Lady Chatterley's Lover*, setting Mellors's triumphant "John Thomas" and Connie's receptive "Lady Jane" against Clifford Chatterley's paralysis and Bertha Coutts's assertive clitoral "beak."[79] And in subsequent decades the pace of this defensive reaction-formation quickened. Miller himself, for example, began to find a virtue in sexual warfare, which, he declared, by reestablishing sex polarity would also resurrect masculinity: "the eternal battle with women," he proclaimed, "sharpens our resistance, develops our strength, enlarges the scope of our cultural achievements."[80] In his novels, moreover, he relished victories that he had achieved through the reification of women in a theology of the cunt that complemented Lawrence's theology of the phallus. "The body is hers, but the cunt's

James Thurber. "The War Between Men and Women: The Overt Act and the Battle on the Stairs," *The Thurber Carnival*, 1945. Copyright © 1943 James Thurber. Copyright © 1971 Helen W. Thurber and Rosemary A. Thurber. From "The War Between Men and Women" Series, *Men, Women and Dogs*, published by Harcourt Brace Jovanovich.

James Thurber. "The War Between Men and Women: Zero Hour, Connecticut, and The Sniper," *The Thurber Carnival*, 1945. Copyright © 1943 James Thurber. Copyright © 1971 Helen W. Thurber and Rosemary A. Thurber. From "The War Between Men and Women" Series, *Men, Women and Dogs*, published by Harcourt Brace Jovanovich.

yours," he insisted in *Sexus* (1949), and in *Tropic of Capricorn* (1939) he outlined his credo in a description of "the best fuck" he ever had: the object of his desire was a "simpleton" about whom he noted that "above the belt . . . she was batty . . . Perhaps that was what made her cunt so marvellously impersonal. It was one cunt out of a million." Indeed, this idealized woman's desire is not threatening precisely because it is bovine: she responds to male sexuality "just as naturally as a cow lowering its head to graze."[81]

The explicit physicality celebrated in most of Miller's texts points to a way in which his contemporaries and descendants would wage their new campaign against women. From Miller himself to Norman Mailer, from Tennessee Williams to Thomas Berger, they would—sometimes with irony but sometimes with savagery—reconstitute the penis as a pistol with which to shoot women into submission. Many factors no doubt contributed to their need for such a strategy. To begin with, the Depression assaulted already fragile male egos by threatening to undermine the economic power of the traditional husband-as-breadwinner. In addition, World War II tended to intensify a male sense of peril, and, as we shall argue in a later volume, it simultaneously fostered a contempt for women as sexual objects (pin-up girls, whores, camp followers) and an ambivalence toward the mothers and sweethearts who were presumed to be safe at home.

Later, what Robert Lowell in *Life Studies* (1959) was to call "the tranquillised *Fifties*" saw the articulation in pop psychology and popular fiction of a suburban ideology of domesticity and "togetherness," which seemed, paradoxically enough, to give extraordinary authority to wives and "moms" even while (as Betty Friedan famously claimed in *The Feminine Mystique* [1963]) it also served to keep women in their proper places.[82] Finally, of course, the so-called "second wave" of feminism, which began in the late 1960s and burgeoned in the 1970s and 1980s, was at least as disturbing to men as the first wave had been, for proponents of women's liberation were now demanding considerably more than the political power emblematized by the vote: they were asserting, and often achieving, professional, economic, and sexual equality—and sometimes they even appeared, to their nervous male contemporaries, to be claiming superiority. Thus if the male worker was economically at risk during the Depression and the male soldier physically at risk during the war, the man in the gray flannel suit felt himself to be psychologically imperiled in the 1950s family room while even the most liberal intellectual felt, and frequently was, threatened by feminist demands in the 1970s and 1980s.

One solution to all these problems was what we might call the domestication of desire, a maneuver that was, interestingly, associated with a complete reversal of just those Victorian values articulated in *The Princess.* Where Tennyson and such contemporaries as Charles Dickens and Coventry Patmore praised women for decorous purity and benevolent maternity, and where turn-of-the-century and modernist men of letters blamed them for destructive desirousness, postmodernist male thinkers asserted antithetical moral priorities, praising women for compliant sexiness while blaming them for prudish frigidity and castrating maternity. Thus the scarlet letter *A* that Hawthorne had used in the nineteenth century to symbolize the crime of the adulteress now dissolved into the pornographic *O* that signified both the emptiness and the openness of an obediently serviceable woman in Pauline Réage's *The Story of O* (1954, 1964).[83]

To be sure, as early as 1918 and 1928, respectively, Marie Stopes in her *Married Love* and Theodoor Henrik van de Velde in *Ideal Marriage: Its Physiology and Technique* had encouraged women to follow Dora Russell's advice and see sex as a "thing of . . . delight."[84] But by the 1950s, after World War II had propelled massive numbers of married women into the work force (where, as William Chafe has noted, they were increasingly to make permanent places for themselves),[85] a new ideology of eroticism redefined woman's sexual delight as virtually compulsory rather than, as Dora Russell had implied, wonderfully voluntary. In other words, just as more and more women were getting paid for using their brains, more and more men represented them in novels, plays, and poems as nothing but bodies, as if to repress by erasing, rather than denouncing, the kinds of ambitions that Princess Ida articulated. Thus in this era, with the proliferation of sexual surveys like the *Kinsey Report* and commercially successful marriage manuals as well as a "sexual revolution" institutionalized in such journals as *Playboy* and *Penthouse,* "coming together" became de rigueur.[86] In fact, a sign of manhood, as the poet W. D. Snodgrass declared in his Pulitzer prize-winning *Heart's Needle* (1959), was the ability to bring a woman to orgasm: "I taught myself . . . To ease my woman so she came."[87]

On the surface, of course, Snodgrass's desire to "ease" his woman "so she came" seems notably generous. But actually such a construction of female desire ultimately implies female dependency: if a man does not "ease" her, Snodgrass suggests, the woman cannot come. In this regard, Freud's theory of woman as a "castrated" man was useful, for it implied a valorization of the implemental (sexual) utility of the penis (as opposed to the clitoris or the vagina) which intensified a widespread cultural assumption of female passivity. Moreover, it followed from such an assumption that women who have "inappropriate" desires—the woman who wants too much (the aggressive nymphomaniac), the woman who wants too little (the frigid bitch), and the woman who is not wantable (the mother, and perhaps also the unattractive "dog")—must be punished. The penis as a therapeutic instrument in the domestication of desire, therefore, was always on the verge of turning into a penis as pistol, an instrument of rape and revenge, and, oddly enough, the raped woman seems to have been fetishized and sanctified as often as the woman who was eased into easily coming.

In William Carlos Williams's *Paterson*, for instance (Book III, 1949), a crucial modernist has a key vision of a "Beautiful Thing" whom he encounters in his medical capacity "flat on [her] back, in a low bed (waiting)" in a basement.[88] The title he gives her—with its allusion to the French "belle chose"—links her to Miller's theology of the cunt, but in his explanation of how he has come to meet her Williams is even more explicit than Miller about the beauty this "thing" has achieved through male-inflicted physical violence. Explaining that "the guys from Paterson / beat up / the guys from Newark and . . . socked you one / across the nose," the New Jersey doctor imagines his patient's ordeal in terms that hint at a gang bang: "Then back to the party! / and they maled / and femaled you . . . Three days in the same dress / up and down" (127). Yet his sympathy for this sexual victim is, curiously, accompanied by voyeuristic absorption in her mutilation. After noting that "You showed me your legs, scarred (as a child) / by the whip," he formulates a worshipful philosophy about her suffering:

> . . . I must believe that all
> desired women have had each
> in the end

> a busted nose
> and live afterward marked up
> Beautiful Thing
> for memory's sake
> to be credible in their deeds. [127]

That this "docile queen" is evidently black, moreover—"—a flame, / black plush, a dark flame" (128)—suggests that the poet is oscillating between a humane sympathy for a victim who is "indifferent, / through loss" and an oddly neo-Swinburnean pleasure in his own difference from, and superiority to, what he sees as ontological pain.

From the perspective of black male writers, of course, such sexual visions of difference are delineated in alternative ways, ways which emphasize the link between the black man's persistent consciousness of racial oppression and a concomitant sense of invisibility or no-manhood. Specifically, the anger of the black male artist often translates into an obsession not with the rape victim but with the existential desires of the would-be "rapist" or the elemental dilemma of the framed-up rapist. In Richard Wright's *A Native Son* (1940), Bigger Thomas—who implicitly dreads being smaller than Law-rence's John Thomas—murders one white woman and one black woman out of pure anxiety, and does so while both are in bed. In the first case, fearing discovery by the girl's parents, he inadvertently suffocates this white woman whom he took to her home because she was drunk; in the second, he murders his black girlfriend be-cause he worries that she will reveal his killing of the first woman. In both cases, however, Bigger's femicides are extensively elaborated: after he has killed the white girl, he has to carve up her body and stuff it into a furnace in a scene that Wright chillingly dramatizes, and the killing of the black woman is brilliantly detailed through Wright's description of Bigger's use of a brick to demolish her head into "a wet wad of cotton," as well as through Wright's analysis of his protagonist's feeling that "She seemed limp; he could act now."[89] That all this violence is directed against women is explained by Big-ger's and Wright's rhetoric of rape, which *A Native Son* defines as "*not* what one did to women" (emphasis ours) but as "what one felt when one's back was against a wall and one had to strike out, whether one wanted to or not, to keep the pack from killing one" (214).

More sardonically, in Ralph Ellison's *Invisible Man*, the underground man who is the book's protagonist encounters an "aggressively receptive" wasteland white woman named Sybil, who pleads,
parodically and drunkenly, "Come on, beat me, daddy—you—you
big black bruiser," to which he responds by writing, just as drunkenly
and parodically, on her belly

SYBIL, YOU WERE RAPED
BY SANTA CLAUS
SURPRISE[90]

Just a little earlier, this black, bleak anti-hero, who had been asked
by his political "Brotherhood" to lecture on "the woman question,"
had mockingly defined himself as a "domesticated rapist, obviously,
an expert on the woman question" (394), and much earlier in the
book he had been forced, at a white man's "smoker," to gaze upon
the naked body of a "magnificent blonde" before engaging in a
blindfolded "battle royal" with a group of his black contemporaries
(15–16). There, on the one hand, he had recognized his commonality
with the exploited woman as he noted the "terror and disgust in
her eyes, almost like my own terror and that which I saw in some
of the other [black] boys" (17); and on the other hand, he had reacted
to her enforced voluptuousness and the cultural fetishization it signaled by wanting to "spit upon her . . . to caress her and destroy
her, to love her and murder her, to hide from her and yet to stroke
where below the small American flag tattooed upon her belly her
thighs formed a capital V" (16).

Comparable and equally ambivalent attitudes toward rape are expressed in a text by Tennessee Williams that was published in the
same decade as *A Native Son, Invisible Man,* and *Paterson* III. But
while William Carlos Williams's poem fetishizes the battered woman,
and Wright's and Ellison's novels both identify with and assault
women, *A Streetcar Named Desire* (1947) dramatizes the dynamics of
the battering of women. Standing apart from heterosexual institutions, the homosexual author of *Streetcar* simultaneously records,
rationalizes, and critiques the use of the penis as weapon that he
perceives as essential to Stanley Kowalski's relations with women.
The play's sensitively self-deluding Blanche DuBois is, of course, a
sympathetic heroine, a woman whose imaginative energy surpasses

the creativity of any of the other characters in the play. Thus her perspective on the relationship between her sister Stella and Stella's husband Stanley is surely one that the author himself regards as valid. As if echoing Lady Psyche's assertion that "Darwinian man" is "only a monkey shav'd," Blanche accuses Stanley of being "apelike" and urges Stella not to "hang back with the brutes."[91] In many ways the drama proves that she is right, for the drunken, sweaty, poker-playing Stanley beats his wife, and the submissive Stella seems sexually enthralled by his violence. From Blanche's point of view, then, as well as from Williams's, the streetcar named heterosexual desire is a runaway trolley that leads, as Blanche explains, through "Cemetery" to the "Elysian Fields" of obliteration (7).

At the same time, however, Williams shows that this neurasthenic former English teacher lives in a fantasy world at least as deadly as the arena of sexual violence inhabited by the Kowalskis. Aging, impoverished, and alcoholic, she pretends to be a pure young lady but was in fact run out of her hometown for flagrant sexual misconduct. Unable to bear the glare of reality, she avoids daylight, clings to shadows, and tries to seduce younger men. Worse still, she was evidently responsible for the suicide of the homosexual "boy" she claims to have married: she admits that after she found him in a room with "an older man who had been his friend for years," she shattered him into shooting himself by saying "I know! I saw! You disgust me!" (68). Thus, when Stanley rapes her, precipitating her into madness, Williams implies that she is getting a punishment that fits her crimes. Because she has seduced and betrayed, used and abused men whose own marginality in the heterosexual world made them especially vulnerable to her fakery—sensitive men, students, and most particularly her homosexual husband—she has had a "date . . . from the beginning" (94) with the masculinist Stanley, who represents in his brutishness the phallic origin of the male species.

Finally, however, despite his depiction of Blanche's culpability, in the last scene of the play Williams produces a scathing critique of the heterosexual imperative which is driving her mad, although, like all the characters in the work except the dead "boy," she has lived by it. In order for the Kowalskis to live happily ever after, Stella must deny the reality of Blanche's experience with Stanley ("I couldn't believe her story and go on living with Stanley!" [96]) and send this troubled and troublesome sister to a madhouse, replacing her in the family circle with a baby boy. Moreover, that Stanley's guilt may be greater than Blanche's is a view expressed even by one of his own poker buddies, who tells him, as the hysterical Blanche is pinned to the floor by a hospital attendant, that "You done this, all a your God-damn' rutting with things you—" (102). Indeed, just before the curtain falls, Williams juxtaposes two speeches which brilliantly indict the law of the phallus and the streetcar named heterosexual desire. As Stanley "voluptuously" comforts the sobbing Stella—"Now, love. Now, now, love"—the male poker game resumes: "All right, boys—this game is seven card *stud*" (103, emphasis ours).

Williams's vision of the brutality with which Stanley has asserted the power of the penis both to punish Blanche and to subjugate Stella is generalized by another homosexual artist into a vision of the connection between the hegemony of the phallus and the horror of modern technocracy. In the "Moloch" section of *Howl* (1956), Allen Ginsberg curses a macho society marred by "demonic industries! spectral nations! invincible madhouses! granite cocks! monstrous bombs!"[92] Yet many of Ginsberg's contemporaries, as he himself notes, were as committed as Stanley Kowalski—or Henry Miller—to the worship of the "granite cock" and the "marvellously impersonal" receptive cunt. In "Sather Gate Illumination" (1956), for example, the rebel of *Howl* wrote admiringly about his and Jack Kerouac's hero Neal Cassidy that "N[eal] sees all girls / as visions of their inner cunts," and Ginsberg's friend Gary Snyder in "For a Far-out Friend" (1957) told a woman whom, he confessed, he had once beaten up, that "visions of your body / Kept me high for weeks" and, in particular, visions of her with "a little golden belt just above / your naked snatch."[93] As if literalizing Snyder's story, moreover, the Beat hero William Burroughs actually did shoot and kill his wife in 1951 while aiming at a champagne glass on her head.[94]

Indeed, if anything, a Kowalskiesque impulse to use the penis and other implements as battering rams with which to assault or destroy women intensified in the 1950s and 1960s. In Hubert Selby's *Last Exit to Brooklyn* (1957), for example, the whorish—that is, inappropriately desirous—Tra La La is gang-raped and finally murdered by being impaled on broomsticks and beer bottles. Even a metaphysical comedy like Thomas Pynchon's *V* (1963) turns on comparable vengeance dreams, dreams that also recall the "invisible man's" urge to spit upon, caress, and murder the capital V of the naked blonde. V's lesbian actress-lover Melanie is skewered by a pole in an onstage act in which she has failed to protect herself with a prop chastity belt, while the supposedly charismatic body of V herself is disassembled by children who steal her wooden legs, fake teeth and wig. And of course V's name not only symbolizes violence and vulgarity, it also stands for the vulva, the vagina, and the horrifying void that these female body parts seem to represent if they have not been properly domesticated by the phallus.[95]

Such a void is directly confronted in Norman Mailer's *An American Dream* (1964), whose hero, Rojack, murders his wife because her body seems to exude what T. S. Eliot once called "that good old hearty female stench."[96] That Rojack subsequently sodomizes a German maid who has the suggestive name of *Ruta* further certifies his heroism. Even though he has purified his life by killing one woman, he is not afraid to enter the stinking darkness of another woman's body. Thus, as Kate Millett has argued, "The reader is given to understand that by murdering one woman and buggering another, Rojack [has become] a 'man.' "[97] Moreover, when this Ruta-rooter does find a compliant and sweet-smelling woman (with the appropriately virginal and luscious name of Cherry), he declares his masculine independence of her desire for reproductive control by flicking out her diaphragm before making love to her.

Interestingly, one of the few major 1960s texts about sexual struggle in which a man is successfully murdered rather than being triumphantly murderous is Imamu Amiri Baraka's (LeRoi Jones's) prize-winning play *Dutchman* (1964), and this anomaly is surely at least in part because the work sets gender hostilities in the same context of racial conflict that marks Wright's *A Native Son* and Ellison's *Invisible Man*. Drawing on a long social and literary tradition that mythologizes the white woman's desireableness to the sexually voracious black man,[98] the drama reverses stereotypes by beginning with a white woman's effort to seduce a black man and ending with her murder of him. Lula, who calls herself "Lena the Hyena . . . [a] poetess," enters a subway car eating an apple and proceeds to tease and taunt Clay, a middle-class passenger who at one point confesses that in college he had thought of himself as a "black Baudelaire."[99]

At first he is intrigued by her advances but he slowly becomes wary of her, and finally he responds to what he realizes is an attack on his manhood by telling her "I could murder you now. Such a tiny ugly throat. I could squeeze it flat. . . ." (33). But though he threatens to "rip your lousy breasts off!" because of her whorishness ("You fuck some black man, and right away you're an expert on black people" [34]), his murderous will fails and, as he is preparing to leave the subway car, she stabs him. To make matters more terrifying, it becomes clear when Lula turns to the other passengers on the train and orders them to dispose of Clay's body that everyone at the scene is somehow in her thrall. Worse still, when Lula begins to make mysterious notes after the event, it becomes plain that she is the executioner of a grand design—a plot whose reenactment is forecast at the end of *Dutchman* when another young black man, obviously her next victim, enters the subway car.

To be sure, Baraka's play is at least as focused on racial relations as it is on sexual ones, but the author's decision to dramatize the inequality of whites and blacks through a struggle between woman and man suggests that he believes the white *female* is specifically the oppressor of the black race. More, that the title of the play alludes to *The Flying Dutchman* is significant, for in Wagner's opera the Dutchman is doomed to sail around the world until he can find a woman who is willing to sacrifice her life for him. Perhaps because neither Clay nor Baraka himself can imagine that such a white woman would step forward to rescue his eternally subway-riding and perpetually sacrificed "Dutchman," the writer later incorporated a fantasy of black male revenge against white women into a poem entitled "Babylon Revisited" (1969).

Cursing the whorish woman who symbolizes white culture's destruction of black manhood as "a vast pusschamber / of pus(sy) memories / with no organs / nothing to make babies," Baraka's speaker seems to echo Mailer's horror at the stinking void of his dead wife's vagina.[100] At the same time, his explanation of the reason for his ritual of revenge recalls the destructiveness of Lawrence's, West's, and Tennessee Williams's female characters: "This bitch killed a friend of mine named Bob Thompson / a black painter, a giant, once, she reduced / to a pitiful imitation faggot." Finally, his

concluding prayer envisions a vengeance as hideous as the fates inflicted on Selby's Tra La La or Pynchon's Melanie and V:

> May this bitch and her sisters, all of them,
> receive my words
> in all their orifices like lye mixed with
> cocola and alaga syrup
>
> feel this shit, bitches, feel it, now laugh your
> hysterectic laughs
> while your flesh burns
> and your eyes peel to red mud

That the villainess of Baraka's "Babylon Revisited" has "no organs /
nothing to make babies" and that she has emasculated his friend
"Bob Thompson" suggests yet another aspect of the postmodernist
sex war: the campaign against mothers. From Philip Wylie to John
Osborne, from Edward Albee to Philip Roth, men of letters excoriate
women for what Wylie famously called "Momism," even while, like
Jones, they reproach them for sterility. In *Generation of Vipers* (1942),
Wylie inveighs against "the destroying mother," defining "moms"
as "five-and-ten-cent-store Lilith[s]"—modern equivalents, therefore,
of the legendary baby-killer—and arguing that "We must face the
dynasty of the dames at once."[101] Though the ideology of the baby-
booming late 1940s and 1950s asserted that woman's place was in
the nursery and the Scout Club carpool, the more diligently mothers
went their appointed rounds, the more their benevolence was
doubted. In 1947, Ferdinand Lundberg's and Marynia Farnham's
Modern Woman—The Lost Sex claimed to show that "the traditional
'mom' " was "the mother of [a] deficient male" and, rhetorically asking "Just what have these women done to their sons?," the authors,
a social historian and a psychiatrist, replied "They have stripped
them of their male powers—that is, they have castrated them."[102]

As if dramatizing Lundberg's and Farnham's theories, Edward
Albee in *The American Dream* (1961) wrote a play about a sterile
"Mommy" who literally blinds and castrates the baby boy she has
purchased from an adoption agency. A year later, Albee produced
in *Who's Afraid of Virginia Woolf?* a modern version of Martha Wash-

ington, the "mother" of our country, who, though she is as sterile as the earlier "Mommy," defines herself as "the Earth Mother" and scorns men for being "impotent lunk-heads": "They get their courage up . . . but that's all, baby."[103] Albee's attack on mothers echoes the earlier onslaughts of John Osborne's Jimmy Porter in *Look Back in Anger* (1957), postwar England's paradigmatic "angry young man" whose rage is directed against, among other things, an "armor-plated" mother-in-law who would even make the worms in her coffin ill: "That old bitch should be dead. . . . My God, those worms will need a good dose of salts the day they get through her!"[104] At the same time, Albee's viperous mommies and vituperative men foreshadow the notoriously stereotypical Jewish mother who reigns over Philip Roth's *Portnoy's Complaint* (1970) and who reveals her love for her son by threatening him with a knife to make him eat. This aggressively "good" mother has figuratively, if not literally, reduced the neurotic Portnoy to an obsession with masturbation that functions as a pathetic revenge against the sexual inhibitions she has instilled in him even while it isolates him from true sexual power. Indeed, like one of Wylie's "five-and-ten-cent-store Lilith[s]," she has gobbled up her baby boy's virility and transformed him into a foolish analysand who begs his psychiatrist to "Bless me with manhood!"[105]

The heterosexual solutions available to victims like Portnoy inevitably continue the fetishizing of the penis as pistol with which countless male characters in male-authored contemporary literature have reclaimed and reasserted the law of the phallus. Though Roth's hero is impotent when, after a passionate wrestling match, he tries to rape the "good" Jewish girl Naomi, he lives out his extraordinary sexual fantasies with a hillbilly from West Virginia called "the Monkey," and he achieves his ultimate sexual dominance over this "Darwinian" woman when he drives her to a suicide attempt. Nevertheless, even while Roth, particularly in his characterization of Sophie Portnoy, depicts women as destructive, he does not see them—the way some of his more consciously anti-feminist contemporaries do—as intentional viragos. Just a year after Roth published *Portnoy's Complaint,* however, Norman Mailer responded to Kate Millett's attack (in *Sexual Politics,* 1969) on *An American Dream* with a masculinist treatise entitled *The Prisoner of Sex,* a tract in which he passionately traced his own literary genealogy back through the Miller of *Tropic of Capricorn* and *Nexus,* the Lawrence of *Lady Chatterley's Lover,* and the Hemingway of "The Short Happy Life of Francis Macomber."

Sardonically quoting the SCUM (Society for Cutting Up Men) manifesto—"It is now technically possible to reproduce without the aid of males . . . and to produce only females. . . .the male is an incomplete female, a walking abortion, aborted at the gene state"[106]—and recounting the story of Valeria Solanis's attempted murder of Andy Warhol, Mailer discussed the "brutal bloody war" between the sexes and compared what he ironically imagined as a feminist evaluation of the penis ("10 cubic inches" out of the "probably 3000 cubic inches" of an "average man or woman['s]" body) to his own assessment of "a firm erection on a delicate fellow" as man's "finest moral product" (36). Such remarks are defensive indeed, coming from the author who had created the viciously virile Rojack some ten years earlier, and they point to a newly anxious self-consciousness with which men responded to the second wave of feminism. Examining "the irrational male response to the emergence of the liberated woman," Christopher Lasch claims in *The Culture of Narcissism* that "modern woman's increasing demand for sexual fulfillment" is experienced as "intimidating" by men who "agonize about their capacity to satisfy it."[107] That Mailer felt he had (with nervous sarcasm) to respond to SCUM's demystifications of biological maleness, for example, suggests that, like Philip Roth, who incarnated one of his protagonists as a "breast" in the same year,[108] he worried that he might be "an incomplete female," and, at the very least, that he was sensitive to his own sense of male "delicacy." And similar worries were recorded by such other contemporary men of letters as John Barth in the short story "Night-Sea Journey" (1966) and Woody Allen in the film *Everything You Wanted To Know About Sex* (1972), both of whom recount the hapless expeditions of fragile sperm up the cavernous labyrinth of the birth canal toward the heart of darkness where the kind of female power valorized by some feminists lurks.[109]

Yet Allen's sperm wait in a kind of high-tech "ready room" and Barth's night-sea journeyer associates himself with the epic hero Odysseus, implying that the old tropes of sexual combat are still operative and have, indeed, been intensified in this period. Certainly

Lasch argues that "Feminism and the ideology of intimacy have discredited the sexual stereotypes which kept women in their place but which also made it possible to acknowledge sexual antagonism without raising it to the level of all-out warfare."[110] As if to document his point, in 1965, the science fiction writer William Tenn published an exceptionally funny short fantasy entitled "The Masculinist Revolt," in which, during the fin de siècle between 1990 and 2015, angry men revive what they see as their lost virility by bringing back "the codpiece" because they feel that "Most of their troubles could be traced to a development that occurred shortly before World War I. . . . 'Man-tailoring' [for women's clothing], the first identifiable villain."[111] In response to such emasculated costuming, Tenn's comic hero, P. Edward Pollyglow, otherwise known as "Old Pep," founds the masculinist movement by advertising his codpieces with the slogan

> MEN ARE DIFFERENT FROM WOMEN!
> Dress *differently!*
> Dress *masculinist!*
> Wear Pollyglow Men's Jumpers
> With the *Special Pollyglow Codpiece!*
> (And join the masculinist club!)   [217]

Later, he philosophizes that " 'Men are a lost sex in America. . . . Who wouldn't rather be strong than limp, hard than soft? Stand up for yourselves, men of America, stand up high!' " (223) and his "national Masculinist constitution" begins with the multiply parodic statement that " '. . . all men are created equal with women . . . that among these rights are life, liberty and the pursuit of the opposite sex . . . from each according to his sperm, to each according to her ova . . .' " (ellipses Tenn's; 223). Empowered by the "bible of Masculinism" entitled *Man: The First Sex*[112] and by an anthem praising one Hank Dorselblad, who came "out of the west, / Through all the wide border, his codpiece is best" (228), Pollyglow's followers seek to repeal the Nineteenth (women's suffrage) Amendment to the Constitution but are confronted and confounded by a "counter-revolution" led by one Elvis P. Borax, who sings in a "delicately whining tenor"

Rule, Maternal! My mother
rules my heart!
Mother never, never, never was
a tart! [239]

Finally Borax and his "avalanche of infuriated women" (250) defeat
the Masculinists and "It was almost as if Masculinism had never been"
(251). But tellingly, the movement's emblematic codpiece

> survived as a part of modern male costume. In motion, it has
> a rhythmic wave that reminds many women of a sternly shaken
> forefinger, warning them that men, at the last, can only be
> pushed so far and no farther. For men, the codpiece is still a
> flag, now a flag of truce perhaps, but it flutters in a war that
> goes on and on. [251]

Tenn, who composed "The Masculinist Revolt" as a futuristic satire in 1961, claimed that he "was subliminally aware of rapidly shift-
ing attitudes toward sexual differentiation in our society, but that
what I noticed as an anticipatory tremor was actually the first rock-
slide of the total cataclysm" (Author's Note). Interestingly, the reaction to the "cataclysm" that Tenn formulated in and as fantasy
was to be literalized within a decade by Eldridge Cleaver, who in
the middle 1970s designed, marketed, and posed for photographs
in men's trousers with codpieces. In a 1976 interview, Cleaver
claimed that he was "against penis binding," adding that he "was
trying to strike a balance between indecent exposure and emasculation, and come up with decent exposure." And two years later, in
another interview, he supplemented his discussion of the codpiece
with a diatribe against most forms of contraception, in which—as
if, again, to literalize a male writer's fantasy (in this case Woody
Allen's)—he declared that "men are the guardians of sperm" so that
"the ideal solution would not be to send sperm on suicide missions. . . ."[113]

The implications of the "cataclysm" to which both Tenn and
Cleaver had in various ways responded, moreover, were fully ex-
plored during the same decade in Thomas Berger's *Regiment of
Women* (1973), whose title alludes to John Knox's *The First Blast of*

the Trumpet Against the Monstrous Regiment of Women (1548), and which is perhaps the most conscious of the recent male novels that deal with sexual combat.[114] Interspersing Orwellian descriptions of a futurist society ruled by women with epigraphs drawn from masculinist *and* feminist thinkers (Martin Luther, Virginia Woolf, Friedrich Nietzsche, George Bernard Shaw, Olive Schreiner), Berger seems at first to satirize the social construction of gender by portraying all the ways in which his novel's subjugated men suffer from feminization: encased in uncomfortable dresses and stockings, convinced that the proper orgasm is an anal one stimulated by a dildo, and incarcerated in Sperm Banks where they are "milked" by female top sergeants, his male characters are as hesitant, insecure, and sentimental as readers of Harlequin romances.[115] But the book's conclusion fantasizes the return of a "natural" biological order. When Berger's "deviant" hero and heroine, Georgie and Harriet, escape to an unpolluted corner of Maine, they notice that, contrary to the unnatural mythology of their culture (which imagines sexual intercourse as deadly to the female of the species), the male rabbit "fucks the female" (304), and they discover, too, that Georgie is "the one with the protuberant organ" (317). Berger thus hints that what Freud called "Some Psychological Consequences of the Anatomical Distinction Between the Sexes" will lead this new Adam and Eve to a Paradise Regained.

At the same time, however, Berger's last words in the novel—a quotation from Nietzsche—are "Woman was God's *second* mistake," and precisely because we must assume that Georgie and Harriet may spawn a culture as unjust to women as their society has been to men, we must also conclude that, in this writer's opinion, both sides in the battle between the sexes are equally culpable.[116] Will the renovated history engendered by his newly gendered Edenic couple lead to the same old stalemate? Such a question is in fact examined— and unanswered—in an even more recent and popular novel, composed by a writer who, like Cleaver, became notorious for having been photographed in a costume designed to emphasize his virility. In John Irving's *The World According to Garp* (1978), Garp's wife bites off her lover's penis in an auto accident that kills one of her sons and partially blinds the other, Garp's famous feminist mother is shot by a reactionary man, and Garp himself is mowed down at the

Christlike age of thirty-three by a women's liberation fanatic who has arranged to have her tongue removed. Though Irving's portrayal of feminists as self-mutilating hysterics is savage, his novel's denouement suggests that, as the battle of the sexes grows increasingly violent, a victory for either side becomes virtually unimaginable.[117]

The lengths to which the poet Robert Bly has quite recently gone in an attempt to energize the new men whom he sees as no-men or "wimps" simply underscore this point. A story in the March 19, 1986, *San Francisco Chronicle* recounts Bly's view that "The men's movement is going through a sea change these days. The sensitive-guy model is being replaced by the Wild Man in search of the primitive roots of his maleness."[118] Deploying "30 conga drummers hammering out a tribal beat" and "men capering about in fearsome masks," Bly sermonizes that "there is something about being a man over the last 20 years that is connected with the feeling of inadequacy," notes grimly that "that 20-year period coincides with the rise of feminism" and adds glumly that "the force field of the mother is very strong." Yet, despite his hopeful drumming and dancing, he mourns that "We've lost some connection with the deep inner roots of power associated with the macho or brute male." The futile ferocity that marks Ted Hughes's "Lovesong," the poem with which we began this meditation on sexual battle, is thus even more characteristic of contemporary sexual rhetoric than it was of Tennyson's. Hilarion does, after all, defeat Ida—and he defeats her through love while making "the woman's cause" his own. But Hughes's vision of female curses and male threats seems to promise a future in which the battle between men and women escalates to an unthinkably apocalyptic denouement:

> His promises were the surgeon's gag
> Her promises took the top off his skull
> She would get a brooch made of it
> His vows pulled out all her sinews
> He showed her how to make a love-knot
> Her vows put his eyes in formalin

It is probably no coincidence, then, that in the late 1950s Ted Hughes's wife, the poet Sylvia Plath, wrote a story entitled "Stone Boy with Dolphin" in which she fictionalized her first meeting with her husband-to-be as a ferocious encounter between a brooding young woman named Dody Ventura and a leonine poet named Leonard who assaults her with a brutal kiss—"Green shadow, moss shadow, raked her mouth"—to which she responds with a vampiric bite:

> Teeth gouged. And held. Salt, warm salt, laving the tastebuds of her tongue. Teeth dug to meet. An ache started far off at their bone root. Mark that, mark that. But he shook. Shook her bang against the solid-grained substance of the wall.[119]

"Kissing—biting— / Where is the difference?" might be Dody's motto, as it was the motto of Kleist's Penthesilea, but, significantly, Sylvia Plath, as a woman of letters, was a citizen of an age in which, as she once remarked, she and her husband were both brought up to "romp through words together,"[120] an age in which she herself had realized many of the ambitions of Tennyson's Ida. Yet, from her point of view, as from Hughes's, it appears that the battle of the sexes which was waged throughout this century meant that sexy seduction was all too often betrayed into stalemated violence.

2 Fighting for Life: The Women's Cause

It seems congenital with some women to have deeply rooted in their innermost nature a smoldering enmity, ay, sometimes a physical disgust to men, it is a kind of kin-feeling to the race-dislike of white men to black.

—George Egerton

How utterly detestable mannishness is; so mighty and strong and comforting when you have been mewed up with women all your life, and then suddenly, in a second, far away, utterly imbecile and aggravating, with a superior self-satisfied smile because a woman says one thing one minute and another the next. Men ought to be horse-whipped, all the grown men, all who have ever had that self-satisfied smile, all, all, horse-whipped until they apologize on their knees.

—Dorothy Richardson

The great civil war, . . . that will come and must come before the world can begin to grow up, will be fought out on this terrain of man and woman, and we must storm and hold Cape Turk before we talk of social justice.

—Sylvia Townsend Warner

If literary men in the late nineteenth and early twentieth centuries portrayed women's invasion of the public sphere as an act of aggression that inaugurated a battle of the sexes, did late nineteenth- and twentieth-century literary women transform their words into weapons in order to wrest authority from men? As if to imply that the man's case is inextricably entangled in the woman's cause, Ted

Hughes' murderous "Lovesong" is countered not only by Sylvia Plath's story "Stone Boy with Dolphin" but also countered in advance by the poem entitled "Words" (1963?), which defines linguistic units as "Axes / After whose stroke the wood rings [.]"[1] While Plath's echoing hatchet strokes may have been a personal response to the familial crowing of Ted Hughes, they also evoke a tradition that goes back to Emily Dickinson, who "took [her] Power in [her] Hand— / And went against the World—" and forward to Olga Broumas, who warns in one text that "I want this poem to be a weapon / I give it authority / To kill."[2] Though, for the most part, nineteenth- and twentieth-century women writers have been far less confident of women's victory than their male contemporaries were, they nevertheless document the casualties of a battle of the sexes, a battle over the zone that many men experienced as a no man's land because it debilitated masculinity but that a number of women defined, if only fleetingly, as a no man's land because it seemed to herald what Charlotte Perkins Gilman called a "Herland."

That women have been less confident may seem paradoxical, in view of the resentment with which such men as W. S. Gilbert, T. S. Eliot, D. H. Lawrence, Ernest Hemingway, and Norman Mailer reacted to what they perceived as unprecedented female power. Yet when we turn to works by women who were contemporaries of these men, we find that female writers have often felt even more imperiled than men did by the sexual combat in which they were obliged to engage. For, as is so frequently the case in the history of sex relations, men view the smallest female steps toward autonomy as threatening strides that will strip them of all authority, while women respond to such anxious reaction-formations with a nervous sense of guilt and a paradoxical sense of vulnerability. At the same time, some women, particularly in the modernist period, have felt empowered by every advance toward cultural centrality, so that the female half of the dialogue is considerably more complicated than the male.[3]

No doubt because of this complexity, where male-authored descriptions of sexual conflict are generally quite straightforward and almost always feature literal duels, battles, or wrestling matches, women's works—though they sometimes include physical confrontations—frequently imagine female victory either through duplicity and subterfuge or through providential circumstance. In women's

texts, men generally win tests of bodily strength, but women outwit
or outlast men who fortuitously succumb to fatal mischances. Unwilling or unable to envision female aggression even in the face of
male assault, a number of literary women create characters who reap
the benefits of battle without having to endure the risks of combat
or who win their struggle with a male antagonist through such sacrificial but murderous gestures as infanticide.[4] In fact, as Dickinson's
"I took my Power in my Hand" suggests, many women writers may
have feared that naked bellicosity boomerangs: after comparing
herself to David and her foe to Goliath, the poet ironically admits
that "I aimed my Pebble—but Myself / Was all the one that fell—."
Thus in an even more telling poem Dickinson prefigures the view
of sexual battle formulated by many of her descendants when she
presents triumph as a kind of coincidence:

> I rose—because He sank—
> I thought it would be opposite—
> But when his power dropped—
> My Soul grew straight.   [J. 616]

That "He" sank, the poet implies, was none of her doing, yet because
"He" just *happened* to sink, her "Soul grew" victoriously "straight."

The contradiction between aggression and femininity that is resolved in this poem posed, of course, a particular problem to women
of Dickinson's period, who, as we argued in *The Madwoman in the
Attic,* constructed the emblematic figure of an enraged but tormented
madwoman in order simultaneously to repress and express their
feelings of anger. But in many ways turn-of-the-century, modernist,
and postmodernist literary women were almost as troubled by their
own fury as Dickinson and her contemporaries were by theirs. Still,
the accelerating entrance of women into the public sphere which so
disturbed literary men did enable some female artists to legitimize
and rationalize the complaints of the madwoman. Moving the woman
rebel from the liminal zone of the third storey in which nineteenth-
century artists had sequestered her to the first storey in which her
own story could become central, Edwardian suffrage polemics, like
much female-authored fiction of the period, employed military imagery, often couched in a rhetoric of sacrifice, in order to glimpse
the possibility of female victory in the battle of the sexes, while mod-

ernist writers reveled in private triumphs that were often facilitated by their new public authority. Moreover, although postmodernist women of letters responded to the male backlash that characterized their era with some vivid nightmares of female defeat, many contemporary literary women have begun to dream with increasing fervor of a triumphant woman warrior, a warrior who has, in some cases, implicitly righted the wrongs of women as they were perceived in the nineteenth century.

Certainly, even at the height of her personal war against Hughes, Sylvia Plath knew that her deadliest sentences transcribed a plot that originated with her ancestresses. Quite early in "Stone Boy with Dolphin," for instance, Dody Ventura meditates in her "third-floor attic room" on the defeats of her precursors: "witches on the rack . . . Joan of Arc crackling at the stake . . . anonymous ladies flaring like torches in the rending metal of Riviera roadsters . . . Zelda enlightened, burning behind the bars of her madness" (*JP* 175). Accepting the inevitability of victimization—"Unwincing, in her mind's eye, she bared her flesh. Here. Strike home" (175)—this character is trapped inside a classic story of female vulnerability in the battle of the sexes. Elsewhere, moreover, Plath hints that she half-consciously associates the writings of at least a few major Victorian precursors—namely, the Brontë sisters—with the depiction of threats to women, indeed with what Joyce Carol Oates, in an essay on *Wuthering Heights,* calls a "bleak, somber, deathly wisdom."[5]

The wife of a Yorkshireman, Plath had visited Haworth, where she reverently toured the Brontë parsonage, noting that "They [the sisters] touched this, wore that, wrote here in a house redolent with ghosts," and then journeyed to Top Withens, the site of *Wuthering Heights* (1847), ironically observing that "There are two ways to the stone house, both tiresome."[6] On the same trip, however, she planned a story entitled "All the Dead Dears," a tale which was to be "set in Yorkshire (*Wuthering Heights* background)" and which, even while it obliquely alludes to the sexual violence of Emily Brontë's novel, suggests Plath's own sense that the story's neo-Victorian protagonist—a "woman who *almost* has second sight"—must herself be killed by her visions of the dead. That Plath's Nelly Meehan, a revision of Brontë's Nelly Dean, becomes a victim as well as a votary of the spirit world, implies Plath's sense that, in the Brontë's territory, female power may be dangerous. Similarly, Plath's statement in a later text, a poem called "Wuthering Heights" (1962), that "The horizons ring me like faggots" (*CP* 167), with its allusion to witch-burning, identifies a key, female-authored nineteenth-century novel with a plot of female sacrifice.

Analyses of such texts as Emily Brontë's *Wuthering Heights,* her Gondal poems, and Charlotte Brontë's *Jane Eyre* indicate that the American writer's impulse was reasonable. For though the Gondal texts concentrate on the imperious autonomy of the queenly A. G. A., who might almost be seen as a prototype of Princess Ida, *Wuthering Heights* dramatizes not only Heathcliff's physical abuse of Isabella Linton and the second Catherine but also the patriarchal world's horrifying defeat of the first Catherine.[7] Even the Gondal verses, moreover, record their author's dreams of triumph achieved primarily through passive resistance and providential redemption. In the well-known "The Prisoner: A Fragment," for example, the defeated female speaker can only imagine herself transfigured when "dawns the Invisible" and when "the Unseen its truth reveals."[8] In a society where, as Emily Dickinson put it, "My portion is Defeat— today— / A paler luck than Victory" (J. 639), it was often necessary for women artists to claim that "Captivity is Consciousness— / So's Liberty" (J. 384).

It is in *Jane Eyre,* however, that, as if to surface the conflicts that haunt both Emily Brontë and Emily Dickinson, a woman trying to escape captivity not through consciousness but through revolt—a woman who inhabits a "third-floor attic room"—is most graphically shown grappling with her husband in a paradigmatic physical combat that may have functioned for many women writers as a kind of primal scene of sexual battle.[9] Describing Bertha Mason Rochester's fight with her husband after his aborted wedding to Jane, Brontë notes that she was "a big woman, in stature almost equalling her husband, and corpulent besides: she showed virile force in the contest—more than once she almost throttled him, athletic as he was" (ch. 26). In this scene, moreover, as in her earlier attack on her brother Richard, Bertha *bites* "like a tigress" (ch. 20) with exactly the vampiric fury of Dody Ventura: "the lunatic sprang and grappled his throat viciously and laid her teeth to his cheek" (ch. 26).

Yet, as we all know, despite her talent for biting and wrestling,

Bertha does not have even the shadow of a chance to win her battle with Rochester, and her husband's refusal to unleash his own powers—"he would not strike; he would only wrestle"—ultimately signifies his confidence in his mastery. In this respect, *Jane Eyre*'s depiction of the marital tussle between the Rochesters suggests that, even in the years when Tennyson was writing *The Princess*, women artists could not help believing that what the creator of Prince Hilarion celebrated as "the woman's cause" was at best a problematic project, at worst a lost cause. Nor is that cause, in Charlotte Brontë's view, likely to be "man's," except in the providentially transformed, happily-ever-after world of *Jane Eyre*'s Ferndean. Before that conclusion, in the grim realm of Thornfield's attic, male confidence and power are unshakeable: after Rochester has pinioned Bertha's arms behind her and bound her to a chair as efficiently as the male minions of Lawrence's Delilah tie up his Samson, he bitterly remarks that "I must shut up my prize." His obvious pain is mingled with triumph, for at least—despite his failure to wed his "true" bride— he has proved his own virility by defeating a woman whose pseudovirility has severely threatened the patriarchal order he represents.

The contrast between Brontë's grotesque madwoman and Tennyson's wayward but learned princess implies a more general distinction between male and female attitudes toward the battle of the sexes in the mid-nineteenth century. Women writers from Charlotte Brontë to George Eliot seem to have felt that the female autonomy which inspired such struggles could only have been dangerous, even monstrous: as we speculated in *The Madwoman in the Attic*, they saw woman's ambition as Satanic because, experiencing such ambition in themselves and understanding its real implications, they realized the nature of the sociocultural changes it might bring about. More importantly, however, such women writers must have understood that there would have to *be* enormous sociocultural changes in order for women to fight openly for power in the real world. Men of Tennyson's generation may have deplored the aspirations of women, but they were able to depict pitched battles between the sexes either because they did not seriously understand the real constraints of women's situation or because they did not view female ambition as genuinely threatening. That Tennyson was inspired by the lonely and tormented rebellion of the real-life Caroline Norton to create not only the haughtily autonomous figure of Ida but also an entire community of followers over whom Ida rules demonstrates yet again the discrepancy between male and female perceptions of the woman's cause and its effects.

The woman who was one of Tennyson's few rivals for the post of poet laureate after Wordsworth's death, for example, regarded *The Princess* as "a fairy tale": writing to her future husband, Elizabeth Barrett Browning—then Elizabeth Barrett—described a poem "called the 'University,' the university-members being all female," and went on to ask, "Now isn't this world too old and fond of steam, for blank verse poems, in ever so many books, to be written on the fairies?"[10] Some three years before Tennyson had begun work on his description of a female community, moreover, Barrett Browning had described a powerful female who rules extensive domains that are realistically criss-crossed by very modern steam engines: as she is presented by her poet-lover Bertram, a marginalized man who relates the story of their relationship, Lady Geraldine of "Lady Geraldine's Courtship" (1844) "has farms and she has manors, she can threaten and command," and she even has—as in some early suffragist's fantasy—"voters in the Commons."[11] Significantly, however, when Bertram reproaches Geraldine for what he assumes is her prideful autonomy, he discovers that, unlike Tennyson's princess, she has always believed that the woman's cause is *man*. Though he claims that he has fallen, "struck down before her" (LXXXVIII), Bertram had wrested a crucial sexual victory from Geraldine when he declared that she must " 'Learn more reverence, madam . . . for Adam's seed, MAN!' " (LXXV). And unlike Ida, whose forces actually defeat Hilarion in battle, Geraldine—in what Barrett Browning evidently intends as an attempt at realism—gains her lover by adopting a time-honored feminine strategy of surrender: as she abases herself to the artist whom she adores, Geraldine indicates that she has always agreed with his self-estimate and seductively adds that she is hardly "worthy of thy poet-heart" (Conclusion, VIII).

To be sure, Barrett Browning's later heroine Aurora Leigh attains precisely the autonomy that Geraldine relinquishes, and she seems to gain it at least in part because she has refused a suitor who appears even more arrogant than the triumphant Bertram. Repudiating her cousin Romney's offer of marriage, Aurora proudly asserts that "I too have my vocation,—work to do" (II, 455). Yet despite Barrett Browning's depiction of Aurora's explicit feminism, this writer takes pains to depict her heroine's struggle for an education in terms that are deliberately anti-utopian compared to those in which Tennyson portrays his "fairy tale" university for women. Enduring a standard Victorian training in ladyhood, Aurora is obliged to learn "cross-stitch" and to spin glass, stuff birds, and model flowers in wax (I, 447, 425); in fact, unlike Princess Ida, she gains her only real learning by stealthily seeking out "the secret of a garret-room" (I, 834) filled with her dead father's books.

Of course, at the end of Barrett Browning's "novel-poem" Aurora achieves what has to be seen as a triumph compared to the defeats of Geraldine and Ida. Unlike Ida's, her literary projects succeed, and unlike Geraldine, she wins her lover not through renunciation but through a providential accident that, like the maiming of Charlotte Brontë's Rochester, softens his spirit. But Barrett Browning's evocation of the same kind of providence on which Charlotte Brontë depended reminds us yet again that Victorian women writers could not imagine female characters who might win sexual struggles through their own direct actions. Blinded and bereft of his patriarchal property, Romney fortuitously "sinks" so that Aurora can fortunately "rise" in just the way that, when Rochester's "power drop[s]," Jane's "Soul [grows] straight." As in *Jane Eyre*, an outright battle between hero and heroine has been evaded, almost certainly because both the author and her protagonist assume that a directly agonistic sexual confrontation would only issue in defeat for the woman.

A similar withdrawal from overt conflict and deployment of providential death also permeate the work of George Eliot, who arranges the coincidental death by water of unpleasant or villainous male characters in fictions from *The Mill on the Floss* (1860) to *Daniel Deronda* (1876).[12] Most dramatically, in *Daniel Deronda* Gwendolyn Harleth sees "my wish outside me" and hears her heart say " 'Die!' " when her cruel husband, Grandcourt, sinks into the sea after a boating mishap (ch. 56). Such women writers as Brontë, Barrett Browning, and Eliot clearly understood that their heroines were embroiled in sexual contests, but they plainly believed that only a madwoman would attempt to win such a battle through "virile force." Rather, both the authors' and the characters' hostility had to be distanced and disguised so that, like Gwendolyn's "wish," it stood "outside" intentionality. Indeed, it almost seems as if Victorian women writers can only express or enact overt hostility when they are discussing issues other than the woman's cause. Like Eliot, whose *Daniel Deronda* increasingly focuses on the politics of Judaism, Barrett Browning frequently uses such political causes as abolitionism or Italian unification to vent the spleen which informs her avowal in "A Curse for a Nation" that "A curse from the depths of womanhood / Is very salt, and bitter, and good" (48).

Yet even when Barrett Browning consciously sets her revulsion against slavery in the context of rage at sexual oppression, she creates a female character who can only battle her male enemy indirectly. The raped black speaker of "The Runaway Slave at Pilgrim's Point" smoulders with rage at her brutal owner, but she displaces her fury onto the white face of her illegitimate child, a face that has "The *master's* look, that used to fall / On my soul like his lash" (XXI). Thus, in a gesture that recalls the vengeful child-murders of mythic or fictional characters from Lilith, Medea, and Procne to Martha Ray in Wordsworth's "The Thorn" (1798) and Hetty Sorel in Eliot's *Adam Bede* (1859), she commits infanticide, and, like some of these characters, she is maddened by the discovery that, even though she has punished the man who betrayed her, she has also murdered and betrayed a part of herself. The act of infanticide, Barrett Browning implies, is a woman's most potent form of revenge against men because it destroys the patrilineage, but at the same time it is a telling sign of female vulnerability because it reveals that one of the few kinds of power a woman has is destructive power over her child.

Another way in which Victorian women of letters evade depictions of direct female aggression against men even while they implicitly represent a battle of the sexes is through the creation of characters who exemplify the dictum of Jane Austen's Henry Tilney that "man has the advantage of choice, woman only the power of refusal" (*Northanger Abbey,* ch. 10). A paradigmatic text here is Christina Rossetti's "Goblin Market" (1862), whose heroic Lizzie subjects herself to the pulpy assaults of a horde of goblin men in order to save her fallen sister Laura from the deleterious side effects of forbidden fruit. Refusing to eat the fruits she wishes to carry away with her, Lizzie passively resists what amounts to a vegetable rape, as the goblins elbow, jostle, claw her, tear her gown, soil her stockings, and twitch her hair out, squeezing "their fruits / Against her mouth to make her eat."[13] Like Emily Dickinson, who defined herself as "Empress of Calvary," Lizzie voluntarily endures her ordeal while refusing to fight back. And like Dickinson, who achieves redemptive authority by allowing herself to be "Born—Bridalled—Shrouded— / In a Day—" (J.1072), Lizzie becomes her sister's savior, urging Laura to feed on, and be healed by, the traces of violation that the goblin men have left on her body: "Never mind my bruises, / Hug me, kiss me, suck my juices" (1.467–68). Though the goblin men have been "Worn out by [Lizzie's] resistance" (1.438) and her sister has been cured, Rossetti's heroine has refrained from actual retaliation. Thus, though a war between goblin men and delicate maidens has been won by the "weaker" sex, a full-scale battle of the sexes has been evaded.

Whether they rely on the intervention of providence to defeat male enemies, whether they revenge themselves on male foes by displacing their anger onto children, or whether they employ strategies of passive resistance, the female characters created by Victorian women writers appear continually conscious of their own vulnerability in the face of male potency and privilege. Perhaps most tellingly, in a surrealistic dream-vision that she recorded in her *Gifts of Power* (c. 1843–45), the black Shaker visionary Rebecca Cox Jackson summarized a dread of male violence that explains why so many nineteenth-century women writers believed that the male gift of strength could only be countered by female gifts of faith, luck, duplicity, and passivity. Jackson's "A Dream of Slaughter" describes a scene in which a mysterious male intruder takes "a lance and [lays] my nose open and then he cut[s] my head on the right side, from the back to the front above my nose [so that] The skin and blood covered me like a veil from my head to my lap."[14] Carving her up as if he were a forerunner of England's infamous turn-of-the-century Jack the Ripper, this phantom antagonist strikes such fear in her that, because she knows "He can show no mercy," Jackson devoutly believes that she must "sit still, as though I was dead, for that was the only thing that would save me" (95). Playing dead and prayerfully hoping that, as Jackson says, "Thy life is hid in Christ"—in the providential image of a redeemer—were crucial nineteenth-century res-

olutions of the terrifying problem posed not only by nightmare intruders but also by such milder men as Tennyson's, along with
Gilbert and Sullivan's, invading heroes.

———————

Male aggression appears to have inspired very different responses
from turn-of-the-century women of letters, many of whom, even
while they may seem to reenact the evasive maneuvers of their high
Victorian ancestresses, self-consciously focus on these maneuvers in
order to emphasize the centrality of the sexual battle in which they
feel themselves to be engaged. No doubt one reason for this newly
keen awareness of sexual warfare was many women's equally intense
realization that the story of *The Princess* was no longer what Barrett
Browning had called "a fairy tale." As Martha Vicinus has shown,
"By 1897 women were largely accepted as part of the world of higher
education, albeit a peripheral and minor part."[15]
   Thus one student at Newnham actually wrote home about a favorite tutor that "She *is* a Princess Ida," and undergraduates at Girton sang a cheerful anthem which expressed in real life a political
determination as strong as that articulated by both Tennyson's and
Gilbert's Ida:

> "Girton my friend, you are young, are young,"
>   Said Cambridge old and grey,
> "And it is not meet that a tree whose growth
> Is centuries old, should plight its troth
>   To the mushroom birth of to-day, to-day,
>   To the mushroom birth of to-day."
>   But full and clear falls on the ear
>   The answer of Girton for all to hear,—
>
> "You may say us Yea, you may say us Nay,
> But the tide has turned and we've left the bay,
> We've crossed the bar and we've felt the spray
> Where the winds and waves have their freest play,—
> We like it, good Sir, and we'll have our way!"[16]

Paradoxically, however, because late nineteenth-century women had
greater expectations of victory, it became crucially important for

them to analyze the dynamics of defeat. Certainly such turn-of-the-century feminist theorists as Olive Schreiner and Charlotte Perkins Gilman consistently strove to outline visions of a world transformed by a transformation of woman's role. For both, as for their many suffragist readers, western culture's traditional gender arrangement was a parasitic one in which men and women fought against, and fed upon, each other.

Schreiner, for example, argued that, since woman was reduced "like a field bug, to the passive exercise of her sex functions alone," she was passed from man to man as an object of sexual exploitation. "Because the larger male has so long and so mercilessly suppressed the weaker and exterminated those who refused to submit," Schreiner claimed in *From Man to Man* (1927) that only "servile" women survived. In the same text, moreover, she followed the Victorian writer William Black in outlining a story about a female Shakespeare comparable to the one that Virginia Woolf constructs in *A Room of One's Own* and she did so by meditating on the aesthetic cost of such suppression, asking,

> What has humanity not lost by the suppression and subjection of the weaker sex by the muscularly stronger sex alone? We have a Shakespeare; but what of the possible Shakespeares we might have had, who passed their life from youth upward brewing currant wine and making pastries for fat country squires to eat, with no glimpse of the freedom of life and action, necessary even to poach on deer in the green forest, stifled out without one line written, simply because, being of the weaker sex, life gave no room for action and grasp on life?[17]

Similarly, Charlotte Perkins Gilman declared in *Woman and Economics* (1898) that, though women may have originally been the first sex, they had been brutally reduced to secondariness by predatory male sexuality.[18]

Both were articulating assumptions about the violence of male sexuality which were more drastically formulated by such crusaders as Christabel Pankhurst, Jane Addams, and Margaret Sanger. Pankhurst's *The Great Scourge and How To End It* (1913), for instance, presents women as innocent sacrifices to the contaminating, even murderous, male phallus: "the vast majority of men," she informed her readers just when Walter Heape was analyzing sex antagonism, "contract sexual disease in one of its forms before they are married. Let every woman learn that to cure a man of such a disease is long and difficult and strictly speaking impossible, since no doctor can give a guarantee that his patient is cured and will not immediately or in years to come infect his wife. . . ."[19] Thus, in an attempt to transcend female vulnerability and transform male violence, all these thinkers sought to imagine a society not unlike the community envisioned by Tennyson's Ida and Hilarion, a world in which the woman's cause is man's.

Because they gained a regiment of followers, moreover, these polemicists had high hopes for success. Such posters as the *Haunted House* helped them dramatize their sense that woman was a titanically rebellious spirit brooding over the house of culture (figure, below). While the figure in *The Haunted House* is almost Gothic in her posture, other texts frequently employed a rousing military rhetoric com-

The Haunted House. Poster. Museum of London.

parable to Princess Ida's. As a major article in the first issue of *Votes for Women* (1907) declared,

> The founders and leaders of the movement must lead, the non-commissioned officers must carry out their instructions, the rank and file must loyally share the burdens of the fight. For there is no compulsion to come into our ranks, but those who come must come as soldiers ready to march onwards in battle array.[20]

Similarly, one of the first women arrested for arson as part of the suffrage struggle claimed in court "that militant Suffragettes stand in an analogous position to soldiers," and the "weekly paper, *Common Cause*, pictured a woman in armor on its front page for over two years (1912–14)."[21] Writing about the political strategies of women who dressed on ceremonial occasions as warriors like Britomart and Joan of Arc, Winifred Holtby observed in 1935 that

> One of the great virtues of the Militant Suffrage Movement was its mastery of the art of ritual. Its great processions, its pageants, banners, badges, its prison uniforms, its martyr's funerals, for a brief time took the place usually held by military or religious ceremony in the imagination of those who saw them.[22]

Yet, as marching and hunger-striking suffragists discovered, and as Holtby's reference to martyrs reveals, even the most militant masses of women were still inexorably subject to the authority of men who, like the intruder in Jackson's dream, could "show no mercy." Passed in 1913, England's infamous Cat and Mouse Act, for instance, provided for the release and subsequent re-arrest of debilitated hunger-strikers, metaphorically reducing women to scurrying victims stalked by inescapable Toms and Tommies (figure, p. 79). The very act of hunger-striking, moreover, along with the torture of the forcible feeding with which authorities countered that act, was surrounded by a rhetoric of sacrifice designed, as Martha Vicinus has shown, to emphasize the way in which "the language of the spirit came naturally to those who gave up their bodies to a moral cause."[23] Politicizing the passive resistance that had enabled Christina Rossetti's Lizzie to redeem her fallen sister, suffragists also

The Cat and Mouse Act. Poster. Museum of London.

followed Rossetti's lead in pointing to the sainthood and sublimity
of women who refused to eat the forbidden fruits offered by men.
Wrote one former prisoner,

> the food, so delicious, so tempting, is offered by man to the
> woman, representative of her sex, and for the sake of her sex
> she must refuse even to taste it. So the woman triumphs over
> the man. . . . in this revolution of womanhood each woman
> strives to remove the old stigma of the story of Adam and Eve.[24]

But ultimately, of course, the way to remove Eve's stigma was by
taking on the stigmata of a Dickinsonian "Empress of Calvary," that
is, by becoming a female Christ, as Emily Wilding Davison sought
to do when she flung herself in front of the king's racehorse after
deciding that "to re-enact the tragedy of Calvary for generations
yet unborn, that is the last consummate sacrifice of the Militant!"[25]

The figure of the sacrificed militant may explain why, even though
loyal crusaders for "the Cause" produced polemics which urged
women to battle men directly, turn-of-the-century women novelists
and poets continued to create characters who are either defeated
by male intransigence or who overcome their sexual opponents
through the same indirect strategies and the same providential luck
delineated by Victorian women. In addition, the iconography of the
martyred suffragist may explain why a number of literary women
continued to deconstruct their male precursors' visions of feminist
power, as if to imply, yet again, that in the real world women could
never achieve the authority attributed to them by some men of letters. In particular, women of letters who did not overtly align themselves with the suffragist movement and who may have questioned
some of its methods, insisted on what seemed to them to be "realism."

In *Ethan Frome* (1911), for instance, Edith Wharton portrays a
Zenobia strikingly different from Hawthorne's proud and beautiful
heroine. A nagging, shrewish wife, seven years older than her unhappy husband, Wharton's Zeena is only able, first, to achieve power
over him by exploiting her rights as an invalid, and then by profiting
from the providential invalidism of his lover, Mattie Silver. Clearly,
for Wharton the glamorous and threatening strength of Hawthorne's Zenobia was as unrealistic as the public and private bonding
of women that her mentor Henry James explored in *The Bostonians*.

Thus, though Wharton does not explicitly examine "the woman question" in *Ethan Frome,* her novel implicitly points to an issue which concerned many of her contemporaries: the issue of what women could realistically expect to attain and at what cost. Significantly, as the hope for a new future merged with revulsion against a contaminated past, and as the vision of a New Woman fused with horror at the traditional woman, much female-authored literature oscillated between extremes of exuberance and despair, between dreams of miraculous victory and nightmares of violent defeat.

Such an oscillation is perhaps most brilliantly depicted in Kate Chopin's terse, O. Henry-like "The Story of an Hour" (1894), whose heroine, Louise Mallard, experiences a private moment of ecstasy after hearing that her husband has been killed in a "railroad disaster" but then, ironically enough, suffers a public shock of horror when she sees that her spouse is still alive.[26] Although her doctors, conscious that she has always had "a heart trouble," decide she has "died of heart disease—of joy that kills," Chopin makes it clear that her protagonist has really died of disappointment. In the hour when Louise thought herself a widow—"Free! Body and soul free!"—there had been "a feverish triumph" in this woman's eyes, "and she carried herself unwittingly like a goddess of Victory" (354). But if, in the first half of the story Louise Mallard "rose because he sank," at the tale's end her situation is "opposite": she sinks because he seems to have literally risen from the dead. Although she has actually thought of her husband as "kind" and "tender," she had realized in a "brief moment of illumination" that she wanted to "live for herself" with "no powerful will bending hers . . ." (353). Yet the fate that appeared to have liberated her has returned her to what she defines as captivity.

Louise's vision of marriage-as-captivity is even more angrily delineated in George Egerton's "Virgin Soil" (in her collection *Discords,* 1894), a story about a runaway wife that is almost entirely devoted to the woman's impassioned denunciation of her husband's brutal sexual will and of her mother's complicity in "deliver[ing] me body and soul into his hands without preparing me in any way for the ordeal I was to go through" (157). Indeed, where Chopin's heroine dreads a coercion she associates as much with kindness as with cruelty, Egerton's Florence depicts her husband as unremittingly cruel, her marriage as a "hateful yoke," and her sexual life as "a nightly degradation" (155). From her point of view, sexuality is nothing but a form of combat which the virginal bride is doomed to lose because of her socially sanctioned ignorance. Reproaching her mother, Florence declares that

> "You gave me not one weapon in my hand to defend myself against the possible attacks of man at his worst. You sent me out to fight the biggest battle of a woman's life, the one in which she ought to know every turn of the game, with a white gauze . . . of maidenly purity as a shield." [157]

As if to illustrate Christabel Pankhurst's claim that men are contaminating, the soiled virgin of "Virgin Soil" graphically describes her revulsion at her husband as well as her own murderous rage: "I loathe him," she exclaims to her mother, "shiver at the touch of his lips, his breath, his hands; . . . my whole body revolts at his touch" (160), adding that her life has been "one long crucifixion . . . " (159).

Despite the declarations of independence sworn by such characters as Florence and such polemicists as Christabel Pankhurst, and despite the redemptive martyrdom sought by Emily Davison, however, the inevitability of female crucifixion—sexual or social, literal or figurative—haunts a number of texts by turn-of-the-century women. Olive Schreiner's "Little African Story" (1893), for example, recounts the brutal sacrifice of a young servant girl who is murdered by three ruffians while trying to warn a family (which has also been brutal to her) that these criminals plan to attack them; and Schreiner's *Story of an African Farm* (1883) also meditates on the inexorability of female victimization in patriarchal culture, more explicitly identifying femininity with martyrdom.[27] But it is in Charlotte Mew's extraordinary "A White Night" (1903) that a staunchly independent New Woman is forced to confront an archaic ceremony of female sacrifice which seems to suggest that, even in an age when the woman's cause has made great progress, the ritual immolation of women persists at the heart of western cultural institutions.

Both Jamesian and Gothic, Mew's story is an account of a Spanish adventure purportedly told to the author by a mining engineer named Cameron, who relates that in 1876 he joined his sister, Ella, and her husband, King, on an expedition into the remote back-country of Spain and specifically to a town of "extreme antiquity."[28] Near this town, the English trio find themselves journeying past a sinister "Calvary" (148) to an old church and convent, where they witness a "bizarre" Mass conducted by a group of monks and priests who, after intoning the Office for the Dead, bury a woman alive before the high altar. Interestingly, though Cameron and, to a lesser extent, King, are horrified by what they see, they ultimately treat the event as a "spectacle," while the New Womanly Ella, who is described as an unfazeable traveler, "would tell you," according to Cameron, "that the horror of those hours hasn't altogether ceased to haunt her, that it visits her in dreams and poisons sleep" (159). Even during the event, indeed, Cameron defines the procession as a "solemn farce" but realizes that in "Ella's presence" this "was not a woman's comedy" (154).

Still more striking than the contrast between Ella's and Cameron's reaction is the distinction between the trauma Ella suffers and the paradoxical triumph that the sacrificed woman attains, as she acquiesces in the martyrdom which puts her, like Poe's Madeline Usher, "living in the tomb."[29] Although, as the procession enters the church, the "grave and passionless" keynotes of male liturgy are counterpointed by "a piercing, intermittent note, an awful discord"— the woman's almost involuntary screams of protest—Cameron observes that even at this point she was "more like a person in some trance of terror or of anguish than a voluntary rebel; her cries bespoke a physical revulsion into which her spirit didn't enter; they were not her own—they were," like the hostile wishes experienced by George Eliot's Gwendolyn in *Daniel Deronda,* "outside herself" (151–152). As the ceremony quickens its pace, therefore, this nameless female martyr abandons the cries that are as inharmonious as the protests voiced by the heroines of Egerton's *Discords* and "with an air of proud surrender, of magnificent disdain," she catches the "trick of . . . quiescence, acquiescence" (153–54). As Cameron comments, "She had, one understood, her part to play," and if she wasn't at the ceremony's beginning "quite prepared," she "played it later with superb effect" (152).

But is this rite of living death a ceremony of innocence or of guilt? One phrase at the end of the story hints that, like Ella, this woman might have been a rebel: she might have "one way or other,

clogged the wheels of an inflexible machine," that is, she might have
defied a transcendent law which has "the face of nothing human"
but is an impersonal and inexorable "system," a "rule" (159). Yet at
the same time, the woman's (and Mew's) complicity in this drama
of sacrifice suggests a belief that defiance can only be momentary,
for defeat is inevitable and eternal. What Ella has to confront is the
extremity of the fact that the *Ur* world of the archaic Church defines
woman as a scapegoat. In addition, that Mew chooses to relate the
timeless nightmare of "A White Night" from the point of view of a
male narrator indicates the author's own belief that the male perspective on the spectacle of female sacrifice is a normative one, and
that the female horror at such a spectacle is unspeakable. The allegorically named Ella, who seems by the end of the story to be
reduced from the New Woman to Everywoman, hastens to lodge a
protest with the British Consul but her expressions of revulsion are
as ineffective as the nameless woman's discordant screams have been.
Silenced like the woman buried at the center of the sanctuary, Ella
can only be heard by the reader through the interstices of her
brother's text.[30]

Yet even when the victimized woman undertakes to act and speak
for herself in turn-of-the-century fiction, she is often forced back
upon strategies comparable to those of her Victorian precursors. In
both George Egerton's "Wedlock" (1894) and Mary E. Wilkins Freeman's "Old Woman Magoun" (1909), women revenge themselves
on men through infanticides like the one described by Barrett
Browning in "The Runaway Slave at Pilgrim's Point." Specifically,
in "Wedlock," a woman resists the brutality of her husband first by
beating and then by murdering his three children from a former
marriage. At the end of the story, as a "ghastly pool" of "thick
sorghum red" blackens in an upstairs bedroom, Egerton's heroine,
Susan, dozes in a chair downstairs, with her hands "crimson as if
she has dipped them in dye" (144). And that significant scenes from
this drama are witnessed with dread and excitement by a female
author who lodges upstairs suggests yet again the New Woman's
preoccupation with the persistence of the traditional plot of sexual
combat. But that the woman writer can only offer tea and sympathy
to her maddened landlady and that she moves out when she has
"an oppressive, inexplicable presentiment" (132) about Susan's fate

even more explicitly dramatize Egerton's sense that it is dangerous to live in the house of heterosexuality. The sociocultural changes that facilitated the rise of an economically independent professional woman like Egerton's female author have highlighted but not infiltrated the heart of the family, where husband and wife "sway together in the passage" (127), locked in the fatal combat of wedlock.

A similar sense of the fatality of adult heterosexuality permeates Freeman's "Old Woman Magoun," whose eponymous protagonist poisons her delicate granddaughter Lily rather than surrender her to a suitor who has won her in a card game with her father. Because Old Woman Magoun is large, aggressive, and self-assertive, with "a mighty sense of reliance upon herself," this rural matriarch might at first seem almost invincible.[31] Certainly Freeman observes that "the weakness of the masculine element in Barry's Ford," the town where she lives, is "laid low before [her] strenuous feminine assertion" and her open contempt" for men (167–68). Yet, as the story shows, Old Woman Magoun is not only powerless in her contest with her granddaughter's father, she is also ineffectual in her effort to persuade a local lawyer to adopt Lily in order to save the girl from the marriage her father has arranged. On the one hand, Lily's father and his gambling companion represent a predatory male sexuality that would transform the virginal Lily into a commodity, sully her virgin soil, and possibly even kill her as it did her own mother, who died a week after childbirth. On the other hand, the censorious lawyer, who refuses to adopt Lily because he regards her blood as tainted, speaks for a legalistic male society preoccupied with the rules of lineage.

Caught between a dangerous nature and a hostile culture, Old Woman Magoun reaches a dead end where she evidently feels she can only save Lily by engineering her death. Watching in silence as the girl nibbles the berries of a bush of deadly nightshade, the desperate grandmother steels herself against the sufferings of the only being she really loves, and when the sick girl complains of "deadly nausea" (186), Old Woman Magoun paints what amounts to a parody of Victorian pictures of heaven. Revenging herself on the men she hates, this maddened woman resists male authority by paradoxically allowing her granddaughter to consume "the evil gifts" of forbidden fruit because she believes that the girl will be better dead than wed.

Yet after the child dies, she herself becomes a madwoman, carrying everywhere, "as one might have carried an infant, Lily's old rag doll" (189). Thus, analyzing the defeat that Old Woman Magoun endures and inflicts, Freeman implies here that, without some radical but perhaps barely imaginable social transformation, women who wish to resist the deadlock of wedlock will either become dead dears like Lily or worshippers of dead dolls like Old Woman Magoun.

To be sure, despite the grim view of heterosexual hostilities that Freeman offers in "Old Woman Magoun," this author herself, along with a number of other turn-of-the-century women of letters, did produce texts which effectively resist or defy male power. From Florence in George Egerton's "Virgin Soil" to the runaway bride of Charlotte Mew's "The Farmer's Bride" (1916), women refuse the erotic advances of husbands whom they dislike or fear.[32] In some cases, moreover, such attempts at separatism even issue in the separate peace of a woman's place. Louisa Ellis in Freeman's "A New England Nun" (1891), for instance, dreads the "coarse masculine presence" of her fiancé and is relieved when she discovers that he has fallen in love with another young woman.[33] Happily sending him away so that she can reign over a small but peaceful domestic world of her own, she feels "like a queen who, after fearing lest her domain be wrested away from her, sees it firmly insured in her possession" (124). Though Freeman's narrative concedes that Louisa may have sold her "birthright" as a woman for a mess of pottage, the author nevertheless comments that "the taste of the pottage was so delicious" (125) and, by redefining the old maid as a consecrated nun who frets not at her convent walls, Freeman suggests that, if looked at in a new way, a traditional female stereotype might, surprisingly enough, offer a blueprint for attaining the autonomy of the New Woman.

In her "The Revolt of 'Mother' " (1891), moreover, Freeman takes a similarly revisionary look at another traditional female stereotype—the figure whom she self-consciously defines through quotation marks in her title as the "mother." A pious but resolute farm-wife and mother, Sarah Penn unsuccessfully tries to get her uncommunicative husband to build the better house he had promised her forty years earlier and protests his decision to build, instead, a new barn. He remains impervious to her impassioned pleas, however, so, when he is suddenly called away on business for a few days, Sarah marshalls the aid of her children and moves all her household belongings into the newly completed barn.

Her insurrection requires courage, for as Freeman explains,

> During the next few hours a feat was performed by this simple, pious, New England mother which was equal in its way to Wolfe's storming of the Heights of Abraham. It took no more genius and audacity of bravery for Wolfe to cheer his wondering soldiers up those steep precipices, under the sleeping eyes of the enemy, than for Sarah Penn, at the head of her children, to move all their household goods into the new barn while her husband was away. [*SS* 308]

But the occupation of enemy territory is successfully carried out, and this conquering heroine subjugates her foe's domain by transforming box-stalls into bedrooms, the harness-room into "a kitchen of her dreams," and "the row of stanchions before the allotted space for cows" (308) into a front entry. Her victory is complete when her returning husband accepts her move as a fait accompli and weeps at his inevitable submission to her will. This formerly inflexible man is now, Freeman shows, "like a fortress whose walls had no active resistance, and went down the instant the right besieging tools were used" (313). Though "mother's" rebellion has employed the stereotypical arts of the homemaker, she has deployed domesticity in a revisionary move that gives her something comparable to the authority dreamed of by the New Woman.

Of course Freeman's stories, like those of Sarah Orne Jewett, can be seen as nostalgic in their attempt to recuperate the potency of an old girls' network for a New Woman's world. But even more overtly New Womanly texts like Egerton's "The Regeneration of Two" (1894), Edith Wharton's "The Other Two" (1904), and Charlotte Perkins Gilman's "When I Was a Witch" (1910) depend not only on the kinds of lucky strikes that win battles in female-authored Victorian literature, but also on revisionary uses of traditional feminine wiles. The widowed heroine of Egerton's "The Regeneration of Two" not only exults in the death that has allowed her, unlike Chopin's falsely hopeful Louise Mallard, to "be[long] to myself again" (168), she also is regenerated when a chance encounter with a censorious male poet convinces her that women live useless lives and in response she founds a charitable community where she gains power by becoming a classic ministering angel. Moreover, at the story's end, she achieves even further power when the reproachful poet falls ill and she nurses him like a Great Mother caring for a feeble child, forcing him to acknowledge his admiration for a "colony of women managed by a woman, going their own way to hold a place in the world in face of opinion" (232). Looking at how she has "grown," the poet admits *"I begin to fear you!,"* a sentiment that makes sense in light of her boast "Methinks, Poet, the pupil has distanced the master!" (245)

If Egerton's heroine not only rises because her poet sinks but also becomes the head of a community of her own by revising the stereotype of the angel in the house, Edith Wharton's heroine in "The Other Two" employs the arts of ladylike seduction to rob her three husbands of "the joy of possessorship" and, instead, to reduce them to "partners" or "members" of a "syndicate" in which each holds "so many shares in [their] wife's personality."[34] Told from the perspective of Alice Haskett-Varick-Waythorn's latest husband, a man who finds his way thorny indeed, this brilliant comedy of manners depicts a woman whose tea and sympathy "sicken" (393) instead of healing the male partners who, unlike the monks in Mew's "White Night," bond as victims rather than victimizers.

Perhaps even more radically, the narrator of Charlotte Perkins Gilman's "When I Was a Witch" is miraculously enabled to work her vindictive will against men by transforming the traditional female fear of being called a witch into a New Womanly fantasy of having witchlike powers that allow her to inflict odd punishments which suit masculine crimes. Yet the fragility of her enterprise is frankly dramatized when she wishes "with all [her] strength—that women, all women, might realize Womanhood at last; its power and pride and place in life," for, as she discovers, that sort of overtly feminist wishing, unlike the black magic which had "fallen" on her earlier, was "white" magic, a form of sorcery which "didn't work at all."[35] It is only in the revision of *The Princess* (and, as we shall argue in our next volume, of Rider Haggard's *She*) called *Herland* (1915) that Gilman was able to imagine the successful implementation of "white magic" in a society where a band of women comparable to Ida and her cohorts demonstrate to three male intruders, whose personalities seem to echo those of Hilarion and his friends, that they have realized "Womanhood at last; its power and pride and place in life."[36]

Indeed, far more radically than Tennyson, Gilman elaborates in *Herland* the vision of triumphant female community that had inspired the marching and hunger-striking suffragists. Where Tennyson's Ida had to secede from a world still ruled by men, Gilman's Herlanders are the lucky heiresses of a queendom where the men have all been destroyed by a series of mischances. Where Ida has to depend on the military skills of her brother Arac in her battle with Hilarion and his forces, the Herlanders mass together to capture and confine the three male interlopers in their country. Where Lady Psyche's "fatal babe" helps convert the princess to sexual submission, the Herlanders reproduce parthenogenetically without the slightest need of male assistance and, far from being converted into erotically eager wives, they either win the men over to their New Womanly cause or expel them ignominiously from the community. Nevertheless, even the wish fulfillments of *Herland* are undermined by the very contradictions between desire and reality that impelled Gilman to fuse feminism and fantasy not only in her utopias but in the more sardonic "When I Was a Witch." For, throughout her career, Gilman's great expectations for victory, like those of most of her contemporaries, were continually qualified by her stubbornly realistic consciousness of the female defeats that she observed in a world she knew was mostly devoid of fairytale enchantment.

How did feminist modernists defend themselves against their precursors' depictions of female defeat as a perpetual possibility? One combative strategy may have been associated with precisely the social and metaphysical crises in masculine confidence that produced such male-authored no-men as Eliot's Fisher King, Lawrence's Loerke, Hemingway's Jake, Joyce's Leopold Bloom, and West's Miss Lonelyhearts. As we have seen, the ideological and theological underpinnings of patriarchal culture had been severely weakened not just by the rise of women but also by the concomitant complex of phenomena which seemed to threaten a decline and fall of western man and of what Charlotte Perkins Gilman called his "androcentric" world:[37] the dark Satanic mills of industrialism, the disappearance of God, the recessional of the British Empire. Paradoxically, therefore, women in the first third of the twentieth century were often empowered to imagine victory in the sexual battle not just because of their own new strength but also because of their antagonists' new weakness.

From those texts that present a threatened but nevertheless supportive female community to those that are still haunted by visions of female scapegoats, to those that dramatize fortuitous male death and those that for the first time depict direct resistance and retaliation by women characters, literary works by feminist modernists often create male characters who are from the start far weaker than, say, Charlotte Brontë's Rochester or Elizabeth Barrett Browning's Romney. At last, therefore, in the absence of male potency, the presence of victorious females becomes imaginable. Yet, inevitably, the fruits of female victory may be bitter and the gifts of power poisoned. Triumph over an unworthy, diminished, or disabled opponent may feel like exploitation of his misfortune and—because women are naturally entangled in the declining culture constructed by men—the cooling of the fire that began to sink "on dune and headland" in Kipling's "Recessional" (1897) may leave them as chilled as their brothers.[38]

To begin with, even in the context of the increasingly notable no man's land that feminist modernists shared with male contemporaries, some of their heroines rely on the revisionary ways of deploying domesticity that energized figures in such turn-of-the-century texts as "The Regeneration of Two" and "The Revolt of 'Mother.' " Susan Glaspell's well-known "Trifles" (1916)—a play that was also published as the short story "A Jury of Her Peers"—elevates housewifely knowledge, first, into detective skills and, then, into a strategy for subverting male authority. When a county attorney, a sheriff, and a neighboring farmer arrive at the scene of a crime (a remote farmhouse where one John Wright has been murdered) they are accompanied by the sheriff's and the farmer's wives, two women whose concerns they consider "trifling." But though they have jailed Wright's wife on suspicion of murder, the men are unable to find evidence to prove their case, despite their swaggering professionalism. The women, however, are able to interpret small signs—an untidy kitchen, a strangely sewn quilt, an empty birdcage, a dead bird—so that, in a tradition that would be continued by Agatha Christie's Miss Jane Marple, they understand the crime even while they implicitly vindicate the woman who committed it.

Once a high-spirited young girl named Minnie Foster, Mrs. Wright has been wronged by the taciturn husband who isolated her—"She didn't even belong to the Ladies Aid"—and who sequestered her in his lonely farmhouse.[39] Thus, when he broke the neck of the canary which represented not only a voice of life but the voice she had had in her former life, she retaliated by strangling him. Justifying her action, the women note that "Wright wouldn't like the bird—a thing that sang. She used to sing. He killed that, too" (25), and gradually they make an unspoken decision to protect her against the law embodied in their own husbands by withholding and destroying the crucial evidence which their husbands have overlooked. That these women have bonded together to liberate another woman who has herself effectively triumphed over a cruel male jailer suggests the new intensity with which twentieth-century writers were beginning to imagine a variety of Ladies Aid societies. But that their duplicitious intervention in the Wright murder case is facilitated by the arrogance that blinds the men to the code of domesticity in which the terms of the drama have been formulated implies that, in the words of Dickens's Mr. Bumble, "the law is a ass." Thus, whether they are dead like John Wright or dupes like the play's three officious investigators, the men in Glaspell's text are far less daunting antagonists than the suitors, fathers, or husbands in Freeman's stories. When, at the end of "Trifles," the county attorney patronizingly asks the "ladies" about the name of a quilting technique and one replies, "we call it—knot it" (30), the implicit pun on "knotting" and "not-ing" negates, indeed annihilates, male authority, for it both recalls and condones the murderous noose that Minnie Foster Wright knotted around her husband's neck.

It is in the more overtly feminist polemics of Virginia Woolf, though, that visions of female triumph are most dramatically set against portraits of male inadequacy. Of course, Woolf's famous description in *A Room of One's Own* (1929) of sumptuous meals at Oxbridge, along with her speculations on the "sacks of gold and silver" that were and still are "shovelled into" men's colleges (20), emphasizes her sense of the lingering power wielded by male bastions of learning. Yet her confrontation, during a luxurious lunch at Oxbridge, with a tailless Manx cat, perhaps a comically allegorical representative of the general world of man as well as the particular Isle of Man, reveals her belief that man is now a "truncated animal" (11), while her conclusion that it is "worse perhaps to be locked in" than locked out (24) hints that men have incarcerated themselves in a prison of tradition from which they cannot escape.

As if to legitimize Princess Ida's failed educational project, Woolf counters the fallen autumn of Oxbridge with the miraculous spring of the woman's college she calls Fernham. Woolf's dream of redemptive women's colleges haunts her entire oeuvre, for, precisely because she knew that "this world is . . . old and fond of steam," she believed that what had seemed like a "fairy tale" to Elizabeth Barrett Browning was a reality, and a reality that could endure and overcome male assaults. Indeed, in *Three Guineas* she even transforms the debilitating poverty that she had in *A Room of One's Own* associated with female institutions of learning into a positive virtue and a reason for women to attack the traditional male university. But Woolf does not just associate male education with enfeebled traditions paradoxically established by wealth and privilege that have been denied to women; she also directly connects the masculine university with patriarchal assaults upon women.

In *A Room of One's Own* Woolf's paradigmatic patriarch is "Professor von X. engaged in writing his monumental work entitled *The Mental, Moral, and Physical Inferiority of the Female Sex*," a man whose pen has literally become a weapon: "His expression suggested that he was labouring under some emotion that made him jab his pen on the paper as if he were killing some noxious insect as he wrote, but even when he had killed it that did not satisfy him; he must go on killing; and even so, some cause for anger and irritation remained" (31). Interestingly, too, Woolf's construction of this figure involves her in an angry attempt at retaliation in which she also uses her pen as a weapon. After she has "drawn" her satiric picture of the Professor, Woolf observes, she begins half-consciously to embellish it with a series of ferocious doodles: "I . . . began drawing cartwheels and circles over the angry professor's face till he looked like a burning bush or a flaming comet—anyhow, an apparition without human semblance or significance. The professor was nothing now but a faggot burning on the top of Hampstead Heath" (32).

Ultimately, Woolf's fictive victory over the Professor illuminates her belief that, where in the past such an authority figure might have definitively defeated her, now—even though he and his kind still rule the world—she can at least imaginatively burn him at the stake like a witch, and she can even begin to envision a future in which women will no longer be at his mercy. This contrast between her sense of past female powerlessness and future female power also shapes two important narratives that are embedded in *A Room of One's Own:* the folk ballad of the four Marys and the parable of Judith Shakespeare. Throughout the text, Woolf alludes to Mary Beton, Mary Seton, and Mary Carmichael, the ladies-in-waiting who attend upon the doomed Mary Hamilton of Scottish legend, gradually revising them so they become increasingly independent New Women who constitute a veritable Ladies Aid society, which might be able to save sacrificial victims like their mistress. At the same time, her meditation on women and fiction turns on the story of a woman Shakespeare that William Black and Olive Schreiner had proposed earlier.

Significantly, however, where Schreiner had imagined this mythical female artist as having been robbed of her creativity by imprisonment in a life of uneventful drudgery and Black had envisioned his rebellious heroine as incapable of artistry, Woolf gives the tale a more melodramatic cast, first by allowing her to revolt against domesticity, and then by outlining the violent fate that patriarchal culture would have inflicted on her for precisely Mary Hamilton's crime of bearing an illegitimate child. Even more tellingly, however, although Woolf identifies the repressed genius of Judith Shakespeare with the suppressed powers of ancient witches and wisewomen, she also reimagines the students of Fernham as yet another kind of Ladies Aid society whose work might bring about Judith Shakespeare's resurrection:

> Now my belief is that this poet who never wrote a word and was buried at the crossroads still lives. She lives in you and me, and in many other women who are not here tonight for they are washing up the dishes and putting the children to bed. But

she lives; for great poets do not die; they are continuing presences; they need only the opportunity to walk among us in the
flesh. This opportunity, as I think, it is now coming within your
power to give her. For my belief is that if we live another century or so . . . if we have the habit of freedom and the courage
to write exactly what we think . . . the dead poet who was
Shakespeare's sister will put on the body which she has so often
laid down. [117–18]

Not all feminist-modernist imaginings of female triumph are as
ecstatic as Virginia Woolf's, but such artists as Willa Cather and H.
D. frequently balance allusions to myths of female sacrifice with depictions of quasi-feminist autonomy and retribution. For example,
the mummified figure of Mother Eve which Tom Outland describes
discovering in an interpolated archaeological narrative at the center
of Cather's *The Professor's House* (1925) is countered by the story of
the ferociously willful Aztec princess who dominates an interpolated
folktale at the center of Cather's "Coming, Aphrodite!" (1920). If
the primordial woman whose history Cather's patriarchal Professor
St. Peter is forced to acknowledge has suffered an archetypal murder—

there was a great wound in her side, the ribs stuck out through
the dried flesh. Her mouth was open as if she were screaming,
and her face, through all those years, had kept a look of terrible
agony[40]

—the potent rainmaking princess whose tale is recounted by the
defensive male artist Don Hedger has not only seduced and betrayed
forty male lovers but also done so through the instrumentality of a
gelded, captured, and captivated prince. Similarly, H. D.'s famous
lyric "Helen" (1924) delineates a sacrificial heroine whom "all Greece
hates," while her vengeful "Eurydice" (1917) depicts a mythic woman
who boasts that "Before I am lost / hell must open like a red rose /
for the dead to pass" and insists that even in death she is more alive
than Orpheus is in life.[41]

But if H. D. constructs a character who imagines triumphing in
death over a living man, a number of her contemporaries create
women who achieve heroic stature through witnessing or facilitating

male death, who feel inexplicably empowered by male deaths, or whose lives yield them fortuitous victories over dead or dying men. Edna St. Vincent Millay's cycle of "Sonnets from an Ungrafted Tree" (1923), for instance, describes the new dignity gained by a woman who comes back into the house of a sick husband from whom she has been separated and "watch[es] beside his bed until he dies[s], / Loving him not at all," while Ellen Glasgow's short story "Jordan's End" (1923) ascribes a comparable dignity to a woman who poisons her mad husband in order to save him from his own insanity. Although after her act of mercy killing this devoted wife looks as tragic as "Antigone . . . on the day of her sacrifice," Glasgow has taken pains to represent the necessity for the woman's deed by symbolizing the decline of the South through the depiction of a tainted patri-lineage.[42] Even more radically, the heroine of Zora Neale Hurston's *Their Eyes Were Watching God* (1937) shoots a spouse who has been maddened by the bite of a rabid dog: though she has been deeply in love with her husband, Tea Cake, the marriage of Hurston's Janey ends in a gun fight during which a "fiend in him" aims a pistol at her with deadly accuracy so that she is forced to fire her own loaded gun and then to fall locked in a murderous embrace with this once beloved man.[43]

Where such women as Glasgow's Judith and Hurston's Janey are clearly pained by the marital losses which have gained them heroism, other female characters achieve notably guilt-free triumphs. In Katherine Mansfield's "The Garden-Party" (1922) and Virginia Woolf's *Mrs. Dalloway* (1925), for example, two major feminist modernists explore moments of being in which women are mysteriously empowered by meditations on dead men. After Laura in "The Garden-Party" has viewed the body of a young workman who "lay . . . fast asleep . . . wonderful, beautiful," she exclaims to her brother that the experience "was simply marvellous," while Clarissa Dalloway responds to the news of Septimus Warren Smith's death by deciding that his sacrificial suicide "made her feel the beauty, made her feel the fun" of her own existence.[44]

But of course neither Laura nor Clarissa is personally involved in either the life or the death of the man whose fall gives her a feeling that she has risen. In Zora Neale Hurston's "Sweat" (1926), however, a female protagonist achieves victory over her hostile hus-

band by allowing his murderous scheme to boomerang. The oppressed laundress Delia Jones, who has been beaten by her husband
Sykes " 'nough tuh kill three women,' " first asserts herself by refusing to let him replace her with his mistress in the house she has
earned by the sweat of her brow.[45] More dramatically, when Sykes
plots to kill Delia by leaving a rattlesnake in her laundry hamper,
she escapes but retaliates by failing to warn him that the serpent is
loose in the house. Crouched outside the window as Sykes—mortally
wounded by the snake—utters a terrible cry, she watches him crawl
toward her and, as she decides not to go for help, realizes that he
will die knowing she has been complicitous in his demise.

Despite the fact that Delia is depicted as beaten and burdened
by her husband, however, Hurston consistently dramatizes the connections between this working woman's economic independence, the
man's economic dependence, and the couple's struggle for possession
of the house. Like so many males imagined by modernists of both
sexes, Sykes is in some sense a hollow man: " 'Mah tub of suds is
filled yo' belly with vittles more times than yo' hands is filled it. Mah
sweat is done paid for this house and Ah reckon Ah kin keep on
sweatin' in it,' " Delia tells him as she "cow[s] him" by brandishing
"an iron skillet from the stove" (40). In addition, the men of her
community, who scorn Sykes, observe that " 'he useter eat some
mighty big hunks uh humble pie tuh get dat li'l 'oman he got' " (43).
Thus, though she is wounded by his philandering, Delia is able to
"build a spiritual earthworks" against him, so that "His shells could
no longer reach her," and, even more crucially, she is ultimately
able to implement her own prediction that " 'Sometime or ruther,
Sykes, like everybody else, is gointer reap his sowing' " (42).

Where the humble Delia's building of "spiritual earthworks" ends
in a moment of melodramatic retribution, Rebecca West creates in
"Indissoluble Matrimony" (1914) a sophisticated female character
whose imperviousness to her husband's assaults leads to a more
ironic, almost farcical, denouement. Both a beautiful dark sensualist
(her husband George insists that she has "black blood" in her)[46] and
an accomplished platform speaker for the cause of socialism, West's
Evadne Silverton maddens her effete, ascetic, and misogynistic husband to the point where, like Hurston's Sykes, he tries to commit
murder; indeed, unlike Sykes, he actually believes he has killed his

wife. Specifically, George becomes enraged at Evadne both because he learns that she has accepted a speaking engagement of which he disapproves and because he has convinced himself that she is having an affair with another man. When she leaves the house in the midst of their fight, he follows her, believing that she is going to meet her lover, but discovers instead that she has simply gone for a swim in a nearby reservoir. Still enraged, he tries to drown her and, though she fights back, he convinces himself that he has succeeded in sinking her when in fact she has just eluded him by swimming away under water. Absolutely sure of his triumph, he decides that, instead of allowing himself to be hanged for killing his wife, he will heroically commit suicide. But when he returns home to find his wife peacefully sleeping in the marital bed, he realizes in a moment of comic epiphany that "Bodies like his do not kill bodies like hers" (1599), that he is and always will be "beaten" by her unquenchable vitality, and that there are no waters deep enough to dissolve the bonds of his marriage.

Yet despite the verve with which West satirizes both George's misogyny and his fantasy of victory, the historical detail that marks her account of the Silvertons' strife points to her more general belief that, as she claimed elsewhere, "Like all terrible and wicked things, sex-antagonism has a sound logical basis."[47] Indeed, for feminist modernists "Indissoluble Matrimony" might have functioned as a witty exploration of the dynamics of sex antagonism, a paradigmatic (female) joke about the neurotic never-never-land inhabited by the lost boys who became the early twentieth century's no-men. For, more than Hurston, West sees the dis-ease of no-manhood as a basis for sexual battle. If "Sweat's" Sykes Jones was a hollow man, "Indissoluble Matrimony's" George Silverton is a miserably wedded and unhappily bedded J. Alfred Prufrock, singing a lovesong that becomes a song of hate because he is obsessed with the "secret obscenity of women!"(1580)

That West, whose story appeared in Wyndham Lewis's *Blast* in 1914, could never have read "Prufrock," which did not appear in Harriet Monroe's *Poetry* until 1915, is beside the point, for George's sexual anxiety, almost a form of male hysteria, is exactly the symptom of masculine cultural enervation that Eliot too would analyze, and within a year. But West not only anticipated Eliot's analysis, she was also—though her story is not the modernist classic that "Prufrock" has become—more radical in her diagnosis of male sexual paranoia. Prufrock, Eliot implies, really does inhabit a world where indifferent women "come and go / Talking of Michelangelo" and, as we saw earlier, in the version of the poem called "Prufrock Among the Women" he really does journey through what seems to be a threatening red-light district. Yet though it is true that Evadne Silverton has had a surprisingly brilliant career as a socialist writer and speaker so that she is perhaps even more disturbingly autonomous than Prufrock's women, West takes pains to show that George's vision of her as an adulteress is nothing but a figment of his own imagination.

In doing this, West makes explicit what is only implicit in Eliot's famous dramatic monologue: the connection between male sexual anxiety and women's entrance into the public sphere. Indeed, this couple's sexual battle is triggered by a handbill on which George "saw her name—his name—," a handbill announcing a platform appearance by "MRS. EVADNE SILVERTON." At first "convulsed with rage," West's weakened hero quickly succumbs to "spiritual nausea [which] made him determined to be a better man than her" [sic] (1582–83). From the start of the story, he has been characterized as prudishly nauseated by the female body and especially by his wife's frank sensuality, so much so that "Wife-desertion seemed to him a beautiful return of the tainted body to cleanliness" (1580). Now it becomes clear that his revulsion at this "depraved, over-sexed creature" (1582) is specifically associated with the freedom and frankness of her desire. Horrified by what he sees as his own diminishment into instrumentality ("Her vitality needed him as it needed the fruit on the table before him" [1582]), he even begins to conflate her intellectual energy with her bodily vigor; at the moment when, unlike the ultimately compliant Verena Tarrant in *The Bostonians*, she refuses to submit to his demand that she withdraw from the platform appearance advertised in the handbill, he decides that "Her face was heavy with intellect, her lips coarse with power" (1583).

Throughout the story, besides linking Evadne's sexual autonomy with her political activism, George also implicitly associates both these troublesome phenomena with what he sees as her "alien" race. At first, he had fallen in love with her because of her "smouldering contralto such as only those of black blood can possess" (1581), but, in the course of their marriage, as he increasingly sinks and she inexorably rises, he has come to define his loathing of her otherness in xenophobic terms. It is because of her "black blood" that she has "indiscreet taste," an "uncanny, Negro way" of humming, "alien beauty," and the "shamelessness of a young animal" (1578–81). Worse still, it is because of her "black blood" that, like some descendant of *Jane Eyre's* Bertha Mason Rochester, she has what he perceives as an insatiable sexual appetite, monstrous strength, and the Satanic subversiveness of Blake's "invisible worm" destroying the rose of the world with its "dark secret love" (1593–94). But worst of all, her passage from song (the "smouldering contralto" he had first loved) to speech (the platform appearances he hates) seems to presage the disruptive entrance of a négritude emblematic of a savage nature into an increasingly vulnerable culture.

Even as she analyzes George's historically constructed sense of vulnerability, however, West satirizes his vindictive passion for retaliation, his sense that "what every man most desires" is "one night of power over a woman for the business of murder or love" (1599). As if deconstructing in advance the hypothesis proposed in T. S. Eliot's *Sweeney Agonistes* that "Any man has to, needs to, wants to / Once in a lifetime, do a girl in," she shows that George's triumphant crowing over his wife's apparent defeat—" 'I must be a very strong man,' " he mutters to himself after he thinks he has drowned Evadne—is really nonsensical babble. Though George believes that he has "saved the earth from corruption by killing Evadne" (1596), he returns home to understand "how absurd it was ever to have thought that he had killed her" (1599). Ferocious as D. H. Lawrence's Gudrun, in a bathing dress that makes her look "as though she were clad in a garment of dark polished mail," West's Evadne elicits in her husband a Lawrentian "ecstasy" of fury (1590–91). But for Lawrence such responsibilities of rage had a moral, even a missionary, seriousness that West feels obliged to parody as she shows that the supposed "adulteress" whom George wishes to "accuse in the law courts and condemn into the street" is "merely his good wife, the faithful attendant of his hearth" (1589).

Ultimately, the asymmetry between Lawrence's solemnity and West's satire, between his earnestness and her irony, can surely be attributed to just the historical change about which both were writing—the emergence of such New Women as Gudrun Brangwen and Evadne Silverton. That George and Evadne struggle to inflict upon each other a virtually mythic "death by water" adds even further resonance to their story. In the nineteenth century, Hawthorne's Zenobia achieves a consummation her author may devoutly wish for her when she drowns like her prototype, Margaret Fuller. Similarly, a number of George Eliot's anti-heroes achieve equally calamitous consummations when they too meet their deaths by water. In the twentieth century, however, fictive deaths are as asymmetrical as fictive lives. On the one hand, such male authors as T. S. Eliot and D. H. Lawrence quite consistently imagine watery catastrophes for their heroes. On the other hand, a female author like Rebecca West fantasizes about an undrownable heroine and also about a hero not worth drowning. On the surface, because George has survived his struggle with his spouse, he might seem different and luckier than such dead husbands as Glaspell's Mr. Wright or Hurston's Sykes Jones. But West's story suggests that, precisely because he is so ineffectual, George does not have to be killed off. For this reason, the tale marks a key moment in the female story of sexual battle, a moment when the woman is seen as unequivocally victorious.

Of course, even Evadne Silverton wins the sexual battle instigated by her husband not through active but through passive resistance: simply swimming away from his murderous grasp, she reveals her realistic understanding—shared with other female-authored heroines—that women are not culturally conditioned to engage in acts of physical aggression. However, even while women in the 1920s and 1930s continued to infiltrate the public sphere—gaining the vote, achieving university degrees, entering the work force—the feminist-modernist vision of a female moment of triumph, a vision perhaps most optimistically as well as comically elaborated in "Indissoluble Matrimony," began to darken. And, curiously, such darkening was manifested in women's texts by what would seem at first glance to be a healthy impulse to depict women actively fighting their male opponents rather than just passively resisting them.

From C. L. Moore's "Shambleau" (1933) to Ann Petry's *The Street*

(1946) and Carson McCullers's "Ballad of the Sad Cafe" (1951), women's fictions of sexual struggle in the 1930s and 1940s portray female characters who are physically powerful enough to inaugurate and sustain combat against men.[48] Ultimately, however, this aggressive power is shown to be not a badge of courage but a horrifying necessity, born of escalating male bellicosity and inexorably leading to female defeat. In addition, it is consistently characterized as tragic, freakish, or monstrous. For, as male writers like Faulkner, Miller, and Wylie mounted intensified attacks on female autonomy, their female contemporaries defended themselves with aggressive fantasies of physical power, a power that the plots of their stories define as necessary for survival. At the same time, these postmodernist women of letters do not seem to have been able to imagine such physical force as effective, for their women combatants are regularly haunted by guilt and frequently punished by defeat. Indeed, the plots constructed by these writers are often so critical of or punitive towards their female protagonists that their authors would seem to have internalized just the horror at independent womanhood which marks the writings of literary men from Faulkner to Wylie.

It is possible to see these dynamics of female defense and defeat most dramatically deployed in what may well be the most noncanonical of female-authored midcentury texts. Specifically, both in the science fiction tradition and in the black tradition women writers seem to feel freest to express their fantasies about the inexorability of sexual battle as well as their fears of female defeat in that conflict. Evidently white women writing in a marginalized "pulp" culture and black women writing in a ghettoized "ethnic" culture had been forced to confront feelings of aggression that were in any case elicited by the labeling of their literary works as secondary. Thus such apparently eccentric texts as Moore's "Shambleau," in science fiction, or Petry's *The Street*, in the black tradition, function as paradigms of the ambivalence with which women writers imagine the guilt and the grief associated with the battle of the sexes in this period. Perhaps, too, these tales function this way because, besides producing feelings of literary subordination or marginalization, the science fiction and black traditions enable female artists to translate the comparatively subtle terms of sexual struggle into the more openly theatrical terms of species or racial struggle. In works from these traditions, that is, the conflict that Rebecca West only allusively embodies through her depiction of a white husband's identification of his wife's otherness with négritude is explicitly allegorized through an examination of the ways in which humans (men) must confront and confound aliens (women) or the ways in which (white) men or their (black) minions confront and constrain subordinated (black) women.

A quintessential battle between the sexes figured as two different species occurs in the classic short story "Shambleau," which relates the poisonously sensual encounter of a white earthman named Northwest Smith with a vampiric and Medusa-like creature called Shambleau, a femme fatale with hideously pulsing, slimy, and snaky locks, who feeds on her man's vital juices in what seems like a fantastic exaggeration of the way in which West's *Eva*dne needs to consume the apple who is her Adam. Particularly notable in this story is its recapitulation of male anxieties about the dangers that Faulkner and Miller, and of course before them Freud, explicitly or implicitly attributed to the female "cunt"—its supposedly slimy, lethal, insatiable, and muscular suction, as well as (for Freud) its failed because multiplied phallicism.[19] Describing the "mound like a mass of entrails" (23) that is the hair of her story's apparently submissive, brown girl, C. L. Moore brings to the surface not just her narrator's horror of the Shambleau but also George Silverton's disgust at "the secret obscenity of women" as well as the horror of Faulkner and Miller at those impersonal cunts which (if only in their voracity) seem to triumph over men. In addition, because Shambleau must be killed by Northwest Smith's friend, as must the "ancient, swamp-born memories" (23) she has awakened, the ending of this story dramatizes not only the male imperative to murder the alien female but also the female author's culturally conditioned self-loathing.

But if Moore, in a frankly fantastic work, has merged both her own socially induced dread of female sexuality and the intense misogyny that marked her historical moment, Ann Petry produces in *The Street*, a dozen years later, a more documentary text representing the battle of the sexes not only as a racial but also as a class struggle. In marked contrast to her black female precursor Zora Neale Hurston, who focuses in *Their Eyes Were Watching God* and "Sweat" on the fortuitous triumphs of powerful country women, Petry mourns the helplessness that even the most determined women experience in the city. Her heroine, Lutie Johnson, battles cold, filth, poverty, and crime on the street in Harlem where, after the breakup of her marriage, she finds a first apartment of her own. But even while she struggles to support herself and her eight-year-old son, she is subjected to sexual assaults by black and white men alike. For Petry suggests that the chain-of-being in Harlem—descending from white men through black men to black women—puts the black woman in a position of double jeopardy: not only is she oppressed by both white and black men, she is also the booty for which they struggle with each other.

The threat of rape hangs over Lutie from the beginning to the end of her life on 116th street. First, the superintendent of her building brutally assaults her; then, it becomes clear that Mr. Junto, a white boss of bars and whorehouses in Harlem, has his eye on her, as if to prove the truth of her grandmother's warning that white men " 'ain't never willin' to let a black woman alone" (33); finally, in the novel's violent denouement, a black employee of Junto's, who has been commissioned to purchase Lutie's sexual favors for the boss, decides to assert his independence of the white man by staking out a prior claim on her body. But when he traps her in his apartment and tries to force himself on her before selling her to Junto, she becomes enraged and, at last expressing "a lifetime of pent-up resentment" (266), she smashes in his head with a heavy candlestick.

As Lutie is killing this man, the narrator clarifies the connections between sexual combat and racial/socioeconomic conflicts:

> First she was venting her rage against the dirty, crowded street . . . Then the limp figure on the sofa became, in turn, Jim [her husband] and the slender girl she'd found him with; became the insult in the moist-eyed glances of white men on the subway; became the unconcealed hostility in the eyes of white women . . . Finally . . . she was striking at the white world which thrust black people into a walled enclosure from which there was no escape . . . She saw the face and head of the man on the sofa through waves of anger in which he represented all these things and she was destroying them. [266–67]

What emerges from this passage is an explanation of the black woman's position at the bottom of the social ladder, for Petry reminds us that, because the black man is unmanned by the white man, he needs to exert special mastery over "his" woman. If a black woman like Lutie Johnson makes money when her husband cannot, he may, like Lutie's spouse, desert her; but if, like Junto's henchman, he has more money than she does, he will use his economic power to enslave her.

Yet ultimately, as *The Street* also makes clear, the urban working-class black woman has no viable way out of her dilemmas short of turning herself into a monster or a freak. Lutie becomes an outcast when she yields to the murderous rage that triggers her crime, and after the killing she is forced to abandon her son and flee the city. And Lutie's story is counterpointed by the monitory tale of a veritable female monster who reigns over 116th street like a freakish queen. Grotesquely fat and hideously scarred from a fire, Mrs. Hedges is the madam of a small whorehouse in Lutie's apartment building, but she is also the partner of Harlem's sinister Mr. Junto. In fact, we learn that Junto went into most of his illicit businesses at her suggestion and that he has "the kind of forthright admiration for her that he would have for . . . a man he regarded as his equal" (153). Yet Mrs. Hedges has won such autonomy at the cost of her femininity, almost indeed of her humanity. Not only does she traffic in women—among other things she repeatedly tries to procure Lutie for Junto—but she is herself so disfigured from flames that "never as long as she lived would any man look at her and want her. . . . No sum of money would be big enough to make [men] pretend to want her" (152). Escaping the cycle of sexual victimization in which Lutie is entrapped, Mrs. Hedges has paid for freedom with freak-ishness, for she has "the appearance of a creature that had strayed from some other planet" (148).

Where in the science fiction and black traditions species warfare and racial combat are conflated with sexual battle, the southern Gothic mode allows Carson McCullers to depict sexual conflict with equal extravagance through the creation of characters who are in their own way at least as freakish as Petry's Mrs. Hedges and C. L. Moore's Shambleau, and through the recounting of the sort of gro-tesque events that are usually the subjects of tall tales or folk ballads. Even more dramatically than Moore and Petry, however, McCullers shows in her dreamlike mythic narrative of "The Ballad of the Sad Cafe" the culturally determined psychic logic that condemns the

autonomous woman as a freak who must necessarily be sentenced
to the defeat that is femininity. In fact, like her friend and contemporary Tennessee Williams, Carson McCullers seems to stand outside
the constructs of gender in order to demonstrate, as Williams did
in *Streetcar*, the pain of what Adrienne Rich has called "compulsory
heterosexuality."[50] But even more than Williams does in *Streetcar*,
McCullers focuses in "Ballad" on the terrifying revenge that the law
of the phallus inflicts on those (women) who defy its imperatives.
Specifically, she dramatizes the punishment meted out to a woman
who has arrogantly supposed that she could live in a no man's land—
first without a real man, and then with a dwarfish no-man.

At the beginning of "Ballad," Miss Amelia Evans has the kind of
physical power, intellectual authority, and personal autonomy that
characterize Rebecca West's Evadne Silverton, but, unlike Evadne,
she does not need men at all, even as instruments of her own pleasure. Six feet two inches tall, frequently "dressed in overalls and
gumboots," the thirty-year-old Amelia Evans is "a woman with bones
and muscles like a man," who has parlayed an inheritance from her
father into a fortune that makes her "the richest woman for miles
around," for she is the proprietor of a store and a still (where she
makes "the best liquor in the county") and the possessor of "mort-
gages on crops and property, a sawmill [and] money in the bank
(45)."[51] In addition, she is an extraordinarily skillful healer, a kind
of self-taught general practitioner about whom McCullers observes
that "no disease was so terrible but what she would undertake to
cure it" (17).

That Miss Amelia's success is associated with a culturally problematic eccentricity is shown not only by her masculine and peculiar
physical appearance (besides being unusually tall and strong for a
woman, she is cross-eyed, "dark and somewhat queer of face" [14])
but also by her anti-social nature (it is "only with people that Miss
Amelia [is] not at ease" [5]), by her litigiousness (only her proclivity
for lawsuits keeps her from being "as rich as a congressman" [5]),
and, most important, by her one failing as a "doctor":

> If a patient came with a female complaint she could do nothing.
> Indeed, at the mere mention of the words her face would slowly
> darken with shame, and she would stand there craning her

neck against the collar of her shirt, or rubbing her swamp boots together, for all the world like a great, shamed, dumb-tongued child. [17]

Taken together, all these traits illustrate this woman's rebellious desire to rule rather than to be ruled. Alienated from the community which she in some sense governs, the indomitable Miss Amelia manipulates social law in order to transcend it, and she refuses to acknowledge the biological law that governs her own body.

Inevitably, then, when Miss Amelia marries one Marvin Macy— for reasons that remain mysterious to the townsfolk as well as to the reader but which seem to have the inexplicable force that motivates actions in fairy tales—the wedding leads to immediate disaster. During the ceremony itself, Miss Amelia rubs "the palm of her right hand down the side of her satin wedding gown" as if "reaching for the pocket of her overalls," and afterwards she hurries out of the church, "walking at least two paces ahead" of her bridegroom (30). But the couple's wedding night is even more catastrophic. Though the townsfolk had "counted on the marriage to tone down Miss Amelia's temper, to put a bit of bride-fat on her, and to change her at last into a calculable woman" (30–31), this incalculable bride refuses to sleep with her husband, instead "stomp[ing] down the stairs in breeches and a khaki jacket" and spending the night, "feet up on the kitchen stove," smoking her father's pipe (31). Worse still, when the humiliated Marvin Macy—who has for love of her transformed himself from the handsome town ne'er-do-well to an exemplary suitor—seeks to placate his resistant wife with presents from "Society City," she offers them for sale in her store; when he signs "over to her the whole of his worldly goods . . . ten acres of timberland," she studies the paper "sternly" and files it away "soberly"; and when, driven to drunkenness by her recalcitrance, he approaches her humbly, she swings "once with her fist and hit[s] his face so hard that he [is] thrown back against the wall and one of his front teeth [is] broken" (32). After ten days of marriage, she turns him off her property and, following much public suffering, he leaves town, writing her a "wild love letter" in which "were also included threats" and vows of revenge (33).

At this point, Miss Amelia seems invincible, not only in her battle with her groom but also in her social and sexual eccentricity. Yet, oddly enough, she can only speak of Marvin Macey "with a terrible and spiteful bitterness" (33) that would not appear to be the natural response of the victor to the vanquished. Given Miss Amelia's fierce independence, along with her excessive hostility to Marvin Macy, it is almost predictable that, having rejected a he-man, she now embraces a no-man like Lymon Willis, the mysterious hunchbacked dwarf who claims to be her cousin. Coming out of nowhere from no one but asserting common ancestry with hers, this physically deformed and spiritually dissolute but emotionally compelling creature is destined, in his consumptive way, to consume most of Miss Amelia's worldly goods, and, significantly, he resembles not only the dwarfish "sewer rat" Loerke in Lawrence's *Women in Love* but also the spiteful cripple Doyle in Nathanael West's *Miss Lonelyhearts*, both paradigmatic no-men who represent for their authors all that is socially bankrupt in contemporary culture.

But while Lawrence and West characterize the dwarf as from first to last a decadent whose perversity signals the end of the species of man, McCullers implies that, at least in the beginning of their relationship, Miss Amelia's Cousin Lymon is an empowering figure for her. Knitting her into the community, he facilitates her creation of the cafe in which her rare liquor can teach its drinkers how to read the truths of their own souls. Offering her (or, more accurately, allowing her to offer) love and friendship, he functions as the family, and hence the identity, she lost when her "Big Papa" died; and that she gives him not only her father's snuff box but her father's (master) bedroom suggests again the dwarf's connection with her patrilineage. Tiny as a child yet charismatic as any gigolo, he seems to be her son and her lover, a link to the ancestral past who might provide her with the future she repudiated when she rejected Marvin Macy. Yet, as McCullers's text gradually and grimly reveals, Miss Amelia's Cousin Lymon is, in the deepest sense, a lie-man, a no-man whose manhood is really a lie. In fact, nebulously related to her mother (ostensibly the son of her mother's half-sister), he is not in any way associated with her patrilineage. Rather, pale and vampiric, he is in Freudian terms the (false) baby as false phallus, whose deformity and fake masculinity represent the deformity and fakery that (as Miss Amelia must learn) are associated with her own self-deluding male impersonation. If she wants a member instead of a wedding, she has to discover that this treacherous imposter is what she will get.

That Lymon as phallus is a lie becomes clear with the liberation of Marvin Macy from the penitentiary where, after Miss Amelia's rejection, he had been incarcerated for a number of years. Unlike George Silverton in Rebecca West's "Indissoluble Matrimony," who had been pruriently obsessed with his wife's supposed adultery and whose no-manhood had led him to the edge of madness, Lymon becomes instantly enthralled to his patroness's unknown husband, with whom he exchanges a look "like the look of two criminals who recognize each other" (47). But once the no-man Lymon, who as the fake thing recognizes the real thing, weds himself to the he-man Marvin, Miss Amelia begins to go into a bizarre decline, a decline that presages a defeat even more radical than Evadne's victory. Relinquishing her overalls for the red dress that she had previously reserved only for Sundays, Miss Amelia has lost her falsely instrumental Lymon Willis and is now, therefore, will-less. Moreover, caught between two phallic beings—the one exploitative, the other vengeful—she tries to please one and poison the other, but in both cases she fails: mendacious cousin Lymon becomes a mad man who is increasingly flirtatious toward Marvin Macy, while Marvin Macy becomes a bad man whose gradual usurpation of the very house and grounds she had granted to the dwarf signifies that, even if the rebellious woman desires the false phallus that she can control, the true phallus will eventually repossess her and all her worldly goods in an ultimate act of masculinist retribution. Indeed, as McCullers shows, though Miss Amelia tries to resist her "mortal enemy," "everything she trie[s] to do against Marvin Macy rebound[s] on herself" (60).

Since the terms of the psychodrama unfolding in McCullers's sad cafe are so inexorable, Miss Amelia is doomed from the start to lose the physical battle with Macy which constitutes the novella's climax. Because she has given up her bed to Lymon (who has given up his to Marvin Macy), her only bed has been an uncomfortable sofa, and perhaps, we are told, "lack of sleep . . . clouded her wits." But in itself, as McCullers makes clear, neither sleeplessness nor the stress of having her house invaded would necessarily have been enough to guarantee Miss Amelia's defeat. "A fine fighter," this powerful woman "know[s] all manner of mean holds and squeezes," so that "the town [is] betting on" her victory, remembering "the great fight between Miss Amelia and a Fork Falls lawyer who had tried to cheat her . . . a huge strapping fellow [who] was left three quarters dead when she had finished with him. And it was not only her talent as a boxer that had impressed everyone—she could demoralize her enemy by making terrifying faces and fierce noises" (61). In spite of Miss Amelia's unnatural strength, though, the sexual subtext represented by the grotesque triangle in which she is involved dooms her to defeat.

For, as McCullers describes it, the spectacular fight in which Marvin Macy and Miss Amelia engage before a mass of spectators in the cleared cafe at seven P.M. on Ground Hog Day is not just a jealous struggle for power over Lymon, it is the primal scene of sexual consummation which did not take place on their wedding night. Stripped for action—Miss Amelia barefoot in overalls rolled up to the knees, Marvin Macy "naked to the waist and heavily greased"— the combatants present themselves as the central figures in a bizarre but ancient ritual, "walk[ing] toward each other with no haste, their fists already gripped, and their eyes like the eyes of dreamers" (66). But as they come together in the match, the specifically sexual nature of this ritual becomes clear, for McCullers's language, whether intentionally or not, is heavy with double entendres. At the beginning of the fight, when the strange and estranged husband and wife are said to produce "the sound of knocks, panting, and thumpings on the floor" as they are "experimenting with various positions" (66), McCullers evokes the idiom of foreplay. Then, when Miss Amelia gets "a grasp around [Marvin Macy's] waist" and "the real fight" begins, the wrestling couple's thrashings not only recall the wrestling match between the unnaturally virile Bertha Mason Rochester and her captor husband but also plainly suggest that, besides being sexual, the battle *is* sex: "For a while the fighters grappled muscle to muscle, their hipbones braced against each other. Backward and forward, from side to side, they swayed in this way" (67).

Unlike Rochester, however, who is so confident in his mastery that he will not "strike," he will "only wrestle," Marvin Macy appears to be on the verge of losing the fight and his manhood, for though he is "tricky to grasp," Miss Amelia is "stronger" (67). In fact, as their bout reaches its climax, she bends "him over backward, and inch by inch she force[s] him to the floor" until she has "him down, and straddled; her strong big hands . . . on his throat" (67). At just this moment of imminent female victory, however, the phallic retribution that must punish Miss Amelia's transgressive behavior is exacted. The hunchback, who has been watching the fight from an elevated position on the counter of the cafe, suddenly utters "a cry . . . that caused a shrill bright shiver to run down the spine" (67) and sails "through the air as though he had grown hawk wings" (68) to land like an incubus on Miss Amelia's back and to allow Marvin Macy to leave her "sprawled on the floor, her arms flung outward and motionless."

Why is the hunchback the agent of Miss Amelia's symbolic defloration as well as her literal defeat and thus the instrument of Marvin Macy's sexual triumph? And why is his leap into the fray accompanied by a mysterious cry? McCullers's text is so complex that we have to read it as overdetermined. From one perspective, if we take the hunchback to represent the false phallus associated with Miss Amelia's presumptuous usurpation of masculine privilege—with, that is, what Freud would call her "penis envy" and her "masculinity complex"—then his intervention in the fight signals the moment when she must be forced to confront the delusional quality of her pseudo-virility.[52] Deformed himself, Lymon lands on her back to dramatize the way in which his physical deformity echoes her sexual deformity. In this reading, then, as Miss Amelia is made to surrender her pretensions to power, true masculinity reasserts itself with a victorious war whoop that sends a shiver down the spines of the onlookers, who realize that they are present at a solemn cultural event.

From another perspective, if we see the hunchback as representing the "little man" that is the female clitoris or, in a more generalized sense, the authentic if truncated female libido that Miss Amelia has refused to acknowledge, then the intervention of the hunchback in the fight signals the moment when she has been forced to confront her desire for Marvin Macy. Certainly from the day Macy returned to town, her behavior has notably changed: abandoning overalls for a dress, feeding Macy at her table, and finally bedding him down in her private quarters, she might almost "[seem] to have lost her will" (53) because she is in a kind of erotic trance, and the hunchback's open flirtation with Marvin Macy might well express her own secret enthrallment. In this reading, therefore, the mysterious cry is a cry of female orgasmic surrender which sends a shiver down the spine of onlookers because they realize that they are voyeurs witnessing a ceremonial sexual event.

Finally, from yet a third perspective, if we define the hunchback not simply as an anatomical or allegorical aspect of Miss Amelia but rather as an autonomous male character, then his intervention in the fight signals the moment when, by eliminating Amelia as a rival, he achieves a homosexual union with the man whom he has been trying to seduce since the moment when they exchanged their first gaze of secret complicity. In this reading, then—a reading that supposes McCullers's text to be haunted by female anxiety about male social and sexual bonding—Miss Amelia is simply the medium whose house and flesh provide the opportunity for Lymon and Marvin Macy to come together, and the mysterious cry at the end of the fight expresses their homoerotic orgasm while sending a shiver down the spines of onlookers because they realize they are witnessing a perverse and subversive event. Moreover, that the two men leave town together after destroying most of Miss Amelia's property re-iterates the point that she not only is no longer necessary to them but that their union requires her obliteration.

Whether one subscribes to all or none of these readings, it is clear that at the conclusion of "Ballad" Miss Amelia has been metamor-phosed from a woman warrior to a helpless madwoman. Her very body has shriveled, for she is "thin as old maids are thin when they go crazy"; her eyes emphasize her isolation because they are "more crossed . . . as though they sought each other out to exchange a little glance of grief and lonely recognition"; and her voice is "broken, soft, and sad" (70). Bereft of her once legendary physical strength, she has also lost her social, intellectual, and economic authority; her cafe is closed; her house is boarded up; and all her "wise doctoring" is over, for she tells "one-half of her patients that they [are] going to die outright, and to the remaining half she recommend[s] cures so far-fetched and agonizing that no one in his right mind would consider them for a moment" (69–70). Incarcerated in a wasteland of a town where "the soul rots with boredom," she resembles not only such paradigmatic mad spinsters as Miss Havisham in Dickens's *Great Expectations* and Miss Emily in Faulkner's "A Rose for Emily" but also a female version of T. S. Eliot's wounded Fisher King.

Even the male prisoners in the novella's mysterious epilogue—a brief coda entitled "THE TWELVE MORTAL MEN"—are happier on their chain gang than is this prisoner of sex in her sad cafe, for as she sits in silence beside the one window of her house "which is not boarded" and turns toward the empty street "a face like the terrible dim faces known in dreams," their voices swell together "until at last it seems that the sound does not come from the twelve men on the gang, but from the earth itself, or the wide sky" (3, 71). Even in the penitentiary, McCullers implies, men are sustained by their own community while a woman like Miss Amelia—who, even at her most powerful, never had a community of women—has been inexorably condemned to the solitary confinement such a singular anomaly deserves.

Like West's "Indissoluble Matrimony," McCullers's "Ballad" tells an extraordinarily detailed and coherent tale of sexual battle. A number of elements that appear in these works, however, recur separately in texts produced by McCullers's female contemporaries and descendants. Between the 1940s and the 1970s, as the conditions that gave rise to the second wave of feminism were taking shape, literary women responded to male attacks with accounts of female freakishness, male willfulness or brutality, female guilt, and female sacrifice. Flannery O'Connor's classic 1955 short story "Good Country People," for instance, introduces a heroine just as freakish as McCullers's Miss Amelia—if not more so. And like Miss Amelia, Hulga/Joy, the weak-hearted, wooden-legged, atheistical Ph.D., is punished for unfeminine arrogance when a seemingly stupid Bible salesman outwits her, teaches her not to judge a book by its cover (he keeps whisky, dirty playing cards, and condoms in a hollowed-out Bible), and absconds with her leg.[53]

More melodramatically, Elizabeth Bowen's equally classic 1945 tale "The Demon Lover" analyzes male willfulness by describing a woman's futile efforts to flee the terrifying advances of the dead lover with whom she has plighted a "sinister troth" and who has returned from the grave to assert his claim on her, while almost two decades later, in *The Bell Jar* (1963), Sylvia Plath examines male brutality by depicting, among other things, the savagery of a woman-hating Argentinian who excoriates and beats Esther Greenwood.[54] A few years later, moreover, as if both to stress the historical weight of such behavior and to emphasize the postmodern woman's horror at its intensification, Jean Rhys rewrites the story of the battle between Bertha Mason Rochester and her husband from the supposed madwoman's point of view. In *Wide Sargasso Sea* (1966), revising Charlotte Brontë's portrait of Rochester, Rhys characterizes the hero of *Jane Eyre* as viciously oppressive and she sympathetically transcribes Bertha's consciousness as the supposedly depraved wife sinks into the madness he has helped to cause.[55] Finally, in "The Child Who Favored Daughter" (1967), a far more extreme account of male brutality, Alice Walker tells the story of a man who has beaten his own wife into a cripple, forcing her to kill herself, and who later, in a moment of rage, slices off his own daughter's breasts, while in *The Bluest Eye* (1970), Toni Morrison recounts the history of a man who rapes his pubescent daughter and catapults her into madness.[56]

From Marge Piercy to May Swenson and Margaret Atwood, poets offer similarly striking portrayals of male sadism. In Piercy's "The friend" (1969), for example, a man tells a woman to "cut off your hands" and to "burn your body. / it is not clean and smells like sex." In Swenson's "Bleeding" (1970), the man is represented as a knife, the woman as a cut who is told—even as the knife penetrates in a grotesque parody of sexual intercourse—to "stop" bleeding "or I will sink in farther." And, in the first poem of her *Power Politics* (1971), Margaret Atwood produces an equally bitter allegory of sexual intercourse as the epitome of male cruelty and female vulnerability:

> you fit into me
> like a hook into an eye
>
> a fish hook
> an open eye[57]

All these texts suggest, in one way or another, that midcentury women writers experience men as telling women to suffer and be still, to bleed and to endure, for not only has the penis now been redefined as a weapon, it has been defined as a weapon whose aggressive onslaughts women ought to want. Thus in this period, even when women achieve victory in their sexual battles with men, their triumphs are tainted with a guilt that was completely absent in, say, "Trifles" or "Indissoluble Matrimony." Paule Marshall's *Brown Girl, Brown Stones* (1959), for example, describes the "war" between a hard-working woman from Barbados and her dreamy ineffectual husband, a war which she wins when she has him deported but whose outcome Marshall shows is a hollow victory because, in destroying him, this woman shatters her relationship with her daughter.[58]

As if meditating on the issue of female culpability, other women writers in this period develop plots that describe the inexorability of female sacrifice, sacrifice that is associated not with the specific guilt that Marshall examines but with the generalized guilt of the scapegoat. In Shirley Jackson's famous "The Lottery" (1948), the protesting Tessie Hutchinson is positioned at the center of a ceremonial arena not unlike the high altar in Mew's "A White Night" or, for that matter, the cleared cafe in McCullers's "Ballad," and, as if to indicate that the sacrifice of woman is at the heart of culture's darkness, she is ritually stoned to death to ensure communal prosperity because "lottery in June" means "corn be heavy soon."[59] And, though the very title of Jackson's tale implies that anyone, male or female, could be marked out for such a fate, it is significant that the story this female writer chose to tell is of a woman who is ceremonially slaughtered as the result of a lottery whose machinery is administered and justified by men.

Less ceremonial and public but equally inexplicable and horrifying is the account of female sacrifice in Joyce Carol Oates's resonant "Where Are You Going, Where Have You Been?" (1970), a modern version of Death and the Maiden in which a fifteen-year-old girl is murderously seduced by a sinister, almost supernaturally powerful hipster named Arnold Friend. Advising her to "Be nice to me, be sweet like you can because what else is there for a girl like you but to be sweet and pretty and give in," Friend persuades her to go with him to what she knows will be her death, in part because she is convinced that in doing so she is somehow saving her family from his bizarre onslaught.[60] Although both Oates's and Jackson's hapless heroines may seem radically different from the aggressive female contestants created by Moore, Petry, and McCullers, their stories constitute important counterpoints to postmodernist fictions of sexual combat, for in "The Lottery" and "Where Are You Going" the dynamic of female defeat is dramatized in its purest form. Precisely because the female protagonists of these tales do not, and cannot, either struggle against or account for the punishment they do not seem to deserve, their authors are able to interrogate the logic of a culture whose feminine mystique tells the wife and mother that she must sacrifice herself for her family while also admonishing the daughter that there is nothing else for "a girl like you but to be sweet and pretty and give in."

With the second wave of feminism, not giving in becomes more than ever before a possibility about which women writers can dream. In the midseventies, for instance, such texts as Alison Lurie's *The War Between the Tates* (1974) and Julia O'Faolain's "Man in the Cellar" (1974) describe hectic sexual struggles which women have more than a chance of winning. In despair over the "battle fatigue" he experiences as he is torn between his estranged wife and his student mistress, Lurie's Brian Tate thinks, "Other wars end eventually in victory, defeat or exhaustion, but the war between men and women goes on forever."[61] And though Lurie concludes by hinting at the possibility of a reconciliation between the warring spouses, her novel climaxes with a depiction of Brian Tate and a male colleague of his as prisoners of sex, locked up in a campus building by a swarm of rabid, radical feminists. Even more dramatically, O'Faolain's short story begins with its English female narrator admitting, about her intransigently macho Italian husband, that "When we fight, he wins: history of the sex war."[62] Yet the tale develops to a point where the maddened wife (with the Spenserian name of Una) has chained her mate with red-velvet-covered iron fetters to a bedstead in their cellar; there, after fifteen days of imprisonment, he has become so "meek and constipated" that he lets her insert a "glycerine suppository" into "his anus, with [her] finger, giving no signs of shame or vindictiveness" (209).

Despite the vividness of Lurie's and O'Faolain's narratives, however, it is particularly in science fiction, fantasy, and lyric poetry—

genres which liberate the political imagination to consider the possible instead of the probable—that literary women from the science
fiction writers Marion Zimmer Bradley, James Tiptree, Jr., and
Joanna Russ, and the fantasists Angela Carter and Maxine Hong
Kingston, to the poets Adrienne Rich, Diane Wakoski, and Susan
Griffin, build on the social analyses implicit in the texts of such precursors as Moore, Petry, McCullers, and Rhys both to protest the
phallic laws these writers are documenting and to imagine a world
elsewhere in which such laws would be eternally and definitively
repealed. In *The Shattered Chain* (1976), for instance, Bradley's vision
of free Amazons is infused with the utopian fervor that also in this
period inspires the French novelist Monique Wittig's *Les Guérillères*.[63]
Similarly, in Tiptree's "Mama Come Home" (1968), a race of alien
"giantesses" invades the earth, raping and enslaving men—the narrator, one of their victims, says that his experience of the sexual
assault was like "being attacked by a . . . vacuum cleaner"—and their
onslaught can only be repelled when a secret service group in Washington enacts a charade designed to convince them that they too
might be vulnerable to such attack.[64] Conversely, in Tiptree's "The
Women Men Don't See" (1975), an apparently mousy woman who
observes that "women have no rights . . . except what men allow us"
decides that, because the struggle naught availeth, she will take her
daughter and go off to another planet. Though the tale's male narrator insists that "Men and women aren't different species," she
triumphantly embraces what she defines as an "extraordinary opportunity for travel" because she feels less alienated from so-called
aliens than she does from the males of her own species.[65]

More strikingly, in Joanna Russ's *The Female Man* (1975), we encounter four psychic avatars of the narrator, Joanna, one of whom,
Janet, represents the feminist serenity of the Herland that is the all-
female planet Whileaway, and another of whom, biblically called
Jael, symbolizes the militant feminist rage that fuels interminable
sexual combat between Manlanders and Womanlanders on a planet
reminiscent of the sexually-conflicted futurist world created by
Thomas Berger. Jael's erotic authority over a lobotomized male sex-
slave named Davie parodically reverses Miller's theology of the cunt,
for as she "play[s] with him. . . , then swallow[s] him whole like a
watermelon seed," he reveals himself to be as idiotically sexual as

Miller's "one cunt in a million," lying below his masterful mistress, "his blue gaze shattered, his whole body uncontrollably arched, all his sensations concentrated in the place where [she holds] him."[66]

But that besides enslaving Davie, who lives in an exercise box, Jael is a trained killer with "talons like a cat's but bigger" and teeth that "are a sham over metal" (181) clarifies the connection between sexual dominance and sex antagonism. In one of the book's climactic scenes, she boastfully describes her murderous engagement with a Manlander she contemptuously calls "Boss":

> I raked him gaily on the neck and chin and when he embraced me in rage, sank my claws into his back. You have to build up the fingers surgically so they'll take the strain. A certain squeamishness prevents me from using my teeth in front of witnesses—the best way to silence an enemy is to bite out his larynx. Forgive me! I dug the hardened cuticle into his neck but he sprang away; he tried a kick but I wasn't there (I told you they rely too much on their strength); he got hold of my arm but I broke the hold and spun him off, adding with my nifty, weighted shoon another bruise on his limping kidneys. Ha ha! He fell on me (you don't feel injuries, in my state) and I reached around and scored him under the ear, letting him spray urgently into the rug; he will stagger to his feet and fall, he will plunge fountainy to the ground; at her feet he bowed, he fell, he lay down; at her feet he bowed, he fell, he lay down dead. [182]

As Russ indicates, Jael is pathological—in her way as maddened as Rhys's Bertha—but the dream in whose service she wreaks mayhem is the widespread twentieth-century fantasy of a Herland where, *while* (the men are) *away*, the women citizens will while away their time "in a blessedness none of us will ever know" (213).

But if science fiction writers like Bradley, Tiptree, and Russ create cultures in which women are either powerful rulers or potent rebels, female fantasists as diverse as Angela Carter and Maxine Hong Kingston dream dreams in which they excavate or transform ancient scripts. In Carter's "The Company of Wolves" (1979), a New Womanly Little Red Riding Hood seduces and subdues her wolfish male antagonist when, as she takes off the garment which has traditionally defined her fate, she redefines herself as "nobody's meat."[67] Similarly, Maxine Hong Kingston's *The Woman Warrior* (1976) reaches back into Chinese legend to translate the word for woman—"slave"—into linguistic gifts of power that are inscribed on her body and to metamorphose herself from a humble reader into "a female avenger."[68]

Poets are comparably passionate in their imaginings of the ecstatic consummation associated with the unleashing of female rage. From Diane Wakoski's *Motorcycle Betrayal Poems* (1971) and *Dancing on the Grave of a Son of a Bitch* (1973)—both collections based on vengeful protofeminist sequences—to Adrienne Rich's "Trying to Talk to A Man" and "The Phenomenology of Anger," both in her influentially feminist *Diving Into the Wreck* (1976), to Susan Griffin's "I Like to Think of Harriet Tubman" (1976), contemporary women poets have vindictively warned their male opponents that, in the words of Griffin's poem,

> I want them to feel fear now
> as I have felt suffering in the womb, and
> I want them
> to know
> that there is always time to make right
> what is wrong,
> there is always a time
> for retribution
> and that time
> is beginning.

To the extent that these writers crafted what Audre Lorde calls *Cables to Rage*, they were not only influenced by but deeply influenced the contemporary feminist movement, with its self-consciously aggressive intent to transform words into weapons that would be effective in the sexual battle over public as well as private territory.[69]

Such an intent is, of course, in itself problematic, for what price victory if one sex annihilates the other? In other words, is the "blessedness" of female separatism a promised end—a one far-off divine event—toward which the whole creation moves? And even if it were, is such an end in sight? No history, after all, not even women's, is wholly progressive. As we have seen, from Charlotte

Brontë's Bertha Mason Rochester and Mary Wilkins Freeman's Old Woman Magoun to Rebecca West's Evadne Silverton, Carson McCullers's Miss Amelia Evans, and Joanna Russ's Jael, women characters created by women writers have repeatedly drafted themselves into what Sylvia Townsend Warner called "the great civil war" between men and women. Although their efforts have been continually baffled and balked, the repeated eruption of fantasies of female victory into their texts qualifies what might seem to be the monolithic historical pattern we have been tracing. Similarly, that pattern is also qualified by dark, female-authored fictions about female defeat, visions which are often themselves signs of feminist rebellion. Some years after such thinkers as Simone de Beauvoir, Betty Friedan, and Kate Millett had begun to reinvent the women's movement, James Tiptree, Jr.—elsewhere the author of fantasies about female autonomy—recorded in "The Screwfly Solution" (1977) a terrifying vision of a femicidal Holocaust. And to return to Sylvia Plath, with whom we began this analysis of the woman's cause, even before the second wave of feminism had made its effects known this artist who sought to recover "a self . . . a queen" (*CP* 215) had imagined not only the female martyrdom claimed by the masochistic Dody Ventura of "Stone Boy with Dolphin" but also a key instance of providential womanly triumph in a subtle sexual contest that is at the heart of the story entitled "The Fifty-Ninth Bear" (1959).

Tiptree's "The Screwfly Solution" describes a mysterious "epidemic" of "murders or massacres of women" associated with the rise of a misogynistic cult called "The Sons of Adam," a cult that is far more ferocious than the perpetrators of P. Edward Pollyglow's comic "Masculinist Revolt."[70] As if echoing the doctrines of Otto Weininger, the leaders of this group agree that the human race must eschew reproduction because "as long as man depends on the old filthy animal why God won't help him. When man gets rid of his animal part which is woman, this is the signal God is awaiting. Then God will reveal the new, true, clean way. . . ." (59). In spite of feminist "Save-the-Women" committees (61) such ideas sweep the world, and, although Pope John IV refuses "to comment officially on the so-called Pauline Purification cults," one Cardinal Fazzoli pontificates that "Women . . . are nowhere defined as human but merely as a

transitional expedient or state." (65) As the massacres continue, fu-
neral homes begin to refuse to accept female cadavers, and harbors
are blocked by female corpses. Even the kindly scientist who is the
story's hero comes down with the disease of misogyny and, despite
his efforts to resist what he understands to be his own illness, he
kills his daughter and cuts his own throat.

Finally it becomes clear, through a number of scientific documents
embedded in Tiptree's text, that an alien race is exterminating humanity by manipulating a *"vulnerable link in the behavioral chain"* (55)
which, in this case, is the connection in the male of the species between "aggression/predation and sexual reproduction" (69). At the
story's end, "the last woman left alive on earth" (74), disguised as a
boy, resigns herself to her own imminent death and the ultimate
death of humankind. When Booth Tarkington's "The Veiled Feminists of Atlantis" concluded with the destruction of a continent, his
narrator had asked, about the battle of the sexes recorded there,
"Who won?" and a comparable question is implicit in Tiptree's tale.
Just in the years, therefore, when such writers as Kingston, Rich,
and Russ were celebrating the potency of women warriors, Tiptree
was articulating a very different, though equally radical, phenomenology of anger by returning to the problem of female sacrifice so
vividly dramatized in Charlotte Mew's "A White Night."

Yet another mode of expressing anger—a quasi-Victorian one—
is explored in Plath's "The Fifty-Ninth Bear" (1959). Here, the story's
apparently childlike and trusting heroine, Sadie, has insisted that
she and her husband will see fifty-nine bears on a visit to a national
park because the number fifty-nine is her "symbol of plenitude"
while Norton, her somewhat smug husband, who frequently imagines himself as a "hollow-cheeked, Hamletesque" widower, has casually bet that they will see seventy-one (*JP*, 108). At the tale's end
Sadie wins the wager when the providential fifty-ninth bear, which
she calls "My bear," appears and kills Norton, who realizes, as he
tries to drive the creature away, that "there is another will working,
a will stronger, even, than his" (*JP* 114). Significantly, as he struggles
in the deadly embrace—the bear hug—of the animal, the vanquished
man tastes "a thick, sweet honey," as if the *Ur*, ursine embrace were
not only deathly but sexual; thus, because the bear is defined as
Sadie's bear, it seems that Norton is being destroyed by a grotesque

conjugal coupling. That, "as from a far and rapidly receding planet," Norton hears "a shrill cry—of terror, or triumph, he could not tell" (*JP* 114) also emphasizes the possibility of Sadie's secret complicity, even indeed her orgasmic pleasure, in this event which has drawn the man away from the planet of his humanity and enfolded him in an alien and annihilating embrace.

But if in the early "The Fifty-Ninth Bear" Plath imagines a female triumph achieved through a fortuitous event which allows her heroine, like Gwendolyn Grandcourt, to see her "wish outside" her, in such famous late poems as "Lady Lazarus" and "Daddy" she fantasizes vengeful victories won by female speakers who openly act for themselves. No wonder, then—to come full circle back to Ted Hughes—that even after Plath's death her poet-husband described in "Love Song" a sexual battle that was not just intensely physical but also notably linguistic, with combat carried on through words, whispers, promises, vows. For, as the battle of the sexes raged in public and in private, between stern Victorian husbands and their maddened wives, between turn-of-the-century misogynists and rebellious suffragists, between modernist no-men and autonomous New Women, between midcentury he-men and ambitious independent women, between contemporary masculinists and second-wave feminists, literary men and women began to wage war not only with but over words themselves. Indeed, both the shape of literary history and the nature of the language out of which that history is constituted became crucial combat zones, since both the man's case and the woman's cause had to be based not only on redefinitions of female and male nature but also on revisions of the aesthetic assumptions and linguistic presumptions of patriarchal culture.

Illustration on preceding page: Aubrey Beardsley. *Book-Plate of the Artist*, from *The Collected Drawings of Aubrey Beardsley*, ed. Bruce S. Harris. Courtesy of the Crown Publishing Group.

Tradition and the Female Talent: Modernism and Masculinism

> Towards the end of the eighteenth century a change came about
> which, if I were re-writing history, I should describe more fully and
> think of greater importance than the Crusades or the Wars of the
> Roses. The middle-class woman began to write.
>
> —Virginia Woolf

> The fact that the recognised heads of literature in the Homeric age
> were the nine muses . . . throws back the suggestion of female
> authorship to a very remote period. . . . If the truth were known, we
> might very likely find that it was man rather than woman who has
> been the interloper in the domain of literature.
>
> —Samuel Butler

> In the nineteenth century men were confident, the women were not
> but in the twentieth century the men have no confidence.
>
> —Dashiell Hammett to Gertrude Stein

> The existing monuments form an ideal order among themselves,
> which is modified by the introduction of the new (the really new) work
> of art among them.
>
> —T. S. Eliot

On December 30, 1927, Max Beerbohm wrote Virginia Woolf a strangely ambiguous fan letter. Praising her criticism for its likeness to her father's work—"if he had been a 'Georgian' and a woman, just so would he have written"—he went on quite unexpectedly to attack her fiction: "Your novels beat me—black and blue. I retire howling, aching, sore; full, moreover, of an acute sense of disgrace.

I return later, I re-submit myself to the discipline. No use: I am
carried out half-dead."[1] What was bothering the incomparable Max?
Certainly, in the context of his admiration for *The Common Reader*
("a book which I have read twice and rate above any modern book
of criticism"), his somewhat paranoid association of Woolf's novels
with bondage and discipline seems inexplicable, almost bizarre.

To be sure, Beerbohm goes on in the same letter to provide an
explanation of his pain which would appear to suggest that his
quarrel with Leslie Stephen's daughter is part of a larger generational conflict in the world of letters. "I don't really, insidious though
you are, believe in your Cambridge argument that a new spirit exacts
a new method . . . of narration," he explains, identifying himself
with "Homer's and Thackeray's method, and Tolstoi's and Tom's,
Dick's, Chaucer's, Maupassant's, and Harry's," all presumably
methods grounded in the modes and manners of traditional realism.
In other words, he sets himself, as a late Victorian man of letters,
against Woolf, as a representative of Cambridge/Bloomsbury modernism. "You may be right in thinking that we are 'on the verge of
one of the great ages of English literature'," he admits, but adds,
"I believe that ten years hence and one hundred years hence fictional
narrative will be thriving only in the old method about which I have
been so stodgy and so longsome. . . ." Despite this explanation,
Beerbohm's description of the effect Woolf's novels have on him,
together with his list of the Toms, Dicks, and Harrys who constitute
his literary patrilineage, implies that more than a conflict of cohorts
is being enacted here. Curiously enough, moreover, the rhetoric of
his letter echoes a story he had published seven years earlier, a story
about a specifically literary battle not between the generations but
between the sexes. Indeed, Beerbohm's image of a generational
struggle may mask a more profound sexual-literary struggle dramatized not only in his fiction but also in the fiction of many of his
contemporaries, a struggle associated with the more general battle
of the sexes we have already discussed.

"The Crime," which was included in Beerbohm's *And Even Now*
(1920), describes the acute "sense of disgrace" experienced by a
nameless narrator who impetuously flings a woman writer's novel
into a fireplace but cannot seem to burn the book up. Vacationing
in a rented cottage in a remote county, this solitary man of letters

compares himself at the outset of the story to "Lear in the hovel on the heath."[2] Idly looking for something to read, he picks up the latest novel by a well-known woman writer whom he has met and been daunted by on several occasions: "She had a sisterly, brotherly way, . . . But I was conscious that my best, under her eye, was not good . . . she said for me just what I had tried to say, and proceeded to show me just why it was wrong" (247). In fact, he reminisces, his few conversations with her led him to speculate on the " 'sex war' " that, "we are often told[,] is to be one of the features of the world's future—women demanding the right to do men's work, and men refusing, resisting, counter-attacking" (248). Although he claims that he himself has never had his "sense of fitness jarred, nor a spark of animosity roused" by most feminist demands, he confesses that he is disturbed by the idea of a woman practicing the art of writing. More specifically, he admits that he is bothered if a woman is "an habitual, professional author, with a passion for her art, and a fountain-pen and an agent, and sums down in advance of royalties on sales in Canada and Australia" (248–49).

But the novelist whose book Beerbohm's man of letters picks up in his country cottage is emphatically all these things and, worse still, her work, as its jacket copy suggests, is characterized by "immense vitality," "intense vitality"; her newest novel, say the critics, is "A book that will live" (247). Furthermore, when he begins reading this book, he soon discovers that the novel is itself a *Kunstlerroman* about a successful woman of letters, a mother who sits "writing in a summer-house at the end of a small garden," her pen traveling "rapidly across the foolscap" (249). He feels "exquisite satisfaction," therefore, when he discovers that, following "an impulse . . . almost before I was conscious of it" (250), he has committed the heinous crime of flinging his landlord's copy of this woman's book into the fire, where it stands for a moment gloriously glowing. But although at first "little tongues of bright colour" (251) leaping from the binding let him exult that "I had scored . . . perfectly" against this "Poor woman!," he soon discovers to his dismay that the text itself refuses to be burnt. Enacting a cross between a ritual rape and a sacrificial burning at the stake, this increasingly obsessed narrator "rakes" the book "fore and aft" with a poker, "carve[s]" it into sections, "subdivide[s] it, spread[s] it, redistribute[s] it" (251–52). Yet still its intense and immense vitality proclaims that "It [is] a book that would live—do what one might" (252), while fragments of its sentences haunt and taunt him—" 'lways loathed you, bu' " for instance. Finally, then, Beerbohm's disgraced man of letters has to concede that his female antagonist has "scored again." Not only has he been unable to destroy her book in "the yawning crimson jaws" of his hearth, her book has itself damped his flames. As his fire goes "darkly, dismally, gradually quite out" (252), he is left alone in a small and chilly room, as dispossessed as a parodic Lear confined to the prison of his consciousness.

Beerbohm's story is, of course, a masterfully comical satire on the futile rage with which men of letters greeted female literary achievement. At the same time, it is also, as the author's own letter to Virginia Woolf suggests, an enactment of that futile rage. Like Beerbohm himself, the narrator of "The Crime" admires his literary woman's "creative work immensely—but only in a bemused and miserable manner." Like Beerbohm, too, he tries to "resubmit himself to the discipline" of reading her text, but ends up experiencing "an acute sense of disgrace." Again, like Beerbohm, he finds the woman novelist's methods "insidious." And, like Beerbohm, he is beaten "black and blue." What the juxtaposition of the letter and the story demonstrates, therefore, is that the existence of a tradition of "habitual, professional" women authors made for a battle of the sexes over the province and provenance of literature, a battle which—like the more general battle over votes and rights—men felt they were losing in the years when Beerbohm wrote.

That Beerbohm was no noncombatant in the war between men and women which had been gathering force since the late nineteenth century is manifest in *Zuleika Dobson* (1906), that ultimate comedy of the femme fatale. Zuleika's narcissistic female charm, after all, causes all the youth of Oxford simultaneously to immolate themselves in the allegorically significant river Isis on the day Judas's boating crew is supposed to bump the crew of Magdalene. Even the dandy Duke of Dorset, a consummate poet in ancient and modern languages, must unwillingly submit to the sorcery of a "She-Wizard" whose conjuring tricks include the Demon Egg-Cup, the Magic Cannister, and the Blazing Ball of Worsted, and Zuleika's beauty is so threatening that, when she comes to town, the grim Roman Emperors whose busts grace Oxford sweat and weep.[3] Always masking his masculinist anxieties with elegant irony, Beerbohm nevertheless understood the deeply dialectical relationship in which men and women found themselves by the fin de siècle, a relationship that was unprecedented in literary history, as Virginia Woolf herself pointed out.

Eight years after Beerbohm wrote "The Crime," Woolf observed, in a passage from *A Room of One's Own* which we have used as an epigraph here, that "Toward the end of the eighteenth century a change came about which, if I were rewriting history, I should describe more fully and think of greater importance than the Crusades or the War of the Roses. The middle-class woman began to write" (68). Earlier, moreover, in just the year when Beerbohm wrote "The Crime," Woolf had analyzed the empowering implications of the entrance of women into literary history, noting in a letter to *The New Statesman* that "the seventeenth century produced more remarkable women than the sixteenth, the eighteenth than the seventeenth, and the nineteenth than all three put together[.] When I compare the Duchess of Newcastle with Jane Austen, the matchless Orinda with Emily Brontë, Mrs. Haywood with George Eliot, Aphra Behn with Charlotte Brontë, Jane Gray with Jane Harrison, the advance in intellectual power seems to me not only sensible but immense."[4] Describing the evolution of a tradition of immense and intense vitality, Woolf's statement almost seems to gloss the dilemma Beerbohm dramatizes in "The Crime." Moreover, the implicit dialogue between Beerbohm and Woolf that we have traced here seems itself to gloss the asymmetrical responses of men and women of letters to the strong new presence of women in the literary marketplace. For, when the middle-class woman began not only to enter the professions but specifically to enter the profession of letters, both sexes reacted with powerful but different changes in their views of the world and themselves.

How did male reactions inflect the engendering of literary history in the twentieth century? To begin with—and most dramatically—writers like James in America and Wilde in England could not help noticing that theirs was among the earliest generations to have female precursors. But what did it mean for such men to have to confront not only the commercial successes of, say, Harriet Beecher Stowe in America and Mary Elizabeth Braddon in England, but also the cultural achievements of, say, George Eliot, Elizabeth Barrett Browning, and Charlotte Brontë in England? Where literary men had traditionally looked for inspiration to the idealized mother or mistress whom convention metaphorized as a muse, turn-of-the-century and twentieth-century men of letters suffered from a disquieting intimation that the goddesses of literature, like the literary women male readers now encountered in increasing numbers, might reserve creative power for themselves. Worse still, these men feared that real-life "sisters of the sacred well" might go beyond what Milton had magisterially defined as "denial vain, and coy excuse" to produce texts that would eclipse or actually obliterate male efforts.[5] The literally castrating "Mommy" of Edward Albee's *The American Dream* may indeed be linked to the literarily castrating female precursor whose rivalrous descendants had to brag *"Who's Afraid of Virginia Woolf?"*

But perhaps even more important, because for late nineteenth- and early twentieth-century literary sons the Oedipal struggle against the father was in some sense doomed from the start, this historical change reinforced the feeling of belatedness—the anxiety about the originatory power of the father—upon which, as Harold Bloom has shown, literary men had already been brooding for several centuries. Where the male precursor had had an acquiescent mother-muse, his heir now confronted rebellious ancestresses and ambitious female peers, literary women whose very existence called the concept of the willing muse into question. Moreover, where the male precursor had himself been an adequate inheritor, capable of articulating a mature authority sufficient to the demands of his lineage, the modernist often felt that, as Wyndham Lewis put it in 1921, his culture was characterized by "a sort of No Man's Land atmosphere" and that, except for a marginalized elite, "[t]here is no mature authority."[6] Thus, what Matthew Arnold called in "The Scholar Gypsy" "this strange disease of modern life" (l. 203) became a literary disease with the "feminine, chattering, canting age" that Basil Ransom had excoriated in *The Bostonians*. At the same time, however, the very dis-ease fostered by this unprecedented cultural crisis worked paradoxically to the advantage of many literary men: as the richness of the (male) modernist tradition attests, for many male writers

Beerbohm's futile rage became fertile rage, fueling the innovations of the avant garde in order to ward off the onslaughts of women.

In 1975 Harold Bloom casually and almost comically declared that "the first true breach with literary continuity will be brought about in generations to come if the burgeoning religion of Liberated Woman spreads from its clusters of enthusiasts to dominate the West. Homer will cease to be the inevitable precursor and the rhetoric and forms of our literature then may break at last from tradition."[7] Bloom seems to have been speculating provisionally about some future catastrophe, yet it is possible to argue that what he described in such ironically apocalyptic terms was an event that had already occurred. Certainly, as early as 1897, Samuel Butler was claiming that *The Odyssey* was actually composed by a woman. Observing, in a passage part of which we have used as an epigraph to this chapter, that "In an age . . . when men were chiefly occupied either with fighting or hunting, the arts of peace, and among them all kinds of literary accomplishments, would be more naturally left to women," he concluded that "If the truth were known, we might very likely find that it was man rather than woman who has been the interloper in the domain of literature." Butler's argument was, of course, regarded as eccentric by most of his contemporaries, yet within two decades the young Aldous Huxley was to dramatize a situation in which a woman seems to dominate "the domain of literature" not in remote antiquity but in the present moment. Published in the same year that Max Beerbohm produced "The Crime," "The Farcical History of Richard Greenow" was the lead work in a volume with the resolutely nihilistic title *Limbo*, and indeed in keeping with such nihilism Huxley's tale traced the misadventures and growing misogyny of a literary man who lives out in his own person the living end of masculine history that Bloom describes.

Dick Greenow, the anti-hero of Huxley's farcical *Kunstlerroman*, starts as a sensitive boy with a domineering younger sister named Millicent, whose dollhouse fascinates him, although, as if she had already read Ibsen, "it simply didn't interest her."[8] Enduring the standard late Victorian male education, first at a public school called Aesop and then at Cantaloup College, Oxford, he falls hopelessly

in love at the age of sixteen with one Francis Quarles, a handsome
dullard (with a literary name) who has "the face and limbs of a
Graeco-Roman statue" (8) and who inspires him to fits of tears and
sentimental verse-writing from which he is luckily awakened by a
sudden sense that he had been "suffering from anemia of the brain"
(23). Later, he dedicates himself to "all that [is] most intellectually
distinguished" (29), but soon unnervingly discovers that he has been
possessed by the spirit of a female novelist named "Pearl Bellairs,"
who takes over his body to write long, saccharine romances while
he is asleep.

Pearl's first work is entitled *Heartsease Fitzroy: The Story of a Young
Girl* and, ironically enough, its instant success helps finance Dick's
"unproductive male labours" (38). After going down from college
in a blaze of glory, therefore, he pragmatically continues his dual
career. While he works on his *New Synthetic Philosophy*, Pearl indefatigably completes *La Belle Dame Sans Morality* and *Daisy's Voyage to
Cytherea,* along with a series of articles "for the girls of Britain" (49).
But, as Dick gradually loses his intellectual potency and becomes
little Dick, Pearl (with her fanciful belle airs) increasingly manifests
herself as the belle-heir, a twentieth-century inheritor of the women's
tradition founded by such precursors as *Jane Eyre.* Worse still, as
his writing becomes increasingly elitist and occult, her work, inspired
by his readings of George Sand, Elizabeth Barrett Browning, and
Mrs. Humphrey Ward, becomes ever more popular.

The crisis of Dick's life, which parodies an intensified historical
crisis for literary men, comes with the advent of World War I. As
he travels toward London, planning to become a conscientious ob-
jector, even the wheels of the train "refus[e] to recite Milton" (65),
as if prophetically warning him about the demise of the cultural
history he had hoped to inherit. Finally, moreover, his experiences
during the war document that demise, for while his sister Millicent
organizes a hospital depot and then supervises three hundred clerks
at the Ministry of Munitions with "unsurpassed efficiency" (95), Pearl
writes jingoistic propaganda for the "Women of England." Distraught about the "horrible Bluebeard's chamber of his own brain"
(67), Dick visits a psychiatrist whose word association test elicits a
response which seems to offer some solution to the mystery of his
schizophrenic seizures, for the word "woman" seems to lead inex-

orably to the word "novelist" (67). Though Dick continues to stage dramatic anti-war protests as an intellectual socialist/pacifist, therefore, he slowly sinks into madness, with Pearl demonically possessing his brain and pen. By the end of the war, when she is strong enough to emerge and register to vote, he is confined as a lunatic and force-fed the way the suffragists had been. Filled with revulsion at Pearl's proliferating vulgarity, he desperately tries to will his body to science, but even here she intervenes, wresting the pen from him and begging to be buried "in a little country church-yard with little marble angels." In the end, his last desperate scribblings, the fragments he has tried to shore against his ruin, are "thrown away as being merely the written ravings of a madman" (115).

Despite the desolation of Dick's fate, Huxley's story is as farcical as its title indicates; like Beerbohm's, it seems to have been intended as a deliciously sardonic diversion. Huxley himself indicates in the text that he is creating a comedy of doubles like Dr. Jekyll and Mr. Hyde in fiction, William Sharp and Fiona McLeod in real life. In addition, Huxley is examining the intellectual and moral impoverishment, the historical weariness, of great male centers of learning like Aesop and Cantaloup. Virginia Woolf, in fact, observed in a 1920 review of *Limbo* that "as one reads one cannot help exclaiming that English society is making it impossible to produce English literature."[9] Huxley himself, she believed, was in a double bind like Dick Greenow's: when he writes satirically, dissecting the culture on which his own literary authority must depend, he inevitably writes his own death warrant; but if he tries to write about what he believes in, "behold, Mr. Huxley can only stammer." Nevertheless, though Woolf is curiously reticent on the subject, it seems significant that Richard Greenow emerges as a prototypically modern alienated intellectual specifically within the context of a tale depicting degrading femininity let loose in a society where the apocalypse Bloom described was already taking place. Little Dick Greenow does seem to be the apotheosis of a *poète maudit*, and he seems to have become such a figure precisely because of the excursions of his sister, Millicent, and the incursions of her double, Pearl.

That Huxley and Beerbohm were not alone in their sense of a literary apocalypse set in motion by the changing literary relations of the sexes is further suggested by a number of Henry James's

short stories. His 1894 "The Death of the Lion," for instance, counterpoints the ignominious demise of a truly great man of letters and
the horrifying rise of two vulgarly popular literary transsexuals, all
brought together in one Mrs. Wimbush's country house. "Guy Wal-
singham" is the pen name of "a lady who goes in for the larger
latitude," transforming herself into a man because " 'Obsessions, by
Miss So-and-so' would look a little odd, but men are more naturally
indelicate," while "Dora Forbes" is " 'the pen-name' of an indubitable
male" with a "big red mustache" who has assumed a feminine personality "because the ladies are such popular favorites" and because
"there's every prospect" of his transformation being "widely imitated."[10] Although these two aesthetic impostors capture the hearts
and minds of the wealthy female culture vultures who populate Mrs.
Wimbush's salon, the literary lion dies unacknowledged, robbed even
of a significant portion of his reputation, for Mrs. Wimbush loses
the only copy of his newest manuscript. As it did for Huxley and
Beerbohm, for James, literature associated with women writers and
women readers threatens the standards of excellence associated with
a traditional literary order.

Similarly, James's "The Next Time" (1895) traces another male
literary fall associated with a female literary rise. Just as "The Death
of the Lion" is narrated by a journalist keenly conscious of the trivial
trends of the age, "The Next Time" is a tale told by a critic keenly
aware of the changing fortunes of the artist. Ralph Limbert, the
subject of this critic's story, is a novelist who tries to descend to the
level of what would be commercially successful in an age of "trash
triumphant" (245), but in spite of all his efforts he fails to write
badly enough to achieve popularity, while such bad popular writing
comes quite naturally to his rival, Mrs. Jane Highmore, who produces voluminous bestsellers with the greatest of ease. Finally,
James's "Greville Fane" (1892) portrays the "imperturbable industry"
of a woman novelist who "could invent stories by the yard, but
couldn't write a page of English" (153, 155). Although James's narrator is in many ways sympathetic to this "dull kind woman" who
has been, as he shows, ruthlessly exploited by her children, he con-
descendingly explains that he "liked her" because "she rested me
so from literature," which was to him "an irritation, a torment" (154).
His sense of his own "admirably absolute" failure, in other words,

his vision of the Ouida-like Greville Fane as "an old sausage-mill" giving forth "any poor verbal scrap that had been dropped into her" (156) and receiving lucrative rewards for such banality. In all three of these James tales, then, the male writer is rarefied, marginalized, and impoverished, while the female writer, like Beerbohm's woman novelist and Huxley's Pearl Bellairs, achieves an "immense vitality" and a sinister centrality.

Even when the female imagination is incarnated in a nonprofessional teller of tales, indeed, its newly established primacy seems able to rob the male interlocutor of his ancient potency. In Saki's comical "The Open Window" (1911), for instance, a "very self-possessed young lady of fifteen" named Vera terrifies a neurasthenic caller (with the appropriate name of Mr. Nuttell) by telling a wild yarn about her aunt, who she assures him has been driven mad with grief over the deaths of her husband and two young brothers in a nearby bog:[11] "Poor aunt always thinks that they will come back some day" (260), she explains, so she leaves the French windows open on the anniversary of their demise. When the aunt comes in and begins talking briskly about the return of her husband and brothers, the mentally fragile Nuttell is horrified by what he thinks is her lunacy, and when the men themselves (who have simply been out hunting) do return, looking "as if they were muddy up to the eyes" (261), he is convinced that he is seeing ghosts and rushes madly into the twilight. But of course he has merely been victimized by Vera's inveracity, her self-possessed fictionalizing. Playing upon his bad nerves, this imaginative woman has sent him out of the house and out of his wits. Worse still, unbeknownst to him, this precocious fifteen-year-old next transforms him into a character in still another fiction, explaining, when her aunt wonders at his behavior, that he was once hunted by a pack of dogs into an open grave near the Ganges. "Romance at short notice," adds Saki, "was her specialty" (262).

Historically speaking, which figure comes first, the neurasthenic man of letters or the imaginative female romancer? Does Pearl Bellairs gain her strength from Dick Greenow's weakness or is Dick weakened by her strength? Huxley's story, like James's tales, emphasizes the second of these alternatives while not discounting the first. To begin with, after all, Dick Greenow is certainly not a powerful heir of his patrilineage, but his physical fragility and mental effeminacy are matched by, say, the bovine stupidity of the physically powerful Francis Quarles, whose name bizarrely echoes the name of the metaphysical poet Francis Quarles. Because neither of these men can be an inheritor, culture inevitably falls into the hands of Pearl and Millicent. But increasingly, as the story progresses, these two female demons of efficiency become themselves the causes of Dick's diminution. Like Beerbohm's woman writer, who says for the narrator "just what I had tried to say" and then proceeds "to show [him] why it [is] wrong" (247), Pearl even usurps Dick's language, as she invades "the sanctities of his private life" and tramples "on his dearest convictions, denying his faith" (62).

As the novella goes on, indeed, Huxley uses the rhetoric of parasitism and vampirism to describe Pearl's insistent and untiring appropriation of Dick's body: she is "greedy for life"; she leaps "upon him and [stamps] him out of existence" (71); "watching perpetually like a hungry tigress for her opportunity," she takes "possession of his conscious faculties" so that he is "lost, blotted off the register of living souls while she [performs] with intense and hideous industry, her self-appointed task" (73–74). Like Zuleika Dobson, she is a femme fatale whose voracity requires the suicide of the literary man; like those of Beerbohm's literary woman—or, indeed, those of Virginia Woolf as Beerbohm envisioned her in his 1927 letter—her "insidious" ways threaten to destroy the male and the culture he represents; like those of James's and Saki's imaginative women, her fantasies cripple man's fancy, her "romance at short notice" warps his mind, and her "hideous industry" and "immense vitality" leave him with "an acute sense of disgrace."

Given the vampiric and parasitic qualities of this paradigmatic literary woman, one cannot help thinking that she seems uncannily like a nonliterary female prototype Thomas Hardy once created: his famous "Ivy Wife" (1898). Looking for a host to feed on, Hardy's vegetable femme fatale tries first "to love a full-boughed beech / And be as high as he," then to give "the grasp of partnership" to a plane tree, but finally in her "affection" she strives "to coll an ash," who "in trust" receives her love.[12] But that the ash accepts her embrace, as the other trees do not, implies in terms of the question we have been raising here, that some secret death wish, some ashen neurasthenia, is in fact a precondition for female triumph. And certainly the victory of the Ivy Wife is in some ways analogous not only to the triumphs of Pearl Bellairs and her fictive sisters, but also to those of Swinburne's, Lawrence's, and Hemingway's hostile heroines, for, as she tells us, "with my soft green claw / I cramped and bound him as I wove / Such was my love: ha-ha!" Like Pearl and the others, she is a tenaciously successful parasite, cramping her host's style with what appears to be her virtue but is really her "hideous industry." Worse still, like the "low, slow ha! ha!" of Rochester's mad wife in *Jane Eyre* (ch. 12), which echoes through the third storey of haunted Thornfield Hall, her exultant exclamation—"Such was my love—ha-ha!"—expresses yet again the alien urgency of female desire, with its threat to male potency.

More than his modernist successors, however, Hardy feels free to imagine a punitive plot in which the vampiric Ivy Wife is destroyed by her own aspirations.

> But in my triumph I lost sight of afterhaps. Soon he
> Being bark-bound, flagged, snapped, fell outright,
> And in his fall felled me.

Although this may in some sense be the story of Pearl Bellairs, it is emphatically not that of Beerbohm's or James's or Saki's women (and even Pearl Bellairs may, after all, live on through her amazingly successful writing). No doubt because Hardy still feels himself hardily embedded in the sexual conventions of Victorian culture, he is able to annihilate his overreaching female Faust. Yet he does also have to kill the male host along with the female guest, and the anxious ambiguities his poem records therefore point to a story he was to publish in the 1890s, a story about an "Ivy Wife" which provides a significant background to the struggles over literary primacy that we have been tracing here.

Hardy's "An Imaginative Woman," which was composed in the 1860s but included in *Life's Little Ironies* (1894), dramatizes the increasing infatuation of a would-be woman poet named Ella Marchmill, who seems in her female submissiveness like a paradigmatic *elle*, for a true poet with the appropriate name of Robert Trewe.[13] The only daughter of a struggling man of letters and the wife of a "commonplace" small-arms manufacturer, Ella publishes what Hardy makes clear is second-rate verse under the pseudonym of John Ivy, and an Ivy Wife is what, metaphorically speaking, she becomes in her relationship both to her husband and to the fantasy lover / double into whom she transforms Robert Trewe. For though the most striking irony in this tale of one of life's little ironies is that Ella never actually meets Trewe, she becomes obsessed with him when she and her family rent his rooms in a seaside resort for a month one summer. A poem of his, Ella recalls, had appeared in large type at the top of a page in a magazine on which her own poem about the same subject was published in small type at the bottom. He had then assembled his poems in a volume that sold successfully, but when she tried to follow his example her own collection had fallen "dead in a fortnight—if it had ever been alive" (9). For some time, indeed, "with sad and hopeless envy Ella Marchmill had often and often scanned the rival poet's work, so much stronger as it always was than her own feeble lines. She had imitated him, and her inability to touch his level would send her into fits of despondency" (9).

When she finds herself actually inhabiting Trewe's room, therefore, Ella feverishly studies the relics of identity he has left behind. Possessed by the Ivy Wife's passion to "be as high as he," she dons his macintosh and hat, imagining his coat as "the mantle of Elijah" and praying "it might inspire me to rival him, glorious genius that he is!" (12). But although "*His* heart had beat inside that coat and *his* brain had worked under that hat," her "weakness beside him [makes] her feel quite sick" (13). Similarly, when she finds his picture secreted behind a photograph of the royal family, she studies his "striking countenance" adoringly (16) but soon confesses that "It's *you* who've so cruelly eclipsed me these many times!" (17) Finally, she scans "the half-obliterated pencillings on the wall-paper" next to his bed (17), perceiving "the least of them" as "so intense, so sweet, so palpitating, that it seemed as if his very breath fanned her cheeks from those walls" (17). Enclosed by the ghostly traces of Trewe's script, she invokes his presence, imagining that "she was sleeping on a poet's lips, immersed in the very essence of him, permeated by his spirit as by an ether" (18). In a number of ways, then, she seems as vulnerable, passive, and secondary as the Ivy Wife. Disciple to master, student to teacher, even Danäe to Zeus, Mary to Holy Spirit, "permeated" by male authority, she appears more threatened than threat.

In the meantime, while Ella continues humbly to hope for a meeting with this deific man of letters, the distant Trewe responds with cursory civility to the letter she writes him as "John Ivy" and misses a meeting she has arranged because, as a friend of his explains, he is horrified by the "lies that he is powerless to refute" in a review that accuses his poetry of being "too erotic and passionate" (24). Trewe, it appears, has gone into a bizarre decline which we soon learn is not unrelated to his new volume of verse, *Lyrics to a Woman Unknown*, a book whose impetus is a mysterious passion for a kind of *Ferne Geliebte*, an "imaginary woman alone," for—he himself insists—in spite of what has been said in some quarters "there is no real woman behind the title" (26). Soon we learn that he has actually committed suicide and that he has done so because of this "imaginary woman." On the one hand, therefore, Trewe appears to have been sapped of strength because there was no mother, sister, or female friend "tenderly devoted" to him (26); on the other hand, although he says "there is no real woman behind the title" of his newest volume, the "imaginary woman" whose absence triggers his death seems suspiciously related to the "imaginative woman" named Ella Marchmill. To make matters worse, although Ella is genuinely distraught at Trewe's demise, she soon, in what Hardy insinuates is one of "life's little ironies," gives birth to the poet's successor, a son who "by an inexplicable trick of Nature" (32) looks uncannily like this man she has never met.

Ella herself dies in labor, confessing to her husband that she has been mysteriously "possessed" (31), for here, as in so many of Hardy's texts, both men and women are subjected to the "little ironies" impelled by "Crass Casualty." But her production of this apparently illegitimate child suggests that, despite her own victimization by fate, she has radically subverted the very patrilineage which refused to acknowledge her poetry, for, by creating an alien heir to the literary man, she has triumphed over both Trewe and her husband, supplanting the one and undermining the other. Like the Ivy Wife, in other words, she "nurtures a love" which "cramp[s] and bind[s]" her male hosts, even though their "fall felled" her; like Saki's teenage romancer, she has an imagination so strong that it transforms the past and future history of the men in her life; like Pearl Bellairs, she leaves a legacy of chaos which dramatically expresses her sense of herself as a second-rate poet and a second-rate person. At least subtextually, Hardy's language implies that Ella's ambition somehow causes the sexual frustration that kills Trewe, since the reality of the fiercely "imaginative woman" annihilates the dream of the nurturing "imaginary woman." Finally, and most ironically, Ella does not merely destroy Trewe; more terribly, she recreates him in diminished form as a vulnerable child. As early as the 1860s, then, Hardy was brooding on just the issues that Beerbohm, Huxley, James, and Saki were later to explore. In dramatizing such issues, moreover, all these writers were creating a tradition that would continue throughout the twentieth century. In 1946, for instance, Somerset Maugham produced a witty tale that drew on many of the same sexual anxieties which informed "An Imaginative Woman."

Maugham's "The Colonel's Lady" recounts the dismay of a pompous country squire who discovers that the wife he considers "the sort of woman you simply didn't notice" has become a famous imaginative woman with the publication of a best-selling volume of verse.[14] Embarrassingly, too, his wife's *When Pyramids Decay* records the history of a passionate love affair she has had with a younger man, an affair that ended tragically when her youthful lover died. Beginning with the colonel's benign neglect of his wife's book—he muses, without really reading her verse, that "several of [her poems] had long lines of irregular length and didn't rhyme. He didn't like that" (590)—Maugham's story traces this smug husband's dawning realization that he has been completely eclipsed by his wife's celebrity and that he has been not only cuckolded but cuckolded in public and for all posterity.

Although Maugham seems to relish this punishment of his self-satisfied colonel, the turns of his story's plot make the relationship between female creativity and (metaphorically speaking) male castration strikingly clear. Thus, as an analysis of the destructive potency of the poet-wife, "The Colonel's Lady" echoes "An Imaginative Woman." Yet, no doubt because Maugham was writing half a century after Hardy did and working in a culture where women had made even greater advances than they had in Hardy's time, the later story shows its literary heroine to be in every way more threatening than Ella Marchmill was. While Ella had dutifully borne her husband several legitimate heirs before producing the uncanny interloper who resembled Robert Trewe, Evie Peregrine, the colonel's lady, is characterized by her husband as "barren," a fact that "was tough on a fellow who wanted an heir of his own loins" (589). While both Ella and Trewe appear to have been in some sense killed by their inexplicable erotic entanglement, Evie's young lover dies but she lives to tell the tale and, as one reader of her work observes in the story, "though she was shattered by his death, in a strange sort of way she welcomed it" (603). In addition, while Ella's desire for Trewe leaves her feeling "cruelly eclipsed," Evie's poems prove the unnerving liberation of her desire: when the colonel justifies an adultery of his own with the explanation that "A man wants it. Women are different," his lawyer dryly replies "We only have men's word for that" (601).

No wonder, then, that Maugham's disgraced protagonist can only remember two lines of poetry, "The boy stood on the burning deck" and "Ruin seize thee, ruthless king" (590), for, compared to Ella's husband, the colonel is a ruined patriarch, a humiliated victim of a bedroom farce played out before a massive audience—the readers of five editions in England and one forthcoming in America. Unlike Ella's husband, who can discount his wife's verse as banal and second-rate, this man must confront the opinions of critics who compare his Evie to Emily Dickinson and Sappho. Even more than Hardy or, for that matter, Beerbohm, Huxley, James, and Saki, Maugham is documenting the "immense" and "intense vitality" of a female literary tradition whose existence might debilitate not only men of letters but all men.

———

The male authors whose stories we have reviewed here were not merely paranoid, for their fictions reflect the astonishing rise of both critically and commercially successful women of letters throughout the middle and late nineteenth century in England and America.[15] The prototypes of such stereotypes as Huxley's Pearl Bellairs, James's Greville Fane, and Maugham's Evie Peregrine were not only, after all, such stellar figures as Harriet Beecher Stowe, Mary Elizabeth

Braddon, and Elizabeth Barrett Browning; they were part of what Hawthorne called "a damned mob of scribbling women," a "mob" that had begun to invade the literary marketplace with alarming success and striking visibility as early as 1855, when—three years after the publication of *The Blithedale Romance*—Hawthorne made his defensive remark.[16]

For several reasons the first impact of this invasion was felt in America by men like Hawthorne. Cut off not only from the long history of the English fatherland but also from the literary patrilineage that, drawing on a tradition from Chaucer and Shakespeare to Milton and the Romantics, endowed the man of letters with the powers of a priest or prophet, American artists felt simultaneously rebellious toward British tradition and emasculated by their alienation from the authority of that tradition. Thus they reacted to the achievements of women more quickly than their British contemporaries did, and reacted by beginning to create a myth of America as a country of aggressive women. Expressing such a male sense of literary assault and invasion, one anonymous commentator complained in 1856 that "France, England, Germany, Sweden, but most of all our own country, has furnished forth an army of women in the walks of literature . . . quite to the shame of manhood."[17] His feelings were confirmed by the fact that out of 558 poems published in the 1870s by the prestigious *Atlantic Monthly*, 201 were by women.[18] By 1896, the poet Louise Guiney felt confident enough about the poetic achievements of her sex to write that "The women over here are regular Atalantas in the poetic race."[19]

As for what Nina Baym has called "Woman's Fiction" and what Henry Nash Smith has defined as the scribbling woman's "cosmic success story," it is arguable that by the midnineteenth century in America such a genre dominated the literary marketplace.[20] According to Larzer Ziff, for instance, Henry James believed that "women, with their free use of leisure, were the chief consumers of novels and therefore were increasingly becoming producers of them. The feminine attitude, now disengaging itself from that of men, was in point of fact coming to be all that the novel was."[21] Commenting on the same phenomenon, the critic Thomas Beer observes that "if you were a proper editor you did not trifle with the Titaness and for her sake you issued tales of women, by women, for women."[22]

Describing such an atmosphere, Edmund Clarence Stedman characterized this period in his *American Anthology* as "the woman's age," and as recently as 1981 Leslie Fiedler defined the nineteenth-century American "struggle of High Art and Low" as a mythic "battle of the sexes" in which the serious male author believed himself to be "condemned to neglect and poverty by a culture simultaneously commercialized and feminized."[23] By the 1920s, therefore, male observers of the American intellectual scene were anxiously noting that, as Van Wyck Brooks put it in 1922, "Samson had lost his virility. The American writer who 'goes wrong' is in a similar state," and that, as Harold Stearns remarked in the same year, "Hardly any intelligent foreigner has failed to observe and comment upon the extraordinary feminization of American social life, and . . . the intellectual anemia or torpor that seems to accompany it," because though "men and women in America [seem to] share their intellectual life. . . . The men have been feminized."[24]

Despite the special historical and social problems with which American men of letters were confronted, however, their response to this "woman's age" provided a crucial paradigm of what was to become comparable anxiety on the other side of the Atlantic. By the turn of the century, even the most supportive Englishmen often expressed reservations about women's writing which suggest that they were as nervous about female literary power as their American precursors. In essays praising Elizabeth Barrett Browning, Charlotte Brontë, and Emily Brontë, for example, Algernon Charles Swinburne took pains to distinguish the works of these few good women from the works of what he sardonically called "the female immortals of whom the happy present hour is so much more than seasonably prolific."[25] Gloatingly predicting the downfall of most female-authored literature, he said that Charlotte Brontë's novels would endure

> when darkness everlasting has long since fallen upon all human memory of their cheap scientific, their vulgar erotic, and their voluminous domestic schools; when even *Daniel Deronda* has gone the way of all waxwork, when even Miss Broughton no longer cometh up as a flower, and even Mrs. Oliphant is at length cut down like the grass. [3]

Similarly, Oscar Wilde, the son of a woman poet, the editor of *Women's World* and the author of an apparently celebratory essay on "English Poetesses," subtly defended himself against the threat posed by female literary productivity. Even while praising "the really remarkable awakening of woman's song that characterizes the latter half of our century in England," he undercut his affirmation of English poetesses by singling out figures like "Eliza Haywood, who is immortalized by the badness of her work, and has a niche in *The Dunciad*," "Mrs. Ratcliffe [sic], who introduced the romantic novel, and has consequently much to answer for," "poor L. E. L., whom Disraeli described in one of his letters as 'the personification of Brompton,'" and "pretty, charming, 'Perdita,' who flirted alternately with poetry and the Prince Regent and has left us a pathetic little poem on a snowdrop."[26] In fact, his principal thesis is that the only great English poetess is Elizabeth Barrett Browning, with all the others being characterized essentially as versions of Ella Marchmill.

In thus defining and deriding "scribbling women" in an 1888 issue of England's *Queen*, Wilde would seem to have been doing exactly what such satirists as Bret Harte and Mark Twain had done earlier in America. Hart's "Miss Mix by Ch - l - tte Br - nte" (1867) is a parody of *Jane Eyre* that the American humorist reinterprets as a muddled and melodramatic farce in which the smugly virtuous heroine leaves her childhood home at "Minerva Cottage" forever to enter the service (and the arms) of "Mr. Rawjester," the polygamous master of "Blunderbore Hall," who bears a "remarkable likeness to a gorilla."[27] As for Twain, one of the most comical characters in his *Huckleberry Finn* (1885) is the lugubrious lyricist Emmeline Grangerford, whose "Ode to Stephen Dowling Bots, Dec'd" is merely one of the inadvertently humorous mortuary verses that she grinds out with fatal fluency: "she could rattle off poetry like nothing," explains Huck. "She didn't ever have to stop to think."[28] Like Wilde's Eliza Haywood and Harte's "Ch - l - tte Br - nte," Emmeline is "immortalized by the badness of her work" and, as we quickly discover, she was killed by her own eager vulgarity just as surely as she is buried by Twain's hilarious recounting of it, for "she pined away and did not live long" after the traumatic occasion when she "hung fire on a rhyme for [a] dead person's name, which was Whistler."

Of course, what Harte and Twain offer are light-hearted caricatures, and yet the motivating force behind their comedy—as behind the comedy of Huxley and Beerbohm—is comparable to the sexual hostility recorded by Hawthorne and James. Perhaps, too, such sexual hostility is what drew D. H. Lawrence to write about what might seem to have been an unlikely subject for him—namely, the masters of the "American Renaissance." His *Studies in Classic American Literature* (1923) was, interestingly enough, one of the first major critical assessments of these artists, and he was clearly attracted to them by a sense of the parallels between their situation and the general battle in which he himself was engaged. From the first, for example, Lawrence traces the roots of American identity to a disruption of patriarchal authority: "Mastery, kingship, fatherhood had their power destroyed at the time of the Renaissance. And it was precisely at this moment that the great drift over the Atlantic started."[29] Thus, he claims that "the American eagle" is "a hen-eagle" (11), and he reads the works of such classic American authors as Crevecoeur, Cooper, Poe, and Hawthorne as accounts of embattled masculinity.

Moreover, in his essays on *The Scarlet Letter*, Lawrence brings to the surface the connections between midnineteenth-century American literature, as he views it, and the late nineteenth-century British literary tradition that had shaped his own art. Flamboyantly comparing Hawthorne and Hardy, he notes that Hester Prynne had

> dished [Dimmesdale] and his spirituality, so he hated her. As Angel Clare was dished, and hated Tess. As Jude in the end hated Sue: or should have done. The women make fools of them, the spiritual men. And when, as men, they've gone flop in their spirituality, they can't pick themselves up whole any more. So they just crawl, and die detesting the female, or the females, who made them fall. [97]

Finally, that the woman Lawrence defines as perniciously seductive is destined to metamorphose into a figure who is fatally intellectual is made clear both in this essay and in Lawrence's piece on *The Blithedale Romance*, where he associates Hester with "the woman out of bounds [who] is a devil" (100) and later describes Zenobia as a "Black Pearl [who] is rotting down," adding that "The cleverer she is, the faster she rots" (117).[30]

In arguing that "European decadence was anticipated in America; and American influence passed over to Europe, was assimilated there, and then returned to this land of innocence as something purplish in its modernity and a little wicked" (43), Lawrence was, among other things, showing that literary men on both sides of the Atlantic felt the need to protect themselves against clever "Pearls"— Pearl in *The Scarlet Letter* (1850); Zenobia, the "Black Pearl" of *The Blithedale Romance;* and Pearl Bellairs—whose vulgar spirituality rots the foundations of male art. For like male novelists from James to Joyce, he was dismayed by what Robert Martin Adams calls the world's "ready acceptance of frank unashamed trash" and specifically by the way in which "lowbrows avidly devoured rhetorical romances by such as Elinor Glyn, Marie Corelli, Mrs. Henry Wood, Miss Rhoda Broughton, Mary Elizabeth Braddon, Maria Susanna Cummins and other weird sisters."[31]

Perhaps the best example of the highbrow male modernists' disgust with the lowbrow scribbler is Joyce's parody of Maria Cummins's *The Lamplighter* (1854) in the "Nausicaa" chapter of *Ulysses* (1922). Unlike the relatively brief and often adulatory stylistic tributes to his literary patrilineage that Joyce incorporated into the "Oxen of the Sun" chapter, this parody indicts the banality and bathos inculcated in young girls by the pulpy fiction of literary women. Writing in a "namby pamby marmalady drawersy style," Joyce satirizes Gerty MacDowell's girls' school language, which both revolts and titillates him, for even as he attacks this vulgarly genteel virgin's sentimentality, he gets to transcribe not only her voice but the vices of one of the foremost of Hawthorne's "damned mob of scribbling women."[32] More recently and far more drastically, as if to clarify the connection between the battle of the sexes and the battle of the books, Nathanael West shows in *Miss Lonelyhearts* how his newspaper reporters revenge themselves against their own nihilism by savoring stories about lady writers with three names: "Mary Roberts Wilcox, Ella Wheeler Catheter, Ford Mary Rinehart"—"what they all needed was a good rape." In particular, West records their special pleasure in an assault on a "hard-boiled" woman writer in a bar frequented by mugs: "They got her into the back room to teach her a new word and put the boots to her. They didn't let her out for three days. On the last day they sold tickets to niggers."[33]

Besides being driven—not just by general cultural disillusionment but also perhaps by specifically sexual anxiety—to dramatize such ferocious misogyny and racism, a number of modernist male writers may have been as disturbed by their economic dependence on women as they were troubled by women's usurpation of the marketplace. A striking characteristic of the twentieth-century avant garde, after all, was its determinedly anti-commercial cast. Perhaps there has been no circle of writers since the sixteenth century which was more dependent on private patronage, and, like such sixteenth-century figures as Sidney and Spenser, many prominent modernists were subsidized by a series of wealthy women or publicized by a set of powerful women. Among others, Yeats was financially dependent on Lady Gregory; Lawrence was sponsored by Lady Ottoline Morrell and Mable Dodge Luhan; Joyce was generously helped not only by Lady Gregory but also by Harriet Weaver and Sylvia Beach; Eliot was aided by May Sinclair, Virginia Woolf, and Lady Rothermere. In addition, all these men were in some sense at the mercy of entrepreneurial female editors like Harriet Monroe, Jane Heap, Margaret Anderson, Dora Marsden, and Marianne Moore. Finally, the careers of these writers were significantly furthered by female mentors like Amy Lowell, Gertrude Stein, Natalie Barney, Peggy Guggenheim, and Bryher, as were the careers of Hemingway, Dos Passos, and Sherwood Anderson.

But obviously the most important aspect of women's entrance into literary history was the fact that some female authors were neither scribblers nor mentors; some were great artists or influential intellectuals. Although many literary men were daunted by this phenomenon, a number of men of letters did, of course, respond by writing admiring memoirs and critical tributes to women precursors and contemporaries. Hawthorne may have covertly attacked Margaret Fuller in *The Blithedale Romance*, but Thomas Wentworth Higginson composed a book-length eulogy for her.[34] Although both Swinburne and Wilde were contemptuous of a number of literary women, both admired Elizabeth Barrett Browning, and Swinburne wrote glowing tributes to Charlotte and Emily Brontë. Similarly, though Henry James was ambivalent toward the mysterious mastery of George Eliot, confiding that she "has a larger circumference than any woman I have ever seen," Leslie Stephen wrote a volume about her for, ironically enough, the English Men of Letters Series.[35] Again, Mark Twain ridiculed what he saw as the narrowness of Jane Austen's art, but in a short story entitled "The Janeites" Rudyard Kipling commemorated her achievement by telling the tale of a World War I regiment that develops an elaborate but effective life-saving code based on characters in her novels.[36] As for the modernists, even some of the more openly misogynistic men of letters, along with those who might be considered quasi feminists, occasionally had kind words for female precursors and contemporaries. Just as Henry James supported and complimented Edith Wharton, Ezra Pound praised Mina Loy and Marianne Moore; William Carlos Williams wrote admiringly of Emily Dickinson, Gertrude Stein, Marianne Moore, and Marcia Nardi; Sherwood Anderson paid tribute to Gertrude Stein; T. S. Eliot celebrated Christina Rossetti, Marianne Moore, and Djuna Barnes; Yeats praised Lady Gregory and Dorothy Wellesley; and Henry Miller wrote enthusiastically about Anaïs Nin.

But although the compliments formulated by these literary men were usually genuine, they were sometimes problematic. As Bonnie Costello has argued, "Male praise [often] undermined women writers by isolating them in conventional gender categories that diminish[ed] their power"[37]: Anderson associates Stein with kitchens, for instance, and T. S. Eliot's "final, and 'magnificent' compliment" to Marianne Moore's poetry is that it "is as 'feminine' as Christina Rossetti's."[38] Still more problematically, William Carlos Williams—the grandson of *Emily Dickenson* Wellcome and a male poet-critic who at one point defined Emily Dickinson as "a beginning, a trembling at the edge of waking" for American verse—also insisted that "Emily Dickinson, starving of passion in her father's garden, is the very nearest [to a true woman poet] we have ever seen—starving. Never a woman: never a poet."[39] In addition, as Costello has also suggested, "Insofar as the 'female writer' became worthy of notice, the writing itself got neglected."[40] Gertrude Stein, for example, lamented all her long life that, though she was personally lionized, no one read her books. In fact, in certain cases, it seems likely that the more a man of letters expresses admiration for a female contemporary or precursor, the more his own feelings of admiration may worry him. In *The White Goddess* (1948) Robert Graves quotes a remark that illustrates this point: a scholar he knew once said of Sappho that she was very good but added "That's the trouble; she was very, *very* good."[41]

Yet if some male writers might have felt threatened by so ghostly a precursor as Sappho because she was "very, *very* good," they were even more disturbed by the competition of female contemporaries who might also be "very, *very* good." Certainly, as modernist encomia to women reveal, men and women in the twentieth century were more than ever before joined in literary enterprises. They were friends, peers, colleagues, coeditors—readers and revisers of each other's work. But at various times a kind of scribbling sibling rivalry may have been established between mutually admiring pairs like James and Wharton, Yeats and Lady Gregory, Hemingway and Stein, Lawrence and Mansfield (or H. D.), Wells and West (or Richardson), Eliot and Woolf, Graves and Riding, Miller and Nin, and in many of these instances each half of the pair recorded anxieties, or at least reservations, about the other. More generally, though, both men of letters and women of letters devised a variety of strategies for defusing anxiety about the literary combat in which they often felt engaged. Among male writers, such strategies included mythologizing women to align them with dread prototypes; fictionalizing them to dramatize their destructive influence; slandering them in essays, memoirs, and poems; prescribing alternative ambitions for them; appropriating their words in order to usurp or trivialize their language; and ignoring or evading their achievements in critical texts.

James, for instance, mythologizes Wharton as "the whirling one . . . the Angel of Destruction,"[42] while Yeats frequently associates women artists and thinkers with self-destructiveness or with the destruction of culture. Though he praised the poems of Dorothy Wellesley and the plays of Lady Augusta Gregory, in "On a Political Prisoner" he describes the mind of the militant Irish nationalist Con Markiewicz as "a bitter, an abstract thing, / Her thought some popular enmity" (181), while it is the dancer Loie Fuller's "dragon of air" that he remembers when he predicts the second coming of Herodias's daughters, and we are reminded that even Maud Gonne's beauty "like a tightened bow" is potentially ruinous when the poet asks "Was there another Troy for her to burn?"[43] As for fictionalized portraits, Lawrence's versions of the artist as a young woman frequently emphasize her sterility as they recount the "frictional white seething" of her aesthetic as well as her sexual desire. In *Women in Love*, as we have seen, he draws on the figure of Katherine Mansfield in creating his portrait of Gudrun, whose "nerve-brain" irony, together with the independence represented by her devotion to her art, suggests that her murderous rejection of Gerald is an expression of the implacable female will that manifests itself when women burst "into self assertion," while in *Kangaroo* (1923) he even more frankly transforms H. D. into one of those "poetesses" his hero "feared and wondered over."[44]

Similarly, in *The Roaring Queen* (written 1936, published 1973), Wyndham Lewis became more than usually vituperative about Virginia Woolf. Fictionalizing her in connection with a caricature of Arnold Bennett as Samuel Shodbutt, he scornfully alluded to her own aggressively sardonic "Mr. Bennett and Mrs. Brown" and misogynistically as well as anti-Semitically delineated her as "Rhoda Hyman," a "lanky and sickly lady in Victorian muslins" who, though she is "the patronizing queen of the highbrow world," is also the "most egregious of bogus Jane Austens."[45] To be sure, Lewis sets his cartoon Woolf in the context of an emasculated literary society ruled by shoddy Shodbutt, the commercial sellout; by warring male homosexuals; by eleven-year-old "girl" novelists; and by sexually voracious Oxonian viragoes (like his "Baby Brooktrout," an impassioned reader of *Lady Chatterley's Lover*). But his portrait of Woolf implies that she is the queen of a literary night whose miasmas have proliferated because there is now no "mature [male] authority" on the scene to safeguard the "new and delicate life" of masculinist inheritors.

If Lawrence and Lewis fictionalize Mansfield, H. D., and Woolf in anxious or angry ways, writers like William Carlos Williams and Hemingway often record distinctly unpleasant memories of such literary women in autobiographies, memoirs, and confessional poems. Williams, for instance, consistently portrays H. D.—a woman toward whom he had once admittedly had romantic feelings—as foolish and pretentious, describes a first meeting with Gertrude Stein in which the hostess of the rue du Fleurus literary salon told him that "writing is not, of course, your *métier*," and even admits about his beloved Marianne Moore that, at their first encounter, he "not a little feared her not only because of her keen wit but for her skill as a writer of poems."[46] More belligerently, Hemingway castigates his one-time mentor Gertrude Stein in a poem entitled "Portrait of a Lady" and throughout *A Moveable Feast.* In "Portrait of a Lady," composed at just the time when the two authors were severing their relationship, he parodies Stein's style in a confessedly "mean poem. A poem written by a man with a grudge. A poem written by a boy who is envious," to declare that "Gertrude Stein was never crazy / Gertrude Stein was very lazy."[47] Later, responding to her criticism of him in *The Autobiography of Alice B. Toklas,* he dramatizes his revulsion against her lesbianism when he describes his horror at overhearing an intimate dialogue between her and Alice. In the same book, moreover, he reacts specifically against her literary accomplishment, observing that this quarrelsome, ambitious "Roman emperor" wrote books that "a more conscientious and less lazy writer would have put in a wastebasket."[48]

More generally, in earlier works from the same period as "Portrait of a Lady," Hemingway had attacked other contemporary women of letters. "To a Tragic Poetess" faults Dorothy Parker for her self-indulgent suicide attempts ("Nothing in her life became her like her almost leaving of it") while lamenting the successful suicides of men who seem destroyed by female indifference.[49] Similarly, "The Lady Poets with Foot Notes" vilifies the voracious mouths and wombs of literary ladies:

One lady poet was a nymphomaniac and wrote for Vanity Fair.[1]
One lady poet's husband was killed in the war.[2]
One lady poet wanted her lover, but was afraid of having a
baby.
When she finally got married, she found she couldn't have a
baby.[3]
One lady poet slept with Bill Reedy got fatter and fatter and
made half a million dollars writing bum plays.[4]
One lady poet never had enough to eat.[5]
One lady poet was big and fat and no fool.[6]
[1]College nymphomania. Favorite lyric poet of leading editorial
writer, N.Y. Tribune.
[2]It sold her stuff.

³Favourite of State University male virgins. Wonderful on unrequited love.
⁴Stomach's gone bad from liquor. Expects to do something really good soon.
⁵It showed in her work.
⁶She smokes cigars all right, but her stuff was no good.[50]

To annotate Hemingway's footnotes, we might mention that behind the misogyny of this catalog lurk Edna St. Vincent Millay, Alice Kilmer, Sara Teasdale, Zoë Atkins, Lola Ridge, and Amy Lowell.

In poems and essays, Yeats, Lawrence, Eliot, and Graves clarify the imperatives that underlie such misogyny when they admonish female contemporaries and descendants to relinquish "self-assertion" and, as Yeats tells his daughter, "become a flourishing hidden tree" since for women in particular "An intellectual hatred is the worst / So let her think opinions are accursed" (*CP* 187). "The great flow of female consciousness is downward," insists Lawrence, so that "the moment woman has got man's ideals and tricks drilled into her, the moment she is competent in the manly world—there's an end of it."[51] Similarly, in a draft of *The Waste Land* (1922), in the course of portraying a loathsome woman writer, Eliot declares that "women grown intellectual grow dull / And lose the mother wit of natural trull," and in *The White Goddess* Graves claims "It is the imitation of male poetry that causes the false ring in the work of almost all women poets," declaring that "A woman who concerns herself with poetry" should either be "a silent Muse" or "should be the Muse in a complete sense . . . and should write with antique authority," an authority which, by its very antiquity, would preclude the threat of contemporary competition.[52]

Paradoxically enough, another way of precluding such a threat seems to have been the usurpation of women's words. Disguised as homage, the tradition of male literary appropriation goes back at least as far as William Wordsworth, who transformed some of his sister Dorothy's journal entries into major poems. But among the modernists such a move seems to have been far more popular than it was with the Romantics. Yeats, for example, metamorphosed his wife George's trance writings into the mystical geometry of *A Vision*, whose "ghostly instructors" claimed to have come to give him "metaphors for poetry," while Lawrence used memoirs written by his childhood sweetheart Jessie Chambers as the bases for long passages in *Sons and Lovers* and rewrote a novel by an obscure Australian nurse as *The Boy in the Bush*.[53] Similarly, F. Scott Fitzgerald famously drew on material provided by his wife, Zelda, and even T. S. Eliot incorporated a few lines contributed by his first wife, Vivien, into *The Waste Land*. More strikingly, William Carlos Williams, who once confessed to being "particularly fond of watercress," rechristened Marcia Nardi, whom Robert Lowell later called a "lacerated and lacerating poetess," as "Cress," the epistolary villainess of *Paterson* II (1948).[54]

Accusing Williams of "the complete damming of all my creative capacities in a particularly disastrous manner such as I have never before experienced," Nardi had sarcastically told Williams that all his "fine talk . . . about woman's need to 'sail free in her own element' as a poet, becomes nothing but empty rhetoric in the light of your behaviour towards me"[55] (107). Thus Williams noted that the long letter from Nardi with which he concluded this section of his magnum opus was a "tail [that] has tried to wag the dog," remarking elsewhere that "It is . . . an attack, a personal attack upon me, by a woman . . . a reply from the female side to many of my male pretensions . . . a strong reply which sought to destroy me." But he also observed that, "If I hid the reply it would be a confession of weakness on my part." And thus, too, his manly willingness to acknowledge Nardi's importance becomes an assertion of strength in which he defuses anxiety about Nardi as a paradigmatic woman of letters by transforming her into a character whom he can control, a creature of his own imagination. Paradoxically, he can only do this by letting her say her say but forcing her to do it on his own terms. Noting that to hide her words "would be a confession of weakness," this man of letters who was later to tell Nardi her poems were so good "that I feel ashamed for my sex" adopts instead the brilliant strategy of the hero of Poe's "The Purloined Letter," concealing the threat implied by the dangerous letters he has purloined by placing them so frankly in the open that no one would suspect their power.[56]

Yet another way of precluding such a threat, however, involves the construction of a literary history that denies the reality of women writers, a gesture that returns us to the act of *Blütbruderschaft* with

American male precursors that Lawrence performed in *Studies* and suggests that the existence of a female tradition may have had to be more generally countered with critical ceremonies of male self-certification. In this respect, the emergence of modern male literary discourse, exemplified by theoretical and canon-forming works like "Tradition and the Individual Talent," *The ABC of Reading* (1934), *Seven Types of Ambiguity* (1930), and *The Well-Wrought Urn* (1947), can be seen as an attempt to construct *his* story of a literary history in which women play no part. This discourse was based on assumptions which were articulated in a sexualized idiom during the early part of the century by, among others, the influential T. E. Hulme who complained in "A Lecture on Modern Poetry" (delivered 1914) that "Imitative poetry springs up like weeds, and women whimper and whine of you and I alas, and roses, roses all the way. It becomes the expression of sentimentality rather than of virile thought."[57]

Of course, as John Guillory has demonstrated, T. S. Eliot's elevation of "an alternative canon," based on "his preference for the Metaphysicals and Dryden over Spenser and Milton, for the Jacobean dramatists over Shakespeare, and his rejection of virtually all Romantic and Victorian poetry," must be seen as a consequence of this influential poet-critic's own sense of belatedness toward the male tradition fathered by Milton and continued in the nineteenth century.[58] At the same time, however, such a consecration of an "orthodox" tradition, and particularly such a yearning for a Golden Age before "the dissociation of sensibility set in" (64) as well as a desire to learn "how to see the world as the Christian Fathers saw it" (291), erases the history associated with the entrance of women into the literary marketplace. Moreover, the Eliotian theory (propounded in "Tradition and the Individual Talent") that poetry involves "an escape from emotion" and "an escape from personality" constructs an implicitly masculine aesthetic of hard, abstract, learned verse that is opposed to the aesthetic of soft, effusive, personal verse supposedly written by women and Romantics (10). Thus in Eliot's critical writing women are implicitly devalued and the Romantics are in some sense feminized as Buckley hinted they had been by Tennyson, but Tennyson himself becomes part of a contaminated and metaphorically emasculated century.

In different ways, e. e. cummings, Ezra Pound, Wallace Stevens, and William Carlos Williams made statements which elaborate the sexual assumptions that shaped Eliot's thinking. In a meditation on "the Cambridge ladies who live in furnished souls," cummings connects mediocre women with dead gods and dull Victorians, declaring that these women are "unbeautiful and have comfortable minds," and suggesting that the worst thing about them is that "they believe in Christ and Longfellow, both dead."[59] In a frequently cited discussion of creativity in verse, Pound claimed that "Poetry speaks phallic direction," and, as Hugh Kenner notes, reflected "on a career of driving ideas into 'the great passive vulva of London.' "[60] In "A High-Toned Old Christian Woman," a poem that is less sexually graphic but has equally masculinist overtones, Wallace Stevens observes with patronizing aplomb that "Poetry is the supreme fiction, madame," adding that "fictive things / Wink as they will. Wink most when widows wince."[61] More explicitly, Williams produced in *Imaginations* (1970) a strikingly sexualized definition of the distinction between "good" and "bad" poetry: "What is good poetry made of," he asks, and answers "Of rats and snails and puppy-dog's tails," and then he adds "What is bad poetry made of," and he answers "Of sugar and spice and everything nice, / That is what bad poetry is made of."[62]

Though such American New Critics as John Crowe Ransom and R. P. Blackmur may not have so overtly sexualized "good" and "bad" poetry, their attempts at evaluation and canonization seem to have been motivated by a nostalgia as strong as Eliot's for the lost powers of "the Christian Fathers," and implicitly for the male strength associated with bygone male sexual hierarchies, a nostalgia which no doubt caused Ransom to refer to Emily Dickinson as "a little homekeeping person" and Blackmur to say, just as patronizingly, that she "wrote indefatigably, as some women cook or knit. Her gift for words and the cultural predicament of her time drove her to poetry instead of antimacassars."[63] To poet-critics from Lawrence, Eliot, Pound, and Williams to Ransom and Blackmur, a literary landscape populated by women, whether they were scribblers, mentors, or great artists, may have seemed like a no man's land, a wasted and wasting country that left them with what Beerbohm called "an acute sense of disgrace."

Indeed, the acute sense of disgrace we associate with such a waste land may arise from the fact that, as much as the industrial revolution and the fall of God, the rise of the female imagination was a central problem for the twentieth-century male imagination. Thus when we focus not only on women's increasingly successful struggle for autonomy in the years from, say, 1880 to 1920, but also on their increasingly successful production of literary texts throughout the nineteenth and twentieth centuries, we find ourselves confronting an entirely different modernism. And it is a modernism constructed not just against the grain of Victorian male precursors, not just in the shadow of a shattered God, but as an integral part of a complex response to *female* precursors and contemporaries. Indeed, it is possible to hypothesize that a reaction-formation against the rise of literary women became not just a theme in modernist writing but a motive for modernism. Even the establishment of a supposedly anti-establishment avant garde can be seen as part of this phenomenon, for the twin strategies of excavation and innovation deployed in experimental works like *The Cantos* (1917–69), *The Waste Land*, and *Ulysses* reconstitute the hierarchies implicit in what T. S. Eliot called in "Tradition and the Individual Talent" "the mind of Europe" (6). As we shall argue in chapter five, the excavation of that mind's fragments functions simultaneously to counter and to recover the noble fatherhood of precursors from Homer to Dante and Shakespeare, while the linguistic innovation associated with the avant garde—the use of puns, allusions, phrases in foreign languages, arcane and fractured forms—functions to occult language so that only an initiated elite can participate in the community of high culture. A few women like Gertrude Stein and Djuna Barnes did intermittently join such a community, but by and large it remained (and may have been unconsciously designed as) a men's club. It is not surprising, therefore, that on his first reading of *The Waste Land* Joyce noted that T. S. Eliot's masterpiece "ends [the] idea of poetry for ladies," which was, after all, no more than what Hulme had called "roses, roses all the way."[64]

The need somehow to "end . . . poetry for ladies" did not end with modernists, for more recently some literary men seem to have felt as strongly as Harold Stearns did in 1922 that they were living in an age of "extraordinary feminization." Describing the Statue of Liberty, Robert Lowell characterizes the spirit of his society as militant and female: noting "the thrilling, chilling silver of your laugh, / the hysterical digging of your accursed spur," he apostrophizes her as an "Amazon, gazing on me, pop-eyed, cool, / ageless, not holding back your war-whoop."[65] Indeed, from James Thurber to Norman Mailer, William Gass, Anthony Burgess, Leroi Jones, and Edward Albee, from Theodore Roethke to John Berryman and Lowell himself, many postmodernist men of letters continued to define their artistic integrity in opposition to either the literary incompetence or the aesthetic hysteria they associated with women.

In "Here Lies Miss Groby" (1942), for instance, Thurber protested against what Ann Douglas has called "the feminization of American culture" by satirizing the high school English teacher who has traditionally been a literary culture bearer. His Miss Groby is presented as a classic battle axe of a schoolmarm who "crucifie[d] sentences" by parsing them on the blackboard, who never "saw any famous work of literature from far enough away to know what it meant," who was so preoccupied with counting that she "would have got an enormous thrill out of Wordsworth's famous lines about Lucy if they had been written" so that Lucy was "Fair as a star when ninety-eight / Are shining in the sky," and who causes the young Thurber to become so obsessed with finding an example of the "Thing Contained for the Container" that he imagines a woman saying to her husband " 'Get away from me or I'll hit you with the milk.' "[66] An antisentimental, bluestocking heiress of the tradition exemplified by Twain's sentimental Emmeline Grangerford, Miss Groby leaves her ex-pupil "tossing and moaning" (39) over her destruction of literary values and her deconstruction of good writing. And thus, though she is not herself a writer, this Miss Groby resembles the stereotypical Mrs. Grundy, whose moralistic strictures contaminate social as well as literary structures.

Where Thurber is genial and comic about his high school English teacher, many of his descendants are far more scornful about the virtually sexual incapacity of women writers. As usual, Norman Mailer—whose *The Prisoner of Sex* was written to counter Kate Millett's attack on him in *Sexual Politics*—is among the most belligerent of these postmodernists. In *Advertisements for Myself* (1959), he makes what he calls a "terrible confession":

> I have nothing to say about any of the talented women who write today . . . I can only say that the sniffs I get from the ink of women are always fey, old-hat . . . too dykily psychotic, crippled creepish, fashionable, frigid . . . or else bright and stillborn. Since I've never been able to read Virginia Woolf, and am sometimes willing to believe it can conceivably be my fault, this verdict may be taken as the twisted tongue of a soured taste, at least by those readers who do not share with me the ground of departure—that a good novelist can do without everything but the remnant of his balls.[67]

Gass and Burgess have also made comparable remarks, with Gass declaring that women writers "lack that blood-congested genital drive which energizes every great style," and Burgess complaining that Jane Austen's work "lacks a strong male thrust."[68] At the same time, despite such efforts to represent women writers as metaphorically castrated, it seems significant that Baraka's Lena the Hyena, the villainess of *Dutchman*, is a woman *poet* and that the reiterated refrain of Albee's Martha is "Who's Afraid of Virginia Woolf?"

To be sure, Roethke, Berryman, and Lowell would seem to be considerably less virulent than, say, Mailer. Yet even when these literary men celebrate female contemporaries and precursors, they tend to single out a token woman for attention, or to qualify in one text the compliment expressed in another. Roethke, for example, writes with admiration about Louise Bogan, Berryman with reverence for Anne Bradstreet, and Lowell with adulation about Elizabeth Bishop. But each has also made critical gestures that suggest some measure of hostility toward literary women. Reviewing Louise Bogan, Roethke prefaces his praise for her with an attack on women poets:

> Two of the charges most frequently levelled against poetry by women are lack of range—in subject matter, in emotional tone—and lack of sense of humor. And one could, in individual instances among writers of real talent, add other aesthetic and

moral shortcomings: the spinning-out; the embroidering of trivial themes; a concern for the mere surfaces of life—that special province of the feminine talent in prose—hiding from the real agonies of the spirit; refusing to face up to what existence is; lyric or religious posturing; running between the boudoir and the altar, stamping a tiny foot against God; or lapsing into sententiousness that implies the author has reinvented integrity; carrying on excessively about Fate, about time; lamenting the lot of the woman; caterwauling; writing the same poem about fifty times, and so on.[69]

Similarly, despite his *Homage to Mistress Anne Bradstreet* (1956), John Berryman explains in *The Dream Songs* (1969) that

> Them lady poets must not marry, pal.
> Miss Dickinson—fancy in Amherst bedding her.
> Fancy a lark with Sappho,
> a tumble in the bushes with Miss Moore,
> a spoon with Emily, while Charlotte glare.
> Miss Bishop's too noble-O.

and adds in the next stanza that "Sylvia Plath is not. / She—she her credentials / has handed in, leaving alone two tots / and widower to what he makes of it— / surviving guy."[70] Finally, though Lowell pays tribute to Jean Stafford and Elizabeth Bishop and though he wrote a preface to the American edition of *Ariel*, he makes a similar but nastier statement about the dead Plath, noting in "Sylvia Plath" that because female English majors now say "*I* am Sylvia, / I hate marriage, I must hate babies . . . sixty thousand American infants a year, / U. I. D., Unexplained Infant Deaths, / born physically whole and hearty, refuse to live." These dead babies, asserts Lowell, are the consequence of the pernicious influence wielded by Plath's *"Miniature mad talent"*: "Sylvia the expanding torrent of your attack."[71]

Earlier, in the dazzling prose memoir "91 Revere Street" that he embedded in *Life Studies* (1959), Lowell had sardonically remembered his family's dislike of their literary ancestress Amy Lowell and obviously relished repeating one of "Commander Billy's" "tiresome, tasteless harangues" against the authoress of "Patterns": "Remember Amy Lowell, that cigar-chawing, guffawing, senseless and meterless,

multimillionheiress, heavyweight mascot on a floating fortress. Damn
the *Patterns!* Full speed ahead on a cigareeto!" (38). In a manner
closer to his critique of Plath, moreover, Lowell addressed a poem
to Adrienne Rich in which, though he conceded that "Your ground-
note is joy," he asked, "disabled veteran, how long will you bay with
the hounds / and beat time with crutches?" (154).[72]

In addition, and more notoriously, after he had left Elizabeth
Hardwick, Lowell versified a number of painful passages from her
letters in an act of usurpation comparable to Williams's quotation
of Marcia Nardi's letters in *Paterson* or, for that matter, to Berryman's
impersonation of Anne Bradstreet. Of course, like Williams and
Berryman, Lowell might be said to have been offering an expiatory
homage to Hardwick in these poems, for just as Nardi's letters portray Williams as culpable and Berryman's poem depicts Bradstreet
as admirable, Hardwick's words reveal both Lowell's guilt and her
strength. Yet, like Williams, Lowell also humiliates the woman whose
pained sentences he exhibits to public view and, like Berryman—
who stresses Bradstreet's suffering sense that "a male great pestle
smashes / small women swarming toward the mortar's rim in vain"—
he manages to speak patronizingly about Hardwick even while he
speaks through and as her.[73] Clearly, for writers in the 1950s, 1960s,
and 1970s, the literary "woman question" was still so urgent that
many of the strongest male artists continued to find their own voices
by entering into an explicit or implicit dialogue with women. Recently, for instance, the British novelist D. M. Thomas became notorious for his controversial appropriation, in *The White Hotel*, of
Dina Pronicheva's account of her experience at Babi Yar.[74] But perhaps more to the point in terms of the battle of the sexes is another
of Lowell's poems: that the "almost impotent almost faithful" speaker
of Lowell's "Loser" has a wife who sits all night "reading Simone de
Beauvoir till day" suggests this male poet's own consciousness of the
implications of the revitalized women's liberation movement.[75]

Throughout the century, then, men of letters persistently expressed feelings of loss and anger, feelings that the mother-muse
had abandoned them. Indeed, as the Oedipal paradigm through
which Harold Bloom has analyzed literary history dissolved into a
far more complicated complex, they ever more deeply understood
the ramifications of what women also, though very differently, ex-

perienced: the incontrovertible fact that the once willing muse had now become self-willing and, they feared, self-willed. Experiencing themselves as belated, stranded, and "suffocating" on the territory that a play by Harold Pinter called *No Man's Land* (1975), they insisted, with Pinter's bleakly drifting anti-hero Spooner, that "I'm a friend of the arts, particularly the art of poetry, and a guide to the young. I keep open house. Young poets come to me. They read me their verses . . . Women are admitted; some of whom are also poets. Some are not." But then they admit their fear that "Some of the men are not. Most of the men are not."[76] Thus, the muse had to be reconstructed either as a passive woman or, more radically, as an empowering and empowered man. In Dylan Thomas's surrealistic "Ballad of the Long-legged Bait," for instance, she is "A girl alive with . . . hooks through her lips" whom a fisherman, in an allegory of creativity, throws to the "swift flood."[77] And in Ezra Pound's "Sage Homme," a comic comment on *The Waste Land*, Milton's maternal muse becomes a transsexual Sire, suggesting that the modernist poet may be in a double bind. Because he no longer has a suitable female muse, he might construct a male surrogate for her. But, as "Sage Homme" hints, such a figure seems at best comic and at worst perverse, indeed potentially capable of inducing a kind of homophobic panic:

> These are the poems of Eliot
> By the Uranian Muse begot;
> A Man their Mother was,
> A Muse their Sire.
>
> How did the printed Infancies result
> From Nuptuals thus doubly difficult?
>
> If you must needs enquire
> Know diligent Reader
> That on each Occasion
> Ezra performed the Caesarean Operation.[78]

Pound's redefinition of the engendering of male creativity certainly helps explain why and how *The Waste Land* ended the "idea of poetry for ladies," but, more, it functions as an acknowledgment that, for both sexes, the shock of the new—and specifically the new

world of women's words—required shocking sociocultural redefinitions. T. S. Eliot himself may not have understood the radical
implications of the relationship between tradition and the individual
talent that he described in 1919 in *The Egoist* (a journal, incidentally,
which began its career as a suffrage periodical called *The Freewoman*
and then *The New Freewoman*). But Eliot's theory that new works of
art alter not only our sense of the past but also our sense of what
art might *be* actually seems to reflect the sexual crisis that underlies
modernism. For inevitably, the "ideal order" of patriarchal literary
history was radically "modified by the introduction of the new (the
really new) work of art"—and, as Woolf remarked, that "really new
work" was women's work.

4

"Forward into the Past": The Female Affiliation Complex

... the road was cut many years ago—by Fanny Burney, by Aphra Behn, by Harriet Martineau, by Jane Austen, by George Eliot—many famous women, and many more unknown and forgotten, have been before me, making the path smooth, and regulating my steps.
—Virginia Woolf

... You leave me sad and self-distrustful,
For older sisters are very sobering things ...
No, you have not seemed strange to me, but near,
Frightfully near, and rather terrifying.
—Amy Lowell

The purpose of the writer is to say what he feels and sees. To those who write fantasies—the Misses Baldwin, Ferber, Norris—I am not at home ... Norris said she never wrote a story unless it was fun to do. I understand Ferber whistles at her typewriter. And there was that poor sucker Flaubert rolling around on his floor for three days looking for the right word. I'm a feminist, and God knows I'm loyal to my sex. ... But when we paraded through the catcalls of men and when we chained ourselves to lamp posts to try to get our equality—dear child, we didn't foresee *those* female writers. Or Clare Boothe Luce, or Perle Mesta, or Oveta Culp Hobby.
—Dorothy Parker

Four years after Max Beerbohm wrote "The Crime," the actress-novelist Elizabeth Robins confronted her sense that his story was a crime against her and other literary women. Although, Robins admitted in a chapter of a feminist treatise entitled *Ancilla's Share*

165

(1924), "One does not think of Mr. Beerbohm as wearing his heart on his sleeve," "The Crime" was to her mind a "breach [of] his nice reserve," a breach "effected by [an] irresistible antagonism toward the non-helplessness of women."[1] When Robins contemplated the question of what was bothering the incomparable Max, she decided that "He would allow woman a homeopathic practice in letters" but, like "The Crime" 's narrator, he would like to experience the "exquisite satisfaction" of dismembering and burning a "lady's literary remains." To be sure, Robins noted, "in his own engaging way [Beerbohm] laughs at himself" but at the same time, tellingly, "he uncovers one aspect of his sex antagonism" (94–95), an antagonism that, in her view, he shared with many of his contemporaries.

Robins's attitude toward Beerbohm's tale was representative of the feelings that many women of letters had toward the hostility with which a number of men greeted their entrance into the literary marketplace. Yet Robins's defensiveness, no less than Beerbohm's, has been largely ignored in standard histories of modernism, and perhaps one reason why both have usually been overlooked has to do with canon formation. Until quite recently, the works of women writers from Olive Schreiner and Kate Chopin to, even, Edith Wharton and Virginia Woolf, have been dismissed or devalued while critical texts like *Ancilla's Share* have been virtually unavailable. Consequently, the dialogue that late nineteenth- and early twentieth-century male writers carried on with female contemporaries went unheard. Even, however, when we do begin to hear the male half of this ongoing literary conversation—as we just have—we may be in danger of misinterpreting the women writers' experience, for the women's part of the dialogue was no more symmetrically equivalent to the men's than was the female response to the battle of the sexes. In fact, what many men defined as "the crime" of female literary ambition had unusually complex origins and consequences for women of letters.

To begin with, women experience the dynamics of maternal literary inheritance differently from the way men do. In the nineteenth century, Elizabeth Barrett Browning had lamented that "England has had many learned women . . . and yet where were the poetesses?", adding that "I look everywhere for grandmothers and see none."[2] But by the twentieth century that situation had obviously changed. Looking everywhere for what Barrett Browning had called "grandmothers"—that is, for representatives of a literary matrilineage—and, for the first time, finding them, women of Robins's generation had entered upon a new relationship with the past, a relationship whose ambivalence is perhaps most succinctly expressed in a poem that the American writer May Sarton addressed to Virginia Woolf four years after her English precursor's death. Remembering in "Letter from Chicago" (1953) what Woolf's demise had meant to her ("Here where you never were, they said, / 'Virginia Woolf is dead.' // The city died. I died in the city . . ."), Sarton goes on to describe the transfiguration of a once alien Chicago by a mysterious moment of recollection and resurrection: "yesterday I found you. / Wherever I looked was love. / Wherever I went I had presents in my hands. / Wherever I went I recognized you."[3] Finally, declaring that "I speak to you and meet my own life," she concludes, "I send you love forward into the past."

Sarton's gesture of amorous salutation is an exemplary one for many modernist women of letters. Also typical, however, are the feelings of abandonment, anger, and alienation expressed by Sarton's confession in the middle of the poem that she was "Witness of unreal tears, my own" and that "I met your death and did not recognize you." Turn-of-the-century and twentieth-century women writers, finding themselves for the first time in possession of a uniquely female literary history, have frequently sought to ensure the viability of their own literary future by paradoxically sending love "forward" into the past, "forward" into the arms of powerful aesthetic foremothers. At the same time, though, such writers have at last begun to experience an anxiety about the binds and burdens of the past that can be understood in terms comparable to (if different from) those Harold Bloom extrapolates from Freud's writings about psychosexual development.[4]

Freud's model of the family romance—particularly as it is outlined in "Female Sexuality" (1931)—becomes a suitable paradigm for the analysis of literary history at just the point when the woman writer confronts both a matrilineal and a patrilineal inheritance, that is, in the twentieth century. According to Freud, the growing girl "may follow one of three lines of development" when, as she enters the Oedipal phase, she definitively confronts the fact of her femininity.[5]

"The first leads to her turning her back on sexuality altogether," because

> frightened by the comparison of herself with boys, [she] . . . gives up her phallic activity . . . and a considerable part of her masculine proclivities in other fields. If she pursues the second line, she clings in obstinate self-assertion to her threatened masculinity . . . whilst the phantasy of really being a man in spite of everything, often dominates long periods of her life. This 'masculinity complex' may also result in a manifestly homosexual object-choice. Only if her development follows the third . . . path does she arrive at the ultimate normal feminine attitude in which she takes her father as love-object, and thus arrives at the Oedipus complex in its feminine form. [FS 198–199]

If we translate this model of female psychosexual development into a map of literary paths, we can see that, whether the female artist turns in what Freud would judge a normative renunciation of her desire for a literary mother to the tradition of the father, whether in what Freud might see as a frigid rejection of both allegiances she attempts to extricate herself altogether from her own aesthetic ambitions, or whether in a move that Freud might define as "defiant" and "homosexual" she claims the maternal tradition as her own, she has at last to struggle with what we would provisionally define as a complicated *female affiliation complex.*

As we argued in *The Madwoman in the Attic,* such a psychoanalytic paradigm could not provide a significant model for nineteenth-century women's literary accomplishments. In our own era, however, the entrance of women into dialogue with male and female precursors has offered female artists a bewildering multiplicity of stances toward the past. Thus the kind of monolithic pattern we traced in earlier women's literary history has been displaced by a variety of patterns. Indeed, because in the twentieth century women have learned to experience themselves as participants in public discourse, such patterns have also been radically qualified—as they were not always in the nineteenth century—by the impact of large cultural events. Even without taking these historical pressures into account, though, the dynamics of female literary inheritance would now be

strikingly various, given the new relevance of the Freudian model
we are advancing. Certainly, as Freud describes it, the girl's path
toward maturity is far more difficult than the boy's because it is
marked by imperatives of object renunciation and libidinal redi-
rection that require enormous investments of psychic energy.

When we apply the model that we have been calling the affiliation
complex to women's literary history, therefore, we inevitably find
women writers oscillating between their matrilineage and their patrilineage in an arduous process of self-definition that, for purposes
of clarity, we will analyze into several phases. But we should quickly
note here that the attitudes toward the precursor which we will sim-
plify into distinct phases often appear simultaneously in the texts
of many major twentieth-century women writers: allegiance to literary fathers does not inevitably sweep away the longing for literary
mothers; anxiety about literary mothers does not always lead to desire for literary fathers. Indeed, for all its flaws, Freud's model is
useful precisely because it implies such a range of reactions to (literary) parentage.

Even as we use Freud, however, we will, like many other feminist
theorists, swerve from Freud, specifically from his interpretation
and valuation of each of the different options available to the growing girl. Perhaps most notably, we see what he considers in "Female
Sexuality" the most mature step possible in female psychosexual development as, at least for the modern literary woman, just as problematic as any other solution to the riddle of femininity, and our
vision of this situation—at least in literary terms—accounts for our
use of the phrase "affiliation complex." For Freud, clearly, the appropriate female developmental strategy entails a repression of the
"pre-Oedipal" desire for the mother and an elaboration of the wish
for the phallus (which possesses the mother) into a desire for the
father, the man who possesses the phallus (and hence the mother).
In the nineteenth-century female tradition, such a strategy was the
principal option available to the daughter-writer; that is, inheriting
a male-dominated literary tradition, she was generally forced to write
out of a desirous (even if agonistic) interaction with that tradition.
For women from Maria Edgeworth to Charlotte Brontë, George
Eliot, and Emily Dickinson, such a revisionary erotic transference
produced great art; wrestling with the master-muse, even as they

sought an invasion of his influence, these writers worked out—and out of—a powerful father-daughter paradigm.

In the twentieth century, however, Freudian concepts like the girl's "secondary Oedipus complex," as well as Freud-derived Bloomian paradigms like the "anxiety of influence" and our own "anxiety of authorship" must give way to a paradigm of ambivalent affiliation, a construct which dramatizes women's intertwined attitudes of anxiety and exuberance about creativity. Etymologically, after all, the word "affiliation" derives from the gender-symmetrical Latin *filia* and *filius*, words which, if not legally at least linguistically, represent an equality of inheritance. To be sure, both the *American Heritage Dictionary* and the *OED* explicitly emphasize sonship and fatherhood, defining "affiliation" as "the act of taking a son, the establishment of sonship" *(OED)* and "in law: to determine the paternity of an illegitimate child" *(American Heritage)*. More generally, however, both dictionaries agree that to affiliate means to "associate oneself as a subordinate or subsidiary with" and, most interestingly, the *American Heritage Dictionary* traces the word back to the Indo-European "dhei," meaning "to suck," a word etymologically connected with "she who suckles." Thus, though lexical evolution may have erased (by reversing) the female origins of this word—emphasizing sonship rather than daughterhood, paternity rather than maternity—the word itself preserves matrilineal traces and specifically the idea of a nurturing and nurtured female. Indeed, the contrast between the secondary but now dominant maleness attributed to the word and its female linguistic roots reiterates Freud's own paradigm of the psychohistorically constructed female Oedipus complex, which obscures the girl's pre-Oedipal phase in just the way the relics of Greek civilization eclipse the remains of Minoan-Mycenaean culture (FS 195).

In its definitional history, therefore, the term "affiliation" itself emblematizes just the problem with which many twentieth-century women writers were obsessed: not only do a number of female artists analyze the relationship between male history and newly imagined female origins, they also perceive themselves as obliged to affiliate themselves with the powers of paternal and/or maternal traditions. In addition, when they confront their newly established maternal tradition, they now sometimes feel as ambivalent toward it as they had toward their paternal tradition, though for different reasons. Thus, where Freud in "Family Romances" (1909) associates fantasies of adoption with hostility to, or disappointment in, biological parents, a different concept of adoption is ambiguously present in our definition of affiliation.[6] The idea of affiliation, as we propose to use it, suggests an evasion of the inexorable lineage of the biological family even while it also implies a power of decision in two historical directions. One may imagine oneself as having been adopted, and thus legitimized, as a literary heiress, but one may also adopt, and thus sanction, others to carry on the tradition one has established. Unlike "influence," then, which connotes an influx or pouring-in of external power, and "authorship," which stands for an originatory primacy, the concept of affiliation carries with it possibilities of both choice and continuity. Choice: one may consciously or not decide with whom to affiliate—align or join—oneself. Continuity: one is thereby linked into a constructed genealogical order which has its own quasi-familial inevitability.

———————

If we examine the first and most traditional stance that this complex offers the woman writer (the turn toward the male precursor which parallels Freud's concept of the girl's positive Oedipal development), we can see at once that the multiplicity of affiliative choices available to late nineteenth- and early twentieth-century women complicates such a resolution. In addition, however, the weakening of patriarchal authority that Bloom describes and which we have already traced inevitably contributed to a dilution of this dominant nineteenth-century script. To be more specific, the turn-of-the-century woman writer was not only haunted by the charisma of her literary fathers, she was for the first time troubled by the simultaneous fragility of their power and ferocity of their anger. Thus, the move that Freud defined as the most "mature" move toward desire for the father sometimes becomes in our own era a vexed, nostalgic, and guilt-ridden service to sustain his name and fame, sometimes becomes an unpremeditated usurpation of his primacy, and sometimes becomes a fearful and guilty propitiation of his outraged authority. In every case, in other words, the traditional father-daughter paradigm is so haunted by history, whether by the

history of male belatedness or by the new record of female achievement, that it cannot by itself provide an entirely satisfactory motive
for female creativity.

Emily Dickinson's "I rose—because He sank—" (J. 616), which
we used earlier to show that women of letters often attributed female
victory in the battle of the sexes to chance or luck, also predicts the
literary-historical dilemma that was to be confronted by a number
of the poet's descendants. At first Dickinson's speaker appears to
be expressing exactly the female exultation that men from Hardy
to Huxley dread: "But when his power dropped— / My Soul grew
straight." But as she recounts the decline of her "fainting Prince,"
Dickinson's speaker becomes oddly nervous, even guilty, and in what
seems like a desperate attempt to revive male power she struggles
to reconstruct her lover's history, telling him of "worlds I knew— /
Where Emperors grew—." Finally, the fallen man becomes a burden
that she claims she has to strain to resurrect:

> And so with Thews of Hymn—
> And Sinew from within—
> And ways I knew not that I knew—till then—
> I lifted Him—

Even if, as Joanne Feit Diehl argues in an analysis of Emily Dickinson's "murderous poetics,"[7] the speaker of this poem is duplici-
tously nursing her male patient into the oblivion of an afterlife where
emperors grow, her anxious narrative, with its urgent insistence on
the male's resurrection, implies that the deconstruction of male primacy is not necessarily matched by a construction of female potency.
To be sure, Dickinson's pun on Hymn/Him may mean that the
speaker herself has usurped some of "his" masculine energy. Yet
her words hint that the deconstruction of "his" primacy must be
countered by a reassuring female commitment to reconstruction.
Thus the "fainting Prince"—no longer an emperor—remained, for
many of Dickinson's descendants, a significant burden.

In 1896, for instance, Mrs. Margaret Oliphant published a semi-
autobiographical Gothic fantasy that seems to define the literary father as no more than a ghostly precursor. "The Library Window"
recounts the obsession of an imaginative young woman with a hal-
lucinatory male figure whom she thinks she glimpses in the window

of a men's college across the road from the home of some relatives she is visiting. Night and day, brooding on the absent presence of this literary father, whose intellectual labors she consistently associates with the work her own "papa" does in his library, she watches him "writing, always writing. . . ."[8] Like Hardy's passionately imaginative heroine, she becomes so completely fixated on the phantom man of letters who is her hero that her aunt must explain that the female line of her family has been haunted for generations by visions of a "Scholar [who] liked his books more than any lady's love" (240), and who was evidently murdered by the brothers of a female ancestress of the girl, who seductively "waved to him and waved to him" from her own window (240).

Like Hardy's Robert Trewe or, for that matter, Huxley's Richard Greenow, Oliphant's scholar seems uncannily insubstantial. Indeed, alluding by implication to the nineteenth-century female novelistic tradition in which heroines are haunted by demonic masters and their mysteries, Oliphant suggests that the imaginative woman may all along have been constructing a fiction of the heroism of the man of letters in order both to romanticize and to rationalize her own sense of secondariness. Nevertheless, if one compares Oliphant's man of letters to Hardy's Robert Trewe, whose story "The Library Window" might almost be glossing, one perceives at once that Hardy's hero is still aesthetically supreme, despite the urgency of his struggle with "John Ivy," while Oliphant's male author is anxiety-producing precisely because he is no more than a figment of the female imagination.

Still, when the literary father is a ghost, he does have an existence even if it is a fictive one. What, though, if he is simply dead? Edith Wharton's "The Angel at the Grave" (1901) confronts this problem head-on at the same time that it continues to delineate the literary daughter's seduction and betrayal by male tradition. Recounting the farcical history of Paulina Anson, "The only granddaughter of the great Orestes Anson,"[9] a monumental figure out of the "American Renaissance" who is no doubt based on the transcendentalist Orestes Brownson, Wharton's story traces the progress of the literary heiress from angel in the house of literary culture to angel at the grave of literary history. At first, dedicating herself like a priestess to the "mystic vocabulary" of her male ancestor's sacred authority, Paulina

defines herself as "the interpreter of the oracle" (248) of her grandfather's wisdom, musing, "What could have been more stimulating
than to construct the theory of a girlish world out of the fragments
of [his] Titanic cosmogony?" (248). But as Wharton's story unfolds,
this heroine suffers an even deeper disillusionment than Oliphant's
narrator. Possessed by her grandfather's house, which she makes
into a shrine to his memory, she is also enthralled by his deathly
presence and renounces her own desires in order to dedicate herself
to the grave task of writing his life. To her astonishment and dismay,
however, she discovers when she has completed his biography that
he has been completely eclipsed: a publisher tells her that people
no longer want to find out who her grandfather was and she goes
home "carrying [her] manuscript like a wounded thing" (251). In
the end, a young male interloper promises, ironically enough, to
revive the reputation of Orestes Anson only because the great man
once stumbled on a scientific theory about the vertebral column of
an obscure fish called the *amphioxus.*

Recounting Paulina's disillusionment, Wharton's story is, of
course, an irreverent glimpse into the vagaries of canon-formation
as well as a snide snipe at "the little knot of [male] Olympians" who
constitute literary history by "continually proclaiming their admiration for each other" and forcing the public to join "as chorus in
this guileless antiphon of praise" (252). More than Oliphant's scholar,
Wharton's Orestes is a helpless protagonist of an *Oresteia* in which
he is not freed from but fractured by the forces of history. That
the enthralled literary granddaughter still continues at the end of
her tale to be "walled alive into a tomb hung with the effigies of
dead ideas" (253) proves, however, that Freud's account of the
woman's inexorable need to turn toward the father is in many literary cases accurate, even while it interrogates his insistence that
such a turn is normative by demonstrating the debilitation wrought
by the "dreary parallel" between the dead father's "fruitless toil"
and the literary daughter's "unprofitable sacrifice" (253).

But what if the daughter's toil seems to profit her at the same
time that it leads to a sacrifice of the (newly and surprisingly) fruitless
father? This is exactly the conundrum confronted in Willa Cather's
"The Willing Muse" (1907), a story that describes the marriage of
Bertha Torrence, a productive popular novelist, to Kenneth Gray,

a rarefied man of letters who seems to stand in the place of father to her because he is, as she confesses, "endlessly more capable of doing than any of us."[10] In fact, however, as we learn in the story, although he would create if he could, she, like Willa, wills and does. Though the "limp" Gray expresses the veneration of "the printed page" instilled by his alma mater in "Olympia, Ohio"—a reverence ostensibly shared by the story's narrator, who was his college roommate—it is Bertha who publishes "better and better" novels, books which testify that she has, exactly like Freud's model daughter, "absorbed" ideas "from Kenneth like a water plant" (117).

From the first, to be sure, Gray's friends have believed that Bertha will make it possible for this aristocrat of art to "mine his vein," but actually he publishes nothing after his marriage and instead becomes Bertha's secretary, responding to her correspondence, reading unsolicited manuscripts, and in all ways proving his "varied usefulness" (115, 118). Gray himself claims that these tasks give him "an excuse for putting off my own work and you know how I welcome any pretext" (119); however, the narrator sees him as aging and bewildered by the incessant "hammer" (123) of his wife's typewriter, while Bertha herself appears ever younger. Finally, like the "anachronism" he is said to be, Gray seems to disappear off the face of the earth— he is last glimpsed in Canton—and Bertha, who has "passed all the limits of nature, not to speak of decorum," typifies the essence of the modern woman, for in her literary triumph, one of the narrator's friends regretfully concedes, she is "a woman of her time and people" (117, 123).

Curiously, then, even while it begins by describing a dutiful wife dedicating herself to an authoritative husband—a relationship modeled on Freud's paradigm of the daughter's devoted turn to the father or his surrogate—Cather's story slyly questions the issue of such a plot, dramatizing the way in which, for the modern woman of letters, wifely decorum functions merely as an apprenticeship to a professional autonomy that threatens male authority. After all, though Bertha Torrence starts out professing to be Kenneth Gray's handmaiden and, as the narrator says, a literary *"fille du regiment"* (117), like both Huxley's Pearl Bellairs and Beerbohm's literary woman this lady of letters achieves "immense" and "intense vitality" at precisely the cost of male energy. But where Beerbohm and Huxley mourned such male diminution, Cather records an ambiguous response to the situation that is simultaneously elegiac toward the defeated man and sympathetic to the triumphant woman. As if to represent the asymmetry of male and female reactions to the rise of female literary power, therefore, even her title expresses ambiguity, for, as between Bertha Torrence and Kenneth Gray, who is the willing and who is the unwilling muse? Musing on such a riddle, Cather's story acknowledges the fact that the female literary eminence she herself seeks may be perceived as pernicious to male preeminence. How, then, would men react? Might the very fragility of the father foster a vengeful impulse to put the woman back in her proper daughterly place?

A number of turn-of-the-century texts by literary women dramatize just such fearful fantasies of male revenge and female filial humiliation. Indeed, whether these stories characterize male readers of female writings as junior or senior mentors, older or younger critics, all the men of letters they depict function as representatives of a hostile paternal tradition. Vernon Lee's novella "Lady Tal" (1892), for instance, explores the ups and downs of the relationship between a Jamesian novelist named Gervaise Marion and an aspiring writer named Lady Atalanta Walkenshaw who is convinced by the end of the story that her literary aspirations are futile, while Edith Wharton's "Writing a War Story" (1919) even more sardonically describes a pretty young VAD's failed attempt to create a fiction commissioned by the editor of *The Man-at-Arms*.[11] But Mary Cholmondeley's *Red Pottage* (1899) and Mary E. Wilkins Freeman's "A Poetess" (1891) reveal the nature of the script behind Lee's and Wharton's apparently comic works by telling tales about the tragic destruction of women's manuscripts and female literary aspirations by censorious male ministers. Even more dramatically, Constance Woolson's "Miss Grief" (1880) excavates the profound grief of the "woman of genius" whose aesthetic passion finds no outlet in a world controlled by jealous scribbling men.

Male contempt for, and anxiety about, female literary ambition is vividly shown in Cholmondeley's *Red Pottage*, whose heroine, an aspiring writer, is horrified to discover that her clergyman-brother has burnt the only manuscript of her novel after it was accepted for publication because he believed "It was a profane, wicked book."[12]

Kneeling over the remains of a huge bonfire he has made in his backyard, she "thrust[s] apart the hot ashes with her bare hands," and mourns "The small writing [that] was plainly visible" as the blackened paper falls "to dust" (216). As if Cholmondely were composing "The Crime" from the perspective of Beerbohm's literary woman, she goes on to dramatize the pain experienced by this woman writer, who can only respond to the annihilation of her words with the maddening realization that "there is no resurrection that I ever heard of for the children of the brain" (261). Where Beerbohm's literary woman—whose book was, after all, already in print in many copies—plainly survives her competitor's assault because of her "immense" and "intense vitality," Cholmondeley's woman of letters is thoroughly devastated, even though her priggish brother is shown to be a fool. To the female writer the male hostility that Beerbohm portrays as comically ineffectual appears both effective and tragic.

In Freeman's "A Poetess," male censoriousness has similarly tragic consequences. Faded Betsy Dole, an impoverished spinster, finds her artistic vocation in the writing of doleful mortuary verses not unlike those composed by Twain's Emmeline Grangerford. Thinking and writing, she looks "like the very genius of gentle, old-fashioned, sentimental poetry," and her commitment to an ascetic but stereotypically female aesthetic is imaged not only in her visions of dead angel-children but also in her garden, which is filled with flowers instead of vegetables; her kitchen, whose larder is conspicuously bare; her costume, which is obsolete; and her sitting room, which is graced by a single canary. Like a parodic version of Emily Dickinson, she writes her poems on odd scraps of paper and the backs of old letters, and for this activity she has achieved a modest reputation in her community which leads to a commission to write an elegy for a dead child, whose parents publish the poem in an amazing run of two dozen broadsides, the equivalent, for her, of "a large edition of a book."[13] To her shame, however, she soon learns that the town's minister considers her verse "in dreadful bad taste" (193). Her first response is to protest: "Would it be fair if that canary bird there, that ain't never done anything but sing, should turn out not to be singin'?" (195) she asks, implicitly questioning this educated man's definitions of art.

Soon, however, she acquiesces in his judgment and burns "all the
love-letters that had passed between her and life," mournfully storing
their ashes in a sugar bowl (195). Then, feeding a lump of sugar to
her canary and renouncing her own supper, she begins to dwindle
away, and by the story's end her decline has become fatal. Ironically,
therefore, she sends for the very minister who has acted as her "executioner" and asks him to write a poem on her demise: "mebbe
my—dyin' [is] goin' to make me—a good subject for—poetry, if I
never wrote none," she speculates (199). Just the tradition that Twain
ridicules, then, becomes the subject of Freeman's sympathetic if
ironic elegy. Yet, she sees that tradition as having been annihilated
not by its own absurdity—Emmeline, after all, died because *she* "hung
fire on a rhyme for Whistler"—but as having been obliterated by
male censure. Betsy Dole yearns for validation by a learned young
man who himself publishes verse in magazines. When such certi-
fication is not forthcoming, she does to herself exactly what Beerbohm's narrator and Cholmondeley's clergyman try to do to their
women of letters: she incinerates her own texts.

A comparable act of self-annihilation occurs at the end of Woolson's "Miss Grief," whose woman of letters responds to editorial rejection first by starving herself and then by asking, on her deathbed,
that all her manuscripts except one be buried with her: "Do not look
at them—my poor dead children!" she tells the narrator; "let them
depart with me—unread, as I have been."[11] Himself a well-known
literary man ("young—strong—rich—praised—loved—successful"
[142]) and therefore all that she is not, the speaker who tells "Miss
Grief's" story has responded to what he recognizes as her genius
with mingled admiration and exasperation. Finding "earnestness,
passion, and power" (130) in her work, he nevertheless also discerns
"absolutely barbarous shortcomings" (134) and is irritated when
"Miss Grief" refuses to listen to his suggestions for revision. Worse
still, he is even more frustrated when, unbeknownst to her, he tries
to rewrite her manuscripts and fails either because "my own powers
were not equal to the task" or else because "her perversities were
as essential a part of her work as her inspirations" (139).

Despite what seems to be his commitment to fostering and pol-
ishing her genius, Woolson's tale reveals that this man is symbolic

of a male-dominated literary establishment which has transformed Miss Crief—or Miss Moncrief, as the woman writer is really called—into the impoverished and suicidal "Miss Grief," the name by which the narrator insists on knowing her. More, at its conclusion, the story dramatizes the secret competitiveness that has in some sense motivated this literary man all along. Confessing that he has kept—but kept unpublished—the one work by "Miss Grief" that she had thought would appear in print, he explains that he sees it "as a memento of my own good fortune for which I should continually give thanks. The want of one grain made all her work void and that one grain was given to me. She, with the greater power, failed—I, with the less, succeeded" (143). Finally, though, the story also shows that by putting herself into the power of this competitor, "Miss Grief" has been as complicitous in her own destruction as Freeman's heroine was. Though her chef d'oeuvre is a drama entitled *Armor*, she is hopelessly vulnerable in her aesthetic isolation, so that as she nears death her aunt places the blame on the narrator and others like him: "And as to who has racked and stabbed her, I say you, *you*—YOU literary men!" (140). Yet, of course, it was "Miss Grief" herself who decided that "her manuscripts covered with violets" should "pillow" her in her coffin, and thus this story in which the daughter, metaphorically speaking, enacts the father's revenge upon her own desire functions, like Freeman's, as an analysis of the father-daughter paradigm which reveals just how problematic such a pattern could be for late- and post-Victorian women.

No matter how she felt herself to have been wounded by her "Master," after all, Emily Dickinson was also consistently empowered by his influence. Indeed, in such poems as "My Life had stood—a Loaded Gun—" (J. 754) and "I Have a King, who does not speak—" (J. 103) she speaks not only to but for him. As Barbara Mossberg has observed, the "daughter construct" functioned paradoxically to energize as well as to oppress Dickinson, and it functioned in a similar way for such diverse figures as Maria Edgeworth, Charlotte Brontë, and Margaret Fuller.[15] Precisely because of the existence of such precursors, however, the paradigm was historicized toward the end of the nineteenth century, and thereby drained of its inevitability; as soon as even the most daughterly woman writer might become a plausible rival, male artists as well as their female contemporaries perceived for the first time the father's potential fragility along with his compensatory ferocity.

Even Freud's privileging of the daughter's turn to the father as the normative move in a girl's development toward "mature" femininity may be seen as an effort to counter such new paternal fragility. Significantly, the father of psychoanalysis formulated the ideas outlined in "Some Psychological Consequences of the Anatomical Distinction between the Sexes" (1925) and in "Female Sexuality" at a time when the structure of the patriarchal family was changing because of the rise of the so-called New Woman.[16] It may be possible, then, that Freud's theories were themselves reaction-formations against the cultural instability generated by the existence of women for whom female anatomy did not necessarily imply an intellectually impoverished destiny. As early as 1880, after all, the young Freud had translated John Stuart Mill's *The Subjection of Women* and three years later he protested to his fiancée Martha Bernays that

> it is really a stillborn thought to send women into the struggle for existence exactly as men. If, for instance, I imagined my gentle sweet girl as a competitor it would only end in my telling her, as I did seventeen months ago, that I am fond of her and that I implore her to withdraw from the strife into the calm uncompetitive activity of my home. It is possible that changes in upbringing may suppress all a woman's tender attributes, needful of protection and yet so victorious, and that she can then earn a livelihood like men. It is also possible that in such an event one would not be justified in mourning the passing away of the most delightful things the world can offer us—our ideal of womanhood.[17]

But by the time Freud began seriously to speculate about female sexuality, he may indeed have felt himself to have already witnessed the "passing away" of his early "ideal of womanhood," for he was surrounded by a circle of active women analysts—including such major figures as Lou Andreas-Salomé, Karen Horney, and Helene Deutsch—some of whom, despite the fact that he had symbolically wedded himself to them with rings bearing an image similar to that of the father god Jupiter, were often threateningly rebellious.[18] Not surprisingly, therefore, Freud's account of female sexuality both described and prescribed a continuation of the patriarchal punitiveness with which, in turn-of-the-century and early twentieth-century texts, fictional ministers and men of letters seek to put the literary daughter in her proper place even while his theories of daughterhood explain the grief felt by literary women when male feelings of diminution seem to require the destruction of female literary ambition.

————

The stories we have grouped under the father/daughter paradigm implicitly provide evidence that the woman writer may be so overwhelmed by the male-female competition her creativity seems to instigate that she might choose to relinquish literary desire altogether. Such a renunciation of desire is, of course, the strategy Freud sees at the heart of female frigidity, for the girl who rebels against "the unpleasant facts" of her situation may, in his view, "tur[n] her back on sexuality [that is, desire] altogether" (FS 198). Analogously, the woman who turns her back on aesthetic ambition would seem to have been so alarmed by "unpleasant facts" that she has become completely inhibited. Though such inhibition is ultimately the fate of the heroines we have just discussed, with the notable exception of Bertha Torrence (about whom Cather herself clearly feels ambivalent), all of them have at least in one way or another tried to woo the male muse. Kate Chopin's "Elizabeth Stock's One Story" (composed in 1898), however, provides a model of the sort of female silence that Tillie Olsen has discussed, a silence which suggests even greater vulnerability to the onslaughts of male authority than that portrayed by, say, Cholmondeley or Freeman.[19] Indeed, what is notable about Chopin's heroine is that she almost seems to have anticipated her fate by repressing her verbal desires in advance.

To be sure, Chopin's Elizabeth Stock does tell "one story"—but it is the tale of her complicity in a male plot that functions to dispossess her from her profession, her place, and even her life. A postmistress in a small town, she is in one sense a stock character, a thirty-eight-year-old spinster who is "not afraid or ashamed to say it."[20] Yet she has always longed to be a woman of letters, "much given," says the frame narrator, "to scribbling . . . scraps and bits of writing in bad prose and impossible verse" (586). But she begins her "one story" by admitting that she could not "acquire a literary style" and, worse still, she "never could think of a plot" (586). Such a confession of inadequacy is particularly notable in view of her position as postmistress, under whose eyes pass a succession of stories inscribed on post cards that she cannot help reading. And indeed, when one such card arrests her attention, her sole story begins—the tale of her own annihilation. Discovering from a message to Nathan Brightman, the town's leading citizen, that he is wanted in St. Louis for a business meeting with a man named Collins, she risks her health by journeying in bad weather to Brightman's palatial mansion to deliver what she sees as an urgent summons. But the outcome of his business transaction proves disastrous to her: as part of his deal with Collins, Brightman exercises his influence to give her job to one of Collins's relatives, a "delicate, poetically-natured young fellow" for whose implied literary ambitions the post office position seems ironically suited (590). Worse still, Elizabeth Stock's journey in the cold proves fatal for her: not only does she react to the news of her dismissal "just like I had a chill," but she also literally takes a chill which turns into the consumption that kills her (590).

The implications of Elizabeth Stock's tale are very bitter, but—interestingly—her tone is acquiescent, even anaesthetized throughout. With equal numbness, she narrates episodes in which she has rejected her suitor, incidents that have led to her downfall, and her refusal to protest that downfall. No doubt it is for this reason that she has only "one story"—the story of her repression of desire, and it is for this reason, too, that she is paradigmatic of what we are calling literary "frigidity." To be sure, Kate Chopin as the author of Elizabeth Stock has asserted her own claim upon literary desire precisely by creating Elizabeth Stock's "one story" as only one of many fictions she successfully produced and published. Nevertheless, it is possible that the writer of *The Awakening* (1899), a novel that also traces the annihilation of female creativity, needed to repudiate her anxieties about such repression by enacting them in this text. Nor was she alone in feeling such a need, for many other women writers confront similar fears by imagining characters who are unable to achieve the aesthetic release their authors themselves attain by the very creation of these figures. Indeed, from Elizabeth Stuart

Phelps Ward's *The Story of Avis* (1877) and Olive Schreiner's *The Story of an African Farm* (1883) to Carson McCullers's *The Heart Is a Lonely Hunter* (1940), Harriet Arnow's *The Dollmaker* (1954), and Doris Lessing's *The Golden Notebook* (1962), the female *Kunstlerroman* tradition frequently explores the lives not just of literary women but of would-be painters, actresses, musicians, and sculptors in order to record the problems posed by the renunciation of artistic desire.[21]

There is a sense in which such aesthetic frigidity is implicit not only in Freud's diagnosis of the girl who rebels against "the unpleasant facts of femininity" but also in his more general analysis of what is normatively "feminine" so that, again, in constructing his theory of female psychosexual development he is not only describing but prescribing the one story about literary women that would be acceptable to their male contemporaries—the story of female defeat in the battle of the sexes. For if, as Freud himself implies, desire is the wellspring of creative energy, it may be that by definition there can be no such thing as a woman artist, since the origin of all desire—the desire for the mother—must be blocked or repressed by the growing girl while the desire Freud sanctions as normative—her erotic transference to the father or his surrogate—is a secondary and artificial construct. On the one hand, Freud believes that the girl is "hampered by remains of the pre-Oedipus mother attachment" while, on the other hand, he claims that when she "represses her previous masculinity a considerable part of her general sexual life is permanently injured" (FS 208).

Thus, if art is created through a process of sublimation or substitution which enables the artist to achieve symbolically what "he" cannot achieve literally, Freud's model suggests that the girl is trapped in a situation that forbids such representational maneuvers. Because her desire for the mother is pre-Oedipal, it is archaic and infantile, dating back to a psychic era that precedes symbolization; but because her turn to the father involves not only what Freud would see as a psychically exhausting primary act of representation—the substitution of father for mother as love object—but also an acquiescence in the hegemony of male desire, she herself becomes a symbolic object for the father, a transformation which necessarily frustrates her development toward her own further creativity in the construction of symbols.[22] That literary women did and do construct symbols reminds us again of how intense the prescriptive strain is in Freud's analysis of female sexuality and suggests in addition that, as we shall argue in our final chapter, the pre-Oedipal mother bond may not forbid but may, in fact, elicit symbolization. Yet that so many literary women were haunted, in their writing about writing, by the most painful options he explores should also remind us that, even in literary terms, his perception of the female dilemma was and may still sometimes be at least partly accurate.

What maternal labors might deliver daughters into literary potency? Here we turn to the last, most distinctively modern and complicated of our Freud-derived paradigms for the female affiliation complex, a pattern based on Freud's late insight that in a number of his female analysands the "primary mother-relation had developed in a very rich and many-sided way. . . . Indeed, . . . many a woman [had remained] arrested at the original mother-attachment and never properly achieve[d] the change-over to men" (FS 195). To be sure, Freud's use of the word "arrested" is arresting, for, as we noted earlier, it implies his valuation of the woman's "first mother-attachment" as a regressive and "negative" phase of the more general Oedipus syndrome, a valuation with which a number of revisionist analysts have recently taken issue. Freud's model must therefore be revised to account, as he does not, for twentieth-century women's visions of autonomous female creativity as well as for their efforts to imagine participating in a literary matrilineage which represents maturity rather than regression. At the same time, his description of female psychosexual development does offer us a definition of one stance toward the mother which accurately reflects a strategy deployed by some twentieth-century literary women: "the masculinity complex."

For Freud, the woman who refuses to acknowledge that her mother has not given her a penis is involved in a "masculinity complex"; she pretends she is a man, and that, like a man, she can possess the mother or a mother-surrogate. Indeed, even as late as the 1920s and 1930s, Freud was associating women's desire for women with a biological as well as psychological masculinization. In "The Psychogenesis of a Case of Homosexuality in a Woman" (1920), for instance, he implies that lesbianism might possibly be "cured" by "removing . . . probably hermaphroditic ovaries, and . . . implanting others which would, it is hoped, be of a single sex," while in "Female Sexuality" he generalizes about the "masculinity" of the clitoris in pre-Oedipal, mother-dominated little girls, all of whom he defines in this stage as quasi boys.[23] Though some of his notions were obviously extreme—one wonders how many "hermaphroditic" ovaries were discovered by early twentieth-century gynecologists!—Freud's concept of the masculinity complex is a useful one. For if we translate this notion into literary terms, we can understand the ways in which a number of twentieth-century women artists have sought to gain aesthetic potency through forms of male mimicry.

Of course, nineteenth-century women writers from the Brontës ("Currer, Acton, and Ellis Bell") to Marianne Evans ("George Eliot") employed male pseudonyms and at times male narrators in an effort to legitimize themselves within a literary patrilineage that denied women full creative authority. For the most part, however, they did not impersonate men in order to possess or usurp male sexual privilege by fantasizing about the possession of female figures. On the contrary, though Charlotte Brontë employed the narrative voices of "Charles Townsend" (in some of her Angrian tales) and "William Crimsworth" (in *The Professor*), she seems always to have experienced herself as inspired by a master-muse whose energizing fire incarnated male sexual and imaginative potency.[24] As for George Eliot, she remained throughout her career what Edith Wharton, quoting Wordsworth's "Ode to Duty," called the "Stern daughter of the voice of God," who constantly reminded readers of the allegiance women owed to what Jacques Lacan calls the "Law of the Father."[25] Rather than being a form of "masculinity complex" in Freud's sense, then, the male mimicry practiced by these Victorian women artists functioned to signify their acquiescence in their own (female) inferiority: by mimicking male precursors, they sought an influx of patriarchal power.

In the twentieth century, however, a number of lesbian writers have in various ways employed the strategy of male impersonation to usurp male authority and to reclaim the mother-muse for themselves. As if illustrating Freud's observation that "there is an antithesis between the attachment to the father and the masculinity-complex" (FS 211), these writers reimagine themselves as men of letters in order to fantasize detaching themselves from patriarchal rule and breaking the father's monopoly over women. Indeed, where nineteenth-century literary women like Brontë and Eliot figuratively speaking accept what Freud calls "the fact of castration," these twentieth-century women seem to exemplify his definition of the "masculinity complex": "a girl may refuse to accept the fact of being castrated, may harden herself in the conviction that she *does* possess a penis and may subsequently be impelled to behave as though she were a man" (FS 188). In doing so, they appropriate (and thereby privilege) the phallus even while they simultaneously acquiesce in and (by refusing to be hindered by the absence of a penis) defy Freud's odd notion that women are castrated. Thus, recovering and reconstituting the child's primordial, pre-Oedipal desire for the mother as an inspiring eroticism, they liberate aesthetic energy.

Accounts of such a liberation of aesthetic energy proliferate in the writings of Renée Vivien, Djuna Barnes, Radclyffe Hall, and Gertrude Stein. In Vivien's *A Woman Appeared to Me* (1904), for instance, the literary "androgyne," San Giovanni, comments on a plot that revolves around the sexual relationships of the central female characters. Specifically, San Giovanni—whose name suggests that she is a purified and sanctified version of Mozart's sexually predatory Don Giovanni—argues that the desire for women is the only true source of artistic inspiration, for woman *is* the aesthetic *"par excellence."*[26] The author of a collection of poems entitled *Bona Dea*, this figure who uncannily assumes the prerogatives of masculinity is at the same time struggling to "restore some very ancient and profoundly wise cult, the cult of the Mother Goddess who conceived Infinity and gave birth to eternity" (15), as if anticipating Freud's late equation of the girl's pre-Oedipal mother-attachment and the matriarchal Minoan-Mycenaean stage in western history. Unlike Freud, however, San Giovanni, along with Vivien, sees the reconstitution of that attachment not as regressive but as redemptive. In formulating such a vision, moreover, she heralds a cult of lesbian literary eroticism in which successors as diverse as Barnes, Hall, and Stein participate.

Certainly, Barnes's characterization of Saint Musset in *The Ladies*

Almanack (1928), a portrait of Vivien's lover Natalie Barney, builds on a vocabulary of the sacred comparable to that deployed in *A Woman Appeared to Me* in order to consecrate a woman born "without the Tools for the Trade" whose conviction that the difference between a daughter and a son is "an inch or so less" would be defined by Freud as a "masculinity complex."[27] The female muse or "musette" of an all-female artistic community, this patron saint of lesbian love has had bestowed upon her the name of a man of letters, Alfred de Musset, who was the lover of the nineteenth-century male mimic George Sand. In addition, because she is saintly, she wields the powers of the theological, and, because she is rakish, she transforms the realm of the sexual. Thus what Barnes calls her triumphant "old-girls' Wisdom" (75) inaugurates the new age of transfigured ladies that is chronicled in the calendar called *The Ladies Almanack*.

That Radclyffe Hall appears as Lady Tilly-Tweed-in-Blood in this liberated milieu suggests her participation in this new age, as does her famous lesbian bestseller, *The Well of Loneliness* (1928). Once again the book's major character, the woman writer named Stephen Gordon, appears to have a "masculinity complex" because of her insistence upon the male right to woo and wed women. Stephen Gordon falls in love with Mary Llewellyn, takes her on a honeymoon, provides her with a household, and ultimately "gives her away" to a male suitor whose heterosexual "normalcy" seems to her more suitable than her own "inversion."[28] This last point, of course, reminds us that the sexual rebellion enacted by all these women was often personally costly. Nevertheless, Stephen's erotic relationships with women foster an aesthetic transformation: it is only after acknowledging her lesbian desire that Stephen is able to write a really successful novel. Thus, as Carroll Smith-Rosenberg and Esther Newton have argued, despite the pain *The Well of Loneliness* summarizes—not least in its title—"Hall was able to burst out of the confining framework of female romantic relations which had denied women an explicit affirmation of their sexuality" and of their creativity.[29]

But the woman writer who most consistently and comically elaborated upon yet subverted Freud's "masculinity complex" was, of course, Gertrude Stein, for both in life and art this woman who believed that "Pablo & Matisse have a maleness that belongs to ge-

nius. Moi aussi, perhaps" frequently made herself into what Virgil
Thomson once called "a Founding Father of her century."[30] Playfully
playing "husband" to Alice B. Toklas as "wife," she yet managed in
The Autobiography of Alice B. Toklas to glorify her victorious possession
of a man of genius's privileges, while at the same time seeming to
possess Alice's voice with a ventriloquist's vigor. Such a narrative
strategy was made possible for her by precisely the sexual liberation
she celebrated in the poetic dialogue called "Lifting Belly," an experiment in lesbian doubletalk produced some fifteen years before
she embarked on *The Autobiography*. In that work, a parodic yet sensual process of female love-making leads to a series of impudent
improvisations:

> Darling wife is so good.
> Little husband would.
> Be as good.
> If he could.
> This was said.
> Now we know how to differ.[31]

Counterpointing two desirous voices in such a way that it is impossible to tell who is speaking which line, Stein's and Toklas's dialogues
re-enact yet ridicule the hierarchies that structure heterosexual
marriage even as they release imaginative energies. Proving that "in
the midst of writing there is merriment," Stein simultaneously usurps
and interrogates male sexual and literary authority.

In practice, moreover, as the masterful mistress of a Paris salon
comparable to the ones hostessed by such other literary Amazons
as Edith Wharton and Natalie Barney, Stein set the scene and directed the action of just the (male) modernist experimentation that
was to create the "twentieth century" as we know it. Making herself
into her own and everybody else's pseudomale precursor, she definitively inherited the place of the father in order to put all the
men she knew in their properly dependent places. From Freud's
point of view, the "masculinity complex" could be carried no further.
The father had been turned into a fat-her.[32]

Some critics have argued, though, that Steinian (s)experimental
innovations like the continuous present are related to the multior-
gasmic rhythms of female and specifically lesbian sexuality.[33]

Whether or not that is the case—and we shall argue in our next volume that it is a problematic idea—such observations remind us that Stein gradually but inexorably moved from a position of male impersonation as the rivalrous father of us all (who once explained that "the cause of women . . . does not happen to be her business") to a more explicitly female stance as a troubled acolyte of Susan B. Anthony, whom she defined as the "mother of us all."[34] Indeed, what Stein's late opera of that title illuminates is her growing recognition that the mother's genius must be sometimes fearfully excavated and sometimes triumphantly confronted. By identifying her own search for a literary voice with the history of nineteenth-century women's struggle for the vote, therefore, she began to evolve out of a "masculinity complex" and toward the recognition of female autonomy that has been perhaps most crucial for twentieth-century women artists.

Turning to an analysis of the literary implications of such female autonomy, we enter an area uncharted by Freud. As Gregory Zilboorg pointed out more than four decades ago, Freud's insistence on women's "phallic inferiority" was shaped not only by a long tradition of misogyny but also by a history of male sexual anxieties which themselves shaped that tradition. Writing in 1944, Zilboorg quotes Ernest Jones's 1927 observation that "men analysts have been led to adopt an unduly phallocentric view of [human psychosexual development], the importance of the female organs being correspondingly underestimated," and he adds that "it is the perennial struggle between . . . the free unenslaved mother, and the man who envies her . . . that is found in religion, philosophy, and sociology [and] reflected in the course of psychoanalytic thought."[35] This struggle had a number of literary and theoretical consequences. Here, however, we want to point out that, even if it was repressed by Freud, the figure of the "free unenslaved mother" became resonant for many English-speaking women of letters who were his contemporaries and who began to explore both the literary benefits and liabilities of such independent female power.

As she did very differently in "The Angel at the Grave," Edith Wharton provides a paradigm, this time in *The Touchstone* (1897), a

novella that was actually the first long, sustained narrative she produced as an adult.[36] Written from the point of view of a struggling
New York lawyer named Glennard, this work recounts the history
of his relationship with Margaret Aubyn, a celebrated woman novelist who had corresponded with him for many years, despite the
fact that he could not reciprocate the romantic feelings she had for
him. The plot of the novella turns on his decision to sell and publish
her letters after her death, even though he realizes that they are
texts revealing not only her genius but also her vulnerability. Significantly, the sale yields enough money to let him marry Alix, a
woman whose domestic grace sets her apart from the more intellectual Margaret. But, in spite of his marital bliss, Glennard is
haunted by guilt over what he comes to see as his betrayal of the
woman novelist. When published without any indication of the re-
cipient's identity, the collection of Margaret's letters becomes a best
seller, and Glennard worries that his wife, who does not know about
his connection with the volume, will loathe his conduct because, like
many of her friends, she is contemptuous of the unknown man who
made such personal documents public.

Worse still, as Glennard broods on what he has done, he is tormented by regret at the missed opportunity of responding to Margaret's greatness. Intellectually, aesthetically, and morally brilliant,
she had been a woman of incomparable genius, and his failure to
return her love was less her loss than his own. Like the woman novelist whose "immense" and "intense vitality" Max Beerbohm's narrator cannot kill in "The Crime," she was "too big" for him, and he
is defeated by her triumphant integrity. Therefore, in a scene by
her tombstone, he in some sense becomes a male version of the
angel at the grave in Wharton's later story of that name. Significantly,
however, where Wharton uses Paulina Anson's long dedication to
the memory of her grandfather Orestes Anson as a means of de-
flating the canon of male authority, she here employs Glennard's
bereavement to announce the continuing vitality of even a dead
woman artist, for Margaret's influence permeates Glennard's life,
and, when his wife at last discovers his role in the publication of the
novelist's letters, Margaret's influence permeates her life too, bringing the couple together in a new way as they jointly resolve to expiate
his crime.

First of all, then, because it is a meditation early in Wharton's career on the risks and rewards of precisely the literary profession she was about to enter, *The Touchstone* is useful as a touchstone for understanding the young writer's fear that creative achievement might entail romantic rejection. To the extent that she identifies with Margaret, after all, Wharton explores an anxious fantasy that the woman writer can never experience the ordinary satisfactions of female life. Moreover, to the extent that she identifies with Glennard—largely telling the tale from his point of view—she might seem to be enacting a masculinity complex, aligning herself with the rejecting male in order to escape the ignominy of being the rejected female. Second, however, as our comparison with "The Angel at the Grave" is meant to suggest, Wharton's story itself finally appears to relish Margaret's posthumous victory. For if Glennard thought that he could barter Margaret's love for money to marry on, what he learns, instead, is that she has had not only the power to give him his wife but also, in forcing him to confront his own corruption, the power, as his wife reminds him, to redefine his identity: "she has given you to yourself," concludes Alix.[37]

Because Wharton also identifies with Alix and all the other women readers in the story who revere Margaret's genius, then, this author is at least in part idealizing the female precursor. For Margaret, whose name recalls Margaret Fuller and whose fame recalls George Eliot, proves that even if these writers had been rejected (as they were not) by lovers like Angelo Ossoli and George Henry Lewes, they would have accomplished precisely as much as they did. Female readers both in and out of the story are thus given an image not of a female muse who erotically empowers the woman artist but of a woman artist who is empowered by her talent to transcend what is supposedly for women the insurmountable pain of unrequited love.

Such a fantasy about both the pain and the power of a female precursor functions for the woman writer as a way of envisioning not only an aesthetic ancestress but a nurturing maternal authority, or so Olive Schreiner's short story " 'The Policy in Favor of Protection—' " (1892) and Kate Chopin's "Miss Witherwell's Mistake" (1891) indicate.[38] In the first tale, a woman of letters tries to facilitate a young woman's marriage to the man she herself loves, while in the second a woman journalist subtly furthers her niece's romance with a suitor of whom the girl's parents disapprove by telling the young woman how to write a story. In both cases, the literary women function, like Wharton's Margaret, as inspiring and strengthening female precursors, even fairy godmothers. Also like Margaret, both evade the plots into which they inscribe younger women, but in doing so, unlike Margaret, they are shown to pay a notable price for their creativity.

Thus Chopin, Wharton, and Schreiner all seem to be dramatizing complex allegiances: first, each wishes to be a decorous daughter protected by a maternal presence who facilitates the neat endings of romance; second, each longs to be a singular and originatory figure who escapes the subjugation of heterosexual love while usurping the traditional patriarchal privilege of giving the daughter in marriage; third, each fears that to become such a figure is to be isolated from the comforts of the heterosexual community. As spinsters, Chopin's Miss Witherwell, Schreiner's literary woman, and Wharton's Margaret all spin plots that enmesh others; at the same time all, as Chopin's sardonically allegorical name for her heroine implies, wither well while their dutiful subjects ripen into acceptable female roles.

Though such conflicted self-portraits may seem problematic, we can see, if we compare them to nineteenth-century portraits of the artist as a woman, that despite their ambivalences they do represent a psychological advance for the female imagination. In George Eliot's writings, for instance, the woman artist is inevitably doomed to anguish or decorous renunciation: the eponymous heroine of *Armgart* (1871), the Princess Halm-Eberstein, and the singer Mirah in *Daniel Deronda*, even the preacher Dinah Morris in *Adam Bede*—all are thwarted in, punished for, or released from their ambition. Similarly, Vashti in Charlotte Brontë's *Villette* (1853) and Jo in Louisa May Alcott's *Little Women* (1869) have either to suffer the torment of self-division or to learn the lessons of self-denial. That fin de siècle and modernist women could even begin to imagine successful and influential, if idiosyncratic, precursors suggests that the nineteenth-century female tradition may have empowered twentieth-century women writers to change the shape and scope of their fiction: instead of the female author functioning, if at all, in women's narratives as a repressed or maddened figure who is eclipsed by the docile heroine, she now appears in the work, though often ambiguously, as the representative of a powerful alternative to the plot which she nevertheless still fashions.

Perhaps no twentieth-century literary woman better exemplifies this shift from the nineteenth-century fictional tradition than Virginia Woolf, in part because no twentieth-century woman was more conscious of the influential existence of her aesthetic foremothers. Depicting such diverse artist-figures as Lily Briscoe (in *To the Lighthouse* [1927]), Orlando (in *Orlando* [1928]), and Miss La Trobe (in *Between the Acts* [1941]), Woolf writes novels which often meditate on all the different phases that we have traced in studying the modernist woman's affiliation complex. But perhaps most crucially, in *The Waves* (1931) she herself enacts Freud's idea of the "masculinity complex" even while she records an ambivalent vision of female literary autonomy. To Bernard, the book's prototypical novelist, she gives a long monologue which constitutes both the work's last chapter and its last word on the meaning of the symbolic day that has passed. There is no question, then, but that he is an avatar of the writer herself, a masculinized version of her novelistic *persona* who allows her to relate to the patrilineal past as "the inheritor . . . the continuer . . . the person miraculously appointed to carry it on."[39]

Nevertheless, it is through this male surrogate that Woolf herself is able to glimpse a woman writer who seems to embody a disruption of just the patriarchal history he has inherited. Early in the book, Bernard and his schoolfriend Susan escape from their classroom to enter (whether in reality or in imagination is not clear) the mysterious precincts of a nearby estate called "Elvedon," where the novelist-to-be has a crucial epiphany.[40] "Look over the wall," he exclaims to his companion, and then proceeds to describe a resonant tableau of a lady sitting between two long windows, writing. Woolf's style conveys that, like the children, she wonders at the amazing grace of this lady of Elvedon. Like Bernard, indeed, she is moved at being the first to see her: "We are the discoverers of an unknown land" (186). Yet even such a glimpse is fraught with fear, for Bernard and Susan experience this mystical lady's estate as "a hostile country" in which they are trespassers.

Is the literary woman's land real or is it a hallucination? Guarded by gardeners with "great brooms," does it represent an Eden forever

closed to female as well as male intruders? Bernard's—and Woolf's—
vocabulary of anxiety suggests a paradigmatic ambivalence toward
female literary inheritance. At the same time, however, their rhetoric
of romance—the "lady," "Elvedon"—seems to consecrate this moment as a revelation of originatory female energy. Perhaps not co-
incidentally, then, Woolf's image of a lady writing in a garden not
only revises and reverses Oliphant's depiction of a ghostly man writing at a library window, it also recalls the vision that Beerbohm's
author has in "The Crime" of a woman with "immense" and "intense
vitality" scribbling in a summer house. Different as they are, Woolf's
fantastic lady and Beerbohm's prolific woman seem, in some sense
at least, to be one, for the two writers share a feeling that this New
Woman inhabits a place which is both separate and significant: if
they are to understand their own situations, each must individually,
whether as trespasser or inheritor, come to terms with the terms
she represents.

That in "Letter from Chicago" May Sarton chose Woolf as *the*
pivotal precursor in whom she lost and found herself is therefore
singularly appropriate. Some years earlier, in a poem called "My
Sisters, O My Sisters" (1948), Sarton had reviewed the difficulties
of a range of other female artists and worried that "writing women"
are "strange monsters."[41] Meditating on Woolf, however, appears
to have forced her to surface an even more deadly anxiety about
"writing women," while it also allowed her to find the "place where
time flows again." For indeed it was Woolf herself who mourned
what she claimed were the distortions, deflections, and deceptions
of the female literary tradition at the same time that she signaled a
way for women to perceive time as flowing rather than static, pur-
posefully historical rather than monstrously random. In *A Room of
One's Own*, after all, though she celebrated the achievements of "the
four great novelists" and predicted the resurrection of Shakespeare's
sister, she had worried that "anger [tampered] with the integrity of
Charlotte Brontë the novelist" (76) and argued that "the whole
structure of the early nineteenth-century novel was raised, if one
was a woman, by a mind which was slightly pulled from the straight"
(77). Given her identification of integrity with aesthetic excellence,

she seemed—somewhat surprisingly—driven to insist that many of the novels of her precursors had a "flaw in the centre that had rotted them" (77).

Perhaps the existence of a series of autonomous authorial mothers inspired feelings of intense ambivalence in turn-of-the-century, modernist, and contemporary women writers. On the one hand, as some feminist critics have suggested and as we ourselves have argued, female artists, looking for literary mothers and grandmothers whose achievements certify the female imagination, have been delighted to recover the writings of their ancestresses. On the other hand, we are now convinced that female artists, looking at and revering such precursors, are also haunted and daunted by the autonomy of these figures. In fact, we suspect that the love women writers send forward into the past is, in patriarchal culture, inexorably contaminated by mingled feelings of rivalry and anxiety. Though there is no mythic paradigm of Jocasta and Antigone which would parallel Bloom's archetype of Laius and Oedipus, strong equals at the crossroads, most literary women do ask—as Sylvia Plath did about women poets—"who rivals" (*J* 211), partly because, as Margaret Atwood explains, "members of what feels like a minority" must compete for a "few coveted places" and partly because those coveted places signify, as Freud's model tells us, the approbation of the father who represents cultural authority.[12] But the woman writer who engages with her autonomous precursor in a rivalrous struggle for primacy often learns that the fruit of victory is bitter: the approbation of the father is almost always accompanied by his revulsion, and the autonomy of the mother is frequently as terrifying as it is attractive, for—as Woolf's comments about Charlotte Brontë suggest—it has been won at great cost.

Far from being unequivocally energized by the example of her female precursor, then, the literary daughter finds herself in a double bind. If she simply admires her aesthetic foremother, she is diminished by the originatory power she locates in that ancestress; but, if she struggles to attain the power she identifies with the mother's autonomy, she must confront what Emily Dickinson, speaking of George Eliot, called the "Losses [that] make our Gains ashamed—" (J. 1562)—that is, the peril of the mother's position in patriarchy, the loss of male emotional approval paradoxically associated with male approbation—as well as the intimacy with the mother that would accompany daughterly subordination. To have a history, therefore, may not be quite so advantageous as some feminists have traditionally supposed. Whether it represents what Laura Riding Jackson has scornfully called a "literary ladies' room"[13] or whether it seems to offer a way toward a men's club whose doors are ultimately closed, the past proposes a series of severe ironies. When there was no past, it was indeed possible for women from Mary Shelley to Elizabeth Barrett Browning and Christina Rossetti to dream of, in Dickinson's words, a "different dawn," a "morn by men unseen—" (J. 24) that would lead to a different future. But once history has unfolded, its ironies proliferate as its documents multiply, so that vision and reality split radically apart. In fact, paradoxically, the powerful literary mother becomes the subject of both matrophilial utopian and matrophobic dystopian meditations, a figure to whose primal relation with tradition the daughter obsessively directs her consistently ambivalent attention, at just the moment when it would seem that maternal potency ought to have healed daughterly dis-ease.

As we have suggested that Sarton intuited, no modernist literary woman wrote more tellingly than Virginia Woolf about both the problems and the possibilities of matrilineal (literary) affiliation, in part because no modernist woman of letters was more intensely conscious of the influential existence of aesthetic foremothers. In her critical essays, in particular, she reveals both the anxiety and the exuberance which she and many of her contemporaries experienced as, for the first time, they confronted a female literary inheritance. Indeed, for Woolf, as for a number of other modernist women of letters, it was the comparatively new enterprise of feminist or protofeminist literary criticism that made possible a voyage of dread and desire, a voyage "forward" into the geography of an unprecedented female past.

It is not irrelevant that in *The Waves* Woolf can be said to have summarized her exploration of the past by depicting a writer's voyeuristic gaze at another writer. From early in her career she herself continually looked with mingled admiration and aversion at the lives of her precursors. Indeed, long before she was a novelist Woolf was a literary critic working in a new genre pioneered by women writers of her generation, and her reconstruction of her aesthetic heritage, like the reconstructions attempted by many of her contemporaries and descendants, frequently involved a visualizing of the primal scene of writing, a kind of spying on the past. In particular, Woolf exemplifies how women of letters indulged in such erotic peering when approaching the forbidden precincts of the female tradition. A 1924 essay with the noteworthy title "Indiscretions: 'Never Seek to Tell Thy Love, Love That Never Told Can Be'—but One's Feelings for Some Writers Outrun all Prudence" perhaps most dramatically demonstrates her sensual pleasure as well as her daughterly satisfaction at the visions her voyeurism reveals, even while it records her anxious ambivalence toward such visions.

To begin with, tiptoeing towards women's literary history, Woolf employs a striking metaphor to explain her illicit excitement: ". . . inevitably, we come to the harem, and tremble slightly as we approach the curtain and catch glimpses of women behind it and even hear ripples of laughter and snatches of conversation."[11] Then, tearing aside the veil, she exposes the newly defined female family she discovers behind the swathings of time. Male readers, she observes, have never understood the truth about female authors: "A hundred years ago [women writers] were stars who shone only in male sunshine; deprived of it, they languished into nonentity— sniffed, bickered, envied each other—so men said" (*WW* 75). Now as she looks for herself, Woolf announces that, contrary to received wisdom,

> it is by no means certain that every woman is inspired by pure envy when she reads what another has written. More probably Emily Brontë was the passion of her youth; Charlotte even she loved with nervous affection; and cherished a quiet sisterly regard for Anne. Mrs. Gaskell wields a maternal sway over readers of her own sex; wise, witty and very large-minded, her readers are devoted to her as to the most admirable of mothers; whereas George Eliot is an Aunt, and, as an Aunt, inimitable. . . . Jane Austen we needs must adore; but she does not want it; she wants nothing; our love is a by-product, an irrelevance. . . ." [*WW* 75–76]

Gazing tremblingly into what she sarcastically calls "the harem" of women's literary history, Woolf repudiates the idea of envy with willful irony as she transforms her precursors first into characters,

then into ancestresses. Clearly, for this archetypal feminist critic the
act of deciding to tear the veil and look freely at the past is pre-
requisite to and inextricable from a decision to adopt and be adopted
by an alternative literary lineage. At the same time, however, the
authorial pride with which Woolf herself recreates the "four great
novelists" and Mrs. Gaskell in a fiction of her own making, while
never making reference to their fictions, suggests some measure of
at least impure envy or rivalry on her part.

Such a combination of voyeuristic exploration, aesthetic rivalry,
and voluntary affiliation characterizes not only Woolf's critical oeuvre
but also much of the criticism of female authors produced by other
women writers of her generation as well as by more recent writers.
However, not only for Woolf but for other feminist critics this combination of exploration, rivalry, and affiliation is risky as well as re-
warding. The passage we have quoted from "Indiscretions," after
all, records a painful if eroticized vision of the female past: the foremothers Woolf espies were in their own lives sequestered and sometimes silenced; their greatest triumph—being "stars who shone only
in male sunshine"—implied invisibility; they were said to be angry
and envious, to sniff and bicker. Thus they constitute a problematic
family indeed, and it is no wonder that immediately after symbolically adoring this matrilineal spectacle the critic withdraws from it.
She has revealed her sisters, her cousins, and her aunts only to re-
veil them and return to the safety of her fathers. Her romantic engagement with these ancestresses pales, she nervously explains, "as
the flirtations of a summer compared with the consuming passions
of a lifetime," and she goes on to confess her enthrallment to Shakespeare, John Donne, and that "large, lame, simple-minded . . . great
writer . . . Walter Scott" (*WW* 76).

Here, as elsewhere, Woolf's stance foreshadows a position most
feminist modernists and their successors have taken toward the female past. To be sure, as its title suggests, "Indiscretions" is a deliberately imprudent and impudent essay, a *jeu* the critic seems simply to have dashed off for *Vogue*. Yet for all its comic hyperbole—
or perhaps because of such hyperbole—it expresses precisely the
ambivalence with which Bernard and Susan responded to the lady
of Elvedon in *The Waves*. For, like the episode that recounts their
vision, this essay records the multiple binds in which the twentieth-

century woman writer feels herself to be caught when she confronts the new reality of her female literary inheritance. First, she sees the pain her precursors experienced and wishes to renounce it: to become a woman writer may be, she fears, to become an invisible star in male sunshine—to be, in other words, marginalized, dispossessed, alienated; or, worse, it may be to sniff and bicker—that is, to become a jealous neurotic or even a madwoman. In addition, though, she acknowledges the power her precursors achieved and worries that she may not be able to equal it: to become a woman writer may be to have to find a way of coming to terms with the accomplishments of other women writers. Finally, however, she fears the consequences of both renunciation and rivalry: to renounce her precursors' pain or to refuse to try to rival them may be to relinquish the originatory authority their achievements represent and to isolate oneself forever in the secondary and belated position of the voyeur.

It is just this complex of problems that the voyeuristic stance addresses. By looking *at* the precursor, the female inheritor distances herself from her foremother's struggle while at the same time participating vicariously in the primal moment of composition. Similarly, it is this complex of problems that the imperative of adoption seeks to correct. By looking *for*—seeking out, choosing, and thus achieving a kind of power over—precursors, the twentieth-century woman writer eases the burden of what Harold Bloom has called the "anxiety of influence" while resisting precisely the masculinist oppression and repression that she fears. Metaphorically speaking, as Bloom has shown, male literary history functions like a biological family, albeit a socially constructed one: it is impossible for Wordsworth to evade Milton's paternity, just as it is impossible for Stevens to evade Wordsworth's. For women, however, female genealogy does not have an inexorable logic because the literary matrilineage has been repeatedly erased, obscured, or fragmented. Thus, when the woman writer "adopts" a "mother" like Mrs. Gaskell or an "aunt" like George Eliot, she is creating a fictive family whose romance is sufficient to her desire. What this means is that, even in the unprecedented presence of female literary history, women do not engage in the kind of purely agonistic struggle that Bloom describes. Rather, after they have overcome what we have defined as the nineteenth-century woman writer's "anxiety of authorship" (the fear that because one is a woman one cannot be a writer), they have to confront other, equally distinctive and disturbing difficulties, problems associated with the affiliation complex.

First, each must inevitably ask, "Have I chosen the right—the most empowering, the most authoritative—ancestors? Have I adopted the right name or names?"—meaning, in our terms, "Given the range of options available to me have I decided upon an appropriate affiliation?" Second, each must also wonder, "Have I betrayed my 'biological' family?" meaning, in Bloom's terms, "Have I relinquished or been traitorous to the patrilineage which gave me a name in the first place?" Third, each must worry, "What is the bloodline that runs through me? What genealogy is really mine?" meaning, in terms of women's literary history, "Do I really, despite my effort to certify myself with august ancestresses, descend from a line of silly scribbling ladies who write silly ladies' novels?" Fourth, each must speculate, "Will I be engulfed or obliterated by the primacy of the foremothers whose power I need to invoke?" Given the almost vertiginous range of issues that the adoptive imperative or affiliation complex raises, looking both *at* and *for* must inevitably, again, become an essential survival strategy. For if voyeuristic looking *at* distances the woman writer from crisis even while it allows her to participate vicariously in creation, voyeuristic looking *for* enables her to validate her selected past and her elected self.

From 1904 on, Woolf's critical essays epitomize such a complex process of looking at and for a matrilineal inheritance like the one emblematized by the lady of Elvedon. Not insignificantly, the first piece she ever had accepted for publication—"Haworth. November 1904"—described a pilgrimage to the Brontës' Yorkshire parsonage and lingered lovingly on the display cases that contained "the little personal relics, the dresses and shoes of the dead woman" (*WW* 123) while confessing an anticipatory "excitement" at nearing Haworth, a pleasure which "had in it an element of suspense that was really painful, as though we were to meet some long-separated friend . . . so clear an image had we" (*WW* 122). Some six years after she wrote this essay, when she was still struggling with the recalcitrant manuscript, *Melymbrosia*, that was to become *The Voyage Out* (1915), Woolf implied in a review of Mrs. Gaskell's works that the texts of a female precursor might be secondary substitutes for the personal presence of the author herself: "We who never saw her, with her manner 'gay but definite,' her beautiful face, and her 'almost perfect arm,' find something of the same delight in her books" (*WW* 149). Five years later, in 1915, in a profile of George Eliot that she produced for *TLS*, Woolf, now herself a published novelist, was still obsessed by the visual details that one of her major precursors evoked: "One cannot," she confided, "escape the conviction that the long, heavy face with its expression of serious and sullen and almost equine power has stamped itself depressingly upon the minds of people who remember George Eliot, so that it looks out upon them from her pages" (*WW* 151).

Six years later still, meditating on Eliot's waning reputation, Woolf reiterated her concern with the relationship between face and page, noting that the novelist's "big nose, her little eyes, her heavy horsey head loom from behind the printed page . . ." (*WW* 72). At around the same time, too, Woolf sought out and scrutinized an image of Jane Austen, imagining the scene of writing by meditating on the look and the looks of the writer. Compared with her vision of George Eliot's equine maturity, her glimpse of Austen as a prim yet powerfully sardonic schoolgirl was comforting, and though she confessed that "Miss Cassandra Austen" feared that "a time might come when strangers would pry," Woolf reassured herself about Austen's powers even further by actually prying into a scene of composition.[15] Studying the unfinished text of *The Watsons*, she imagined how the novelist might have finished it. As she, figuratively speaking, watched Austen force her "pen to go through pages of preliminary drudgery," Woolf exulted in her precursor's triumphant creation of a successful episode, confiding that her "senses quicken" at the "peculiar intensity which [this novelist] alone can impart" (*CR* 141).

Similar acts of literary voyeurism mark other essays Woolf published throughout her career. Her study of "The Duchess of Newcastle" (1925) begins with a "curious student" who "quails before the mass of [the Duchess's] mausoleum, peers in, looks about . . . and hurries out again, shutting the door" (*CR* 70), and culminates with a vision of people crowding the streets to look at "the crazy Duchess . . . in her silver coach" (*CR* 78). In addition, Woolf's essay on "Dorothy Wordsworth" (1932) continues the critic's emphasis on vision in three interestingly different ways. First, Dorothy herself becomes a kind of heroine of perception. Distinguished by her expert powers of observation, "she scarcely," in Woolf's phrase, "seemed to shut her eyes" and, looking along the sight-lines that Dorothy's journal "points," Woolf sees precisely what this precursor saw.[16] Second, Woolf dwells with voyeuristic fascination on the "strange love" between the woman see-er and her poet-brother, quoting extensively from the journal passages in which Dorothy describes the pleasures of her relationship with "my Beloved" and transforming the Romantic pair into a real-life version of Emily Brontë's Cathy and Heathcliff: "one could not act without the other. They must feel, they must think, they must be together" (*CR2* 153). Third, evoking her "cheeks . . . brown as a gipsy's. . . . her gait . . . rapid and ungainly," Woolf sees Dorothy seeing (*CR2* 155).

Finally, in an appreciation of Christina Rossetti that appeared in the same volume as "Dorothy Wordsworth," Woolf both uses the voyeuristic strategies that she had employed throughout many other pieces and disrupts those strategies as she imagines the annihilation of the space that separates her from her foremother as well as a quasi-erotic engagement with the object of her admiration. Beginning with an image of Rossetti as an inhabitant of a "miraculously sealed . . . magic tank" (*CR2* 214), Woolf confides that "one might go on looking and listening forever. There is no limit to the strangeness, amusement, and oddity of the past sealed in a tank" (*CR2* 217). But as she explores "this extraordinary territory," she tells us, the figure of Christina Rossetti suddenly utters a sentence which shatters the pane of time that divides the watcher and the watched, "as if a fish . . . suddenly dashed at the glass and broke it" (*CR2* 217). The words that break the glass are spoken in a mysteriously surrealistic scene Woolf reconstructs from a biography of the poet. At a tea-party, "suddenly there uprose from a chair and paced forward into the center of the room a little woman dressed in black, who announced solemnly, 'I am Christina Rossetti!' and having so said, returned to her chair" (*CR2* 217). Woolf's interpretation of the event further narrows the distance between her and the Victorian writer, for indeed the critic supplies the secret meaning of Rossetti's gesture: "Yes . . . I am a poet."

As she meditates on the meaning of such a statement from "a short elderly woman in black," Woolf enters into a passionate dialogue with her precursor—"O Christina Rossetti . . . your instinct was so sure, so direct, so intense that it produced poems that sing like music in one's ears" (*CR2* 219)—and assures her that her miraculous lines will generate a new lineage replacing male monuments of unaging intellect: "some of the poems you wrote in your little back room will be found adhering in perfect symmetry when the Albert Memorial is dust and tinsel" (*CR2* 220). At last, then, the critic admits that, had she been present at that tea-party, she "should certainly have committed some romantic indiscretion" comparable to the imaginative trespasses she confesses in the 1924 essay "Indiscretions": she would have "broken a paper-knife or smashed a tea-cup in the awkward ardour of my admiration when [the poet] said, 'I am Christina Rossetti'" (*CR2* 221). Breaking the implements of gentility that would distance her from her own emotion, Woolf re-enacts Rossetti's own smashing of the glass that intervenes between generations and particularly between generations of women. Indeed, it is as if the lady of Elvedon had stepped through the long windows to address Bernard and Susan and as if they had been able to reply with "awkward ardour." Further, it is even as if they had been able momentarily to identify with the originatory woman, for the title of Woolf's Rossetti essay—"I am Christina Rossetti"—is so notably ambiguous as almost to turn the piece into a dramatic monologue.

That Woolf wished both to identify with Christina Rossetti and to adopt her as an empowering ancestress in order, among other things, to ward off the threat of involuntary participation in what she saw as a trivial and trivializing female tradition is made clear by her speculation that Rossetti's self-defining proclamation was uttered in response to "something [that] was said in a casual, frivolous, tea-party way about poetry" (*CR2* 217).[17] Like George Eliot, Woolf strives to dissociate herself from silly lady readers and silly lady writers. Indeed, her voyeuristic visions of adoptive foremothers are shadowed by a few virulent essays, virtually poison pen letters, in which she definitively distances herself from "scribbling" women. In "A Scribbling Dame (Eliza Haywood)" (1916), for instance, she elaborated a conceit based on a comparison of the eighteenth-century romancer to a "domestic house fly" (*WW* 92), noting "that [Haywood] was a writer of no importance, that no one read her for pleasure, and that nothing is known of her life" (*WW* 93), and adding that the only virtue of Haywood's works was that one "could read 'with a tea-cup in one hand without danger of spilling the tea' " (*WW* 94). A few years later, in a sardonic review entitled "Wilcoxiana (Ella Wheeler Wilcox)" (1919), Woolf did an equally ferocious hatchet-job on a woman poet. Pinning the "Madame de Staël of Milwaukee" (*WW* 173) to a wall of scorn, she described forty photographs of the American author who wrote "Laugh and the world laughs with you, / Weep and you weep alone"—lines at which Woolf herself obviously wanted to laugh—and she observed with voyeuristic revulsion that "Rather than look like a blue-stocking [Wilcox] would have forsaken literature altogether" (*WW* 174).

But the hostility that so triumphantly surfaces in these revisionary versions of George Eliot's "Silly Novels by Lady Novelists" also more subtly haunts even the most laudatory of Woolf's other works of protofeminist criticism. "Haworth, November 1904," for instance, focuses on the relics of an emphatically "dead woman" and "The Duchess of Newcastle" similarly italicizes the demise of the precursor, whose mausoleum causes onlookers to "quail." George Eliot has a "heavy, horsey head," while Christina Rossetti is "a short elderly woman in black" whose religious, social and sartorial eccentricities embody the "oddity of the past sealed in a tank." As she transforms these precursors into characters in search of an author named Virginia Woolf, the author of *A Room of One's Own* often verges upon caricature. Moreover, concentrating on their bodies rather than their books, she frequently seems to be evading a serious consideration of texts whose powers might make her tremble even more than does the "awkward ardour" of her admiration for Christina Rossetti.

Indeed, Woolf's treatment of her foremothers' writings is at times more than implicitly dismissive. In some of this critic's "appreciations" of texts, for example, there is overt ambivalence. "*Aurora Leigh*," she explains in a *Common Reader* essay, "is not . . . the masterpiece that it might have been," which is perhaps "why it has left no successors" (*CR2* 188, 192). Similarly, but more famously, she complains in *A Room of One's Own* that "an acidity . . . a buried suffering . . . a rancour . . . contracts" *Jane Eyre*, although—as she notes with what may be an equally subtle manifestation of hostility—even her beloved Jane Austen had "less genius for writing than Charlotte Brontë" (76, 80). More generally, she asserts elsewhere that "the effect of . . . repressions is still clearly to be traced in women's work, and the effect is wholly to the bad," even though "the effort to free themselves . . . has [also] told disastrously upon the writing of women."[48]

———————

In psychoanalytic terms, Woolf could be said in these passages to be expressing not only rivalry with the aesthetic mother but also exactly the daughterly complaints that Freud outlined in "Female Sexuality" as "the strongest motive[s] for turning away from" the mother: the "reproach that her mother has not given her a proper genital, i.e., that she was born a woman" (and hence with only second-rate literary powers), and the lament "that the mother gave [her] too little milk and did not suckle her long enough" (in other words, that the mother did not nurture her emergent creativity) (FS 202–03). In this regard, Woolf's generalized feelings replicate the even more general revulsion articulated by Willa Cather when, implying that all or almost all women writers were scribbling women, she declared in 1897 that "when I see the announcement of a new book by a woman, I—well, I take one by a man instead" and by Rebecca West when she mused in 1912 that "It would be hard to say why women have refused to become great writers."[49] In addition, they summarize the gist of Amy Lowell's satiric self-analysis in a poem entitled "A Critical Fable" (1922):

> "My dear Sir," I exclaimed, "if you'd not been afraid
> Of Margaret Fuller's success, you'd have stayed
> Your hand in her case and more justly have rated her."
> Here he murmured morosely, "My God, how I hated her!
> But have you no women, whom you must hate too?
> I shall think all the better of you if you do.
> And of them I may add." I assured him, "A few.
> But I scarcely think man feels the same contradictory
> Desire to love them and shear them of victory?"   [*CP* 409]

Lowell's fear—expressed in a passage from "The Sisters" (1925) which we have used as one of our epigraphs—that her literary "sisters" leave her "sad and self-distrustful" also foreshadows Louise Bogan's rivalrous yet reproachful confession that the works of Vic-

torian "poetesses in the parlor" elicit from her "howls, I can assure
you," as well as Margaret Atwood's claim that "woman-woman rivalry" is "likely to take the form of *wanting* another woman writer
to be better than she [that woman writer] is" and Adrienne Rich's
admission about the "Heroines" of the nineteenth century that,
triumphantly "deviant" though they were, their "exact / legacy as it
is" is "not enough."[50] Moreover, the attitudes that Woolf often expresses when she "thinks back" through specific mothers echo Alice
Meynell's scorn of Harriet Martineau as a woman who "could not
thread her way safely in and out of two or three negatives" as well
as Meynell's contempt for Fanny Burney's *Evelina* as "an unabashed
manifestation of waste thoughts."[51] At the same time, Woolf's attitudes look forward to Dorothy Parker's disdain for mindlessly productive female writers of what she considers fantasy—"the Misses
Baldwin, Ferber, Norris"—whom, in a passage we have used as another epigraph to this chapter, Parker contrasts with the truly scru-
pulous artist Flaubert. In addition, they forecast Louise Bogan's
anxious and angry sense that Woolf herself "is frequently intellectually pretentious and always emotionally immature" as well as Sylvia
Plath's feeling that Woolf's "novels make mine possible [but] I shall
go better than she."[52] Furthermore, they look forward to Anne Sexton's "secret fear" of being "a reincarnation" of Edna St. Vincent
Millay, a poet she considered soggily sentimental, as well as to Plath's
determination not to be "quailing or whining like [Sara] Teasdale
or [to write] simple lyrics like Millay" (*LH* 244) and to Edith Sitwell's
anxiety that women's poetry is as a rule "simply *awful*—incompetent,
floppy, whining, arch, trivial, self-pitying" except for "a few poems"
by Christina Rossetti, Emily Dickinson, and Sappho.[53]

By reminding herself of Rossetti, Dickinson, and Sappho—notable
and notably brilliant women writers—yet diminishing their achievements to "a few poems," Sitwell is of course not only expressing her
feelings of rivalry with powerful precursors but also defending herself against her anxiety about what we have seen is the male modernist mythology that all women writers are scribbling women writers, Pearl Bellairses or Ella Marchmills, fat lady poets with footnotes
or Ella Wheeler Catheters. Thus, as she grapples with what male
(and female) writers assert about literary women, Sitwell explains
why so many female modernists began writing protofeminist criti-

cism at this time, for they too sought to assert their own authority in part by drawing on the authorship of their precursors, and in part by disentangling themselves from their own reproachful attitudes toward their foremothers as well as from the damaging charges leveled by masculinist contemporaries. In a sense, then, the turn-of-the-century emergence of literary criticism by and about women is an anxious but healing response to wounding male assaults against women as well as to female fears about contaminated bloodlines. At the same time, however, as we have speculated, this criticism is often specifically characterized by its obsession with a timeless moment during which the female precursor is inspected, respected, suspected.

Such a transcendent interval of voyeuristic inspection not only bypasses chronology and history, it annihilates sequentiality, a point which explains why so many of these women artists chose to validate their heritage through critical essays rather than narrative fictions. In the novel (or indeed the short story) each event inexorably leads to another and is therefore always threatened by ironic qualifications, by the metaphysics of causality. Thus, the stories we have studied frequently undercut themselves, with the aesthetic empowerment of the woman artist sometimes leading to debilitating consequences in the world either for herself or for others, and sometimes so qualified and circumscribed as to lead nowhere. Woolf's critical portraits of women artists, however, concentrating on the scene rather than the sequence of creativity, can ecstatically celebrate or sardonically castigate moments of pure literary being along with moments of literary mutuality. Furthermore, although criticism is perhaps inherently voyeuristic and thus implies a belatedness toward or dependency upon its subject, literary criticism was a new field of endeavor for twentieth-century literary women, one which their precursors had not fully explored, so that it allowed female writers to be truly original while still fantasizing about the true originatory act.

To be sure, nineteenth-century and turn-of-the-century women of letters from Geraldine Jewsbury, Mrs. Gaskell, and Margaret Fuller to Mary Elizabeth Coleridge and Alice Meynell composed various and variously ambivalent tributes to the triumphs and tribulations of their contemporaries and in a few cases their foremoth-

ers.[54] In the twentieth century, however, the pace of such critical
activity quickened, with writers from Willa Cather to Eudora Welty,
from Adrienne Rich to Alice Walker producing biographies, appreciations, and analyses of the lives, works, and difficulties of female
peers and precursors.[55] Whether biographies, appreciations, or
analyses, all these efforts function to help the critic-writer affiliate
herself with a heretofore obscured past. When Vita Sackville-West
explained about Aphra Behn that "her work may not be read, but
it is as a pioneer that she should, to her eternal honour, be remembered" or when Katherine Anne Porter imagined Willa Cather as
"a curiously immoveable shape . . . like certain churches . . . or exemplary women, revered and neglected," they articulated both the
anxiety and the reverence informing countless feminist biographies:
on the one hand, Behn's "work may not be read" and Cather is
"immoveable" as well as "neglected"; on the other hand, Behn is "a
pioneer" and Cather is "an exemplary woman."[56]

Another way of relating to such a lineage, though, is through the
creation of parodic and allusive texts—novels, stories, and plays that
function quasi-critically and refer to or revise female pre-texts. Although they do question the logic of prior narrative causality, these
works can never, of course, discover the timeless moments that critical appreciation reveals. Nevertheless, they work off and out of
such moments, implicitly critiquing and explicitly paying a tribute
to the plots fashioned by precursors. From Jean Rhys to Margaret
Drabble and Joyce Carol Oates, twentieth-century women novelists
have played variations on the themes of their foremothers in order
to strengthen themselves by restoring and revising the past while
restructuring the future. Jean Rhys's *Wide Sargasso Sea,* for example,
both celebrates and interrogates Charlotte Brontë's *Jane Eyre* by retelling the tale from the silenced perspective of Bertha Mason Rochester, while Margaret Drabble's *The Waterfall* (1969) rewrites the story
of *The Mill on the Floss* from an ironic contemporary perspective,
with Drabble's narrator bitterly commenting, "those fictitious heroines, how they haunt me. . . . Maggie Tulliver never slept with her
man: she did all the damage there was to be done, to Lucy, to herself,
to the two men who loved her, and then, like a woman of another
age, she refrained," and concluding bleakly, "I worry about the sexual doom of womanhood, its sad inheritance."[57]

More comically, Joyce Carol Oates's *Mysteries of Winterthurn* (1984) recreates Emily Dickinson as the eccentric Georgina Kilgarvan, five hundred of whose "incoherent scribblings were to be found in packets of creamy-rose stationery, held together by yarn looped through them in the spine amidst the spinster's personal effects."[58] Refusing to acquiesce in what T. E. Hulme called "roses, roses all the way," this "willfully unfeminine" Dickinsonian figure occasionally publishes, under the pseudonym "Iphigenia," texts marked by "rude jarring images, and dashed off lines" (57)—for instance

> If I—am You—
> Shall You—be me?
> If You—scorn I—
> Where then—We
> Be—?   [1]

Of course, Oates is herself a passionate admirer of Dickinson who has produced glowing tributes to "the Myth of Amherst."[59] But her loving parodies function both as tributes to and critiques of the nineteenth-century poet's striking idiosyncrasies.

Two plays, one modern and one contemporary, perform similarly ambivalent acts of obeisance to female precursors, with the first in fact using a version of Emily Dickinson—albeit one that is very different from Oates's—as its central image of the female artist. Susan Glaspell's *Alison's House* (1930) dramatizes a family's struggle to come to terms with "the sexual doom of womanhood, its sad inheritance," as revealed in the poems discovered after the death of Alison Stanhope, the Dickinson avatar. Saintly in a white dress, this lost heroine had told in her verses the story of an illicit "love that never died— loneliness that never died" so that most of her relatives feel they ought to burn what they believe to be letters to the world that the world should not see.[60] The tensions in this text are made particularly explicit when the poet's niece remarks that, perhaps like Margaret's in *The Touchstone*, Alison's love was "death to her. But she made it— life eternal" (141), and those tensions are only ambiguously resolved when, at the end of the play, the poet's brother painfully decides *not* to burn her work. On the one hand, Alison is an imaginative woman whose gifts give "life eternal" to the house of Alison; on the other hand, she is a monitory example of loneliness that never died, loneliness which her descendants must therefore eternally confront.

Such monitory examples, as well as such eternal gifts, are perhaps

even more theatrically analyzed in Caryl Churchill's *Top Girls* (1982),
where the newly promoted head of a women's employment agency
conjures up the spirits of five historical or fictive precursors at a
celebratory dinner party. Isabella Bird, the Victorian traveler; Lady
Nijo, a Japanese courtesan and Buddhist nun; Dull Gret, a key figure
in a Breugel painting; Pope Joan, the legendary medieval female
Pope; and Patient Griselda, the protagonist of stories told by both
Boccaccio and Chaucer—all these women are brought to life in
Churchill's dreamlike first act, and all, in the course of the scene,
confess the cost at which their ambitions were realized: hostile men,
lost children, and even, in the case of Joan, a hideous public exe-
cution. Thus, while the optimistically liberated modern woman
Marlene exclaims "magnificent all of you," Joan intones grim phrases
from Lucretius' *De Rerum Natura,* and Gret asserts that "most of us
is fighting the devils. There's lots of little devils, our size, and we
get them down all right and give them a beating."[61]

Of course, most of these women are neither Marlene's nor
Churchill's *literary* precursors, but in their complex mix of defeat
and victory they represent precisely the historical narratives of which
twentieth-century women writers have now become so intensely
aware. "We've come a long way," says Marlene (13), but, as it unfolds,
even the story of her own life—involving the renunciation of child
and family—implies a script for female achievement that entails a
frightening repetition compulsion. Yet still, despite such ironies, the
gorgeous costuming of Act I's dinner party evokes both the pa-
geantry of the militant suffrage movement that Winifred Holtby
recounted in 1935 and the festive *Dinner Party* of women that Judy
Chicago mounted in 1979.[62] Painfully, mournfully, exuberantly, all
these female descendants of women who experienced "love that
never died—loneliness that never died" seem, at least in some part
of themselves, to want to say "Magnificent, all of you."

———

Perhaps, however, the most distinctive way of confronting the
problems and possibilities of a literary matrilineage is through the
composition of lyric poetry. Though both criticism and fiction based
on critical revision attempt to recover timeless instances of female
literary authority, even criticism is to some extent constrained by

causality. To contextualize a text, after all, is to historicize it. The lyric, however, can evoke fantastic (utopian or dystopian) moments of being in which the female precursor may openly function as a muse or an anti-muse for the daughter artist. Emily Dickinson in the nineteenth century, for instance, celebrated the achievements of such foremothers as Elizabeth Barrett Browning, George Eliot, and Charlotte Brontë with a kind of ecstasy, while a certain rueful animosity seems to have animated Barrett Browning's two sonnets to George Sand, a writer whom the English poet praises for being "True genius, but true woman," yet censures for her "vain denial" of her "woman's nature."[63]

In the twentieth century, however, the production of such ambivalent eulogies to precursors almost became an initiatory ritual gesture for women poets, who now confronted the ineradicable existence of what Barrett Browning had called "grandmothers." From Amy Lowell's "The Sisters" to Erica Jong's "Alcestis on the Poetry Circuit" (1973), modernist and postmodernist women poets have written verses defining the blessings and curses conferred on them by aesthetic ancestresses and peers.[64] A particularly magical example of a poem that blesses the female precursor is offered by Elizabeth Bishop's subversively celebratory "Invitation to Miss Marianne Moore" (1955). Here, revising Pablo Neruda's "Alberto Rojas Jimenez Comes Flying," Bishop appropriates a male-invented structure to call up the powers of a woman who had been not only her literary but her literal mentor. More specifically, in what resembles the classical poet's traditional invocation of the muse, this admirer of Moore's repeatedly asks her older friend to "please come flying" (as the ghost of Jimenez had come flying to Neruda), and the woman she evokes at first seems to be a spirit of place, in particular a spirit of Brooklyn, soaring over the Brooklyn Bridge—perhaps, indeed, over the poetic tradition embodied by Hart Crane's *The Bridge* (1930)—and over the rivers, skyscrapers, libraries, and museums of Manhattan.[65] But Bishop's Moore also seems to be a bit of a witch, "with the pointed toe of each black shoe / trailing a sapphire highlight" and "with a black capeful of butterfly wings and bon-mots." Indeed, the consummation Bishop devoutly wishes to achieve in her confrontation with this woman artist seems not only erotic but also apocalyptic: erotic because Bishop envisions Moore "com[ing]" and

"mounting" the "white mackerel sky / . . . like a daytime comet,"
apocalyptic because Moore's "com[ing]" and "mounting" herald what
Adrienne Rich calls "a whole new poetry beginning here."[66]

Pictured first as a sort of Old Testament deity "In a cloud of fiery
pale chemicals," and later "with heaven knows how many angels all
riding / on the broad black rim of [her] hat," Moore flies over a
Manhattan "all awash with morals," a society corrupted by "taxicabs
and injustices at large." Transcending "the accidents . . . the malig-
nant movies," she seems to presage an "uninvented music" that ac-
companies the disintegration of culture as her female poetic hier-
ophant knows it. For, like a woman Orpheus, Moore, says Bishop,
will tame the lions "on the steps of the Public Library" so that they
will "rise and follow through the doors / up into the reading rooms,"
presumably to range through the shelves devouring unacceptable
poetry. What Bishop wants to share with Moore is a shopping spree
or a good cry ("We can sit down and weep; we can go shopping");
what she fears is that the two will be forced to analyze their own
alienation ("We can . . . play at a game of constantly being wrong /
with a priceless set of vocabularies, / or we can bravely deplore").

But in any case, Moore offers Bishop a cleansing apotheosis of
linguistic destruction—"dynasties of negative constructions / darkening and dying around you / . . . grammar that suddenly turns and
shines"—a vocabulary of annihilation which implies that the union
of the woman poet with her precursor might constitute a healing
break with the past, a break motivated by "natural heroism." Moreover, in its combination of an ostensibly decorous tea-party title
("*Invitation* to *Miss* Marianne Moore") with an exuberantly transfigured landscape ("The waves are running in verses this fine morning"), Bishop's daughterly incantation suggests that the woman who
comes bearing "a long unnebulous train of words" might be greeted
at, and with, a reception that would definitively inspire Bishop's own
poetic future as well as that of the daughter-poet's readers. At the
same time, it is impossible not to notice that, perhaps precisely because "Invitation to Miss Marianne Moore" is about a real woman
toward whom—as Bishop's memoir of Moore reveals—Bishop had
ambivalent feelings, it is also a fantasy, a daydreaming fairy tale
about a literary fairy godmother in witch's clothing who could never
actually "come flying" across the Brooklyn Bridge as this wishful

invocation asks her to do, and whose "soft uninvented music" may well have, as Woolf said of Barrett Browning's *Aurora Leigh,* "no successors." Just as Bishop's ostensibly laudatory essay on Moore incorporates irony into its title—"*Efforts* of Affection" [italics ours]— Moore's own faintly ironic reading of the piece as a "magic poem— every word a living wonder" tacitly acknowledges this point.[67] Here, as in so many of Woolf's essays and fictions, the modernist woman's female precursor, newly substantial though she may be, is still associated with the equivocal sorcery Emily Dickinson in the nineteenth century attributed to what she called Elizabeth Barrett Browning's "Tomes of solid Witchcraft" (J. 593).

A similar air of fantasy permeates Sarton's "Letter from Chicago," the poem with which we began this meditation on matrilineage. To be sure, where Bishop's poem is from the first an incantatory invitation and thus frankly wishful, Sarton's starts as an elegiac farewell, a piece that is openly wistful. Recording her abandonment in a "city of departures" by a dead literary mother, the poet sees herself as dead and surrounded by death, cut off from a maternal heritage which is itself morbid and moribund: "I met your death," she tells Woolf, "and did not recognize you." But then, interestingly, the poem's turn from lamentation to affirmation is manifested through a series of paradoxes and oxymorons which follow a four-year period that has passed since "the world [was] arrested at the instant of [the literary mother's] death." Becoming "the city of arrival," Chicago is transformed into a place where Woolf can be present—and can be given "presents"—precisely because she is absent. Because Woolf is "not, never to be again," she is "Never, never to be dead, / Never to be dead again in this city." "Detached from time, but given to the moment," Woolf makes time flow for the American poet even while this English precursor herself, like the objects of so many of her own critical essays, inhabits an eternally inspiring moment of being. Thus time itself is finally both transformed and transcended. When Sarton concludes her love letter to Woolf with the line "I send you love forward into the past," she implies that for literary women redemptive time must flow oxymoronically: in order to move "forward" into one's own life, one must quest backward into the lives and lines of foremothers like Woolf.

That Sarton's excavation of Woolf's vitality begins not with the novelist's life but with her death—a death, indeed, which was self-chosen, self-inflicted—suggests that what the younger woman has specifically had to come to terms with is the older woman's inexorable autonomy and the pain associated with that autonomy. Thus, when we place this poem in the context of the affiliation complex, we can see that the literary daughter who turns for empowerment to a powerful mother must work through a sense of anxiety about the mother's independence to a recognition that just such independence both undermines and validates her own search for literary authority. More, that Sarton's account of her own and her foremother's metamorphoses is couched in a rhetoric of paradox, just as Bishop's invocation of Moore is filtered through fairytale metaphors while Woolf's own critical essays often include elements of voyeuristic fantasizing, inevitably reminds us that all these writers did continue to inhabit a male-dominated culture, and specifically a culture in which it was still, as Freud's work implied, more "realistic" for a daughter to turn to the father than to the mother. If twentieth-century "writing women"—to go back to Sarton's "My Sisters, O My Sisters"—were no longer "strange monsters" without matrilineal options, they nevertheless had to struggle to find images and metaphors in which they could envision "the deep place where the poet becomes woman . . . And that great sanity, that sun, the feminine power."

———

Not only must the female precursor be invoked, then, but, by implication, threatening male precursors and contemporaries must be annihilated, their "dynasties of negative constructions" must darken and die. A number of female-authored fictions and critical statements attempt to perform either comically or seriously such acts of destruction, though as usually happens in the battle of the sexes, there is an asymmetry between the (literary) man's case and the (literary) woman's cause, with women often seeming to fear that any hostile gesture might subject them to swift and merciless reprisals.

"Lady Tal," the novella by Vernon Lee which we mentioned in connection with father-daughter affiliation, also analyzes the dynamics of the relationship between a James figure, Gervaise Marion, and the would-be novelist Lady Atalanta Walkenshaw in what is clearly an attempt to discredit the real Henry James, and, as James himself believed, "Lady Tal" is in many ways a successful attack on the author of *The Bostonians* because it is a portrait of the artist as an effete expatriate who is more properly characterized as "Mary Anne" than "Marion" (107). When the "huge, strongly-knit" (81) Lady Tal manages to bully Marion into revising her novel-in-progress, he feels himself to become "a kind of male daily governess" (111). Worse still, he is gradually degraded into a figure of fun, clumsily carrying packages for his so-called pupil, who is a philanthropist as well as a woman of letters. Most woundingly, however, even while Lee's story caricatures James/Marion's "spinsterish" foibles, it anatomizes the novelist's more serious defects. This writer's interest in Lady Tal, the narrator suggests, is not really pedagogical but, rather, aesthetic, for he yearns to make her into a character; "the demon of psychological study [has] got the better" of him (95). No wonder, then, that after hearing about this satiric tale, James himself called Lee a "tiger cat."[68]

Yet though James is clearly the target of Vernon Lee's ridicule, even in her satiric portrait of his heartless voyeurism she gives him growing power over the aspiring woman novelist. As the expert who corrects her mistakes, he teaches her that she is "a poor, helpless ignoramus with literary aspirations" (90) and actually forces her to conclude that she will never again attempt an ambitious artistic project. Indeed, by the end of the work, she has virtually proposed marriage to him (as well as a collaboration in which she would be a foolish junior partner), a gesture that is particularly draconian in view of the fact that she will lose her late husband's great estate if she remarries. Moreover, diminished as he is by Lady Tal, Marion even more severely diminishes her, noting that her novel is so imitative that "as a matter of fact she had not produced that novel at all" (88).[69]

Similarly ambivalent attacks on literary men are incorporated into a range of other fictions by women, from Dorothy Richardson's portrait of H. G. Wells as Hypo Wilson in *Pilgrimage* to Doris Lessing's depiction of Clancy Segal as Saul Green in *The Golden Notebook* and Joyce Carol Oates's caricature of Mark Twain in *A Bloodsmoor Romance.*[70] In both public and private critical statements, however, but especially in private ones, twentieth-century women are often

considerably more biting about their male rivals. Dorothy Richardson, for instance, characterized Henry James's style "as a non-stop
waggling of the backside" which leaves readers feeling as if they are
in "a resounding box, where no star shines and no bird sings."[71]
More famously, Virginia Woolf complained in her diary that James
Joyce was "a queasy undergraduate scratching his pimples. . . . a he-
goat," called her friend T. S. Eliot "anaemic," and fumed that in
his moralistic prose D. H. Lawrence "pants and jerks."[72] Against
T. S. Eliot in particular, even more vitriolic charges were leveled by
Genevieve Taggard and Meridel Le Sueur. "In Prufrock," wrote
Taggard to a correspondent, "Eliot shows the first grown-up evidence of his hatred of humanity—his rejection of one half of the
human race," while in *The Waste Land* "Eliot comes out against
everything that democracy in its growing expanding health stands
for" so that she hopes "he is . . . in our time, utterly defeated."[73]
Even more grimly, Meridel Le Sueur once confided to an interviewer
that "I consider the darkest time of my life in '23 when T. S. Eliot
published The Wasteland" [sic], adding that the poem "is about death
. . . straw men, going out with a whimper . . . a terrible influence."
To another interviewer she remarked, "Fortunately, Eliot didn't
speak of hollow women."[74]

The competitiveness that underlies such attacks comes to the surface in a well-known remark that Gertrude Stein once made about
James Joyce:

> Joyce is good. He is a good writer. People like him because he
> is incomprehensible and nobody can understand him. But who
> came first, Gertrude Stein or James Joyce? Do not forget that
> my first great book, *Three Lives*, was published in 1908. That
> was long before *Ulysses*.[75]

Similarly, the anxiety that shadows competitiveness, the fear of male
exploitation or reprisal, was formulated in various ways by both Anaïs Nin and Elizabeth Bishop. Nin, a woman who was often adulatory
about men of letters—for example, about D. H. Lawrence and Henry
Miller—protested the treatment that Zelda Fitzgerald and Caitlin
Thomas received from their literary husbands, declaring that "For
too many centuries women have been busy being muses to the art-

ists."[76] And Bishop, who was, besides being Moore's disciple, usually supportive of male colleagues, complained about William Carlos Williams's publication of Marcia Nardi's letters in *Paterson* and about Robert Lowell's invasion of Elizabeth Hardwick's privacy in *The Dolphin*.[77]

But again it is in lyric poetry, especially in poems which develop fantastic scripts, that the literary daughter's reconstruction of female literary potency is often balanced by a vengeful deconstruction of male literary authority; blessings (albeit ambivalent ones) are shadowed by curses. Not surprisingly, in other words, for at least a few women writers one crucial act of aesthetic assertion is an act of figurative murder, an assault. Unpleasant as this may seem, it is perhaps inevitable that it should be so, given the historical struggle in which so many twentieth-century women writers have been enmeshed— the battles of father against mother, brother against sister that we have recounted in these chapters. Thus Gertrude Stein fulminates against "Patriarchal Poetry," which she sees as everyone's "history their origin," and Amy Lowell produces in "The Revenge" (1922) a ballad whose plot curiously recapitulates the contours of Beerbohm's "The Crime."[78]

Explaining how "All night I read a little book" which was a "hellish thing" authored by a man who "squeezed and drained" others "to give him drink" and whose wife had "gone mad," Lowell's speaker confesses in "The Revenge" that

> I took that little shy, sleek book
> And set a crimson match to it.
> It crinkled like a freshet brook,
> And flaked and vanished, bit by bit.
>
> There was no book my hands could hold,
> No book my eyes could ever see
> But round my head it ran, a bold
> Ironical phylactery.   [*CP* 571–72]

Unlike Beerbohm's narrator, in other words, this vengeful reader does manage to incinerate the text that offends her, yet even so she too fails to annihilate the words that have enraged her, for she has, to her own horror, internalized them. Ultimately, then, the only successful vendetta she can imagine is, amusingly enough, one based on scholarship and criticism:

> I'll write down his biography
> So that the world will die of laughter.
> I'll pin him like a squirming fly,
> A comic spasm of hereafter. . . .
>
> I'll leave him not a decent rag
> Of tragedy to wrap about him.
> I'll hang him up as a red flag
> Till every street boy learns to shout him. . . .
>
> He slew me for a time, admitted;
> But I shall slay him for all time.
> Poor shrivelled clown whom I've outwitted,
> I pardon you your poisoned rhyme.

In "real life," of course, Lowell's own major act of scholarship was a loving one: her adulatory biography of John Keats.[79] Nevertheless, in her long, ambitious *A Critical Fable*, whose structure she admitted borrowing from her uncle James Russell Lowell's *A Fable for Critics*, she did seek to "slay . . . for all time" what she regarded as the "poisoned rhyme" of such male contemporaries as Ezra Pound and T. S. Eliot. Loosely-accented and wide-ranging, this compendious work includes many lines of homage to female peers like Sara Teasdale and (especially) H. D., as well as tributes to a number of Lowell's favorite male colleagues.[80] But significantly, as if determined to revenge herself on Pound and his circle for their scornful characterization of Imagism as "Amygism," she singles out the authors of *The Cantos* and *The Waste Land* as "a few odds and ends" who deserve special vituperation, vituperation which occupies three closely set pages and which includes such savage lines as:

> In order of merit, if not of publicity,
> I will take Eliot first, though it smacks of duplicity

To award Ezra Pound the inferior place
As he simply won't run if not first in a race.
Years ago, 'twould have been the other way round,
With Eliot a rather bad second to Pound.
But Pound has been woefully free with the mustard
And so occupied has quite ruined his custard.
No poems from his pen, just spleen on the loose,
And a man who goes on in that way cooks his goose.
T. S. Eliot's a very unlike proposition,
He has simply won through by process of attrition.
When Pound played the fool, Eliot acted the wiseacre;
Eliot works in his garden, Pound stultifies his acre.
Eliot's always engaged digging fruit out of dust;
Pound was born in an orchard, but his trees have the rust. . . .
Pound believes he's a thinker, but he's far too romantic;
Eliot's sure he's a poet when he's only pedantic.
But Eliot has raised pedantry to a pitch,
While Pound has upset romance into a ditch. . . .
Eliot knows what he knows, though he cannot digest it;
Pound knows nothing at all, but has frequently guessed it.
Eliot builds up his essays but a process of massing;
Pound's are mostly hot air, what the vulgar call 'gassing.'
Eliot lives like a snail in his shell, pen protruding;
Pound struts like a cock, self-adored, self-adored, self-
   deluding. . . .
Each despises his fellows, for varying reasons;
Each one is a traitor, but with different treasons.   [*CP* 429–30]

In fact, she adds in a final paroxysm of vindictiveness, Eliot's poems
are "chilly and dead like corpses on ice" and Pound is a "consummate
quack" (*CP* 431–32).

Lowell's anger at Pound and Eliot may have been unusually intense, and it certainly had understandable historical roots, but judg-
ing by the verses, comic and serious, produced by other women
poets, it was not altogether idiosyncratic. Dorothy Parker's hilarious
"A Pig's-Eye View of Literature" (1928), for instance, treats eminent
male precursors scathingly. Among other things, Parker takes on

that "trio of lyrical treats / . . . Byron and Shelley and Keats," notes
that

> Dante Gabriel Rossetti
> Buried all of his *libretti*,
> Thought the matter over—then
> Went and dug them up again [,]

observes that "Carlyle combined the lit'ry life / With throwing tea-
cups at his wife," and prays

> Should Heaven send me any son,
> I hope he's not like Tennyson.
> I'd rather have him play a fiddle
> Than rise and bow and speak an idyll.[81]

More recently, Julia Randall's "To William Wordsworth" (1961) indicts the Romantic prophet of nature as an "old bone," while Denise
Levertov's "Hypocrite Women" (1964) inveighs against a misogynistic
"white sweating bull of a poet," and Cynthia MacDonald's "Instructions from Bly" (1973) satirically critiques some sententious advice
once offered by the male writer who was destined to become a star
of the contemporary "wild man movement" ("if I was serious / I must
isolate myself for at least a year").[82]

But it is in Sylvia Plath's "Burning the Letters" (1962) that we
find the most passionate, poignant, and in a sense representative
spell cast against a figure whom we have seen in this volume as a
paradigmatic man of letters. Written on the other side of a draft of
Ted Hughes's frequently anthologized "The Thought Fox" (1956)
that Plath herself had typed,[83] this caustic curse responds to Plath's
husband's famous poem just as bitterly as Lowell's *A Critical Fable*
reacts against the works of Pound and Eliot, but with far more pain.
Indeed, like Lowell's "The Revenge," Plath's poem re-enacts the basic
situation dramatized in Beerbohm's "The Crime," and it revises, as
well, the dramatic actions of Mary Cholmondeley's *Red Pottage* and
Mary E. Wilkins Freeman's "A Poetess." For in "Burning the Letters"
Plath's speaker attempts to commit exactly the same crime that
Beerbohm and Lowell record—and to reverse exactly the tragedies
that Cholmondeley and Freeman recount—but in her case the

"crime" is a murder of the "immense" and "intense vitality" expressed in the "white fists" of her literary husband's old letters.

Like Beerbohm's character, Plath's speaker wonders about the words she finds—"What did they know that I didn't?"—and, like Beerbohm's character, she tries to destroy the language of her sexual opposite: in the manuscript version of the poem, she exults that "The mouth of this house is shut. With the butt of a rake / I open the white words that would save themselves," and in the work's final form she crows that her husband's words have "nothing to say to anybody. / I have seen to that. / With the butt of a rake / I flake up papers that breathe like people." In fact, her claim to have achieved an obliteration of her patrilineal past's linguistic traces seems definitive, at least at first: "This fire may lick and fawn, but it is merciless," she boasts, adding that "here is an end to the writing. . . ." Just as the narrator of Beerbohm's "The Crime" at first seems confident that he has "triumphed" over his female literary rival, and just as Lowell's speaker is initially sure that the offending book has "flaked and vanished, bit by bit," Plath's speaker at first appears certain of her victory over the literary man who has betrayed her.

Oddly, however, Plath's poem ends with a mysterious vision of immortality and, even more oddly, with a vision of immortality that is associated with the death of a fox. Earlier in the piece, the cardboard cartons of letters that the speaker wants to burn have been somewhat bizarrely compared to "a dog pack / Holding in its hate / Dully, under a pack of men in red jackets." Then, in the last stanza, as the speaker herself becomes the fire that consumes contaminated language—"My veins glow like trees"—she quite suddenly imagines "dogs . . . tearing a fox" and with horror notes that "This is what it is like— / A red burst and a cry / That . . . goes on

> Dyeing the air
> Telling the particles of the clouds, the leaves, the water
> What immortality is. That it is immortal.

What "are" the dogs here, and who "is" the fox? The poem's early association of the letters with a "dog pack" would suggest that the letters themselves are the dogs and that their dull hate is a canine rage which gnaws at the incendiary speaker no matter how she assaults them "with the butt of a rake," that, indeed, even when they flake into "carbon birds" and punningly dye (in) the air, the words of the letters are ineradicable, so immortal that they propose a tautological definition of immortality, telling the landscape "What immortality is. That it is immortal." In that case, however—if the letters "are" the dogs—then the speaker "is" the fox: even while she seeks to annihilate their "spry hooks" they tear at her, eliciting "a red burst and a cry" of rage, the poem that must go on enacting its own defeat over and over again, immortally.

Yet the literal as well as literary association of Plath's fox-haunted "Burning the Letters" with Hughes's "The Thought Fox" implies another possibility: because the "thought-fox" is an emblem of Hughes's own creativity enigmatically emerging from a midnight forest,[84] his estranged wife's positioning of her poem on the verso side of a manuscript draft of his lyric implies that both metonymically and metaphorically Hughes may "be" the fox here, with the enraged Plath's wishes transformed into a pack of dogs tearing at *him*. But again, even if that is the case, "Burning the Letters" records the defeat of its own intentions. For though the fox splits, bursts, and cries, its shriek of death nevertheless "goes on" to propose a definition of immortality. Whether the speaker or her betrayer "is" the fox, in other words, the poem ultimately fails to accomplish the promised "end to the writing": on the one hand, if she "is" the fox, the work enacts the immortality of her *defeat;* on the other hand, if he "is" the fox, the work dramatizes the *immortality* of his defeat. Like Beerbohm's narrator, then, Plath's speaker discovers that she cannot extinguish the "immense" and "intense vitality" of her sexual opposite/opponent. Wielding rakes, incinerating language, both have sought to obliterate the sentences of a sexual other who would, they fear, sentence them to secondariness, and both—to use Beerbohm's words—have "failed miserably."

There is a significant difference, however, between "The Crime," on the one hand, and "Burning the Letters" (or "The Revenge") on the other, a difference that may allow us a few further speculations about the male/female literary dialectic that is so often embodied in the writings of premodernists, modernists, and postmodernists from Beerbohm to Plath. While Beerbohm's narrator's "crime" against his woman novelist's text ends up putting *his* fire out, Plath's speaker's attempted murder of male letters sets *her* on fire (and, comparably, though less theatrically, Lowell finds in "The Revenge" that her rage "scalds my head," for "Hate is a torch"). Alone in the dark, Beerbohm's literary man feels himself to be out in the cold, ashen, impotent. Torn up by rage, Plath's arsonist of the alphabet has to concede that her "veins glow like trees." Beerbohm's anxiety at his impotence—his failure to ravage the print of a woman of letters—is matched by Plath's anger at her own defeat by what the last line of Hughes's poem victoriously calls "the page [that] is printed," Hughes's page, indelibly printed on the other side of her own.

If we set Plath's curse of a male counterpart against Bishop's blessing of a female precursor and, by implication, against the conflicted attitudes expressed in all the fictional, critical, and poetic visions of a literary ancestry that we have explored in this chapter, what do we learn? We would argue that such a juxtaposition teaches us something about the magnitude of the problem faced by twentieth-century women writers, who perceived themselves as seriously threatened by many of their male contemporaries even while they also experienced with profound ambivalence their own new potency in literary history. Certainly a number of twentieth-century men of letters, in defending themselves against the emergent frailties of literature's patrilineage, have surrounded literary women with a wall of resistance and rage. Countless texts build that wall and affirm its strength, texts including the works of James, Joyce, Eliot, Hemingway, and Williams that we have studied here. And perhaps in this context, a particularly telling gesture was made by Hughes: though Plath's poem may or may not record a fantasy about burning *his* letters, he did—as he revealed a few years ago—incinerate an entire volume of her journal shortly after she had gassed herself in the oven of her London flat in the winter of 1963.[85]

At the same time, however, even while many women writers in this period felt themselves to be threatened by male resistance, these artists had also, as they struggled forward into the past, to explore the implications of Amy Lowell's claim that her female literary relatives were suddenly "near, / Frightfully near and rather terrifying" (*CP*, 409). To these literary daughters, it may have seemed that female as well as male precursors and contemporaries taught a lesson comparable to the one Plath learned at the end of "Burning the Letters": "What immortality is. That it is immortal." In particular, it was through the complexities of the female affiliation complex that twentieth-century literary women confronted the aesthetic immortality of their newly found foremothers, an immortality that inspired many of these thinkers to dream of revising and mythologizing the mother tongue itself.

Sexual Linguistics:
Women's Sentence,
Men's Sentencing

> Books must be read as deliberately and reservedly as they were written. It is not enough even to be able to speak the language of that nation by which they are written, for there is a memorable interval between the spoken and the written language, the language heard and the language read. The one is commonly transitory, a sound, a tongue, a dialect merely, almost brutish, and we learn it unconsciously, like the brutes, of our mothers. The other is the maturity and experience of that; if that is our mother tongue, this is our father tongue, a reserved and select expression, too significant to be heard by the ear, which we must be born again in order to speak.
>
> —Henry David Thoreau

> Give me initiative, spermatic, prophesying, man-making words.
>
> —Ralph Waldo Emerson

> I know, I feel
> the meaning that words hide;
>
> they are anagrams, cryptograms,
> little boxes, conditioned
>
> to hatch butterflies . . .
>
> —H. D.

> My words now must be as slow, as new, as single, as tentative as the steps I took going down the path away from the house, between the dark-branching tall dancers motionless against the winter shining.
>
> —Ursula K. Le Guin

Is anatomy linguistic destiny? Is a womb a metaphorical mouth, a pen a metaphorical penis? Throughout the last hundred years, masculinist and feminist theorists alike have toyed with the idea of an anatomically determined body language which translates the terms and articulations of the body into that body of articulated terminology we call language. That language has such a sexual charge, moreover, is evident not only from these theoretical speculations but also from the belligerent dramas enacted by, say, Max Beerbohm and Amy Lowell, Ted Hughes and Sylvia Plath. For all these figures, words, at one point or another, become not only weapons but booty to be gained, spoil to be incinerated, or hostages to be massacred, suggesting that a major campaign in the battle of the sexes is the conflict over language and, specifically, over competing male and female claims to linguistic primacy.

Lately, in particular, linguistically minded critics and philosophers have increasingly called attention to the indeterminacy of the terms through which we think we know the world, while psychoanalytic theorists have increasingly emphasized the psychological forces that determine the apparently logical terms in which we think we think. Inevitably, therefore, schools of "phallologocentrists," anti-"phallologocentrists," and what we might call "vulvalogocentrists" have arisen to meditate on the sexuality of linguistics and the linguistics of sexuality. For if language is a process of cultural artifice that both distances and defines nature, then it would seem that its words and workings might well embody the bodily differences through which each human being first confronts the fundamental sexuality of his or her own nature. It might seem, in other words, that as Julia Kristeva puts it, "Sexual difference—which is at once biological, physiological, and relative to reproduction—is translated by and translates a difference in the relationship of subjects to the symbolic contract which *is* the social contract; a difference, then, in the relationship to power, language, and meaning."[1]

In this chapter, attempting to integrate the divergent forces of power, language, and meaning, we will examine this relationship between sexual difference and the symbolic contract in an effort primarily to trace the permutations of the modern battle over language and secondarily to place recent ideas about sexual linguistics in a larger historical context. For, as we shall suggest, contemporary language theorists—female and male—participate in a long, bifurcated tradition of feminist and masculinist linguistic fantasy. That such a tradition demonstrably exists, moreover, implies an intuition of the primacy of the mother rather than the father in the process of language acquisition that assimilates the child into what Kristeva calls the "symbolic contract." Thus, questioning Kristeva's identification of the symbolic contract with the social contract, we will draw upon precisely the complex literary history that we have already discussed—the history of the last one hundred years in England and America—to argue that the female subject is not necessarily alienated from the words she writes and speaks.

Significantly, the English woman who most publicly entered into the linguistic fray by defining a female literary tradition saw gender-marked words as potentially central to that tradition's vitality. In one of the most famous yet most opaque passages in *A Room of One's Own*, Virginia Woolf introduces her notoriously puzzling concept of "a woman's sentence." Remarking that the early nineteenth-century woman novelist found that "there was no common sentence ready for her use," she declared that the "man's sentence" inherited by "Thackeray and Dickens and Balzac" from "Johnson, Gibbon and the rest" was as alien to her mind as "the [hardened and set] older forms of literature" were to her imagination (78–80). Her comment, like the literary history in which it is embedded, seems appealingly empirical. Those of us who wish to understand the relationship between genre and gender, Woolf seems to imply—even those who wish to examine the more ontological connection between sexuality and creativity—need merely analyze and classify linguistic structures.

Yet despite Woolf's ardor, no serious research into empirical linguistics has definitively disclosed what might be the special traits of "a woman's sentence" or has even revealed those secondary sexual characteristics which define Woolf's normative "man's sentence." Although such American and British linguists as Robin Lakoff and Dale Spender have recently shown that there are notably different male and female speech behaviors and vocabularies, their research does not really prove Woolf's point. For—in spite of their critique of lexical asymmetries and "he-man" pronouns, as well as their analyses of gender-related syntactic patterns, interruption frequencies, and even vocabulary preferences—they do not agree on whether women speak a distinctive language or whether they are perceived to speak such a language.[2] Indeed, thinkers seem to come much closer to the heart of the matter when they abandon empirical projects altogether and study those theories about the "hierarchized oppositions" of patriarchal language that have been so compellingly articulated by Hélène Cixous and other contemporary French feminists as part of their effort to imagine a female body language, a *"parler femme"* or *"écriture féminine."*

At the same time, however, where the moderate claims of empirical linguistics are both too moderate and too empirical to reveal the theoretical fullness Woolf's passage seems to promise, the words of Cixous and, say, Luce Irigaray often seem almost immoderately mystical in their straining to "invent the other history," to describe woman as "only this space, always virginal, matter subjected to the desire that [man] wishes to imprint," and to imagine a female language which is *"always in the process of weaving itself, of embracing itself with words, but also of getting rid of words in order not to become fixed, congealed in them."*[3] Indeed, it seems singularly odd for Julia Kristeva to observe that in Woolf's own writing "language seems to be seen from a foreign land . . . from the point of view of an asymbolic, spastic body."[4] For Woolf—always a practical literary critic and a conscious historian of the female tradition—may have felt that women's language would provide passwords into a land as new and foreign as Elvedon, but she would surely never have recognized herself in Kristeva's peculiarly medicalized portrait. What, then, did she mean when she dreamt of, yet did not define, "a woman's sentence"?

Provisionally, we want to suggest that Woolf used what was essentially a *fantasy* about a utopian linguistic structure—a "woman's sentence"—to define (and perhaps disguise) her desire to revise not woman's language but woman's relation to language. In fact, we want to argue that, when in *A Room of One's Own* she elaborates upon her dream of the woman writer Mary Carmichael, Woolf at least half-consciously means that her fictive Mary has triumphed not by creating a new sentence-as-grammatical unit but by overturning the sentence-as-definitive-judgment, the sentence-as-decree-or-interdiction, by which woman has been kept from feeling that she can be in full command of language. The utopian concept of woman's grammatical sentence is thus for Woolf, as also perhaps for contemporary American and French linguists, a veil that conceals the more practical idea of woman's legal sentence. More, the ambiguity of the phrase "woman's sentence"—for who is being sentenced? and who is sentencing whom?—is a veil behind which Woolf may be imagining feats of epic prestidigitation: woman, who has been sentenced by man, will now sentence man; and woman, who has been sentenced to confinement and dispossession, will now sentence herself to freedom and five hundred pounds a year. Finally, we want to suggest that, in articulating this visionary revision of the "common" English sentence, Woolf was working in a mode of linguistic fantasy that has been increasingly important since the turn of the century.

As a number of feminist literary critics have recently shown, the traditional masculinist conclusion to the supposition that anatomy is linguistic destiny is far from flattering to the female speaker or writer. In the Middle Ages, the alleged loquacity of women was diagnosed as a biological disorder, a disease of logorrhea, and Renaissance conduct books instructed women against "babbl[ing] out all at large," for they "haue no regarde what they say, but what so euer cometh on theyr tonges ende."[5] Furthermore, from Spenser to Swift, the "Goddesses" of Errour and Criticism were said to exude a poisonous, contaminating language, and Pope thought "th' hysteric or poetic fit" was especially dangerous in a woman, while Edward Young proclaimed, "With skill she vibrates her eternal tongue, / For ever most divinely in the wrong."[6] If it was not actually defined as virulent, moreover, the mouth of woman was thought to gabble in a nonlanguage of garbled syntax and lexical confusion. From Fielding's Mrs. Slipslop to Sheridan's Mrs. Malaprop, such verbose creatures dramatize the idea that the more pretensions women have to learning, the less they know.[7]

Despite this long history of linguistic misogyny, male defenses against female speech became even more fierce once the middle-class woman began to write. William Faulkner makes explicit the implicit assumption behind these attacks on woman's garrulousness when one of his male characters, celebrating the feminine ideal as "a virgin with no legs to leave me, no arms to hold me, no head to talk to me," defines woman generically as "merely [an] articulated genital organ."[8] Whether like Joyce's fluidly fluent Anna Livia Plurabelle, woman ceaselessly burbles and babbles on her way to her "cold mad feary father," or whether like his fluently fluid Molly Bloom, she dribbles and drivels as she dreams of male jinglings, her artless jingles are secondary and asyntactic.[9] Molly's bewilderment at the classical concept of "metempsychosis" and her implicit metamorphosis of it into the babble of "Met him pike hoses" exemplify the parrot-like blankness with which Joyce's women respond to abstract concepts.[10] Another, and perhaps more poignant example is their inability to name, and thus claim, even the functions of their own bodies, an incapacity manifested in Gertie McDowell's speculation that "that thing must be coming on" (361) and Molly's similar worry about "getting that thing like that every week" as well as her bemusement by the word "vagina" and her significant transformation of "emissions" into "omissions" (770). But the "omission" of intellect such problems represent is probably best summarized by Bloom's musicological meditations in "Sirens," first on the notion that female singers "can't manage men's intervals" and have a "*Gap* in their voices too" (emphasis ours), then on the "chamber music" of his wife's "tinkling," which leads him to conclude that "Empty vessels make most noise" (282), then on the virgin female's "Blank face" which needs to be written on like a "page" (for "If not what becomes of them?"), and finally on the female body as a "flute alive" on which man must "Blow gentle" or "Loud" because "Three holes all women" (285). Clearly, in endowing Bloom with such speculations, Joyce is taking upon himself the Holy Office of pronouncing that woman, both linguistically and biologically, is wholly orifice.

At bottom, for Joyce, woman's scattered logos is a scatologos, a Swiftian language that issues from the many obscene mouths of the female body. When she speaks as Molly in Joyce's passages, she passes blood and water; when Joyce implores her to write, as he does Nora in 1909, she is begged to express a calligraphy of shit: "Write the dirty words big and underline them and kiss them and hold them for a moment to your sweet hot cunt, darling, and also pull up your dress a moment and hold them in under your dear little farting bum. Do *more* if you wish and send the letter then to me, my darling brown-arsed fuckbird."[11] Furthermore, when, like

Joyce's Gertie, a woman attempts to etherealize herself, the author wants his readers to realize that she can only ascend to sentimentality. Thus, while Gertie's female bloomers titillate Bloom as Nora's did Joyce, the commercial crap of her genteel Victorian diction is at least in part associated with the reaction-formation of intensified misogyny with which male writers greeted the entrance of women into the literary marketplace.

That such a reaction-formation not only motivated metaphors of feminine blankness and babble but also led to visions of female evil is evidenced by a number of late-nineteenth-century, modernist, and postmodernist works of art. To go back to the fin de siècle, for instance, George de Feure's 1895 oil painting, *The Voice of Evil*,[12] usefully condenses male fantasies about female linguistic power into a single narrative tableau (figure, p. 234). Produced by a leading designer of the art nouveau movement who was also a sometime disciple of Baudelaire, *The Voice of Evil* seems at first to be little more than a misogynistic piece of exotic erotica that might not be out of place in the later chapters of Mario Praz's *The Romantic Agony*. Pale and Byronic, a woman sits before a bizarrely cushioned writing table, facing a blank sheet of paper and a quill pen. She seems to have discarded her jewels (or is she about to put them on?) and a tall, hermaphroditic-looking but distinctly art nouveau *fleur du mal* rises surrealistically to one side of her, framing her and (in its emblematizing of forbidden desire) framing her up. In the background toward which her dreaming gaze is turned, a dark-skinned, red-haired, horned woman makes love to a pale woman who seems certainly to figure this dreaming foreground woman. And both the woman in the fantasy and the woman in the no less fantastic reality are attending, it appears, to "the voice of evil," a title that crucially expresses the male artist's anxiety about the voice of woman's linguistic desire as well as about the speech of her mysteriously alien sexual desire. Does de Feure, for instance, fear that, as the horned muse-woman in the dream whispers and touches her troubled rapt desirous friend, the musing woman in the foreground may sweep away the mind-forged manacles of her rings and bracelets, and begin to write her woman's words? Possessed by passion, she may usurp and possess language, both the voice of evil and the pen of power. Clearly, when she writes, her language will be *other*. Autonomous

Georges de Feure. *The Voice of Evil.* 1895. Collection Robert Walker, Paris. Photo: Cooper Bridgeman Library.

and opaque, it will be the speech of evil. So Georges de Feure has elegantly indicted and sentenced her before she can indite the sentence of her own freedom.

Like Basil Ransom in James's *The Bostonians,* a number of male modernists react against the voices of evil they associate with "a feminine, a nervous, hysterical, chattering, canting age. . . ." Such an entrance of hysteria into history is vividly dramatized by the young T. S. Eliot, James's Bostonian successor. The speaker of the prose-poem "Hysteria," for instance, stares into the deep throat of a laughing woman until he is "drawn in by short gasps" and "lost finally in the dark caverns of her throat, bruised by the ripple of unseen muscles" (24).[13] Although the poem implicitly examines (and perhaps ironically enacts) the madness of its male speaker, it also hints that this man suffers from a hysteria he has caught from his female companion, a hysteria about her *hyster,* her womb and its mysterious "hystery." Contaminated by the woman, he has been feminized and paralyzed in just the way Eliot's indecisive persona is in "The Love Song of J. Alfred Prufrock." "*Blood—mucous—shreds of mucous—purulent offensive discharge":* with this litany of words, underlined on a page torn from *The Midwives' Gazette,* Eliot responded to Conrad Aiken's praise of his *Poems* (1919), as if to suggest that the letters of literary men had been permanently polluted by the effusions of the *hyster.*[14] Similarly, for Pound, civilization is an "old bitch gone in the teeth," and his "Portrait d'une Femme" implies that woman is herself botched.[15] Asserting that "Your mind and you are our Sargasso Sea," he defines her as both the debris and the destroyer of a shipwrecked civilization: her "Ideas, old gossip, oddments of all things, / Strange spars of knowledge" are not fragments she has shored against her ruins; rather, they represent the ruinousness of a mind replete with "Nothing that's quite [her] own."

Finally, then, it is no wonder that the wastings of *The Waste Land* are epitomized by the hysterical speech of women who can "connect nothing with nothing." From the querulous questions of the neurasthenic lady in "A Game of Chess," to the abortion-haunted monologue of toothless Lil's faithless friend, to the fragmentary complaints of the ruined Thames daughters in "The Fire Sermon," the "Shakespehearian rag" intoned by Mrs. Porter and her daughter, and the evil "whisper music" that the vampire woman fiddles on the strings of her hair in "What the Thunder Said," the language of these women embodies "the horror, the horror" that the poet spells from an impotent sibyl's leaves and leavings.[16] For ultimately, like Joyce, Eliot transcribes female language in order to transcend it, thus justifying Joyce's claim that *The Waste Land* ended the "idea of poetry for ladies." But, as we have seen in such texts as Hemingway's "Lady Poets with Footnotes," Lawrence's *Women in Love*, West's *Miss Lonelyhearts*, and Faulkner's *Light in August*, a number of other male modernists who attacked creative or intellectual women were also attempting to end the idea of poetry for ladies, and they were often attempting to do so specifically by castigating what they defined as the incoherence or destructiveness of female language.

It was against such scorn as that expressed by, say, Eliot and Joyce that the new words of New Women's linguistic fictions had to contend, in a battle of the sexes that centered on the crucial issue of woman's command of language as against language's command of woman, a battle that redirects our attention to women's historic efforts to come to terms with the urgent need for female literary authority through fantasies about the possession of a mother tongue. As was the case in both the social and aesthetic struggles we have examined, however, female-authored theories of language were not and are not precisely symmetrical with male ones. Though Woolf wrote with some ambivalence about the "man's sentence" and though, more recently, feminist thinkers from Monique Wittig and Madeleine Gagnon to Adrienne Rich and Jane Gallop have inveighed against the "oppressor's language" spoken by patriarchal culture, women writers do not for the most part deride *men's* language in the way that men chastise women's speech.[17] On the contrary, where male writers often seem to define "woman talk" as a contaminated subset of the general category "language," women writers tend to assume that "men's language" *is* "language." Hence the female linguistic project is in many ways more urgent, more radical, and—as we shall see—more contradictory than the male one, for the women's revisionary imperative frequently involves a desperate effort to renovate the entire process of verbal symbolization, a process that, they feel, has historically subordinated women.

"Unhappy one," lament the heroines of Monique Wittig's *Les Guér-illères,*

> men have expelled you from the world of symbols and yet they
> have given you names, they have called you slave, you unhappy
> slave. Masters, they have exercised their right as master. They
> write, of their authority to accord names, that it goes back so
> far that the origin of language itself may be considered an act
> of authority emanating from those who dominate . . . the lan-
> guage you speak is made up of words that are killing you.[18]

As Wittig's concern with the originatory male "authority to accord
names" suggests, then, the female need to achieve a command over
language has, to begin with, been most practically expressed through
strategies of unnaming and renaming, strategies that directly address
the problem of woman's patronymically defined identity in western
culture. Any human subject, as Jacques Lacan points out, is in a
sense "the slave . . . of a discourse . . . in which his place is already
inscribed at birth, if only by virtue of his proper name."[19] At the
same time, though, the (male) linguistic preserve of history begins,
as Jacques Derrida has observed, with the empowering, rather than
enslaving, preservation of (male) names.[20] For woman in our culture,
however, a proper name is at best problematic; even as it "inscribes"
her into the present discourse of society by designating her role as
her father's daughter, her patronymic effaces her matrilineage and
thus erases her own position in the discourse of the future. Her
"proper" name, therefore, is always in a way *im*proper because it is
not, in the French sense, *propre*, her own, either to have or to give.
With what letters, then, can a woman of letters preserve herself?
How can she employ the alphabet to perpetuate the most elementary
trace of her identity?

Two twentieth-century works by women writers reveal both the
parameters and the persistence of this problem even while they hint
at the outlines of a solution that literary women have explored for
some centuries, but in the last one hundred years with increasing
intensity, in order to fortify themselves against male contempt. First,
Zora Neale Hurston's *Their Eyes Were Watching God* recounts the history of a heroine named Janie Crawford but nicknamed "Alphabet
'cause so many people had done named me different names" (21),

a point that reflects not only the primary dispossession of all women from "proper" nomenclature but also the double dispossession of black women, who have been exiled from their African heritage as well as from their matronymic. Becoming "Alphabet," moreover— or so Hurston implies—this woman would seem to have become no more than a character (like the letter of the alphabet) who signifies nothing for herself while facilitating the "circulation of signs" that reinforces communication among men.[21]

More recently, and even more explicitly, Ruth Stone mourns the lost names of her matrilineage in a poem named "Names":

> My grandmother's name was Nora Swan.
> Old Aden Swan was her father. But who was her mother?
> I don't know my great-grandmother's name.
> I don't know how many children she bore.
> Like rings of a tree the years of woman's fertility.
>   Who were my great aunt Swans?
>   . . . As anemone in mid-summer, the air
> cannot find them and grandmother's been at rest for forty
>   years. . . .[22]

If a woman is not a signifier in an alphabet possessed by men ("Old Aden Swan was her father"), speculates Stone, she would seem to be no more than a sort of function of the landscape. For instead of being graphed by distinguished inscriptions, women leave indistinguishable traces, natural accretions like the "rings of a tree" whose very presence attests to the absence of cultural identity. After all, adds Stone, "Who can bother naming all those women churning butter, / leaning on scrub boards, holding to iron bedposts / sweating in labor?"

Paradoxically, however, the terms in which Hurston and Stone put woman's linguistic problem begin to provide significant solutions which allow for female self-signification. The variety of "Alphabet's" social experience, for instance—represented by the range of her names—finally enables her to learn "de maiden language all over" (173). ". . . [N]ew thoughts had tuh be thought and *new words said*" (emphasis ours), Janie Crawford Killocks Starks Woods thinks after she has survived a succession of marital identities, and at the end of the novel, empowered by the saying of such words to tell her own story, she has become a sort of goddess who pulls "in her horizon like a great fish-net. [Pulls] it from around the waist of the world and [drapes] it over her shoulder" (286).

Similarly, though using a rather different strategy, Ruth Stone empowers herself in "Names" by imagining an alternative to patriarchal naming:

. . . My grandmother knew the names
of all the plants on the mountain. Those were the names
she spoke of to me. Sorrel, lamb's ear, spleenwort, heal-all;
never go hungry, she said, when you can gather a pot of greens.

Thus, though Stone doesn't know "who . . . the women [are] who nurtured" her grandmother for her, though "the air / cannot find" their names,

In me are all the names I can remember—pennyroyal, boneset,
bedstraw, toadflax—from whom I did descend in perpetuity.

What this poet recovers are names of power, regal autographs drawn from a feminized nature. Where Hurston prophesies a new ("maiden") language which postdates the inscriptions and descriptions of patriarchy, that is, Stone dreams of an archaic language which predates the patronymics of culture. Both, however, are gaining strength through fantasies of either an original or an originatory linguistic matrilineage, a "grandmatology" which they implicitly set against the patrilineal linguistics of the grammatology that they see as having historically subordinated them and their ancestresses.

Hurston's and Stone's fantasies are paradigmatic because, since the late nineteenth century, women of letters have defended themselves against the intimations of linguistic mortality conveyed to them, both by the nature of patriarchal culture and by the anger of literary men, through fantasies about names, letters, and languages, fantasies which consistently mythologize the female sign even as they authorize the female signature and validate womanly words. As is so often the case, Emily Dickinson is the foremother who articulates a fantasy about female linguistic power that empowers not only her verse but the voices of both her precursors and her successors. In the poem about Elizabeth Barrett Browning that begins "I think I was enchanted / When first a sombre Girl— / I read that

Foreign Lady," Dickinson appears to respond to Romney's charge in *Aurora Leigh* that his cousin Aurora's poetry is merely "witchcraft" (J. 593). Performing a proto-Derridean "renversement," this American artist subversively celebrates the "Divine Insanity" produced by Barrett Browning's "Tomes of solid Witchcraft." In particular, she redefines madness as the source of incantations by which "that Foreign Lady" the woman poet transforms even the most ordinary objects, metamorphosing bees to butterflies and quotidian nature into "Titanic Opera."

For Dickinson, moreover, such "Witchcraft has not a Pedigree / T'is early as our Breath" (J. 1708), the breath of a new life of female speech that she associates with the life breathed into her by Barrett Browning's enchanting chants. At the same time, she shows that, even without the authority of a recorded pedigree, such witchcraft establishes a secret ancestry outside the lines of any public genealogical tree, so that it serves as a linguistic/literary model through which the woman poet can express a sense of the primacy of her own words and their commonality with the words of other women writers. Thus, even while she concedes that "Witchcraft was hung, in History" (J. 1583), Dickinson not only emphasizes the historical sacrifice of the female associated with (illegitimate) speech and (illicit) sexuality, she also neatly turns the screw by identifying herself with (an implicitly alternative) history, as she predicts the continuing triumphs of this underground poetic community dedicated to "Conversions of the Mind" (J. 593).

That women like Dickinson should feel the need for a secret ancestry is made clear by the fact that, on the most literal level, the new words as well as the transformative new meanings of women artists have often been expressed by the new names they have conferred on themselves.[23] To be sure, from James MacPherson ("Ossian") to Samuel Clemens ("Mark Twain"), men have also employed noms de plume, but their motives for doing so have had neither the same consistency nor the same urgency as those which impelled literary women. Certainly, as we noted earlier, by the late nineteenth century the male pseudonym was quite specifically a mask behind which the female writer could hide her disreputable femininity, as did Charlotte Brontë ("Currer Bell"), Mary Ann Evans ("George Eliot"), Aurore Dupin Dudevant ("George Sand"), Mary Chavelita

Dunne ("George Egerton"), Katharine Bradley and Edith Cooper ("Michael Field"), Violet Paget ("Vernon Lee") and Ethel Florence Lindesay ("Henry Handel Richardson").

But a changing attitude toward female names was also evident in this period as well as later, and it was very likely related to the self-consciously revolutionary theories of feminists and suffragists who either kept their maiden names after marriage or used three names, a tradition that instantly became popular for women writers, especially in America. While such Victorian Englishwomen as Mrs. Gaskell, Mrs. Braddon, Mrs. Oliphant, and Mrs. Humphrey Ward had established their allegiance to marital respectability by acquiescing in the couverture of "Mrs.," such Americans as Charlotte Perkins [Stetson] Gilman, Mary E. Wilkins Freeman, Elizabeth Cady Stanton, Elizabeth Stuart Phelps Ward, and Edith Summers Kelly defined themselves through an accumulation of names that reflected compound identities and preserved a lineage that would otherwise be lost. From a male point of view, in fact, the power of such female genealogies was infuriating enough to instigate the sort of "jokes" about "Mary Roberts Wilcox, Ella Wheeler Catheter . . ." that Nathanael West records in *Miss Lonelyhearts.*

Even while women writers used accretions of real names to expand their identities, however, the pseudonym began to function more prominently as a name of power, the mark of a private christening into a second self, a rebirth into linguistic primacy. Olive Schreiner, for instance, married a man who took her maiden name as his own last name. But at the same time she published several works under the name of "Ralph Iron," employing "Ralph" as a tribute to Ralph Waldo Emerson and "Iron" as a signifier of an invulnerable new spirit achieved in the forge of change. To be sure, some twentieth-century women writers wanted to repudiate a stereotypically feminine gender identity: Lulu McCullers was happier with the androgynous family name "Carson," just as Mary O'Connor opted for "Flannery," and "Willa" Cather was so circumspect about her given name that, even after her death, Leon Edel had great difficulty establishing the fact that it was originally "Wilella."[21] But, like "Fanny Fern" or "Sarah Grand" in the late nineteenth century, a number of modernist women sought to make their names into icons of female artistry.

Born Cicely Fairfield, "Rebecca West" named herself after the feminist heroine of Ibsen's *Rosmersholm*, while Karen Dinesen went through the names "Tanne," "Karen Blixen," "Baroness," "The Lioness," and, as a writer, "Isak Dinesen."[25] Laura Gottschalk, nee Riechenthall, used the name "Laura Riding" until she began to sign her work "Laura (Riding) Jackson," while Winifred Ellerman renamed herself "Bryher" after one of the Scilly Isles.[26] What all these redefinitions have in common is an effort on the part of women to rid themselves of or transform the patronymic, an effort perhaps most dramatically enacted in the metamorphosis of the Anglo-American Pauline Tarn into the French poet "Renée Vivien." Born in the United States and raised in England, the woman artist called "Renée Vivien" renounced not only her familial but also her national origins when she took up residency in Paris and began to write fin de siècle verse in French. Her shift in identity gains particular resonance in her 1906 poem "Viviane," where she imagines herself as "born anew"—"Elle renait," in the original—because "Elle a changé de nom, de voix et de visage" ("She has changed names, voice, and visage").[27] Throughout her writing life, however, reborn ("Renée") as "Vivien," she took on the power ascribed to the seductive Vivien of Arthurian legend, who wrests from Merlin the book that represents and contains his magical authority, a scene depicted in the Burne-Jones painting that we have used as a frontispiece to this chapter.

While Pauline Tarn usurped and revised a male legend in order to become "Renée Vivien," another twentieth-century poet—Hilda Doolittle—would seem to have acquiesced in an identity bestowed by patriarchal power, for, understandably hesitant about using her surname, she accepted the camouflage Ezra Pound provided when he baptized her "H. D., *Imagiste*." Yet the power of names and the names of power were as crucial in H. D.'s life as they were in Vivien's. She was quite clear, for instance, about her fascination with a name composed of initials, explaining in *Tribute to Freud* that, "I have used my initials H. D. consistently as my writing signet or sign-manual, though it is only, at this very moment, as I check up on the word 'signet' in my Chambers' English Dictionary that I realize that my writing signature has anything remotely suggesting sovereignty or the royal manner."[28] As Adalaide Morris has noted, moreover, this writer meditates continually on the letter *H*, which signals not only her own name, Hilda, but her mother's name, Helen, as well as the names of many of her heroes and heroines: Helmsman, Huntress, Hermione, Hippolytus, Hippolyta, Hermes, Helios, Heliodora, and Helen of Egypt.[29] In addition, however, she broods on the mirror imagery of "H. D." and "D. H.," which indicates to her that the novelist-poet D. H. Lawrence is her male counterpart, and on the doubling of "H. D." and "H. D.," which tells her that Lord Hugh Dowding, England's Chief Air Marshall in World War II, is her reincarnated consort. Finally, she mythologizes the letters "H. D." so that they stand for the "Hermetic Definitions" that she makes out of the book-length poems which extricate her art from Pound's diminution of her as *"Imagiste."*[30]

But that H. D. should have most persistently extrapolated a series of classical pseudonyms from her initials illuminates yet another problem that literary women from George Eliot to Virginia Woolf, H. D. herself, and more recent writers confront, and that Emily Dickinson implicitly addressed when she sought to establish an alternative ancestry associated with the occult language presumably inscribed in "Tomes of solid Witchcraft": the problem of women's historical exclusion from serious, formal training in just those classics which form the foundation of western literary and linguistic tradition. Specifically, all these "daughters of educated men" may well have intuited that, until the late nineteenth century saw the entrance of large numbers of women into colleges and universities, the education in the classics which their brothers received—that is, education in Latin and Greek—functioned as just the crucial step in gender demarcation that Walter Ong has shown it to be.[31] As Ong notes both in *The Presence of the Word* (1967) and *Fighting for Life* (1981), in boys' schools a classical education instilled masculinist values through a rhetorical training in "agonistic" oral competition which represented a puberty rite that further developed male identity. These men and boys, in other words, had access to a privileged priestly language, what Ong calls a *"patrius sermo"* (a "father speech") as opposed to the *"materna lingua"* (or "mother tongue"). Some women had long sought to counter this language with the vocabulary of witchcraft that we have seen Dickinson employing, the male Mass masked as a female Black Mass; but some, as the male monopoly over the classics was broken, felt free to challenge it with perverse and subversive meditations on Greek and Latin; and still others, as they also observed such male linguistic debilitations, were liberated to try to undermine it through fantasies that bestowed originatory power on the mother tongue.

George Eliot, of course, transcribed in *The Mill on the Floss* the envy that her imaginative heroine, Maggie Tulliver, felt for what she saw as her brother Tom's good luck in being forced to learn Latin. Indeed, even when Tom petulantly becomes "more like a girl" because his own dullness makes the Latin lessons feel like a series of "bruises and crushes" and even when he nonetheless insists that "no girls could learn" this classical language, Maggie delights in his Latin grammar book: "Those mysterious sentences, snatched from an unknown context,—like strange horns of beasts, and leaves of unknown plants, brought from some far-off region,—gave boundless scope to her imagination, and were all the more fascinating because they were in a peculiar tongue of their own, which she could learn to interpret." Despite Maggie's perspicacity, Tom's teacher argues that, although girls can "pick up a little of everything," they can't "go far into anything. They're quick and shallow," a judgment that helps explain why Maggie, like the narrator of *The Mill on the Floss*, continues to find not in classical books but in natural scenes "the mother tongue of our imagination, the language that is laden with all the subtle inextricable associations the fleeting hours of our childhood left behind them."[32]

But for twentieth-century literary women the classics had more ambiguous connotations. Virginia Woolf—who studied Greek with Walter Pater's sister Clara and who deeply admired the classicist Jane Ellen Harrison (the "J- H-" of *A Room of One's Own*)—nevertheless imagined in moments of madness that the birds were speaking Greek to her, and Rachel Vinrace, the protagonist of her early *The Voyage Out*, has to puzzle over what Woolf shows to be an absurd question from her scholarly uncle Ambrose Ridley: "What's the use of reading if you can't read Greek?"[33] Two of Woolf's descendants, moreover, represent the ambivalence of women writers who seek both to usurp and parody the historical exclusiveness of a (masculinist and classical) linguistic code. Louie Pollit, the heroine of

Christina Stead's *Kunstlerroman, The Man Who Loved Children* (1940), creates a witchlike private language that sounds suspiciously like a bizarre mixture of Latin and Greek. "TRAGOS: HERPES ROM. JOST 1," which means "TRAGEDY: THE SNAKEMAN. ACT 1," is the play she produces in it, and when her father expresses annoyance at his dependence on her translation—"Why couldn't it be in English?"—she enlightens him: "Did Euripides write in English?"[31] Even as she ambitiously models herself on a classical playwright, however, Louie also believes that a "secret language" will allow her "to write what she [wishes], she [can] invent an extensive language to express every shade of her ideas" (360). In other words, like Woolf, she suspects that "if you can't read Greek," you should at least write something like it.

More recently and more radically, Suzette Haden Elgin has produced in *Native Tongue* (1984) and *The Judas Rose* (1987), a sequence of science-fiction novels which center on the struggle for verbal and political liberation of oppressed female linguists in a drastically misogynistic future world where the Nineteenth Amendment to the U.S. Constitution has been repealed, and women have no public rights at all. Pretending to create a woman's language called "Langlish," these rebels actually create "A language to say the things that women wanted to say, and about which men always said "Why would anybody want to talk about *that?*" This secret women's language is called "Láadan" or "Ladin . . . lahadin . . . Latin? Almost like Latin, but with a lilt to it."[35] Mournfully aware that "the only song a woman knows is the song she learns at birth; / a sorrowin' song with the words all wrong in the manly tongues of Earth," these heroines long to recreate the communal tongue that they imagine "the 'international' Latin must have been like," but they fear that "Láadan will die, as every language of women must have died, since the beginning of time" (*NT* 265, 251). So threateningly magical, however, is their "Ládan," with its evocation not just of Latin but of Aladdin's lamp, that their male antagonists swear that "it represents danger, and it represents corruption—and it shall not happen" (*NT* 281). By the end of *The Judas Rose*, though, these feminist linguists are convinced that "the language had spread too far to root out" and that "Ládan would spread. . . . It would continue to keep . . . all the women who knew it . . . immune to the state of violence that the men struggled with so incessantly," for as Elgin, herself a linguist, observes, "language can change reality" (*JR* 354–55).

Where Woolf, Stead, and Elgin appropriate and transform the classics, their female cohorts from Edith Wharton on develop a female dream of linguistic witchcraft into other visions of female verbal power. In a short story called "Xingu" (1911) for instance, Wharton hinted at the existence of a language with Amazonian connections and Eleusinian connotations.[36] Renée Vivien, writing in the same period, learned Greek to read Sappho in the original, translated Sappho's lyrics into French and wrote her own "sapphistries."[37] Distancing herself chronologically rather than geographically from the sentences of patriarchy, Djuna Barnes composed in an English that predates the emergence of women writers, as if to reclaim lost dictions for her sex, in works like *Ryder* (1928), *Nightwood* (1937), and *The Antiphon* (1958) that exploit, respectively, eighteenth-century, Renaissance, and Jacobean idioms. In addition, as if teasing out the relationship between "The Voice of Evil" and *The Bostonians*, she symbolized her desire to speak in tongues through baroque fantasies of the eroticism of the tongue. Susan Sniader Lanser points out, for instance, that Barnes's *Ladies Almanack* deploys archaisms, neologisms, a mingling of registers and metaphors, obscure oxymorons, and rhetorical questions to encode a subversive critique of phallic supremacy through a myth of the eternal pleasures of the tongue in the mouth and the clitoris in the "furrow, nook, path, keyhole, whorl, crevice, conch shell."[38]

If Barnes reconstituted an older English for her New Women, Gertrude Stein remade English itself into a foreign language when she seemed really to speak in tongues, testifying to the authority of her own experience. For, as most of her bemused readers realize, many of Stein's books are fantastic experiments in alternative speech: in her *Tender Buttons* (1914), for instance, she provides a new lexicon of old words; in *Three Lives* (1909), she experiments with the continuous present; in *The Making of Americans* (1925), she exchanges the sentence for the paragraph as the unit of meaning. Throughout her canon, clearly, she is attempting to follow her own advice to "only, only excreate, only excreate a no since" in order to excrete a "nonsense" language which would attack the causality of "since" at the same time that it would *X* out those male definitions of female "excrescence" which led to Joyce's demand for a female expression of pure excrement.[39] Furthermore, writing in France, happily surrounded by "people who know no english," Stein dramatized her own (sexual) difference in poems like "Lifting Belly," "As a Wife Has a Cow," and "Pink Melon Joy," where she creates an elaborate private code to describe the delights of an erotic linguistics that translates, say, sacred cows into sexual "cows."[40] Not surprisingly, then, even William Carlos Williams, who met her in Paris with some suspicion, observed that she had disentangled words from the weight of history, from "the burden science, philosophy and every higgledy-piggledy figment of law and order have been laying upon them in the past."[41]

Perhaps most strikingly, H. D.—even while redefining herself as a character out of Greek mythology and reappropriating *Hellas* as a country identified with the name of her mother, *Helen*—developed Dickinson's idea of witchcraft into an "echoing spell" of what Robert Duncan has called her "mothering language."[42] In particular, at the center of her book-length meditative poem *Trilogy* (1944–46), she reconstitutes a new language through a magical, alchemical process. By recovering the "candle and script and bell" that "the new church spat upon," she translates a word like "venereous" into "venerate" to resanctify the lost goddess, Venus. Seasoning holy words for a liturgy that has gone misnamed or unnamed (she translates the Hebrew word *"marah,"* bitter, into "Mother," for example), she whips up a batch of medicinal herbs from the poison she has etymologically uprooted. For H. D., a word is a jewel in a jar, incense in a bowl, a pearl in a shell, a sort of mystic egg that can "hatch" multiple meanings. Therefore she is multiply, almost endlessly, inspired in *Tribute to Freud* by pictographic writing on a wall, and therefore she punningly revises words to turn "ruins," say, into "runes." Indeed, all words, as she meditates on them, become palimpsests: in their palpable ambiguity, her hermetic redefinitions convert "translation" into "transubstantiation," "fever" into "fervour," "savor" into "saviour," and "haven" into a "heaven" of her own devising.[43]

Where in *Trilogy* H. D. carries the covertly feminist concept of alternative tongues to a theological extreme by linking her redefinitions of words to a retelling of the New Testament nativity story, in *Pilgrimage* (1915–38) her friend and associate Dorothy Richardson frequently meditated on the problems of communication which result from the fact that, as her heroine Miriam argues, "by every word they use men and women mean different things." Deploring what the critic Gillian E. Hanscombe calls "the masculinization of language," Miriam comes to believe that "In speech with a man a woman is at a disadvantage—because they speak different languages. She may understand his. Hers he will never speak nor understand."[14] At the same time, however, although Miriam feels herself to be in a sense sexually bilingual, her women's language seems more private, less developed than men's: "There was a woman," she broods, "not this thinking self who talked with men in their own language, but one whose words could be spoken only from the heart's knowledge," but this woman is still "waiting to be born."[15] Nevertheless, despite Miriam's uncertainty, Richardson herself clearly believed that she had managed to capture the cadences of that unborn woman's speech in the many volumes of *Pilgrimage*. Indeed, in a foreword to the 1938 edition, she described her magnum opus as an effort "to produce a feminine equivalent of the current masculine realism," adding that "Feminine prose" should be (like her own) "unpunctuated, moving from point to point without formal obstructions."[16]

In an early review of Richardson's work Virginia Woolf seemed at first to want to debate this point, for even while she agreed that Richardson's "is a woman's sentence," she observed that it was only so "in the sense that it is used to describe a woman's mind." Ultimately, however, she too saw Richardson's major achievement as the invention of "a more elastic" prose, "capable of stretching to the extreme of suspending the frailest particles, of enveloping the vaguest shapes," and she praised the author of *Pilgrimage* for having devised "the psychological sentence of the feminine gender."[17] Even as she theorized in this way, moreover, calling for a new "woman's sentence" and decrying the semi-literate sentences of women like Florinda and Clara in *Jacob's Room* (1922), Woolf often interpolated female linguistic fantasies into her own revisionary narratives of women's histories.[18]

To begin with, as if to document in advance Rich's (or Wittig's) notion that patriarchal speech is "the oppressor's language," Woolf continually creates characters who experience themselves as alienated from the ordinary sense of language. In *The Voyage Out*, for example, Rachel Vinrace hears her lover reading the words of *Comus* and thinks that "they sounded strange; they meant different things from what they usually meant" (326). Similarly, in *Mrs. Dalloway* a skywriting airplane produces an ambiguous trail of smoke which might mean "Glaxo," "Kreemo," "toffee," or "K E Y" (29–32). Again, in *To the Lighthouse* (1927), Lily Briscoe translates Mr. Ramsay's mystifying concern with "subject and object and the nature of reality" into a vision of a kitchen table suspended among the trees and, more to the point, she thinks ironically of how his "splendid mind" struggles to explore thought which, "like the alphabet," is "ranged in twenty-six letters" (53). In *A Room of One's Own*, too, the Woolfian narrator puzzles over the "straight dark bar" formed "like the [implicitly male] letter 'I'. . . . honest and logical; as hard as a nut, and polished for centuries by good teaching and good feeding" but in whose shadow "all is shapeless as mist" (103–04). Finally, in *The Years* (1937), the sibylline Sara Pargiter insistently asks "What's 'I'?" (140) while in *The Waves*, for Rhoda, figures on a blackboard are "white loops" through which she steps "into emptiness, alone" (189), and in *Between the Acts* (1941), the mysterious Miss La Trobe imagines "Words of one syllable" rising from mud, "Words without meaning— wonderful words" (212). For Woolf's heroines, and sometimes even her heroes, then, language often becomes (as in Rhoda's and Woolf's own crucial moments of existential crisis) a patriarchal puddle over which they cannot step.[49]

At the same time, however, Woolf offers her heroines, and a few heroes, the benediction of fantastic new languages. In *Night and Day* (1919), for instance, Katharine Hilbery articulates her feelings through enigmatic visions of "algebraic symbols' " (300). Similarly, in *Mrs. Dalloway*, the shellshocked Septimus expresses *his* strong emotions in pictographic "writings" while an ancient woman "opposite Regent's Park Tube Station" sings a famously enigmatic song that goes "ee um fah um so / foo swee too eem oo" (122).[50] Again, in *Orlando* (1928), Woolf's androgynous hero/heroine wires her husband a comically encoded comment on the meaning of literary achievement: " 'Rattigan Glumphoboo,' which summed it up precisely" (282) while in *The Years* the two "children of the caretaker"— descendants of the Tube Station crone—provide a fitting climax to the Pargiters' family reunion with a shrill ditty that begins "Etho passo tanno hai, / Fai donk to tu do, / Mai to, kai to, lai to see / Toh dom to tuh do—" (429).

Finally, throughout her oeuvre, Woolf emphasizes the fact that both the alienation from language her books describe and the revision of lexicography her books detail are functions of the dispossession of women, as well as of women's natural resources in the face of this dispossession, and she does this by presenting a dramatic succession of female figures whose ancient voices seem to endure from a time before the neat categories of culture restrained female energy. The most notable of these figures is, of course, the tube station crone in *Mrs. Dalloway*. But clearly the ancestor of this woman is the "old blind woman" who, in *Jacob's Room*, sits long past sunset "singing out loud . . . from the depths of her gay wild heart . . ." (67). And her descendants appear in *To the Lighthouse* as the force that lurches through Mrs. McNab's groaning and Mrs. Bast's creaking as they stay the corruption at work on the Ramsays' summer house.

But if, beleaguered though they are, these ancient voices seem to speak of a primal regeneration in direct opposition to the dead gilt letters inscribed on tablets and tombs, with their natural energy they significantly resemble the force that inspires female singers in several of Willa Cather's stories and novels. Thea Kronborg in *The Song of the Lark* (1915), for instance, finds her true voice by visiting a "cleft in the world" called Panther Canyon, where the relics of an archaic civilization still remain intact. Inside "this hollow (like a great fold in the rock)," an "Ancient People" had worn down paths that inspire Thea to re-imagine her voice in terms of the crafts of prehistoric women:

> What was any art but an effort to make a sheath, a mould in which to imprison for a moment the shining, elusive element which is life itself,—life hurrying past us and running away, too strong to stop, too sweet to lose? The Indian women had held it in their jars . . . In singing, one made a vessel of one's throat and nostrils and held it on one's breath, caught the stream in a scale of natural intervals.[51]

Patterned on uniquely female skills, Thea's operatic art draws strength from the same "ancient spring spouting from the earth" that infuses the less trained voices of Woolf's battered women.

Yet to the fatherly priests who populate Cather's later fiction, the earthly voice that sanctifies Thea's art is understandably terrifying and faintly disgusting. In *Death Comes to the Archbishop* (1927), the bishop who takes refuge from a snowstorm inside "two rounded ledges, one directly over the other, with a mouthlike opening between," is revolted not only by a "fetid odour" but also by "a hole" between two "stone lips" inside the cave, through which he hears "an extraordinary vibration."[52] To this European man of God, the speech of what was once an Indian oracle conveys no more than the horror of its own enigmatic existence. How, Cather seems to ask, can a "civilized" adult male come to terms with what Wallace Stevens once called "Words of the fragrant portals . . . / And of ourselves and of our origins. . . ."?[53] Her implicit question reminds us once again of the male modernist anxiety about female Babel to which so many of the women of letters we have discussed here were responding through their construction of fantasy languages. Perhaps more importantly, however, her awareness of the bishop's dilemma as he listens to the speech of (Mother) earth also reminds us that male artists have long contended with their own linguistic anxieties through the invention of fantasy languages, not just degraded tongues attributed to women but languages for themselves, languages, that is, which did not primarily diminish femaleness but principally aggrandized maleness.

Of course, the historical range of male linguistic fantasies shows that not all such variations on the theme of language function to confirm (masculinist) sexual self-definitions. From the mad brilliance of Shakespeare's fools to the brilliant madness of "Anon.'s" "Tom O'Bedlam's Song," from the counterfeit archaisms of Ossian and Chatterton to the counterfeit heroism of Carroll's neologistic "Jabberwocky," from the encoded common sense of Samuel Pepys' *Journal* to the encoded "little language" of Swift's *Journal to Stella*, male writers have sought to overcome the constrictions of language. It hardly seems necessary to say, moreover, that male thinkers from Plato to Derrida have concerned themselves with the constraints of language. However, as Ong's account of the relationship between the common *materna lingua* and the "civilized" *patrius sermo* implies, European male writers have, since the High Middle Ages, been deeply involved in a struggle into (and with) the vernacular, a project which has continually forced them to usurp and transform the daily speech of women and children so as to make it into a suitable instrument for (cultivated) male art.[54]

"Our first tongue," writes Ong, "is called our 'mother tongue' in English and in many other languages," adding that the only "father speech" is a language such as, for example, Latin or Greek, "inherited as land is, an external possession [which] refers to a [legalistic] line of conveyance, not to personal origins" (*Fighting* 37). (By such a distinction, we should note, we take him to mean that the mother tongue, far from being a unique women's language, is what we would ordinarily mean by the phrase "ordinary language.") Certainly when, meditating on reading and writing in *Walden*, Henry David Thoreau, in a passage we have used as an epigraph here, contrasted the "brutish. . . . mother tongue" with the "reserved and select" expression of the "father tongue," he implied that the spoken vernacular is as far below the written classics as dialect is below dialectic or as the literate is below the literary. If men were anxious about the vernacular that their mothers, wives, and daughters also fluently spoke, however, it becomes necessary to speculate that since the thirteenth and fourteenth centuries male writers may have thought linguistic culture to be holding linguistic anarchy at bay because they have had to translate the "high themes" of the classics into what they fear is a low language whose very accessibility might seem to vulgarize those themes.

Still, although male intellectuals from Dante and Chaucer on composed their verses in a vernacular they defined as "maternal," their possession of the classics diminished anxiety. Virgil was Dante's guide, and interestingly, T. S. Eliot, meditating on the "universality" of Dante's language, attributed the power of that poet's " 'Florentine' speech" to its origins in universally understood medieval Latin, a tongue which "tended to concentrate on what men of various races and lands could think together."[55] But according to Ezra Pound, speculating on the same issue, Chaucer "was more compendious than Dante" because he "wrote while England was still a part of Europe" and thus his language was still, if only metaphorically, a branch of a larger "father speech" which constituted the (father) state rather than the (mother) nation. In fact, Pound goes on to say, Chaucer is *"Le Grand Translateur"*—that is, he is the man who brings over the *patrius sermo* of the Latin Middle Ages into the *materna lingua* of the vernacular Renaissance: "He had found a new language, *he had it largely to himself*, with the grand opportunity. Nothing spoiled, nothing worn out" [emphasis ours]. Similarly, says Pound, Milton, "chock a block with Latin," brings over that *patrius sermo* into English.[56] That one turns to Eliot's and Pound's commentaries on these major male *"translateurs"* of classical culture into the vulgar vernacular, however, suggests the historical intensity of the linguistic issue that has haunted male writers since the nineteenth century, eliciting linguistic fantasies at least as forceful as (though very different from) those that many French feminists propose uniquely for women. For, as we have seen that Ong has also noted, the teaching of Latin and Greek as part of the standard curriculum that functioned as a male initiation ritual had begun to die out by the end of the nineteenth century because of the entrance of women into higher education.[57]

Thus if turn-of-the-century, modernist, and postmodernist men responded to the entrance of scribbling women into the literary marketplace with a misogyny that defined the words of those women as merely babble, they also seem to have met their own awareness that they now shared (indeed were confined to) the language of such women with intensified fantasies about what they *as men* could do with that common language. In general, these masculine linguistic fantasies fall into four categories: (1) a mystification (and corollary appropriation) of the powers of the *materna lingua* itself; (2) a revision of the *materna lingua* which would assert (male) power over it; (3) a recuperation (or a wish for recuperation) of what are seen as the lost powers of the *patrius sermo;* (4) a transformation of the *materna lingua* into a powerful new kind of *patrius sermo*. Obviously, in a number of cases these categories overlap, but almost always, at least since the early nineteenth century, the (male) elaboration of linguistic fantasies that can be classified in any of these ways reveals anxiety about the potentially anarchic implications of the vernacular together with a nostalgia for the lost cultural authority of the classics. For, perhaps inevitably, men of letters felt that the obligation to speak and write in a *materna lingua* not only accompanied but signified what Harold Bloom would call the sense of historical belatedness that has been a major creative impediment for male artists since at least the Romantic period.

To mystify the (mother) tongue that one must speak is, of course, the simplest way of defending oneself against that tongue's linguistic contamination; it is to say that, "ordinary" as "ordinary language" appears, a privileged speaker can perceive that it is not ordinary, that what seems to be a *materna lingua* is really a *patrius sermo*. Thus Emerson, meditating on the common (vernacular) speech of poets, calls (in one of our epigraphs) for "spermatic, man-making words," while T. S. Eliot celebrates the implicitly generative energy of Lancelot Andrewes, who "takes a word and derives the world from it; squeezing and squeezing the word until it yields a full juice of meaning which we should never have supposed any word to possess" (*SP*, 305). Similarly, Whitman, that sane son of the *materna lingua* who so notoriously implored the Muse to abandon the classics and "migrate from Greece and Ionia; / Cross out, please, those immensely overpaid accounts," defensively asserts in his "Carol of Words" that there "are vast words to be said," and adds that though "the workmanship of souls is by the inaudible words of the earth; / the great masters know the earth's words, and use them more than the audible words."[58]

A comparable linguistic mysticism imbues the work of many nineteenth- and twentieth-century writers. Perhaps most famously, in "Correspondances" Baudelaire declares that "Nature is a temple" whose "living / Columns sometimes breathe a mingled speech," while Rimbaud prophesies the "latent births" of sounds by proposing synaesthetic definitions—"A black, E white, I red, U green, O blue"— in "Voyelles." A century later, as if to bring to the surface the implications of such statements, Sartre confesses in *Les Mots* (1964) that to "exist was to have an official title somewhere on the infinite Tables of the Word," and "to write was to engrave new beings upon them."[59] As for Stevens, his perception of the threatening earth-voice heard by Cather's Bishop as uttering "words of the fragrant" (rather than fetid) "portals" suggests at least one of the ways he found to counter the anxiety induced by the language he associated in "Esthetique du Mal" with the "brother half-spoken in the mother's throat" (317), the anxiety, that is, of the *materna lingua*. More radically, as he went on writing and confronting such anxiety, Stevens came, in a poem called "Men Made Out of Words," to the proto-Derridean (and in the strictest sense fantastic) conclusion that "Life consists / Of propositions about life. . . . The whole race is a poet that writes down / The eccentric propositions of its fate" (355–56). Most radically, he imagined the poet as a man who, through his mastery of language, "held the world upon his nose / And this-a-way he gave a fling. // His robes and symbols, ai-yi-yi— / And that-a-way he twirled the thing" (178) while, even more desirously, he called for "A new text of the world / . . . A text of intelligent men / At the centre of the unintelligible . . ." (494–95).

From Coleridge to Poe to Hopkins, from Lawrence to Williams to Olson, the category of male linguistic fantasies we have called a revision of the *materna lingua* is frequently exploited by male prosodic theorists who begin with mystifications of language similar to those essayed by Whitman, Baudelaire, Rimbaud, Sartre, and Stevens, visions of the *materna lingua* by which a privileged seer is enabled to perceive the extraordinary powers of ordinary words or the extraordinary words that are "spoken" by ordinary things. Thus, for instance, Lawrence shamanistically intuits that "Tuscan cypresses" are "folded in like a dark thought, / For which the language is lost," but allays his own fear that "our words [are] no good" by reimagining the "echoing / Etruscan syllables" on which (as he implies he alone can tell) these cypresses "darkly concentrate."[60] Williams too—who also worries (in *Paterson*) that "the language is worn out"—refreshes his vocabulary with a similar but even more fantastic imagining of tree speech:

> Wha ha ha ha
> Wheeeee
> Clacka tacka tacka
>
> tacka tacka
> Wha ha ha ha ha
> ha ha ha[61]

More drastically, however, these literary men attempt to demonstrate their power over the vernacular by using its inflections as the bases for revisionary systems of metric mastery—mystical ideas of, say, "organic form" (Coleridge), "sprung rhythm" (Hopkins), "poetry of the present" (Lawrence), "the variable foot" (Williams), or the "breath unit" (Olson). Paradoxically, though such prosodic systems often seem to depend upon a submission to the exigencies of the *materna lingua* (its "natural" rhythms, its "organic" phrases), they too require the mediation of a privileged speaker who can intuit the secret shape of the rhythmic body "darkly concentrate[d]" in what at first appears to be "mere" ordinary language.

As Lawrence's "Cypresses" intimates, however, the very perception of such a darkly rhythmic body secreted in language is often associated also with a belief in the prior existence of that body: to intuit the language of trees, in other words, may be to intuit the ghost of a patriarchal *Ur-Sprache* which has been lost or forgotten. Not surprisingly, then, a number of great modernist poets respond to a sense of the historical belatedness implicit in their confinement to the vernacular *materna lingua* by seeking to reconstitute a vanished father-speech. Yeats's valorization of Gaelic mythology, and especially his obsession with lost names—Cuchulain, Maeve, Naoisi—is germane here (as indeed is his precursor Blake's Ossianic [re]-invention of mysteriously signified gods and goddesses like Los, Orc, Thel, and Urizen). Even more pertinent is Lawrence's yearning for the "dead speech" of the Etruscans, whose language is still so "darkly monumental" in the trees he perceives and praises (*CP* 296). Most to the point, however, is Lawrence's elaborate attempt to revitalize the lost Aztec mythology he celebrates in *The Plumed Serpent* (1926). For, writing hymns to the omnipotent Quetzalcoatl, the submissive Malintzi, and the fierce "red Huitzilopochtli," he reinscribes a language predicated precisely on the divine immolation of the (mothering) female whose tongue this poet loathes but has to speak.[62]

Just as important here, though, are the injunctions and experiments of Pound, Eliot, and Beckett. For, after all, when Pound vigorously asserted that "You cannot learn to write by reading English" (*ABC* 71), he was coming directly to grips with the need for the disintegrated language of that "great humane culture" in which Chaucer still, luckily, participated. Thus, in his own poetic *praxis*,

Pound shored countless fragments of that western *sermo* (and of China's eastern one) against his ruin, while Eliot, paying tribute to *"Il Miglior Fabbro,"* searched among *his* ruin for fragments of Virgil, Ovid, Dante, Wagner, and other representatives of a "great humane culture" to bolster his sense of a self anxiously committed to the vertigo of the vernacular. Similarly, Lucky in Samuel Beckett's *Waiting for Godot* (1954) peppers his desperately metaphysical speeches with Latin *quas* and *quid pro quos*, as if not just to parody but also to echo and enact the last lost quackings of a father tongue.[63] If such a speech is no longer available *in toto*, these male writers imply, perhaps at least it can be used *in partibus* to distinguish their work from what Thoreau called the "brutish . . . mother tongue."

But of course, as Lucky's nihilism suggests, the remembrance of what Beckett calls "all the dead voices" provides only a partial assuagement of the anxiety induced by the vernacular.[64] Indeed, even the fragmentary revival of such voices reminds these writers to a man that they feel themselves to be dependent on the very linguistic sources they seek to transmute. Therefore, for all their modernity, they find themselves in the unenviable position of Tennyson's Merlin, who explains to Vivien in Book VI of *The Idylls of the King* (1859) that his magical powers derive from an ancient volume whose "every square of text [has] an awful charm," but then goes on to confess the secondary, belated character of his relationship to this paradigmatic book of patriarchal authority. It is, he notes,

> Writ in a language that has long gone by . . .
> And every margin scribbled, crost, and cramm'd
> With comment, densest condensation, hard . . .
> And none can read the text, not even I;
> And none can read the comment but myself;
> And in the comment did I find the charm.[65]

Significantly, the "charm" Merlin found "in the comment" is a spell of power which was originally used by a jealous king to subordinate his proud queen: he charmed her "In such-wise that no man could see her more, / Nor saw she save the king, who wrought the charm, / Coming and going, and she lay as dead, / And lost all use of life" (640–45). Just as significantly, the sinister Vivien seduces Merlin into giving *her* the "charm" and, as if predicting the dilemma of so many of his (and Tennyson's) literary descendants, uses it to shut him up in the hollow tower of his own consciousness. Although, as we have seen, Renée Vivien exploits exactly this legend to challenge the erotic and aesthetic privilege of men, Tennyson's message for male readers is clear: even if the (male) magician no longer knows "the language that has long since gone," he must at all costs retain the charm that resides in the comment on the sacred text of power. Thus the transformation of the *materna lingua* into a new *patrius sermo*—the occulting of common language, the transformation of the comment into the charm—seems to offer a definitive cure of the male linguistic wound.

Such a transformation of the comment into the charm is most notably accomplished in a number of different ways by the most radical, even avant-garde fantasists of language, men who, from Mallarmé to Joyce to Derrida, repossess the ancient strength of the *patrius sermo* through the creation of a literature of "comment, densest condensation, hard. . . ." Mallarmé, for instance, reinscribes the world as a text of his own graphing in *"Un Coup de Dés,"* demonstrating that he can cast the dice of language to his own advantage by using the apparently common words of the *materna lingua* to create a charm which both comments upon and constitutes "things" as thoughts.[66] More dramatically, the signatories of Eugene Jolas' "Manifesto: The Revolution of the Word" rebel against "the spectacle of [literature] still under the hegemony of the banal word" with the assertion that "the literary creator has the right to disintegrate the primal matter of words imposed on him. . . . He has the right to use words of his own fashioning. . . ."[67]

The charm that some of Jolas's signatories find in this comment leads to fantastic, neo-*patrii sermones* like the occult speech of Hugo Ball's "Clouds" ("elomen elomen lefitalominai/wolminuscaio . . ." etc., [*T* 175]), the liturgical chanting of Kurt Schwitters' "priimiitittiii" ("priimiitittiii   tisch / tesch / priimiitiitiii   tesch / tusch / priimiitittiii tischa / tescho / priimiitittiii tescho / tuschi. . . ." etc., [*T* 177]), and the frankly masculinist (and Latinate) nostalgia of William Saroyan's "Fragment" ("In my room I slept, dreaming language, Pater hemon, father in heaven, ho en tois ouranois, worded and named, sanctificetur nomen tuum, hallowed. . . ." [*T* 193]). In just about every case, that is, these linguistic revolutionaries became latter-day Merlins seeking, through "densest condensation," to regain the mastery lost when male artists were forced by history to operate within the degrading confines of the vernacular mother tongue, a point best made in a *transition* essay called "Dichtung and Diction" by Stuart Gilbert, who observes that the

> language of the old incantations [a language the *transition* writers were trying to revive] was speech and sound and diction strained to breaking point, a frenzied quest for *names of power* which would evoke the dark personified emotions of the underworld. 'By Adonai, Eloim Jehova, Adonai Sabaoth, Metraton On Agla Adonai Mathon, the pythonic word, the mystery of the salamander, the assembly of the sylphs, the grotto of the gnomes, the demons of the heaven of God, Almousin, Gioor, Jehosua, Evam, Zariatnatmik, "Come! Come! Come!" ' [emphasis ours, *T* 182]

But of course, though the exercises and experiments of Mallarmé, Jolas, Saroyan, and others are both interesting and exemplary, the twentieth century's greatest master of linguistic transformation— the man who definitively converted the comment into the charm— was James Joyce, whose "densest condensation, hard," with its proliferation of puns, parodies, paradoxes, and parables transforms what Hélène Cixous calls "the old single-grooved mother tongue"[68] into what we are calling a *patrius sermo* that can only be comprehended by those who, like Merlin and like Joyce himself, can translate what has been "scribbled, crost, and cramm'd" on the margins of literature into a spell of power. The editors of *transition*, who first published the "work in progress" that was to become *Finnegans Wake*, clearly knew this, as their admiring *Exagmination round His Factification for Incamination of a Work in Progress* indicates, and as their printing of Joyce's own wittily worded self-advertisement for the *Wake*, with its reminder that "Humptydump Dublin's granddada of all rogues," also suggests by evoking the self-serving lexical arrogance of Lewis Carroll's Humpty Dumpty (188).[69] But even before *Finnegans Wake* condensed all European (and some Asian) tongues into a neologistic language whose Viconian loops form a perfect Möbius

strip of what we might call patrilinguistic history, *Ulysses* performed
a similar task, transforming a comment on Homer's antique epic
into a charm that inaugurated a new patrilinguistic epoch.

It would be impossible here to review all the verbal strategies by
which Joyce performed this feat of legerdemain in which the *materna
lingua* dissolved and resolved itself into a newly empowered *patrius
sermo:* his appropriation of dreams in "Circe," his mimicry of music
in "the Sirens," his usurpation of the Mass (and the Black Mass) in
"Telemachus" and elsewhere, his parodying of female speech in
"Nausicaa" and "Penelope," all certainly contribute to the spell of
power he created by deriding or disintegrating what Jolas's revolutionaries of the word called "the primal matter" of the mother
tongue. But perhaps, for our purposes here, the most striking examples of his linguistic prestidigitation are the dazzling parodies
Joyce incorporates into the scene at the Lying-In Hospital (the "Oxen
of the Sun") and the dizzying puns he increasingly invents throughout his oeuvre.

The "Oxen of the Sun" chapter, after all, records the conception,
incubation, and birth—"Hoopsa Boyaboy Hoopsa"—of a magical-
sounding boy through a series of stylistic metamorphoses which seem
to prove that (male) linguistic ontogeny recapitulates (male) linguistic
phylogeny. The borning "Boyaboy" *is* his language, a patriarchal
Word made flesh in the extended *patrius sermo* of history, and though
he is undoubtedly torn out of the prostrate *materna lingua* represented by silent Mrs. Purefoy, he is triumphantly flung (in a Carlylean birth passage) into "God's air, the Allfather's air" (423). As
for his human father, Theodore Purefoy is both comically and seriously "the remarkablest progenitor barring none in this chaffering
allincluding most farraginous chronicle" (423), for, like Joyce himself, he generated this miniature patriarchal Word in the very womb
of the *materna lingua* by "fructifying" a "Godframed Godgiven pre-
formed possibility . . . with [his] modicum of man's work" (423).

If the "Oxen of the Sun" presents us with a parabolic wresting
of patriarchal power from the mother tongue, moreover, Joyce's
puns offer more consistently assertive instances of the ways in which
male writers can transform the *materna lingua* into a *patrius sermo.*
For, containing the powerful charm of etymological commentary
within themselves, such multiple usages suggest not a linguistic

jouissance rebelliously disrupting the decorum of the text, but a linguistic *puissance* fortifying the writer's sentences with "densest condensation, hard." As we do in the presence of all puns, we (laughingly) groan at the author's authoritative neologisms because he has defeated us, even charmed us, by demonstrating his mastery of the mystery of multiple etymologies. We (grudgingly) laugh, indeed, because he has proven his primacy over words, for which he can produce more "ordinary" senses than we ourselves have been able to imagine. A virtuoso of vocabulary, he has surveyed the babble of Babel and, like the "God of the creation, indifferent, paring his fingernails," he has reduced it to order.[70] He has in fact silenced precisely the chaos which seemed to refuse to be silenced—what Julia Kristeva sees as the uncontrollable *"semiotique"* of non-sense—into a cosmos of controllable common sense(s).[71]

Provisionally, tentatively, we would suggest that a similar maneuver may be at the heart of what Geoffrey Hartman calls Derridadaism, in particular at the heart of an otherwise opaque enterprise like Derrida's *Glas* (1974) and an otherwise baroque exercise like Hartman's own *Saving the Text* (1981). For while much recent French feminist theory about *"écriture féminine"* may be contextualized in terms of a tradition of female linguistic fantasy, much recent male theory bears a striking resemblance to some of the masculine linguistic fantasies we have just examined. Certainly, even while Hartman speculates that *Glas* may be either "a Hegelian Rag" or "a fashionable meditation in the graveyard of Western Culture," he admits that, though "It may seem ingenious to characterize Derrida as a conservative thinker," it is nevertheless the case that in *Glas*'s radical weave of radically unravelled significations "the *'Monuments of unageing intellect' are not pulled down. They are . . .* so strong, or our desire is so engaged with them, that the deconstructive activity becomes part of their structure" (emphasis ours).[72] Exactly so, and exactly as in both the title and the text of *Saving the Text* itself or in *Ulysses* or in the *Wake*. Mourning and waking a lost *patrius sermo*, all these male modernists and postmodernists transform the maternal vernacular into a new morning of patriarchy in which they can wake the old powers of the "Allfather's" Word. The motto "Hoopsa Boyaboy Hoopsa" is thus the charm they consistently find in the commentary they ceaselessly study.

This is not to say that all these writers and thinkers are always able completely to allay the anxieties about the vernacular that their construction of fantasy languages seems to disallow. No doubt in his late "Madame La Fleurie" Wallace Stevens speaks in some sense for all of them when he describes the death of the poet and his reabsorption into the *materna lingua* from which, in Joyce's "Oxen of the Sun," he was born. The speech of the dead poet, Stevens sorrows, was finally ineffectual:

> It was a language he spoke, because he must, yet did not
>   know.
> It was a page he had found in the handbook of heartbreak.

And now, without the Word of the "Allfather" as defense against the ferocity of the mother tongue and the mother's tongue, he is given up to what is, at least metaphorically speaking, the anxiety of the vernacular:

> The black fugatos are strumming the blacknesses of black . . .
> The thick strings stutter the finial gutturals.
> He does not lie there remembering the blue-jay, say the jay.
> His grief is that his mother should feed on him, himself and
>   what he saw,
> In that distant chamber, a bearded queen, wicked in her dead
>   light.   [*CP* 507]

———————

What distinguishes the male linguistic fantasies we have reviewed here from the female fantasies we discussed earlier? It seems clear that women's imaginary languages, unlike men's, are for the most part founded on a celebration of the primacy both of the mother tongue and the tongue of the mother.[73] Intuiting the empowerment that daughters might win from literal and literary mothers, women from Dickinson to Woolf and her descendants subversively transform classical languages into female native tongues and praise matriarchal witchcraft. For these artists, the lure of the mother's lore always takes precedence over what Lacan calls the "Law of the Father." To be sure, male writers also seem to intuit this maternal primacy. Indeed, from Stevens and Lawrence to Robert Bly, Charles

Simic, and Donald Hall, they see themselves as sons and lovers of original and originatory women. Stevens's "one of fictive music," unlike his "bearded queen," is "sister and mother and diviner love" (*CP* 87); Lawrence confesses that he loves his mother "like a lover"; Bly proclaims that he "came out of the Mother naked"; Hall imagines the earliest poetic impulse as arising from a "milktongue"; Simic declares that "Poetry is the orphan of . . . maternal silence."[71]

Despite all their fictions of their fictive mothers and their "earthly mothers waiting sleeplessly," however, most of these men and their precursors are either reacting against or seeking to appropriate the primal verbal fertility of the mother, and they are doing so precisely because, to cite Ong once more, "Our first tongue is called our 'mother tongue' in English and in many other languages, and perhaps in all languages is designated by direct or indirect reference to mother. There are no father tongues—a truth that calls for deeper reflection than it commonly commands" (*Fighting*, 36). Clearly, it is this "deeper reflection" that is reflected in the incongruent linguistic fantasies of male and female writers. For whether they are misogynistic deridings of female scatologos, or self-valorizing demands for "Pater hemon, father in heaven . . . worded and named," male vindications of what Lacan terms the "Name of the Father" seem ultimately to be vilifications of the Gnosis of the Mother, vilifications that can be explained by Christiane Olivier's argument that "sexism in language [may be] the result of man's fear of using the same words as women, his fear of finding himself in the same place as the mother."[75]

Perhaps, too, we see the culmination of this tradition of male discrediting of female originating in the extraordinary swerve Lacan himself has to perform as part of his attempt to make the moment of the child's accession to language coincide with the moment of the Oedipus complex, so that woman can be defined "as excluded by the nature of things which is the nature of words."[76] As both Anika Lemaire and C. Stein observe, "at the time of [the Oedipus] complex . . . linguistic communication has already been established, and logically, therefore, the complex itself cannot bring about the primal repression which establishes meaning."[77] It is possible, then, that the Oedipal moment functions as a repetitive revision of an earlier moment, and that the power of the father, while obviously representing the law of patriarchy, need not be inextricably bound to the power of language. Indeed, the fact that the father is a supreme fiction in this now widely disseminated French Freudian theory points, paradoxically enough, to the primordial supremacy of the mother. For if, as language acquisition researchers have demonstrated, and as most mothers know, it is in many cultures the mother who feeds the child words even as she furnishes her or him with food, then, as Freud himself observed (in his analysis of a child's creation and use of symbols to cope with maternal separation), the birth into language delivers the child from helplessness at the goings and the comings, the "oo" and the "ah," the "Fort" and the "Da," of the mother.[78]

In that case, if the primary moment of symbolization occurs when the child identifies difference with distance from the mother, it is not only the presence of the mother's words that teaches the child words, but also the absence of the mother's flesh that requires the child to acquire words. As for the supposedly mediating and essential term of the father—the *"Nom du Père"*—we are suggesting that what makes this name secondary is precisely the fact that it symbolizes no more than the autonomy of the mother—the *Aplomb du Mère*. Moreover, if, as Lévi-Strauss concedes, a woman is not "just a sign" but "a generator of signs,"[79] then it is the example of her self-possessed linguistic generations that impresses the child with the possibility that, because mom is not mum, one might bridge the grievous gulf of absence by expressing desire in language and reconstituting a lost presence through symbolization.

Is it possible, then, that the idea that language is in its essence or nature patriarchal may be a reaction-formation against the linguistic (as well as the biological) primacy of the mother? As long ago as 1954, Bruno Bettelheim observed in *Symbolic Wounds* that "penis envy in girls and castration anxiety in boys have been overemphasized, and a possibly much deeper psychological layer in boys has been relatively neglected . . . a complex of desires and emotions which . . . might be called 'vagina envy' [but which includes] in addition, envy of and fascination with female breasts and lactation, with pregnancy and childbirth."[80] Even earlier, Gregory Zilboorg had begun to call for further studies of "the fundamental envy with which man treats woman," and Karen Horney had claimed that man's "dread of woman" is a consequence of "womb envy."[81] Suppose we follow out such insights by speculating that the biblical story of creation, with its linguistically powerful Adam and its anxious, tongue-tied Eve, is just a male fantasy devised to soothe men's feelings of secondariness, sexual dread, womb and breast envy. Suppose that, instead of postulating a necessary linguistic connection between a lass and a lack, we accept Susan Lurie's speculation that "the sight of woman as castrated is [a] mature male wish-fulfillment fantasy, designed to counter the real terror the sight of woman inspires: *that she is not castrated* despite the fact that she has 'no penis,' and does inspire male fear for his castration."[82] In that case, as Lurie observes, "Psychoanalytic discourse participates in a broad cultural project . . . of constructing woman as castrated precisely because the sight of her does *not* signify her castration," a point that would confirm our earlier claim that Freud himself was at least in part reacting against the rise of the self-sufficient New Woman.

In *The Great Mother* (1955), a useful text that has lately been too often ignored in favor of more fatherly words by Freud and Lacan, Erich Neumann points out that "The positive femininity of the womb appears as a mouth . . . and on the basis of this positive symbolic equation the mouth, as 'upper womb,' is the birthplace of the breath and the word, the Logos."[83] But the very fact that one can metaphorize the mouth as a womb, the Word as the child of female power, implies that women need not experience any ontological alienation from the idea of language as we know it. If the female does have a crucial linguistic role, moreover, isn't it also possible that the primordial self/other couple from whom we learn the couplings, doublings, and splittings of "hierarchy" is the couple called "mother/ child" rather than the one called "man/woman"? If this is so, isn't it also possible that verbal signification arises not from a confrontation with the "Law of the Father" but from a consciousness of the lure and the lore of the mother?

Nancy Chodorow's influential study of *The Reproduction of Mothering* (1978) seems to suggest that, because the pre-Oedipal daughter has a special intimacy with the mother, the growing girl would have a special linguistic privilege.[84] But Chodorow's own concept of the "fluid boundaries" between mother and daughter calls this idea into question because precisely the interidentification Chodorow posits could be said to deny girls the space language negotiates. Indeed, the pre-Oedipal linguistic relationship between mother and daughter *versus* that between mother and son can be and has been theorized in so many different ways that finally we would speculate that boy and girl babies have fundamentally the same pre-Oedipal linguistic relationship to the mother. It may not be necessary, then, to postulate (as Julia Kristeva has) that sexual difference issues in different (male/female) relationships to the symbolic contract. Indeed, it may be important to see that since the symbolic contract is "signed" before the social contract which in patriarchal culture constructs gender difference, these two contracts are notably different treaties with the world. The very fact that, throughout this chapter we have had to maneuver between theory and history, had to contemplate the questions of psychoanalysis while also confronting the constructions of literary history, would seem to reinforce this point, namely the discontinuity between what *has to be* (that is, what is psychically necessary, given western childrearing arrangements) and what *has been* (that is, what is culturally determined). For if any of our speculations have any validity, we must also ask whether the whole structure of "hierarchized" oppositions that some of us have thought essentially patriarchal has been historically erected as a massive defense against the deep throat of the mother and the astonishing priority of that mother tongue which is common to both men and women.

In "Thoughts on Writing" (1980), the American feminist poet Susan Griffin expresses the exhilaration that such an intimation of female linguistic power has already begun to foster in some women writers:

> And now the words 'mother tongue,' language, widen out to me as I see that our relationship to the one who has given us birth, and to that universe which engendered our being, might be the same as our relationship to language; we must trust words and the coming of words.[85]

A century ago, moreover, Emily Dickinson affirmed the same intuition of the mother tongue's nurturing strength, declaring that "A Word made Flesh" can be "tasted" with "ecstasies of stealth" when

"The very food debated" is matched "To our specific strength—."
Emphasizing the connection between language and the sacred, she
asked "Could [Christ's] condescension be / Like this consent of Language / This loved Philology?" (J. 1651). And indeed, for women
writers in general it may be this "*consent* of language" (emphasis
ours) that constitutes a "loved Philology" whose implications a number of thinkers have already understood and celebrated.

For significantly, Dickinson's "A Word made Flesh" almost seems
to be glossing some crucial comments by her famous "Tutor,"
Thomas Wentworth Higginson, who in 1859 answered his own
question—"Ought Women to Learn the Alphabet?"—with evidence
that, although men from Aristotle to Voltaire have thought women
should only employ the alphabet to spell the verb *amo*, many female
spellers, along with a few insightful men, have known that (in a
passage he quoted from the introduction to Elizabeth Elstob's pioneering Anglo-Saxon grammar [1715]), " 'Our earthly possessions
are indeed our patrimony, as derived to us by the industry of our
fathers; but the language in which we speak is our mother tongue,
and who so proper to play the critic in this as the females?' "[86] Higginson therefore viewed the alphabet as the heart of the feminist
matter, for "Once yield the alphabet, and we abandon the whole
long theory of subjection and couverture" (32). Indeed, although
he claimed that woman's subordination had until the nineteenth
century been historically necessary (22), he also, as we noted earlier,
argued that "woman's appointed era" was at hand in a new epoch
that "is initiating an empire of the higher reason, of arts, affections,
aspirations; and for that epoch the genius of woman has been reserved" (25–26). Thus, he proclaimed, Margaret Fuller Ossoli's
motto, "Earth waits for her queen," had to be revised, for "the queen
[who] has waited for her earth" (26) would now claim the alphabet
to capitalize (on) her own initials and her own initiatives.

To carry Fuller's, Higginson's, and Dickinson's intuitions one step
further and match them with Griffin's insight: can it be that—even
as they anxiously or eagerly engaged in social, literary, and linguistic
battles with men of letters—women writers have increasingly looked
beyond the traditional alphabetizings of history, with its masculinist
syntax of subordination, to discover and recover woman as the Alpha
and Omega of both the life of letters and the letters of life? To be

sure, in response to the masculinist deprecations of female language that we have traced here, a number of recent women writers continue to express the kind of alphabetic anxiety that Virginia Woolf dramatized in *To the Lighthouse* and elsewhere. As if echoing Woolf, for instance, Sylvia Plath has her Esther Greenwood write in *The Bell Jar* (1971) about the problem of reading the "alphabet soup of letters" that marks the "fall" in *Finnegans Wake.*[87] Similarly, and expressing the same sense of linguistic marginality, Sue Owen observes in her *Nursery Rhymes for the Dead* (1980) that "THE DEVIL / Will build his kingdom / with a capital letter. / He will claim the first / letter of the alphabet // because it is susceptible. / Then he will start to write / in longhand on anger."[88] Finally, for Ruth Stone, whose meditation on "Names" was paradigmatic earlier in this chapter, the conventions of the alphabet present a series of problems in alienation. A Stone poem significantly entitled "Poetry" (1981) presents its speaker, for instance, sitting "with my cup / to catch the crazy falling alphabet," and goes on through an estranged description of "High rise L's, without windows" and "Subway G's, Y's, twisted, / collapsing underground" to worry that "no one, no one at all, / is sifting through the rubble."[89]

In addition, for such novelists as Margaret Atwood and Doris Lessing, alphabetic writing becomes a crucial issue on which narrators and characters alike frequently brood. The multiply named heroine of Atwood's *Lady Oracle* (1976), for example, who identifies herself variously as "Joan Crawford," "Louise K. Delacourt," and "Joan Foster," is obsessed with the curious code created by an Italian typewriter without the letter *k.* More crucially, she describes entranced literary journeys which yield uniquely female automatic writings in familiar yet strange words out of which she makes the poems which constitute her subversively self-defining volume called "Lady Oracle."[90] Elsewhere, in a poem entitled "It is dangerous to read newspapers," Atwood makes a point which explains this woman's need to reappropriate and redeem patriarchal language, observing that "Each time I hit a key / on my electric typewriter . . . another village explodes."[91] Her linguistic anxiety, as well as her sense of linguistic estrangement, illuminates not only her own covertly revolutionary procedures for underground revisions of alphabetic writing but also those of central characters in Doris Lessing's novels—Mark and Dorothy in *Four-Gated City* (1969), or Anna Wulf in *The Golden Notebook*—all of whom, as if revising the plot of Charlotte Perkins Gilman's "The Yellow Wallpaper" (1892), try to decipher the relationship between oppression and "sentencing" by papering rooms with newspaper clippings, letters, and charts, or by reordering their lives in symbolically significant notebooks. From the perspective of women like Plath, Owen, Stone, Atwood, and Lessing, the alphabet both might be and should be "rubble": whether it annihilates or is annihilated by women, its cryptic elements are both distant and questionable in ways that they rarely are for men of letters.[92]

At the same time, however, even while these literary women ironically isolate themselves from patriarchal dead letters, they and many of their colleagues struggle to excavate what Plath once called "pristine alphabets" from beneath the "rubble."[93] Where male writers, in other words, struggle to certify themselves by appropriating the potency of Thoreau's "father tongue," these female thinkers try to transcend the alphabetizings of history and the history of the alphabet to dream about—in Elinor Wylie's phrase—"The immaculate bosom of the mother-tongue," which, as Wylie also notes, is expressed through a mystical "alphabet with astral fire seasoned."[94] Thus, the complex process of reinventing, relearning, or re-viewing the alphabet—as much as the current French fantasy of writing in the "white ink" of maternal milk[95]—becomes for these writers a crucial act of both self-definition and self-assertion. Such women as Monique Wittig, Sande Zeig, and Olga Broumas, for example, use the alphabet to configure anti-patriarchal, lesbian erotic arrangements. Wittig and Zeig reorganize the world in their *Lesbian Peoples/ Material for a Dictionary* by allowing the ancient sequences of the alphabet to guide them toward new definitions of such words as "Alphabet" ("invented" by Carmenta, Thetis, Kali), "Amazons" ("companion lovers"), "Love" ("an exchange of tattoos") and "word" ("to write one's life with one's blood").[96] And, as if echoing Wittig's reiteration of "O" throughout *Les Guérillères* or critiquing Pauline Réages' use of that letter in *The Story of O*, Broumas writes as "Artemis" in *Beginning with O* about a mystically "curviform alphabet / that defies // decoding" and "appears / to consist of vowels, beginning with O, the O- / mega, horseshoe, the cave of sound"—the simultaneously phonographic and pictographic cave of female desire.[97]

It is in Denise Levertov's "Relearning the Alphabet" (1966), however, that woman's desire to reimagine the alphabet becomes most passionately manifest. As if responding to Higginson's century-old question—"Ought women to learn the Alphabet?"—Levertov sanctifies the primal elements of writing so that they can function to express her own, distinctively female feelings: *A* represents for her a sound that has its own intrinsic meaning—"the ah! of knowing in unthinking / joy"—and *B* signifies "To be. To love another only for being."[98] At the same time, Levertov's mystical letters do not represent the authoritative presence that Jacques Derrida would see as the "phallogocentric" voice of authority. Rather, "lost in the alphabet" of tradition, Levertov recreates her alphabet as a landscape, not of someone else's authority, but of her own desire. Thus, presenting herself as the questor who seeks instead of the lady who is traditionally sought, she sets out from the authentic "ah!" of *A* and the absolute "to be" of *B* toward the *V* of vision, past the will of *W*, through *Y*'s yearnings, to the "blazing addresses" of "wing-tipped" *Z*, its "different darkness." Supple and flexible, her sequence of letters graphs a self whose range of sighs and sounds proclaims that in her womanliness she can both conceive and command the primordial Alpha and the ultimate Omega. Finally, then, with the young Chicana writer, Margarita Cota-Cardena, Levertov might declare

> letters of the alphabet
>   we are
> sisters   we
>   germinate man
>   conjugate his all[.][99]

Clearly many literary women find fantasies of female linguistic power increasingly plausible, and in a recent parable entitled "She Unnames Them," Ursula K. Le Guin might be said to speak for all of them. Here, this writer of speculative fiction, who has consistently meditated on the dynamics of gender, imagines a new Eve redefining and thereby liberating Adam's world. Her first woman gives back to the first man the name given to her by "you and your father" because though "It's been really useful . . . it doesn't exactly seem to fit very well lately." In addition, as she unnames the animals, she decides that "they see[m] far closer than when their names had stood between myself and them like a clear barrier". Finally, as she leaves the oppressively enclosed Garden of patriarchal vocabulary, she determines, in a passage we have used as an epigraph here, that "My words now must be as slow, as new, as single, as tentative, as the steps I [take] going down the path away from the house, between the dark-branching tall dancers motionless against the winter shining."[100] Stepping out of, and beyond, the battle of the sexes, this revisionary female linguist implies that the relationship between anatomy and verbal destiny, between sexual difference and the symbolic contract, at last promises not just female *jouissance* but feminist *puissance*. Perhaps, her authoritative gesture hints, women of letters can now assert that Fuller's and Higginson's queen has put on her royal robes not to murder but to create, not to indict male penmanship but to indite her own powerful characters.

Notes

EPIGRAPHS ON PAGE VII: Adams, *The Education of Henry Adams*, in *Democracy, Esther, Mont Saint Michel and Chartres, The Education of Henry Adams* (New York: Library of America, 1983), p. 1126; Woolf, *A Room of One's Own* (New York: Harcourt, 1929), p. 57; Lawrence, "The Real Thing," *Phoenix: The Posthumous Papers of D. H. Lawrence* (1936), ed. Edward D. McDonald (New York: Penguin, 1978), p. 196; "Do You Strive to Capture the Symbols of Your Reaction? If Not, You Are Quite Old-Fashioned," *New York Evening Sun* (February 13, 1917), p. 10.

Chapter 1

EPIGRAPHS: Lawrence, *Fantasia of the Unconscious* (1922; New York: Penguin, 1977), p. 191; Woolf, *A Room of One's Own*, p. 103 (further references to *A Room* will appear parenthetically in the text); Bly, quoted in the *San Francisco Chronicle*, March 19, 1986, p. 36.

1 Hughes, "Lovesong," *Crow* (New York: Harper & Row, 1971) p. 74.
2 For a discussion of this subject, see Abby Wettan Kleinbaum, *The War Against the Amazons* (New York: McGraw-Hill, 1983), pp. 24–25, 91; we thank Winfried Schleiner for bringing this book to our attention. See also Quintus Smyrnaeus, Book I, "The Arrival, Deeds, and Death of Penthesileia the Amazon Queen," in *The War at Troy; What Homer Didn't Tell*, by Quintus of Smyrna, trans. and with an intro. by Frederick M. Combellack (Norman: University of Oklahoma Press, 1968), pp. 24–46; and Torquato Tasso, *Jerusalem Delivered*, trans. Edward Fairfax, ed. Henry Morley (London: Routledge, 1890). Kleinbaum notes that Virgil briefly depicts Penthesilea and her Amazons in the *Aeneid* but observes that although he could have praised the Amazons because they fought on the side of Troy, he instead gave Aeneas an Amazon opponent to overcome (p. 26).
3 Edmund Spenser, *The Faerie Queene*, V, vii, 42, lines 5–6; on this see Katharine Rogers, *The Troublesome Helpmate: A History of Misogyny in Literature* (Seattle: University of Washington Press, 1966), p. 138. Of course, from Shakespeare's *The Taming of the Shrew* to Pope's *The Rape of the Lock*, battles between men and women are both dramatized and satirized to imply that what Pope calls woman's "love of sway" must be confronted and corrected.
4 Kleist, *Penthesilea*, trans. Humphrey Trevelyan, in *The Classic Theatre, Vol. II: Five German Plays*, ed. Eric Bentley, (New York: Doubleday, 1959), pp. 213–419,

scenes 23, 24; quoted in Kleinbaum, *The War Against the Amazons*, p. 178. See also Hélène Cixous's discussion of Penthesilea in *The Newly Born Woman*, trans. Betsy Wing (Minneapolis: University of Minnesota Press, 1986), pp. 112–22.

5 Tennyson, *The Princess* I.149, in *The Poetical Works of Tennyson*, ed. G. Robert Stange, Cambridge ed. (Boston: Houghton Mifflin, 1974). Further references to part and line number will be included in the text.

6 For a discussion of Hilarion's victory by loss, see Eve Kosofsky Sedgwick, *Between Men: English Literature and Male Homosocial Desire* (New York: Columbia University Press, 1985), p. 123.

7 For example, compare James Kincaid, *Tennyson's Major Poems: The Comic and Ironic Patterns* (New Haven: Yale University Press, 1978), pp. 58–79, and Kate Millett, *Sexual Politics* (New York: Avon, 1971), pp. 110–15.

8 On Tennyson's epilepsy and the history of epilepsy in his family, see Robert Bernard Martin, *Tennyson: The Unquiet Heart* (New York: Oxford University Press, 1980), pp. 10–11, and passim.

9 S. E. Dawson, *Study of the Princess* (Montreal, 1884); quoted in Stange, p. 631.

10 Buckley, *Tennyson: The Growth of a Poet* (Cambridge: Harvard University Press, 1960), pp. 101–03.

11 Carlyle, *Sartor Resartus*, ed. Charles Frederick Harrold (New York: Odyssey, 1937), p. 197.

12 Killham, *Tennyson and The Princess: Reflections of an Age* (London: Athlone, 1958), p. 106. More generally, Gail Cunningham observes in *The New Woman and the Victorian Novel* (London and Basingstoke: Macmillan 1978) that "the 'woman question' had formed an essential part of Victorian thought during most of the reign, and there had already been much agonising over both the formal status of women and general conceptions of the female role" (p. 4).

13 *Edinburgh Review*, quoted in Stange, p. 630.

14 Fiedler, "The Politics of Realism: A Mythological Approach," *Salmagundi* 42 (Summer/Fall 1978): 31–43.

15 Kingsley is quoted in Stange, p. 630; his belief in higher education for women is recorded by Margaret Farrand Thorp, *Charles Kingsley*, p. 65, quoted in Virginia Woolf, *Three Guineas* (1938; New York: Harcourt, 1966), p. 173; see also *The Complete Works of Elizabeth Barrett Browning*, ed. Charlotte Porter and Helen A. Clarke, 6 vols. (1900; New York: AMS Press, 1973), pp. 168–239.

16 [Nicholas Francis Cooke], *Satan in Society* [1870] (by a Physician) (Cincinnati: C. F. Vent, 1898), p. 86.

17 Quoted in Christopher Hibbert, *Gilbert and Sullivan and Their Victorian World* (New York: American Heritage, 1976), p. 161.

18 The uncharacteristic blank verse in which Gilbert cast the speeches in *Princess Ida* no doubt constitutes an act of homage to Tennyson; but the more typical "patter" of his lyrics is ironic in its parody of the arguments made by Tennyson's characters. For another feminist perspective on Gilbert and Sullivan, see Adrienne Munich, " 'Capture the Heart of a Queen': Gilbert and Sullivan's Rites of Conquest," *Centennial Review* 28 (Winter 1984):23–44.

19 Gilbert and Sullivan, *Princess Ida*, in the *Complete Plays of Gilbert and Sullivan*

(New York: W. W. Norton, 1976), p. 263. Further references will be to page numbers in this edition and will be included in the text.

20 These targets are satirized, respectively, in *Iolanthe, The H.M.S. Pinafore, Patience,* and *The Mikado;* "all one sees / That's Japanese" comes from *Patience, Complete Plays,* p. 168.

21 Also built in Chicago was the "Temple" of the Women's Christian Temperance Union; construction began in 1891, only four years after the women began raising funds. On both the Woman's Building and the "Temple," see Jeanne Madeline Weimann, *The Fair Women* (Chicago: Academy Chicago, 1981), esp. p. 16; see also Judith Fryer's discussion of the Woman's Building as an embodiment of "the contradictions of women's self-presentation during this period" as well as her analysis of the library at the Exposition in *Felicitous Space: The Imaginative Structures of Edith Wharton and Willa Cather* (Chapel Hill: University of North Carolina Press, 1986), pp. 23 and 41–42.

22 See Mary Kingsley, *Travels in West Africa: Congo, francais Corisco and Camaroons* (1897; London: Virago, 1981). On women travelers in Africa, see also Katherine Frank, "Voyages Out: Nineteenth-Century Women Travelers in Africa," in *Gender, Ideology, and Action: Historical Perspectives on Women's Public Lives,* ed. Janet Sharistanian (Westport, Conn.: Greenwood Press, 1986), pp. 67–94.

23 Dorothy Middleton, *Victorian Lady Travellers* (London: Routledge, 1965), p. 96.

24 Middleton, *Victorian Lady Travellers,* p. 14.

25 See Ray Strachey, *The Cause: A Short History of the Women's Movement in Great Britain* (1928; London: Virago, 1978); Virginia Woolf, *Three Guineas* (1938; New York: Harcourt, 1966), and *A Room of One's Own;* and Eleanor Flexner, *Century of Struggle: The Women's Rights Movement in the United States* (1959; Cambridge: Harvard University Press, 1973). See also the collection of British suffrage writings *Shoulder to Shoulder,* ed. Midge MacKenzie (New York: Alfred A. Knopf, 1975).

26 Stern, " 'When the Women Reign': Fantasy Literature in the Suffragette Era," *Critical Matrix,* vol. 3 (Spring 1987). Besides *The War of the Sexes* by F. E. Young [Florence Ethel Mills] (London: John Long, 1905), *The Sex Triumphant* by A. C. Fox-Davies (London: Routledge, 1909), and *When the Women Reign. 1930* by Jesse Wilson (London: Stockwell, 1909), Stern cites such other telling titles as *The Revolt of Man* by Sir Walter Besant (London: Chatto & Windus, 1882; rpt. 1896), *New Amazonia: A Foretaste of the Future* by Mrs. George Corbett (London: Tower, 1889), *Lesbia Newman* by Henry Roberts Dalton (London: 1889), *Anno Domini 2000: or, Woman's Destiny* by Sir Julius Vogel (London: Hutchinson, 1889), *A Woman of Tomorrow: A Tale of the Twentieth Century* by Alice Coralie Glyn (London: 1896), *The Raid of Dover: A Romance of the Reign of Woman A.D. 1940* by Douglas Morey Ford (London: 1910), and *When Woman Rules: A Tale of the First Women's Government . . . By a Well-known Member of Parliament* (London: John Long, 1923).

27 Higginson, "Ought Women to Learn the Alphabet?," *Women and the Alphabet* (Boston: Houghton Mifflin, 1900), p. 26–27.

28 Mill, *The Subjection of Women* (Cambridge: MIT Press, 1970), p. 3.

29 *The Education of Henry Adams* in Adams, *Novels, Mont St. Michel, The Education,* p. 1126.

30 Hynes, *The Edwardian Turn of Mind* (Princeton: Princeton University Press, 1968), p. 172. Hynes adds that "This social revolution had many implications besides the sexual: it also involved legal, political, and economic issues, and touched on property ownership, the franchise, higher education, the birth rate, laws of marriage and divorce, the protocol of the court, and the future of the Empire—in short, on nearly every aspect of Edwardian society. In all these aspects, the question asked was what should be the role of woman here?" (p. 172).

31 Roszak, "The Hard and the Soft: The Force of Feminism in Modern Times," in *Masculine/Feminine: Readings in Sexual Mythology and the Liberation of Women,* ed. Betty Roszak and Theodore Roszak (New York: Harper, 1969), p. 88. More recently, Bram Dijkstra has made a similar point and explored the masculinist backlash through studies of fin-de-siècle painting and writing in *Idols of Perversity: Fantasies of Feminine Evil in Fin-de-Siècle Culture* (New York: Oxford University Press, 1986).

32 Weininger, *Sex and Character* (London: Heinemann, 1906), p. 286; Ford Madox Ford (F. M. Hueffer), *Women and Men* (Paris: Three Mountains Press, 1923; 1st. pub. *Little Review* (1919). Noting how "odd" it was that the "Young Liberals . . . were extraordinarily angry with Miss Pankhurst and her followers" (p. 31), Ford goes on to observe sardonically that Weininger, "the young doctor who went mad and died at the age of twenty-three had proved to them that women were inferior animals. He had proved it to the satisfaction of their intelligences. . . . And they were—all these Young Liberals—unfeignedly thankful. They were more thankful than any men that I have ever known. The burden of years had fallen from their shoulders. For, for years and years they had had, as Liberal minded men, to live up to the idea that women should have justice done to them. Now Dr. Weininger had come along and proved that women were inferior animals [and] it meant that the Young Liberal Party need not any more be burdened with the woman question" (p. 31).

33 Quoted in Roszak, "The Hard and the Soft," p. 91. In *The Reactionaries* (New York: Schocken, 1967), John R. Harrison discusses the general political conservatism, even in certain cases fascism, of such major modernists as Pound, Yeats, Eliot, and Lewis. In an early letter, Lawrence conceded that the Futurists were *too* "male": *Collected Letters,* ed. Harry T. Moore (New York: Viking, 1962), p. 280.

34 Haggard, *She* (New York: Hart, 1976), p. 122.

35 Hawthorne, "The Christmas Banquet," *Tales and Sketches* (New York: Library of America, 1982), pp. 850, 865.

36 Hawthorne, *The Blithedale Romance* (New York: Penguin, 1983), pp. 121, 122. Further references will be to this edition and will be included in the text.

37 James, *The Bostonians,* ed. Alfred Habegger (Indianapolis: Bobbs-Merrill, 1976), p. 318. Further references will be to this edition and will appear in the text.

38 For a discussion of the relationship between *The Blithedale Romance* and *The Bostonians,* see Thaddeo K. Babiiha, *The James-Hawthorne Relation: Bibliographical*

Essays (Boston: G. K. Hall, 1980), pp. 171–86; for a more recent discussion, see Richard H. Brodhead, *The School of Hawthorne* (New York: Oxford University Press, 1986), pp. 147–57. Although we link Zenobia's drowning to Margaret Fuller's, it is of course the case that Hawthorne had gone in search of the drowned body of one "Miss Hunt," an episode he describes in a journal entry dated July 1845 which is reprinted in the Norton Critical Edition of *The Blithedale Romance*, ed. Seymour Gross and Rosalie Murphy (New York: W. W. Norton, 1978), pp. 253–57. Also see Nina Baym's quite different reading of this novel, where she argues against the identification of Zenobia with Fuller, claiming that Priscilla is linked to Fuller: "*The* Blithedale Romance: A Radical Reading" in the Norton Critical Edition of *The Blithedale Romance*, p. 362.

39 For feminist readings of *The Bostonians* which, unlike ours, suggest that James is fundamentally sympathetic to Olive, see, for instance, Nina Auerbach, *Communities of Women: An Idea in Fiction* (Cambridge: Harvard University Press, 1978), pp. 119–41, and Judith Fetterley, *The Resisting Reader: A Feminist Approach to American Fiction* (Bloomington: Indiana University Press, 1978), pp. 101–53.

40 LeFanu, "Carmilla," *In a Glass Darkly* (London: Lehmann, 1947), pp. 291, 240, and 244.

41 Swinburne, "Anactoria," in *Poems and Ballads*, p. 65; further references to poems by Swinburne will be to this edition, and page numbers will appear in the text.

42 Wilde, *Salome: A Tragedy in One Act: Translated from the French of Oscar Wilde by Lord Alfred Douglas: Pictured by Aubrey Beardsley* (New York: Dover, 1967), p. 63. We will offer a more detailed discussion of the femme fatale in a later volume, but for a discussion of *Salome*, Beardsley, and the battle of the sexes, see Elliot L. Gilbert, " 'Tumult of Images': Wilde, Beardsley, and *Salome*," *Victorian Studies*, 26:2 (Winter 1983). Interestingly, as Dijkstra points out in *Idols of Perversity*, even such American naturalist texts as William Dean Howells's *A Hazard of New Fortunes* (1890) and Frank Norris's *McTeague* (1899) draw on the iconography of the femme fatale. In the first, Angus Beaton is charmed by a woman, Christine Dryfoos, who experiences "the frenzy that makes a woman kill the man she loves, or fling vitriol to destroy the beauty she cannot have"; in the second, the central character's "brutality" makes the woman with whom he is involved "all the more affectionate; arouse[s] in her a morbid, unwholesome love of submission, a strange unnatural pleasure in yielding, in surrendering herself to the will of an irresistible, virile power." (Both cited in Dijkstra, *Idols of Perversity*, pp. 289, 102.)

43 Praz, *The Romantic Agony*, tr. Angus Davidson, second ed. (New York: Oxford University Press, 1970); Marcus, *The Other Victorians: A Study of Sexuality and Pornography in Mid-Nineteenth-Century England* (New York: Basic Books, 1966); Auerbach, *Woman and the Demon: The Life of a Victorian Myth* (Cambridge: Harvard University Press, 1982); Dijkstra, *Idols of Perversity*.

44 Heape, *Sex Antagonism* (London: Constable, 1913), pp. 2–3. Further references will be to this edition, and page numbers will appear in the text.

45 Ford articulated his feminist sympathies in an early suffrage pamphlet, *This Monstrous Regiment of Women* (London: Women's Freedom League, n.d.) as well

as in "Women and Men," but in a later volume we will also discuss the sex antagonism that he dramatizes in the four books of *Parades End* (1924, 1925, 1926,
1928).

46 Ford, *The Good Soldier: A Tale of Passion* (1927; New York: Vintage, 1955), pp.
123 and 186. Further references will be to this edition and will appear in the
text.

47 Interestingly, this description of Edward Ashburnham as a sacrifice, flayed alive,
echoes the denouement of Flaubert's *Salammbo* (1862), in which Matho, the lover
of the femme fatale Salammbo, is ritually flayed alive.

48 A manuscript of "The Love Song of St. Sebastian" is held in the Berg Collection
of the New York Public Library; for fuller discussions of this text, see Lyndall
Gordon, *Eliot's Early Years* (New York: Oxford University Press, 1977), pp. 55–
62; Ronald Bush, *T. S. Eliot: A Study in Character and Style* (New York: Oxford
University Press, 1983), pp. 19, 58; and Peter Ackroyd, *T. S. Eliot: A Life* (New
York: Simon & Schuster, 1984), p. 52.

49 Swinburne, *The Novels of A. C. Swinburne* (New York: Farrar, 1962), p. 225.

50 The manuscript of "Petit Epître" is held in the Berg Collection of the New York
Public Library; for "Cousin Nancy," see Eliot's *Collected Poems, 1909–1962* (New
York: Harcourt, 1963), p. 22; further references to the poetry of T. S. Eliot will
be to this edition, and page numbers will appear in the text.

51 A manuscript of "Prufrock Among the Women" is held in the Berg collection
of the New York Public Library.

52 Yeats, *Collected Poems of W. B. Yeats* (New York: Macmillan, 1956), p. 342; further
references to the poetry of Yeats will be to this edition, and page numbers will
appear in the text.

53 Holtby, *Virginia Woolf: A Critical Memoir* (1932; Chicago: Academy, 1978), pp.
90–91.

54 Chafe, *The American Woman: Her Changing Social, Economic, and Political Roles,
1920–1970* (New York: Oxford University Press, 1972), p. 89. In Britain, the
numbers of women in higher education were comparatively small—only thirteen-
thousand women in universities by 1930—but they were so troublesome to authorities that in 1926 Oxford and Cambridge imposed strict limits on the ad-
missions of female students. Far more dramatic was the more than nine-fold
gain (up to one-hundred-eighty-five thousand) in female secondary school enrollment in England during the first two decades of the twentieth century. See
Ernest Barker, *Universities in Great Britain: Their Position and Their Problems* (London: Student Christian Movement Press, 1931), p. 59; S. J. Curtis, *Higher Education in Britain Since 1900* (1952; Westport, Conn.: Greenwood, 1970), pp.
184–85; Josephine Kamm, *Hope Deferred: Girls' Education in English History* (London: Methuen, 1965), p. 233. The Abdullah cigarette advertisement appeared
in the March 30, 1920, issue of *Isis*, and we are grateful to Susan Leonardi for
bringing it to our attention.

55 See, for instance, Freud, "Female Sexuality" (1931) in Freud, *Sexuality and the
Psychology of Love*, ed. Philip Rieff (New York: Collier, 1963); further references
to this important essay will be to this edition. For a fuller discussion of this essay,
see chapter 4 of the present volume.

56 On passionlessness, see Nancy Cott, "Passionlessness: A Reinterpretation of Victorian Sexual Ideology, 1790–1850," *Signs* 4 (1978):219–36. This point has recently been challenged by Peter Gay in volume 1, *Education of the Senses*, of *The Bourgeois Experience: Victoria to Freud* (New York: Oxford University Press, 1984); see esp. "Sweet Bourgeois Communions," pp. 109–68.

57 Linda Gordon discusses the history of birth control in *Woman's Body, Woman's Right: A Social History of Birth Control in America* (New York: Penguin, 1977). See especially pp. 186–300.

58 Russell, *Hypatia* (New York: Dutton, 1925), p. 33. Further references to this volume will appear in the text.

59 A selection of articles from the first fifteen years of that journal is available in *Time and Tide Wait for No Man*, ed. Dale Spender (London: Pandora, 1984).

60 On Arthur's situation in *The Idylls of the King*, see Elliot L. Gilbert, "The Female King: Tennyson's Arthurian Apocalypse," *PMLA* 98 (1983):863–78.

61 For a study which examines such figures from a somewhat different perspective, see Peter Hays, *The Limping Hero: Grotesques in Literature* (New York: New York University Press, 1971).

62 Williams, *Autobiography* (New York: New Directions, 1967), p. 229.

63 Hemingway, *A Moveable Feast* (New York: Scribner's, 1964), p. 191.

64 See Ackroyd, pp. 143, 246.

65 Eliot, *The Family Reunion*, in *The Complete Plays of T. S. Eliot* (New York: Harcourt, 1967), p. 62 (act 1, scene 1).

66 For Eliot's relationship with Vivien Haigh-Wood Eliot, see Gordon, pp. 72–80, and Ackroyd, passim.

67 Lawrence, "Samson and Delilah," *Complete Short Stories*, 3 vols. (New York: Viking, 1977) 2: 424, 426.

68 See Lawrence, "Women Are So Cocksure," in *Phoenix: The Posthumous Papers of D. H. Lawrence*, ed. Edward D. McDonald (New York: Viking, 1936), pp. 167–69. In the same collection, "The Real Thing" describes woman's struggle for freedom as a fight in which "man has fallen" (196). See also "Cocksure Women and Hensure Men," in *Phoenix II: Uncollected, Unpublished and Other Prose Works by D. H. Lawrence*, ed. Warren Roberts and Harry T. Moore (New York: Viking, 1968), pp. 553–55.

69 Lawrence, "Figs," *Complete Poems*, ed. Vivian de Sola Pinto and Warren Roberts, 2 vols. (New York: Viking, 1964), 1: 284.

70 Lawrence, *Women in Love* (New York: Penguin, 1976), p. 238. Further references will be to this edition, and page numbers will appear in the text. For discussions, from various perspectives, of Lawrence's identification with women, his sense of male secondariness, and what seem to some critics to be his intermittent feminist sympathies, see Carol Dix, *D. H. Lawrence and Women* (Totowa, New Jersey: Rowman and Littlefield, 1980); Judith Ruderman, *D. H. Lawrence and the Devouring Mother: The search for a patriarchal ideal of leadership* (Durham: Duke University Press, 1984); and Sandra M. Gilbert, "Potent Griselda: D. H. Lawrence and the Great Mother," in Peter Balbert and Phillip Marcus, ed., *Centenary Essays on D. H. Lawrence* (Ithaca: Cornell University Press, 1985).

71 Comparable enactments of male-female combat characterize Lawrence's short

stories "Tickets, Please" (in which a streetcar inspector with the Lawrentian name *John Thomas* has to ward off the erotic and aggressive assaults of a band of wartime female tram conductors) and "The Princess" (whose virginal heroine shoots her Spanish guide, Romero, after he has sexually assaulted her high in the mountains of New Mexico). See D. H. Lawrence, *The Complete Short Stories*, vol. 2.

72 Tarkington's story is included in *The World Does Move; The Works of Booth Tarkington*, 26 vols. (Garden City, New York: Doubleday, 1922–32) 23:266–79. It is briefly discussed by Joanna Russ in "*Amor Vincit Foeminam:* The Battle of the Sexes in Science Fiction," *Science Fiction Studies* 7 (1980) 2–15; rpt. in *Gender Studies: New Directions in Feminist Criticism*, ed. Judith Spector (Bowling Green, Ohio: Bowling Green State University Popular Press, 1986), pp. 60–69. We are grateful to William Collins for calling this story to our attention. Collins has also referred us to Owen M. Johnson's *The Coming of the Amazons* (New York: Longmans, Green, 1931), a work by the author of *Stover at Yale* in which a man who has been frozen in 1929 awakens in 2075 to find that, in Collins's words, "Seven-foot, blonde giantesses rule the world. A woman scientist had invented a death ray which decimated much of the earth . . . Women seized power, and the remaining men are second-class citizens. . . . The thawed hero organizes the men and wins equality when they use a reversal of the Lysistrata ploy." (William Collins, personal letter.)

73 Hemingway, "The Short Happy Life of Francis Macomber," *The Snows of Kilimanjaro and other Stories* (New York: Scribner's, 1970), pp. 127, 154.

74 Faulkner, *Light in August* (New York: Random House, 1959) pp. 221–22, pp. 247–48.

75 Oates, " 'At Least I Have Made a Woman of Her': Images of Women in Yeats, Lawrence, Faulkner," *The Profane Art: Essays and Reviews* (New York: Dutton, 1983), pp. 61–62.

76 West, *Miss Lonelyhearts & The Day of the Locust* (New York: New Directions, 1969), pp. 27–28. Further references will be to this edition, and page numbers will be included in the text.

77 Quoted in Norman Mailer, *The Prisoner of Sex* (New York: Signet, 1971), p. 91. Further references to passages from this work will be to this edition and page numbers will appear in the text.

78 Thurber, "The War Between Men and Women," in *The Thurber Carnival* (New York: Grosset and Dunlap, 1945), pp. 295–305.

79 Lawrence, *Lady Chatterley's Lover* (Harmondsworth: Penguin, 1961), pp. 219, 209.

80 Quoted in Mailer, *Prisoner of Sex*, p. 91.

81 Miller, *Sexus* (New York: Grove, 1965), p. 83, and *Tropic of Capricorn* (London: Calder, 1964), pp. 164–66. See also Kate Millett's chapter on Miller in *Sexual Politics*, pp. 387–411.

82 Lowell, "Memories of West Street and Lepke," in *Life Studies*, Lowell, *Selected Poems* (New York: Farrar Straus, 1976), p. 91; Friedan, *The Feminine Mystique* (New York: Laurel, 1984); in different ways, this point is examined by the recent documentary film *Rosie the Riveter*, and by Barbara Ehrenreich in *The Hearts of Men: American Dreams and the Flight from Commitment* (Garden City, New York: Anchor, 1983).

83 The debate about the identity of "Pauline Réage" has not led to a definitive identification of the gender of the author. Paradoxically, Réage's precursor the Marquis de Sade has often been viewed as a sexual liberator, even by some feminists; see, for example, Susan Sontag, "The Pornographic Imagination," *Styles of Radical Will* (1966; New York: Delta, 1969), p. 45; Angela Carter, *The Sadeian Woman and the Ideology of Pornography* (New York: Pantheon, 1978); and Jane Gallop, *Intersections. A Reading of Sade with Bataille, Blanchot, and Klossowski* (Lincoln: University of Nebraska Press, 1981).

84 Stopes, *Married Love: A New Contribution to the Solution of Sex Differences* (London: Fifield, 1918); van der Velde, *Ideal Marriage,* tr. Stella Brown (New York: Random House, 1930).

85 Despite the fact that, as the film *Rosie the Riveter* demonstrates, many women workers were forced out of the lucrative factory jobs they occupied in World War II, these workers did remain in the labor force. See Chafe, pp. 174–84.

86 Stephen Heath discusses this cultural view of sex in *The Sexual Fix* (New York: Schocken, 1984), esp. pp. 1–5, 149–50.

87 Snodgrass, "April Inventory," *Heart's Needle* (New York: Alfred A. Knopf, 1961), p. 38.

88 Williams, *Paterson* (New York: New Directions, 1963), p. 125. Further references will be to this edition and page numbers will appear in the text.

89 Wright, *A Native Son,* with an introduction, "How 'Bigger' Was Born," by the author, (New York: Harper & Row, 1940), pp. 222–23. Further references will be to this edition and page numbers will appear in the text.

90 Ellison, *Invisible Man* (New York: Random House, 1952), p. 394. Further references will be to this edition and page numbers will appear in the text.

91 Williams, *A Streetcar Named Desire* (New York: Dramatists Play Service, 1953), pp. 50–51. Further references will be to this edition and page numbers will appear in the text.

92 Ginsberg, *Collected Poems, 1947–1980* (New York: Harper & Row, 1984), p. 132.

93 Ginsberg, *Collected Poems,* p. 144; Snyder, *RIPRAP & Cold Mountain Poems* (San Francisco: City Lights, 1965), pp. 17, 18.

94 On Burroughs, see John Tytell, *Naked Angels: The Lives and Literature of the Beat Generation* (New York: McGraw-Hill, 1976), p. 45.

95 Mary Allen makes some of these points in *The Necessary Blankness: Women in Major American Fiction of the Sixties* (Urbana: University of Illinois Press, 1976), pp. 37–46. To be sure, Pynchon's complex text can be read as a quasi-feminist protest against the construction of woman-as-artifice by a masculinist technological culture, but it seems significant that his portrayal of V draws upon a tradition of literary misogyny that dates back at least to Spenser's portrait of Duessa and Swift's "The Progress of Love."

96 Eliot, *The Waste Land: A Facsimile and Transcript . . . ,* ed. Valerie Eliot (New York: Harcourt, 1971), p. 23.

97 Millett, *Sexual Politics,* p. 32.

98 See, for instance, William Faulkner, "Dry September," *The Penguin Collected Stories of William Faulkner* (Harmondsworth: Penguin, 1985), pp. 169–83.

99 Baraka [Jones], *Dutchman & The Slave* (New York: Morrow, 1964), scene 1,

pp. 14, 19. Further references will be to this edition and will appear in the text.

100 Baraka, "Babylon Revisited," *Selected Poetry of Amiri Baraka/LeRoi Jones* (New York: Morrow, 1979), p. 119.

101 Wylie, *Generation of Vipers* (New York: Rinehart, 1942), p. 203. Perhaps paradoxically, however, in *The Disappearance* (New York: Rinehart, 1951), Wylie produced a fantasy about two unisex worlds existing side by side—women disappear from the sight of men, men disappear from the sight of women—in which the manless women do considerably better than the womanless men. His comments on the construction of sex roles are strikingly feminist, moreover: at one point, his male protagonist speculates that "woman's . . . place, essentially 'inferior,' was not in any way the place nature had created her to fill" (263), and at another point this philosophical hero comments directly on the battle of the sexes, asking "If their sexes so revile each other, *how can a species love?* How, if one sex regards itself as superior, can it refrain from detesting the 'inferior' sex?" (264) In conclusion, he decides that "we desperately need a new word, now, that means man-plus-woman and turns everybody away from the cockeyed idea that one without the other means anything—that there are *differences*—that there are relative superiorities and inferiorities" (403).

102 Lundberg and Farnham, *Modern Woman—The Lost Sex* (New York: Harper & Row, 1947), p. 319.

103 Albee, *Who's Afraid of Virginia Woolf?* (New York: Pocket, 1963), p. 189.

104 Osborne, *Look Back in Anger* (New York: Bantam, 1967), pp. 60, 62.

105 Roth, *Portnoy's Complaint* (New York: Random House, 1969), p. 37.

106 Mailer, *The Prisoner of Sex*, p. 37.

107 Lasch, *The Culture of Narcissism* (New York: W. W. Norton, 1978), pp. 189–93.

108 See Roth, *The Breast* (New York: Holt, 1972).

109 See Barth, "Night-Sea Journey," *Lost in the Funhouse: Fiction for Print, Tape, Live Voice* (Garden City, New York: Doubleday, 1968), pp. 3–13.

110 Lasch, *Culture*, p. 195.

111 Tenn, "The Masculinist Revolt," in *The Wooden Star* (New York: Ballantine, 1968), p. 214; further references will be to this edition, and page numbers will be included in the text.

112 Ironically, a few years later Elizabeth Gould Davis actually published a book about women entitled *The First Sex* (New York: Putnam, 1971), but Tenn may, of course, have been alluding to Simone de Beauvoir's *The Second Sex* (1949).

113 See "Cleaver Reveals Why He Didn't Surrender In His Sexy Suit," in *Jet* 51 (November 18, 1976), p. 29. In this interview Cleaver also commented that "I consider my basic design to be one of the greatest artistic triumphs of this 20th Century . . . because for the first time someone has illustrated graphically that ideology and morality are structured into our clothes." See also, for Cleaver's comments on contraception, "Cleaver: Any Man Can," in *Mother Jones* (April 30, 1978), p. 10.

114 But see also Ford Madox Ford's feminist polemic *This Monstrous Regiment of Women* (cited in note 45 above).

115 Berger, *Regiment of Women* (New York: Popular Library, 1973); further references will be to this edition, and page numbers will appear in the text.
116 For further elaborations of this view in contemporary male-authored fiction see, for instance, George Stade, *Confessions of A Lady-Killer* (New York: W. W. Norton, 1979); D. M. Thomas, *The White Hotel* (1981; New York: Pocket Books, 1982); Leonard Michaels, *The Men's Club* (New York: Farrar Straus, 1981); and Ishmael Reed, *Reckless Eyeballing* (New York: St. Martin's, 1986). Particularly in *The Men's Club*, the men feel that women have monopolized "Anger, identity, politics, rights, wrongs. I envied them," and therefore they raid and ransack the refrigerator in which one of their wives has stored food for a women's consciousness-raising meeting; but when this wife returns she hits her husband over the head with a "black iron pot."
117 Irving, *The World According to Garp* (New York: Pocket, 1979); for a discussion of the novel's inscription of patriarchal power, see Janice Doane and Devon Hodges, "Women and the Word According to *Garp*," in *Gender Studies*, pp. 60–69. For the photograph of Irving, see Annie Leibovitz, *Photographs* (New York: Pantheon, 1982).
118 Bly, *San Francisco Chronicle*, pp. 36, 38. For a fuller and even more recent discussion of what we might call the "wild man movement" (and Bly's place in it) as well as a review of some feminist reactions to it, see Steve Chapple, "In Search of the Beast Within," *San Francisco Examiner: Image* (Sunday magazine, January 11, 1987), 12–19, 36–37.
119 Plath, *Johnny Panic and the Bible of Dreams: Short Stories, Prose, and Diary Excerpts* (New York: Harper Colophon, 1980), p. 184. Further references to stories in this collection will be included in the text, preceded by the letters *JP*.
120 Plath, *Letters Home*, ed. Aurelia Schober Plath (New York: Harper & Row, 1975), p. 270. Further references to this volume will be designated *LH*, and page numbers will appear in the text.

Chapter 2

EPIGRAPHS: Egerton, "The Spell of The White Elf" in *Keynotes* (1893), *Keynotes and Discords* (London: Virago, 1983), pp. 80–81; further references to stories in both *Keynotes* and *Discords* will be to the Virago edition and will appear in the text; Richardson, *Honeycomb* (1917), in *Pilgrimage*, vol. 1 (New York: Alfred A. Knopf, 1967), p. 423; Warner, letter to Nancy Cunard, April 28, 1944, in *Letters*, ed. William Maxwell (London: Chatto & Windus, 1982), p. 84.
1 Plath, "Words," *Collected Poems of Sylvia Plath* (New York: Harper & Row, 1981), p. 270. Further references to Plath's poems will be to this edition, and page numbers will appear in the text, preceded by the citation *CP*.
2 *The Poems of Emily Dickinson*, ed. Thomas Johnson, 3 vols. (Cambridge: The Belknap Press of Harvard University Press, 1955), J. 540. Further references

to Dickinson's poems will be to this edition and will be cited in the text by their Johnson number. Olga Broumas is quoted in an epigraph to Barbara Clarke Mossberg, *When A Writer Is A Daughter* (Bloomington: Indiana University Press, 1982).

3 In a very different context, Natalie Zemon Davis has observed, in a study of Pardon tales in sixteenth-century France, that even though women in the sixteenth century (unlike women in the nineteenth and twentieth centuries) "were told . . . that they were uncontrollably angry, as they were also uncontrollably libidinous," female supplicants for pardon—unlike their male counterparts—rarely attributed their crimes to anger but instead adduced such emotions as fear, despair, or jealousy. See Natalie Zemon Davis, "Bloodshed and the Woman's Voice," in *Fiction in the Archives: Pardon Tales and Their Tellers in Sixteenth-Century France* (Stanford: Stanford University Press, 1987.)

4 In " 'When the Women Reign': Fantasy Literature of the Suffragette Era," Katherine Stern makes a comparable point about popular novels, noting that in female-authored utopias and male-authored dystopias about sexual battle "Men tend to invoke the notion of a 'war between the sexes' quite literally while women envision more subtle political manoeuvres and compromises." (*Critical Matrix*, 3 [Spring 1987]).

5 Oates, "The Magnanimity of *Wuthering Heights*," *The Profane Art*, p. 72.

6 Plath, *The Journals of Sylvia Plath*, ed. Ted Hughes and Francis McCullough (New York: Dial, 1982), p. 148. Further references to this volume will be included in the text and will be cited as *J*.

7 For a more extended discussion of this issue, see our *The Madwoman in the Attic*, (New Haven: Yale University Press, 1979), chapter 8.

8 *The Complete Poems of Emily Jane Brontë*, ed. C. W. Hatfield (New York: Columbia University Press, 1941), p. 239.

9 For a discussion of the battle between Bertha Mason Rochester and Rochester as a kind of primal scene, see Elaine Showalter, *A Literature of Their Own: British Women Novelists from Brontë to Lessing* (Princeton: Princeton University Press, 1977), pp. 118–22.

10 Quoted in Virginia L. Radley, *Elizabeth Barrett Browning* (New York: Twayne, 1972), p. 79.

11 See "Lady Geraldine's Courtship" in *The Complete Works of Elizabeth Barrett Browning*, ed. Porter and Clarke, stanza VII. Subsequent references will also be to stanza numbers, or—in the case of *Aurora Leigh*—to book and line numbers, and they will appear in the text.

12 For a discussion of this issue, see Carol Christ, "Aggression and Providential Death in George Eliot's Fiction," *Novel* (Winter 1976), 130–40.

13 Rossetti, *The Complete Poems of Christina Rossetti*, ed. R. W. Crump (Baton Rouge: Louisiana State University Press, 1979), vol. I, lines 406–07. Further references will be to line numbers and will appear in the text.

14 Jackson, *Gifts of Power: The Writings of Rebecca Jackson, Black Visionary, Shaker Eldress*, ed. Jean McMahon Humez (Amherst: University of Massachusetts Press, 1981), p. 94. Further references will be to this volume and page numbers will appear in the text.

15 Vicinus, *Independent Women: Work and Community for Single Women, 1850–1920* (Chicago: University of Chicago Press, 1985), p. 127.

16 Quoted in Vicinus, *Independent Women*, pp. 151, 142–43.

17 Schreiner, *From Man To Man*, with an introductory note by S. C. Cronwright-Schreiner (1927; Chicago: Cassandra-Academy Press, 1977), p. 196. In *Continuing Presences: Virginia Woolf's Use of Literary Allusion* (University Park: Pennsylvania State University Press, 1979), Beverly Ann Schlack observes that Virginia Woolf most likely knew William Black's book *Judith Shakespeare* (1883): p. 146. See Black, *Judith Shakespeare: A Romance* (New and Revised Edition, New York: Harper, 1893); in this somewhat melodramatic novel, Judith Shakespeare is actually the dramatist's daughter, but, though she is not an aspiring writer, she is for most of the work notably rebellious and imaginative.

18 Gilman, *Women and Economics*, ed. Carl N. Degler (1898; New York: Harper & Row, 1966). Gilman argues, for example, that "The life of the female savage is freedom itself . . . compared with the increasing constriction of custom closing in upon the woman, as civilization advances, like the iron torture chamber of romance" (p. 65).

19 Quoted in Andrew Rosen, *Rise Up, Women: The Militant Campaign of the Women's Social and Political Union, 1903–1914* (London: Routledge, 1974), p. 207. Also see the discussion of suffragist militancy in Vicinus, *Independent Women*, pp. 247–80.

20 Quoted by Rosen, *Rise Up, Women*, p. 93.

21 Vicinus, *Independent Women*, p. 261.

22 Holtby, *Women and a Changing Civilization* (1935; Chicago: Cassandra-Academy Press, 1978), p. 103.

23 Vicinus, *Independent Women*, p. 277.

24 Helen Gordon [Liddle], *The Prison: A Sketch* (Letchworth: Garden City Press, 1911), pp. 63–64.

25 Davison, "The Price of Liberty," *Suffragette* 5 (June 1914), p. 10. Also see Rosen, *Rise Up, Women*, pp. 198–200.

26 Chopin, "The Story of an Hour," *The Complete Works of Kate Chopin*, ed. Per Seyersted, 2 vols. (Baton Rouge: Louisiana State University Press, 1969), 1:352. Further references to Chopin's stories will be to this edition, and page numbers will appear in the text.

27 Schreiner, "A Little African Story," in *Dream Life and Real Life* (Chicago: Cassandra-Academy Press, 1977), pp. 9–45.

28 "A White Night" is reprinted in *Charlotte Mew: Collected Poems and Prose*, ed. Val Warner (London: Virago, 1981), p. 147. Further references will be to this edition and page numbers will appear in the text.

29 Edgar Allan Poe, "The Fall of the House of Usher," *Poetry and Tales* (New York: Library of America, 1984), p. 334.

30 In Chopin's "Desiree's Baby" a similar sacrifice is enacted. Indeed, the mother who is accused of black ancestry in that story destroys herself and her baby, although the husband whose racism drove her to this fate is finally proven to be of black descent himself; see *The Complete Works of Kate Chopin*, pp. 240–45.

31 Freeman, "Old Woman Magoun," *The Best Short Stories of Mary E. Wilkins* (New York: Harper's, 1927), p. 169. Further references will be to this edition and page numbers will appear in the text.

32 Sarah Orne Jewett's "A White Heron" is a good example of a story about a heroine's symbolic resistance to male sexuality; that the young protagonist refuses to help the hunter find and kill the heron suggests that she has also refused to be inducted into the heterosexual order. See *The Country of the Pointed Firs and Other Stories*, ed. Willa Cather (Garden City, New York: Doubleday, 1956), pp. 161–71. "The Farmer's Bride," a dramatic monologue spoken by a sexually-frustrated husband, tells the story of such resistance from a male point of view. See Mew, *Collected Poems and Prose*, pp. 1–3.

33 "A New England Nun" is reprinted in *Selected Stories of Mary E. Wilkins Freeman*, ed. with an intro. by Marjorie Pryse (New York: W. W. Norton, 1983), pp. 109–25. Page numbers for other Freeman stories collected in this anthology will appear in the text preceded by the citation *SS*.

34 Wharton, "The Other Two," *Collected Short Stories*, ed. R. W. B. Lewis, 2 vols. (New York: Scribner's, 1968), 1:386 and 393. Further references to Wharton stories will be to this edition and page numbers will be included in the text.

35 Gilman, "When I Was a Witch," is reprinted in *The Charlotte Perkins Gilman Reader*, ed. Ann J. Lane (New York: Pantheon, 1980), p. 31.

36 Gilman, *Herland* (New York: Pantheon, 1979).

37 Gilman's *The Man-Made World; or, Our Androcentric Culture* (New York: Charlton Co., 1911) is her most explicit work on this subject.

38 Rudyard Kipling, "Recessional," in *Rudyard Kipling's Verse, inclusive edition, 1885–1926* (New York: Doubleday, 1927), p. 379.

39 Glaspell, "Trifles," in her *Plays* (Boston: Small, Maynard, 1920), p. 14. Further references will be to this edition and page numbers will be included in the text.

40 Cather, *The Professor's House* (New York: Vintage, 1973), p. 214, and "Coming, Aphrodite!" in *Youth and the Bright Medusa* (New York: Vintage, 1975), pp. 3–63.

41 "Helen" and "Eurydice" appear in *H. D.: Collected Poems, 1912–1944*, ed. Louis L. Martz (New York: New Directions, 1983), pp. 154 and 51–55. Further references to H. D.'s poems in this edition will appear in the text, with page numbers preceded by the citation *CP*. H. D.'s ambivalence about female militancy and triumph is also made clear in the poem "Telesila" (1924), whose protagonist is a woman warrior/poet (according to Pausanius the head of a woman's army) torn between love and war: the piece begins with the following epigraph: *"In Argos—that statue of her; / at her feet the scroll of her / love-poetry, in her hand a helmet"* (*CP*, 184). We are grateful to Gary Burnett for bringing this text to our attention.

42 Millay, *Collected Poems*, ed. Norma Millay (New York: Harper, 1956), p. 606; Glasgow, "Jordan's End," *Collected Stories of Ellen Glasgow*, ed. Richard K. Meeker (Baton Rouge: Louisiana State University Press, 1963), p. 214.

43 Hurston, *Their Eyes Were Watching God* (Urbana: University of Illinois Press, 1978), p. 273. Earlier in the novel Janie has rebelled against the domination of her

second husband by attacking his potency and has effectively catapulted him into a decline that he claims results in his death.

44 Mansfield, "The Garden-Party," in *The Short Stories of Katherine Mansfield* (New York: Knopf, 1976), p. 548; Virginia Woolf, *Mrs. Dalloway* (New York: Harcourt, 1925), p. 284. But see also Mansfield's "The Woman at the Store" (1912) which presents a female character who enters the battle of the sexes in order to right the wrongs marriage has inflicted upon her and who manages only provisionally to survive. The heroine of this tale claims that her husband is " 'away shearin' " but visiting travelers learn otherwise from a picture that the woman's child draws "of the woman shooting at a man with a rook rifle and then digging a hole to bury him in" (134). Although the nameless storekeeper has attempted to stop her child from representing this scene, she has also testified to her belief that her rage against her husband was justified:

"It's six years since I was married, and four miscarriages. I says to 'im, I says, what do you think I'm doing up 'ere? If you was back at the Coast, I'd 'ave you lynched for child murder. Over and over I tells 'em—you've broken my spirit and spoiled my looks, and wot for—that's wot I'm driving at . . ." (131).

In spite of her retaliation against a man who " 'shut [her] up 'ere like a broody 'en' " (132), however, Mansfield's rural woman has been "broken" both by her husband and by her own revenge against him. Looking like "a figure of fun," she is said to be "nothing but sticks and wires" and "her front teeth were knocked out . . ." (126). She has effected the fall of her husband but she herself has not risen.

45 Hurston, "Sweat," in *Spunk* (Berkeley: Turtle Island Foundation, 1985). Further references will be to this edition and will appear in the text. Sykes's name, along with his brutality, suggests that Hurston is consciously or unconsciously revising the plot of sexual battle that Dickens constructs around Bill Sykes and his girlfriend Nancy in *Oliver Twist* (1837).

46 West, "Indissoluble Matrimony," is reprinted in the *Norton Anthology of Literature by Women: The Tradition in English*, ed. Sandra M. Gilbert and Susan Gubar (New York: W. W. Norton, 1985), pp. 1577–99. Further references will be to this edition and page numbers will appear in the text.

47 *The Young Rebecca: Writings of Rebecca West, 1911–1917*, ed. Jane Marcus (New York: Viking, 1982), p. 101.

48 Moore, "Shambleau," in *The Best of C. L. Moore*, ed. Lester Del Rey (New York: Ballantine, 1975), pp. 1–32 (further references will be to this edition, and page numbers will appear in the text); Petry, *The Street* (New York: Pyramid, 1961); further references will be to this edition, and page numbers will appear in the text); McCullers, *The Ballad of the Sad Cafe and Other Stories* (New York: Bantam, 1981; further references will be to this edition, and page numbers will appear in the text).

49 See Freud, "The Medusa's Head" (1922) in *Collected Papers*, vol. 5, ed. James Strachey (London: Hogarth Press, 1950), pp. 105–06. About Moore, it should be noted that she was married to and collaborated with Henry Kuttner, also the

author of science fiction about female power. See, for instance, Kuttner's and Moore's *The Mask of Circe* (1948; New York: CBS Publications, 1975); although the title page names both as authors, the cover of this edition represents the novel as the sole work of Kuttner.

50 Rich's essay, "Compulsory Heterosexuality and Lesbian Existence," originally appeared in *Signs* (1980) and is reprinted in *Women: Sex and Sexuality*, ed. Catharine R. Stimpson and Ethel Spector Person (Chicago: University of Chicago Press, 1980), pp. 62–91.

51 Claire Kahane offers a brief discussion of this point in "The Gothic Mirror," in *The (M)other Tongue: Essays in Feminist Psychoanalytic Interpretation*, ed. Shirley Nelson Garner, Claire Kahane, and Madelon Sprengnether (Ithaca: Cornell University Press, 1985), pp. 347–48.

52 See Freud, "Female Sexuality" (1931), in *Sexuality and the Psychology of Love*, pp. 98–99.

53 O'Connor, "Good Country People," *The Complete Stories of Flannery O'Connor* (New York: Farrar, 1971), pp. 271–91.

54 Bowen, "The Demon Lover," *The Collected Stories of Elizabeth Bowen*, with an introduction by Angus Wilson (New York: Vintage, 1981), pp. 661–66; Sylvia Plath, *The Bell Jar* (New York: Bantam, 1972).

55 Rhys, *Wide Sargasso Sea* (New York: W. W. Norton, 1967).

56 Walker, "The Child Who Favored Daughter," *In Love and Trouble: Stories of Black Women* (New York: Harcourt, 1963), pp. 35–46; Morrison, *The Bluest Eye* (New York: Washington Square Press, 1972).

57 Piercy, "The friend," *Circles on the Water* (New York: Knopf, 1982), p. 39; May Swenson, "Bleeding," *New & Selected Things Taking Place* (Boston: Little, 1978), p. 104; Atwood, *Power Politics* (New York: Harper & Row, 1978), p. 1.

58 Marshall, *Brown Girl, Brownstones* (Old Westbury, New York: Feminist Press, 1981).

59 Jackson, "The Lottery," *The Lottery* (New York: Avon, 1960), p. 215.

60 Oates, *Where Are You Going? Where Have You Been?: Stories of Young America* (Greenwich, Conn.: Fawcett, 1974), p. 66.

61 Lurie, *The War Between the Tates* (New York: Warner Paperback Library, 1975), pp. 206, 300.

62 O'Faolain, "Man in the Cellar," in *Bitches and Sad Ladies*, ed. Pat Rotter (New York: Dell, 1976), p. 179. Further references will be to this edition, and page numbers will be included in the text. We are grateful to Mary Davidson for bringing this text and others to our attention.

63 Bradley, *The Shattered Chain* (New York: Daw Books, 1976); Monique Wittig, *Les Guérillères*, trans. by David Le Vay (New York: Avon, 1973).

64 Tiptree, "Mama Come Home," *Ten Thousand Light-Years from Home* (New York: Ace, 1973), pp. 77, 69.

65 Tiptree, "The Women Men Don't See," *Warm Worlds and Otherwise* (New York: Ballantine, 1975), pp. 153, 154, and 163.

66 Russ, *The Female Man* (New York: Bantam, 1975), p. 197. Further references will be to this edition, and page numbers will appear in the text.

67 Carter, "The Company of Wolves," *The Bloody Chamber* (New York: Harper & Row, 1979), p. 153.

68 Kingston, *The Woman Warrior* (New York: Alfred A. Knopf, 1976), pp. 47 and 43.

69 Wakoski, *The Motorcycle Betrayal Poems* (New York: Simon & Schuster, 1971) and *Dancing on the Grave of a Son of a Bitch* (Los Angeles: Black Sparrow, 1973); Rich, *Diving Into the Wreck* (New York: W. W. Norton, 1973); Griffin, "I Like to Think of Harriet Tubman," in *Like the Iris of an Eye* (New York: Harper & Row, 1976), p. 12; Lorde, *Cables to Rage* (Detroit: Broadside, 1970).

70 Tiptree, "The Screwfly Solution," in *Out of the Everywhere and Other Extraordinary Visions* (New York: Dell Ray, 1981), p. 54. Further references will be to this edition, and page numbers will appear in the text. We are grateful to Elissa Sparks for bringing this text to our attention. More recently, Margaret Atwood has produced a comparable fable about the subordination and—in some cases—extermination of women: see Atwood, *The Handmaid's Tale* (Boston: Houghton Mifflin, 1986).

Chapter 3

EPIGRAPHS: Woolf, *A Room of One's Own*, p. 68; Butler, *The Authoress of the Odyssey*, with a new introduction by David Grene (1897; Chicago: University of Chicago Press, 1967), p. 13; Stein, *Everybody's Autobiography* (1937; New York: Vintage, 1973), p. 5; Eliot, "Tradition and the Individual Talent," in *Selected Essays of T. S. Eliot* (1919; New York: Harcourt, 1950), p. 5. Further references to this essay will be to this edition, and page numbers will appear in the text.

1 Beerbohm's letter to Woolf is held in the Robert H. Taylor Collection of the Firestone Library at Princeton University. This remarkable letter will be quoted in full in Sir Rupert Hart-Davis's forthcoming *Letters of Max Beerbohm* (1988).

2 "The Crime," in Beerbohm, *And Even Now* (London: Heinemann, 1920), p. 246. Subsequent references will be to this edition, and page numbers will be included in the text.

3 Beerbohm, *Zuleika Dobson; Or, An Oxford Love Story* (New York: Heritage, 1960).

4 Woolf, "Response to 'Affable Hawk' [Desmond MacCarthy]," in *The New Statesman*, 2 October 1920; reprinted in Virginia Woolf, *Women and Writing*, ed. Michele Barrett (New York: Harcourt, 1979), pp. 55–56.

5 "Lycidas," lines 15, 18. Harold Bloom, of course, discusses the relationship between the (female) muse and the (male) poet extensively throughout *The Anxiety of Influence* (New York: Oxford, 1973) and its companion volumes.

6 Lewis, "The Children of the New Epoch," *The Tyro* I (April 1921): 3; reprinted in *Wyndham Lewis on Art: Collected Writings 1913–1956*, ed. Walter Michel and C. J. Fox (New York: Funk & Wagnalls, 1969), p. 195. We are grateful to Elyse Blankley for bringing this remark to our attention.

7 Bloom, *A Map of Misreading* (New York: Oxford, 1975), p. 33.

8 Huxley, *Limbo* (New York: Doran, 1920), p. 2. Further references will be to this edition, and page numbers will be included in the text. In "The Manx Cat Again,"

in the *Virginia Woolf Miscellany* (Fall 1984), Joanna Lipking also offers an illuminating discussion of this Huxley tale.

9   Woolf's review of *Limbo* is reprinted in her *Contemporary Writers*, with a preface by Jean Guignet (New York: Harcourt, 1965), p. 150.

10 All the James stories cited here are included in Henry James, *Stories of Writers and Artists*, ed. F. O. Matthiessen (New York: New Directions, 1944). "Death of the Lion": pp. 220–21. Subsequent references will be to this edition, and page numbers will be included in the text.

11 Saki, "The Open Window," *Complete Works of Saki* (New York: Doubleday, 1976), p. 254. Further references will be to this edition, and page numbers will be included in the text.

12 Hardy, "The Ivy Wife," in *The Complete Poems of Thomas Hardy*, ed. James Gibson (New York: Macmillan, 1976), p. 57.

13 Hardy, *Life's Little Ironies* (London: Macmillan, 1953). In a prefatory note, Hardy explains that "An Imaginative Woman" originally appeared in *Wessex Tales* (1888) "but was brought into this volume as being more nearly its place, turning as it does upon a trick of Nature, so to speak . . .", p. 9. Further references will be to this edition, and page numbers will be included in the text.

14 Maugham, "The Colonel's Lady," *Complete Short Stories of Somerset Maugham*, 2 vols. (New York: Doubleday, 1952), 2:589. Further references will be to this edition, and page numbers will be included in the text.

15 To be sure, as Dale Spender argues in *Mothers of the Novel: 100 Good Women Writers before Jane Austen* (London: Pandora, 1986), significant numbers of women were writing and publishing before 1800 and were especially prominent during the eighteenth century. Indeed, the proliferation of satires attacking literary women in the eighteenth century could be said to foreshadow the dynamics we are tracing here. By the middle of the nineteenth century, however, the achievements of most of those female authors had been erased or neglected by literary historians.

16 Hawthorne's comment is quoted by Caroline Ticknor in *Hawthorne and His Publishers* (Boston: Houghton Mifflin, 1913), p. 142.

17 Quoted in Alfred Habegger, *Gender, Fantasy and Realism in American Literature* (New York: Columbia University Press, 1982), p. 239.

18 Quoted in Cheryl Walker, *The Nightingale's Burden: Women Poets and American Culture Before 1900* (Bloomington: Indiana University Press, 1982), p. 117.

19 Walker, p. 125.

20 See Baym, *Woman's Fiction: A Guide to Novels by and about Women in America, 1820–1870* (Ithaca: Cornell University Press, 1978), and Smith, "The Scribbling Woman and the Cosmic Success Story," *Critical Inquiry*, 1 (1974): 47–70.

21 Ziff is describing James's *Essays in London and Elsewhere* in *The American 1890s: Life and Times of a Lost Generation* (New York: Viking, 1966), p. 275.

22 Beer, *The Mauve Decade* (New York: Vintage, 1960), pp. 31–32.

23 On Stedman, see Walker, p. 201; Fiedler, "Literature and Lucre," *The New York Times Book Review*, 31 May 1981:7. For other historical and theoretical discussions of this subject, see Ann Douglas, *The Feminization of American Culture* (New York:

Alfred A. Knopf, 1977); and Nina Baym, "Melodramas of Beset Manhood," in *The New Feminist* Criticism, ed. Elaine Showalter (New York: Pantheon, 1985), pp. 63–80.

24 Brooks, "The Literary Life," *Civilization in the United States* (New York: Harcourt, 1922), p. 182, and Stearns, "The Intellectual Life," in *Civilization in the United States*, p. 135, 143. We are grateful to Elyse Blankley for bringing these texts to our attention.

25 Swinburne, *The Complete Works of Algernon Charles Swinburne*, ed. Sir Edmund Gosse and Thomas James Wise, 20 vols. (London and New York: Heinemann and Wells, 1925–27): "Aurora Leigh," 16:3–8; "A Note on Charlotte Brontë," 14:3–42; "Emily Brontë," 14:45–54. Further references to these essays will be to this edition, and page numbers will be included in the text.

26 *The Artist as Critic: Critical Writings of Oscar Wilde*, ed. Richard Ellmann (Chicago: University of Chicago Press, 1982), pp. 105, 107–08. Further references will be to this edition, and page numbers will appear in the text.

27 Harte, "Miss Mix by Ch-l-tte Br-nte," in *American Literature, Tradition and Innovation*, II. *Romantic and Realistic Writing*, ed. Harrison T. Meserole, Walter Sutton, and Brom Weber (Lexington, Mass.: D. C. Heath, 1969); text taken from Harte, *Condensed Novels and Other Papers* (New York, 1967).

28 Twain [Samuel L. Clemens], *Adventures of Huckleberry Finn*, ed. James K. Bowen and Richard Vanderbeets (Glenview, Ill.: Scott, Foresman, 1970), pp. 120–21.

29 Lawrence, *Studies in Classic American Literature*, (1923; New York: Penguin, 1977), p. 10. Further references will be to this edition and, page numbers will appear in the text.

30 On p. 92 of *Studies*, Lawrence describes his father and mother in comparable terms:

My father hated books, hated the sight of anyone reading or writing.
My mother hated the thought that any of her sons should be condemned to manual labor. Her sons must have something higher than that.
She won. But she died first.
He laughs longest who laughs last.
There is a basic hostility in all of us between the physical and the mental, the blood and the spirit. The mind is 'ashamed' of the blood. And the blood is destroyed by the mind, actually. Hence pale-faces.

31 Adams, *After Joyce: Studies in Fiction after Ulysses* (New York: Oxford University Press, 1977), p. 5.

32 On Joyce's use of Maria Cummins's *The Lamplighter*, see Anthony Burgess, *Joysprick: An Introduction to the Language of James Joyce* (New York: Harcourt, 1973), p. 103.

33 West, *Miss Lonelyhearts and the Day of the Locust* (New York: New Directions, 1962), pp. 13–14.

34 Higginson, *Margaret Fuller Ossoli* (Boston: Houghton Mifflin, 1884).

35 James, letter to his father (10 May 1869), in *Letters*, ed. Leon Edel, 4 vols. (Cambridge: Belknap Press of Harvard University Press, 1974–84) 1:117.

36 Twain to William Dean Howells, January 18, 1909, reprinted in *The Portable Mark Twain*, ed. Bernard DeVoto (New York: Viking, 1946), p. 785; Kipling, "The Janeites," *The Writings in Prose and Verse of Rudyard Kipling*, 31 vols. (New York: Scribner's, 1916–26), 31:159–91.

37 Costello, "Response to 'Tradition and the Female Talent,' " in *Literary History: Theory and Practice, Proceedings of the Northeastern University Center for Literary Studies*, vol. 2 (1984), ed. Herbert L. Sussman (Boston: Northeastern University Press), p. 28.

38 Anderson's comments appear in Edmund Wilson, *Axel's Castle* (New York: Scribner's, 1931), p. 253, while Eliot's are in his review of Moore's *Poems* and *Marriage The Dial* 75:5 (November, 1923):597.

39 Williams, *In the American Grain* (1925; New York: New Directions, 1956), pp. 178–79.

40 Costello, "Response," p. 29.

41 Graves, *The White Goddess: A Historical Grammar of Poetic Myth*, amended and enlarged ed. (New York: Farrar, 1966), p. 447.

42 For James on Wharton, see Cynthia Griffin Wolff, *A Feast of Words: The Triumph of Edith Wharton* (New York: Oxford, 1977), pp. 144–45.

43 Yeats, "Nineteen Hundred and Nineteen" and "No Second Troy," *Collected Poems*, pp. 205, 208, 89.

44 Lawrence, *Women in Love*, pp. 454–55, and *Kangaroo* (New York: Viking, 1960), p. 253. Besides at least in part fictionalizing Mansfield as Gudrun, Lawrence concluded their long friendship with a cruel note: "I loathe you. You revolt me stewing in your own consumption" (Katherine Mansfield's *Letters to J. Middleton Murry*, ed. Murry [New York: Alfred A. Knopf, 1951], p. 470).

45 Lewis, *The Roaring Queen* (London: Secker, 1973), pp. 80 and 96. For Woolf's response to the chapter entitled "Mr. Bennett and Mrs. Woolf" in Lewis's *Men Without Art* (London: Cassell, 1934), see the October 11, 1934, entry in her diary in which Woolf, explaining that she has "taken the arrow of W. L. to my heart," hopes that "the pain is over," admits that "I can't write," and adds that "there is the odd pleasure too of being abused and the feeling of being dismissed into obscurity is also pleasant and salutary"; see *A Writer's Diary*, ed. by Leonard Woolf (New York: New American Library, 1968), pp. 213–14.

46 For Williams on H. D., see his *Autobiography*, pp. 67–60, 215; on his first meeting with Stein, see his *Autobiography*, p. 254; his confession about Moore appears in Williams, *I Wanted to Write a Poem: The Autobiography of the Works of a Poet*, reported and ed. by Edith Heal (1958; rpt. New York: New Directions, 1978), p. 20.

47 Hemingway, "Portrait of a Lady," *88 Poems*, ed. Nicholas Georgiannis (New York: Harcourt, 1979), p. 90.

48 Hemingway, *A Moveable Feast*, pp. 119 and 18. See also Williams's remark about Stein's unpublished manuscripts in his *Autobiography*, p. 254.

49 Hemingway, "To a Tragic Poetess," *88 Poems*, p. 87.

50 Hemingway, "The Lady Poets With Foot Notes," *88 Poems*, p. 77. We are indebted to Cara Chell for bringing this poem to our attention.

51 Lawrence, *Psychoanalysis and the Unconscious and Fantasia of the Unconscious* (1921, 1922; New York: Viking, 1960), pp. 188–89.

52 Eliot, *The Waste Land: Facsimile and Transcript* . . . , ed. Valerie Eliot, p. 27; Graves, *The White Goddess*, p. 447.

53 For the mutual involvement of Yeats and his wife George with the Order of the Golden Dawn, see George Mills Harper, *Yeats's Golden Dawn* (London: Macmillan, 1974), esp., for references to George, pp. 128–30, 134–36, 162; for a more specific discussion of George's automatic writing, see the Editorial Introduction to *A Critical Edition of Yeats's A Vision (1925)*, ed. George Mills Harper and Walter Kelly Hood (London: Macmillan, 1978). On Lawrence's relationship with Jessie Chambers, see Harry T. Moore, *The Priest of Love: A Life of D. H. Lawrence* (revised edition; Carbondale: Southern Illinois University Press, 1974), esp. pp. 36–38, 43–60, 73–75; on Lawrence's revision of the manuscript given him by the Australian nurse Mollie Skinner, see Moore, pp. 51, 349, 375–76.

54 On Fitzgerald's use of Zelda's notes and diaries, see Nancy Milford, *Zelda: A Biography* (New York: Harper & Row, 1970), pp. 35, 44, 55, 58, 71, 76, 81, 89, 102, 177–78, 284–85; for Vivien Eliot's contribution to *The Waste Land*, see *The Waste Land: Facsimile and Transcript* . . . , p. 15. Williams confesses his fondness for watercress in his *Autobiography*, p. 253; Lowell called Nardi a "lacerated and lacerating poetess" in his review of *Paterson II*, *The Nation*, June 19, 1948: 692–94, reprinted in Jerome Mazzaro, *Profiles of William Carlos Williams* (Columbus, Ohio: Charles E. Merril Publishing Co., 1971), p. 75. On Williams's revision of Marcia Nardi's texts, see Theodora Graham, " 'Her Heigh Compleynte': The Cress Letters of William Carlos Williams' *Paterson*," in *Ezra Pound and William Carlos Williams: The University of Pennsylvania Conference Papers*, ed. Daniel Hoffman (Philadelphia: University of Pennsylvania Press, 1983), pp. 164–93.

55 Williams, *Paterson*, pp. 59, 107.

56 Williams spoke of the Nardi letter as "a tail that tried to wag the dog" in a 1948 letter to Horace Gregory, *Selected Letters of William Carlos Williams*, ed. John L. Thirlwall (New York: McDowell, Obolensky, 1957), p. 266; his comment about "a reply from the female side" was made in a letter of August 21, 1961, to Robert D. Pepper, quoted in Mike Weaver, *William Carlos Williams: The American Background* (Cambridge: Cambridge University Press, 1971), pp. 208–09; his remark that he felt "ashamed for" his "sex" was made in a September 1949 letter to Marcia Nardi that is quoted in Paul Mariani, *William Carlos Williams: A New World Naked* (New York: McGraw-Hill, 1981), p. 587. We are grateful to A. Walton Litz for helping us with this Williams material. For a fuller analysis of this issue, see Sandra M. Gilbert, "Purloined Letters: William Carlos Williams and 'Cress,' " *William Carlos Williams Review* 10:2 (Fall 1985):5–15.

57 Hulme, "A Lecture on Modern Poetry," in Hulme, *Further Speculations*, ed. Samuel Hynes (Minneapolis: University of Minnesota Press, 1955), p. 69; we are grateful to Jackie Osherow for bringing this passage to our attention.

58 Guillory, "The Ideology of Canon Formation: T. S. Eliot and Cleanth Brooks," *Critical Inquiry* 10 (1983):179. Further references are included in the text.

59 cummings, *Complete Poems 1913–1962* (New York: Harcourt, 1972), p. 70.

60 Pound quoted in Hugh Kenner, *The Pound Era* (Berkeley: University of California Press, 1971), pp. 104 and 256.

61 Stevens, "A High-Toned Old Christian Woman," *The Collected Poems of Wallace Stevens* (New York: Alfred A. Knopf, 1954), p. 59.

62 Williams, *Imaginations*, ed. Webster Schott (New York: New Directions, 1970), p. 169.

63 Ransom, "Emily Dickinson: A Poet Restored," in *Emily Dickinson: A Collection of Critical Essays*, ed. Richard B. Sewall (Englewood Cliffs, New Jersey: Prentice-Hall, 1963), p. 89; Blackmur is quoted in Reeves, "Introduction," *Selected Poems of Emily Dickinson* (New York: Macmillan, 1960), p. 119.

64 Quoted in Richard Ellmann, *James Joyce* (New York: Oxford University Press, 1959), p. 510.

65 Lowell, "Statue of Liberty," *History* (New York: Farrar, Staus, 1973), p. 147.

66 Thurber, *Thurber Carnival*, pp. 38–39.

67 Mailer, *Advertisements for Myself* (New York: Berkeley, 1966), p. 434–35.

68 Burgess, "The Book Is Not For Reading," *New York Times Book Review*, 4 December 1966, pp. 1, 74, and Gass, on Mailer's *Genius and Lust*, *New York Times Book Review*, 24 October 1976, p. 2.

69 Roethke, "The Poetry of Louise Bogan," *On the Poet and His Craft: Selected Prose of Theodore Roethke*, ed. Ralph J. Mills, Jr. (Seattle: University of Washington Press, 1965), pp. 133–34.

70 Berryman, 187 ("Them lady poets") in *The Dream Songs* (New York: Farrar, Straus, 1974), p. 206.

71 Lowell, "Sylvia Plath," *History*, p. 135.

72 For Lowell on Amy Lowell, see *Life Studies and For the Union Dead* (New York: Noonday, 1967), p. 38; on Rich, see *History*, p. 154. Also worth considering in this context is Auden's famous introduction to Adrienne Rich's *A Change of Worlds* (1951), vol. 48 in the Yale Younger Poets series: her poems, he says, "are neatly and modestly dressed, speak quietly but do not mumble, respect their elders but are not cowed by them, and do not tell fibs" (p. 11); as well as Randall Jarrell's observation about Rich's *The Diamond Cutters* (1955) that the "poet whom we see behind" these poems "cannot help seeming to us a sort of princess in a fairy tale" (Jarrell, "Five Poets," *Yale Review* 46:1 [Autumn 1956]:100).

73 For Lowell's use of Hardwick's letters, see *The Selected Poems of Robert Lowell* (New York: Farrar, Straus, 1976): "Voices," 223; "Records," p. 226; "In the Mail," p. 229; "Exorcism," p. 230; "The Couple," p. 231; and "Christmas," p. 237.

74 For a discussion of this from the point of view of a holocaust scholar, see Alvin H. Rosenfeld, *Imagining Hitler* (Bloomington: Indiana University Press, 1985), p. 57.

75 Lowell, "Loser," *History*, p. 182.

76 Pinter, *No Man's Land* (New York: Grove, 1975), pp. 36, 18.

77 Thomas, "The Ballad of the Long-legged Bait," *The Collected Poems of Dylan Thomas* (New York: New Directions, 1957), p. 167.

78 Pound, "Sage Homme," *The Letters of Ezra Pound, 1907–1941*, ed. D. D. Paige (New York: Harcourt, 1950), p. 170. The "Uranian Muse" might be an allusion to the male homosexuals Edward Carpenter associates with the "third sex" and calls "Uranians" or "Urnings" in *The Intermediate Sex: A Study of Some Transitional Types of Men and Women* (London: G. Allen and Unwin, 1908) and *Intermediate Types among Primitive Folk: A Study in Social Evolution* (London: G. Allen, 1914).

Chapter 4

EPIGRAPHS: Woolf, "Professions for Women," *Women and Writing*, ed. Michele Barrett, p. 57; Lowell, "The Sisters," *Complete Poetical Works* (Boston: Houghton Mifflin, 1955), p. 461 (further references to poems by Amy Lowell will be to this edition, and page numbers will be included in the text); Parker, *Paris Review Interview* in *Writers at Work: The Paris Review Interviews*, ed. Malcoln Cowley (New York: Viking, 1959), pp. 76–77.

 1 Robins, *Ancilla's Share* (1924; Westport, Conn.: Hyperion, 1976), p. 94. Further references will be to this edition, and page numbers will appear in the text.

 2 *The Letters of Elizabeth Barrett Browning*, ed. Frederic G. Kenyon, 2 vols. (New York: Macmillan, 1897), 1:231–32.

 3 Sarton, "Letter from Chicago," *The Collected Poems of May Sarton* (New York: Norton, 1974), pp. 153–4.

 4 See Bloom, *The Anxiety of Influence* and companion volumes, passim.

 5 See Freud, "Female Sexuality" (1931), in *Sigmund Freud: Sexuality and the Psychology of Love*, ed. Philip Rieff (New York: Macmillan, 1963), pp. 194–211; further references to this essay will be to this edition, and page numbers will appear in the text preceded by the citation FS.

 6 Freud, "Family Romances" (1909), in *The Complete Psychological Works of Sigmund Freud* (London: Hogarth, 1959), vol. 9, 235–41.

 7 Diehl, "Murderous Poetics: Dickinson, the Father, and the Text," in Lynda Booze and Betty Flowers, ed., *Fathers and Daughters* (Baltimore: Johns Hopkins University Press, forthcoming).

 8 Oliphant, "The Library Window" in *A Treasury of Victorian Ghost Stories*, ed. Everett F. Bleiler (New York: Scribner's, 1983), p. 222. Further references will be to this edition and page numbers will appear in the text.

 9 Wharton, "The Angel at the Grave," *Collected Short Stories of Edith Wharton*, 1:145. Further references will be to this edition and page numbers will appear in the text.

10 Cather, "The Willing Muse," *Collected Short Fiction 1892–1912*, ed. Mildred R. Bennett (Lincoln: University of Nebraska Press, 1965), p. 115. Further references will be to this edition and page numbers will appear in the text.

11 Lee, "Lady Tal," in *Vanitas: Polite Stories* (London, 1892), pp. 7–119. Further references will be to this edition, and page numbers will appear in the text; Edith Wharton, "Writing a War Story," in *Complete Short Stories of Edith Wharton*, 2:359–70.

12 Cholmondeley, *Red Pottage* (London: Blond, 1968), p. 215. Further references

will be to this edition, and page numbers will appear in the text. We are grateful to Margaret Doody for calling this work to our attention.

13 Freeman, "A Poetess," *Selected Stories of Mary E. Wilkins Freeman,* ed. Marjorie Pryse, p. 191. Further references will be to this edition, and page numbers will appear in the text.

14 Woolson, "Miss Grief," in *For the Major and Selected Short Stories,* ed. Rayburn S. Moore (New Haven: College & University Press, 1967), p. 142. Further references will be to this edition, and page numbers will appear in the text.

15 Mossberg, *Emily Dickinson: When a Writer Is a Daughter,* pp. 33–96.

16 Freud, "Some Psychological Consequences of the Anatomical Distinction between the Sexes," in *Sexuality and the Psychology of Love,* pp. 183–93.

17 Freud's letter to Martha Bernays is quoted in Ernest Jones, *The Life and Work of Sigmund Freud: Volume I, The Formative Years and the Great Discoveries* (New York: Basic Books, 1953), pp. 176–77; a slightly different translation is also available in Ernst L. Freud, ed., *Selected Letters of Sigmund Freud,* trans. Tania and James Stern (New York: Basic Books, 1960), pp. 75–76.

18 See Lucy Freeman and Dr. Herbert Strean, *Freud and Women* (New York: Frederick Unger, 1981), p. 123. To be sure, men, as well as women, were the recipients of these rings, but the ring as symbolizing marriage may have had a special meaning for women.

19 See Olsen, "One Out of Twelve: Writers Who Are Women in Our Century" (1971) and "Silences in Literature" (1962) in Olsen, *Silences* (New York: Delacorte, 1978).

20 Chopin, "Elizabeth Stock's One Story," *Complete Works of Kate Chopin,* 2:587. Further references will be to this edition and will appear in the text.

21 On the female-authored *Kunstlerroman,* see Linda Huff, *A Portrait of the Artist as a Young Woman* (New York: Unger, 1983).

22 For various views of this issue, see Jacques Lacan, "The Signification of the Phallus," in *Ecrits: A Selection,* tr. Alan Sheridan (New York: W. W. Norton, 1977); Anika Lemaire, *Jacques Lacan,* tr. David Macey (London: Routledge, 1977), pp. 67–71, 78–92; and Jacqueline Rose and Juliet Mitchell, "Introduction I" and "Introduction II" in Lacan, *Feminine Sexuality: Jacques Lacan and the école freudienne* ed. Mitchell and Rose; trans. Rose (New York: W. W. Norton, 1982).

23 Freud, "The Psychogenesis of a Case of Homosexuality in a Woman," in *Sexuality and the Psychology of Love,* p. 159.

24 On Brontë's male muse, see, for instance, *The Madwoman in the Attic,* pp. 604–05.

25 For Wharton on Eliot, see Edith Wharton, review of Leslie Stephen, *George Eliot, Bookman* 15 (May 1902):250; for a more general comment on this subject, see Sandra M. Gilbert, "Life's Empty Pack: Notes toward a Literary Daughteronomy," *Critical Inquiry,* 11:3 (March 1985).

26 Vivien, *A Woman Appeared to Me,* trans. Jeannette H. Foster (1904; The Naiad Press, 1979), p. 334.

27 Barnes, *The Ladies Almanack* (1928; New York: Harper & Row, 1972), p. 8. Further references will be to this edition and will appear in the text.

28 Hall, *The Well of Loneliness* (1928; New York: Avon Books, 1981).

29 See Smith-Rosenberg, "The New Woman as Androgyne: Social Disorder and Gender Crisis, 1870–1936," in Smith-Rosenberg, *Disorderly Conduct: Visions of Gender in Victorian America* (New York: Knopf, 1985); and Newton, "The Mythic Mannish Lesbian: Radclyffe Hall and the New Woman," *Signs* 9 (1984):557–75; reprinted in *The Lesbian Issue: Essays from Signs,* ed. Estelle B. Freedman, Barbara C. Gelpi, Susan L. Johnson, Kathleen M. Weston (Chicago: University of Chicago Press, 1985), pp. 7–25. Specifically Newton argues that "The mythic mannish lesbian proposes to usurp the son's place in the Oedipal triangle" (p. 21).

30 This notebook entry by Stein is quoted by Marianne DeKoven in *A Different Language* (Madison: University of Wisconsin Press, 1983), p. 136; Thomson's remarks are quoted in Carl Van Vechten, "A Stein Song," *Selected Writings of Gertrude Stein,* ed. Carl Van Vechten (1933; New York: Vintage Books, 1972), p. xx.

31 Stein, "Lifting Belly," *The Yale Gertrude Stein,* ed. Richard Kostelanetz (New Haven: Yale University Press, 1980), pp. 49 and 54.

32 We are grateful to Molly Gubar for calling this linguistic possibility to our attention at the age of six.

33 See, for example, Elizabeth Fifer, "Is Flesh Advisable? The Interior Theater of Gertrude Stein," *Signs* 4:3 (Spring 1979): 472–83 as well as Neil Schmitz, *Of Huck and Alice: Humorous Writing in American Literature* (Minneapolis: University of Minnesota Press, 1983), pp. 176–78.

34 Stein, *The Mother of Us All* in *Gertrude Stein: Last Operas and Plays,* ed. with an introduction by Carl Van Vechten (1946; New York: Vintage Books, 1975). Stein's comment on feminism appears in *The Autobiography of Alice B. Toklas* in *Selected Writings of Gertrude Stein,* p. 78.

35 Zilboorg, "Masculine and Feminine: Some Biological and Cultural Aspects," in *Psychiatry* 7 (1944):271, 294.

36 Writing under the pseudonym "David Olivieri," Wharton had actually produced her first novel at the age of fifteen; see *Fast and Loose: A Novelette* (Charlottesville: University Press of Virginia, 1977).

37 Wharton, *The Touchstone* (New York: Scribner's, 1900), p. 156.

38 Schreiner, " 'The Policy in Favor of Protection—,' " in *Dream Life and Real Life* (Chicago: Cassandra-Academy, 1977); Kate Chopin, "Miss Witherwell's Mistake" in *Complete Works* 1:59–66.

39 Woolf, *The Waves* in *Jacob's Room and The Waves* (New York: Harcourt, 1959), p. 195. Further references will be to this edition, and page numbers will appear in the text.

40 For a reading of the Elvedon passage, see Joseph Allen Boone, "The Meaning of Elvedon in *The Waves*: A Key to Bernard's Experience and Woolf's Vision," *Modern Fiction Studies* 27:4 (1981–82): 629–37.

41 Sarton, "My Sisters, O My Sisters," *Collected Poems,* pp. 74–77.

42 Atwood, *Second Words: Selected Criticism and Prose* (Toronto: Anansi, 1982), p. 202.

43 Jackson, unpublished letter to the authors, summer 1984.
44 Woolf, "Indiscretions," reprinted in *Virginia Woolf: Women and Writing*, p. 75. Further references to works included in this volume will appear in the text with page numbers preceded by the citation *WW*.
45 Woolf, "Jane Austen," *The Common Reader* (1925; New York: Harcourt, 1955), p. 137. Further references to essays in this volume will appear in the text with page numbers preceded by the citation *CR*.
46 Woolf, "Dorothy Wordsworth," *The Common Reader: Second Series* (1932; New York: Harcourt, 1956), p. 152. Further references to essays in this volume will appear in the text with page numbers preceded by the citation *CR2*.
47 For a discussion of Rossetti's own attitude toward "tea-party" statements about poetry, see the analysis of her novella *Maude* in *The Madwoman in the Attic*, pp. 549–54.
48 Woolf, *Contemporary Writers*, with a preface by Jean Guiguet (New York: Harcourt, 1965), p. 25.
49 Cather, *The World and the Parish: Willa Cather's Articles and Reviews, 1893–1902*, selected and edited with commentary by William M. Curtin (Lincoln: University of Nebraska Press, 1970), 1:362; West, "So Simple" (1912), reprinted in *The Young Rebecca: Writings of Rebecca West, 1911–1917*, ed. Jane Marcus (New York: Viking, 1982), p. 71. In a useful discussion of this subject, Sharon O'Brien quotes Cather's 1895 statement that "Sometimes I wonder why God ever trusts talent in the hands of women . . . they usually make such an infernal mess of it. He must do it as a ghastly joke": see *Willa Cather: The Emerging Voice* (New York: Oxford University Press, 1987), p. 174.
50 Bogan, *What the Woman Lived: Letters of Louise Bogan, 1920–1970*, ed. Ruth Limmer (New York: W. W. Norton, 1984), p. 295; Atwood, *Second Words*, p. 203; and Rich, *The Fact of a Doorframe: Poems Selected and New, 1950–1984* (New York: W. W. Norton, 1984), p. 295.
51 Meynell, *Hearts of Controversy* (London: Pelican Press, n.d.), p. 82; Meynell, *Wares of Autolycus: Selected Literary Essays of Alice Meynell*, chosen and introduced by P. M. Fraser (London: Oxford University Press, 1965), p. 169.
52 Bogan, *What the Woman Lived*, p. 375; Plath, *Journals*, p. 168.
53 Sexton, "The Uncensored Poet: Letters of Anne Sexton," *Ms.* (November 1977), p. 53; Sitwell, *Selected Letters, 1919–1964*, ed. John Lehmann and Derek Parker (New York: Vanguard Press, 1979), p. 113.
54 See *Selections from the Letters of Geraldine Endsor Jewsbury to Jane Welsh Carlyle*, ed. Mrs. Alexander Ireland (London: Longmans, Green, 1892), pp. 347–49; Gaskell, *The Life of Charlotte Brontë*, ed. Alan Shelstron (Baltimore: Penguin, 1975); Fuller, "Miss Barrett's Poems" (1845), "On George Sand" (1839), and "On Meeting George Sand" (1847) in *The Woman and the Myth: Margaret Fuller's Life and Writings*, ed. Bell Gale Chevigny (Old Westbury, New York: Feminist Press, 1976), pp. 101–05, 57–58, and 360–63; and Meynell, "Charlotte and Emily Brontë," in *Hearts of Controversy*, pp. 77–100, as well as "A Woman of Masculine Understanding" (on Harriet Martineau), "Miss Mitford," "The English Women Humorists," "Elizabeth Barrett Browning," and *"Evelina"* in *The Wares of Autolycus*, pp. 8–12, 82–85, 111–26, 166–67, 167–74.

55 Welty, "The Radiance of Jane Austen," "Katherine Anne Porter," and "The House of Willa Cather," in *The Eye of the Story: Selected Essays and Reviews* (New York: Vintage, 1979), pp. 3–13, 30–40, 41–60; Rich, "The Tensions of Anne Bradstreet," "*Jane Eyre:* The Temptations of a Motherless Woman," and "Vesuvius at Home: The Power of Emily Dickinson," in *On Lies, Secrets, and Silence: Selected Prose, 1966–1978* (New York: W. W. Norton, 1979), pp. 21–32, 89–106, 157–84; Walker, "Zora Neale Hurston: A Cautionary Tale and a Partisan View" and "Looking for Zora," in *In Search of Our Mothers' Gardens* (New York: Harcourt, 1983), pp. 83–92, 93–116; also see Marianne Moore, "Emily Dickinson" (1st. pub. 1933) in *The Complete Prose of Marianne Moore*, ed. and with an introduction by Patricia C. Willis (New York: Viking, 1986), pp. 290–93.

56 Sackville-West, *Aphra Behn: The Incomparable Astrea* (New York: Viking, 1928), p. 13; Porter, "Reflections on Willa Cather" in *The Collected Essays* (New York: Delacorte, 1970), pp. 38–39. Also see Cather, "The Best Stories of Sarah Orne Jewett" and "Katherine Mansfield," in *Willa Cather on Writing: Critical Studies on Writing as an Art*, with a foreword by Stephen Tennant (New York: Knopf, 1949), pp. 47–59, 107–20.

57 Drabble, *The Waterfall* (New York: Alfred A. Knopf, 1969), p. 184. Also see May Sinclair, *The Three Sisters* (New York: Macmillan, 1914), which at least in part fictionalizes the lives of the Brontë sisters, as well as Dorothy Richardson, *Pointed Roofs* (1915), in *Pilgrimage*, Vol. I, and May Sarton, *The Small Room* (New York: W. W. Norton, 1961), both of which rewrite and revise Charlotte Brontë's *Villette*.

58 Oates, *Mysteries of Winterthurn* (London: Arena, 1986), pp. 57–58.

59 See Oates, "Soul at the White Heat: The Romance of Emily Dickinson's Poetry," *Critical Inquiry* 13:4 (Summer 1987): 806–24.

60 Glaspell, *Alison's House* (New York: Samuel French, 1930), p. 139. Further references will be to this edition, and page numbers will appear in the text.

61 Churchill, *Top Girls* (London: Methuen, 1982), pp. 12, 28.

62 On the feminist rationale for Judy Chicago's *Dinner Party*, see Chicago, *The Dinner Party* (Garden City, New York: Anchor, 1979), pp. 8–20 and passim.

63 Dickinson, J. 312, 593, and 1562; Browning, "To George Sand: A Desire" and "To George Sand: A Recognition," in *Complete Works*, 2:239.

64 See, for instance, Lowell, "The Sisters" and "On Looking at a Copy of Alice Meynell's Poems," *Complete Poetical Works*, pp. 459–61; 536–37; see also Kay Boyle, "The Invitation in It," *American Citizen* (New York: Simon & Schuster, 1944), pp. 6–7 on Carson McCullers; Muriel Rukeyser, "For Kay Boyle," *The Collected Poems of Muriel Rukeyser* (New York: McGraw Hill, 1978), p. 549; and Lyn Strongin, "Emily Dickinson Postage Stamp," in *No More Masks!*, ed. Florence Howe and Ellen Bass (Garden City, New York: Anchor Doubleday, 1973), p. 274.

65 Bishop, "Invitation to Miss Marianne Moore," *The Complete Poems of Elizabeth Bishop, 1927–1979* (New York: Farrar, Straus & Giroux, 1983), pp. 82–83.

66 Rich, "Transcendental Etude," *The Dream of A Common Language* (New York: Norton, 1978), p. 76.

67 Moore to Bishop, August 24, 1948; quoted by Bonnie Costello, "Marianne Moore and Elizabeth Bishop: Friendship and Influence," unpublished paper delivered

at the MLA Convention, 1982; we are grateful to Bonnie Costello for sharing this paper with us.

68 James's reference to Lee as a "tiger cat" was made in a letter to William James, January 20, 1893, which is quoted in Carl J. Weber, "Henry James and His Tiger-Cat," *PMLA* 68 (Sept. 1953):683.

69 In dramatizing Marion/James's attack on Lady Tal and her novel, Vernon Lee is, ironically enough, also recording her own feeling that she herself has been or might be assaulted, for the book that her heroine struggles to write is a novel about a woman named Violet—the real name (Violet Paget) of the pseudonymous Vernon Lee. Beginning to read Lady Tal's novel with "a melancholy little moan" (83), Marion/James "ejaculate[s]" to himself, "Violet! And her name's Violet, too!" (83)

70 See Richardson, esp. *Dawn's Left Hand* (1931) in *Pilgrimage*, vol. IV, pp. 239–41; Lessing, *The Golden Notebook*, (1962; New York: Bantam, 1979), esp. pp. 549–607 and 639–43; Oates, *A Bloodsmoor Romance* (New York: Dutton, 1982), pp. 447–65.

71 Quoted by Gillian E. Hanscombe, *The Art of Life: Dorothy Richardson and the Development of Feminist Consciousness* (London: Peter Owen, 1982), p. 80.

72 Woolf, *A Writer's Diary*, ed. by Leonard Woolf (New York: New American Library, 1968), pp. 54, 57, and 178.

73 Taggard, unpublished letter to Henry W. Wells, n.d., held at the Columbia University Library. We are indebted to Elaine Showalter for bringing this manuscript to our attention.

74 Both interviews with Le Sueur are quoted by Blanche H. Gelfant in *Women Writing in America: Voices in Collage* (Hanover, New Hampshire: University Press of New England, 1984), p. 78.

75 Stein is quoted in Samuel Putnam, *Paris Was Our Mistress: Memoirs of the Lost and Found Generation* (New York: Viking, 1947), p. 153. Shari Benstock points out that "Stein is mistaken about the publication date of *Three Lives*, which appeared in 1909" (Benstock, *Women of the Left Bank* [Austin: University of Texas Press, 1986], p. 457).

76 Nin, "The New Woman," *In Favor of the Sensitive Man and Other Essays* (New York: Harcourt, 1976), p. 13.

77 Bishop's protests against Williams's use of Nardi's letters and Lowell's use of Hardwick's letters are recorded, respectively, in Theodora Graham, "Her Heigh Compleynte," p. 186, and Ian Hamilton, *Robert Lowell: A Biography* (New York: Random House, 1982), p. 423.

78 Stein, *Bee Time Vine* (New Haven: Yale University Press, 1953), p. 263.

79 See Lowell, *John Keats*, 2 vols. (Boston: Houghton Mifflin, 1925).

80 *A Critical Fable* includes tributes (some of them ambivalent) to Carl Sandburg, Edwin Arlington Robinson, Vachel Lindsay, H. D., Sara Teasdale, Jean Starr Untermeyer, and Louis Untermeyer.

81 *The Portable Dorothy Parker*, with an intro. by W. Somerset Maugham (New York: Viking, 1944), pp. 321–23.

82 Levertov, "Hypocrite Women"; Randall, "To William Wordsworth from Vir-

ginia"; and Macdonald, "Instructions from Bly," all in Florence Howe and Ellen Bass, ed., *No More Masks!*, pp. 149, 158–59, 207–08.

83 The manuscript of "Burning the Letters" is held in the Sylvia Plath Collection at the Smith College Rare Book Room. In " 'More Terrible than She Ever Was': The Manuscripts of Sylvia Plath's Bee Poems," *Sylvia Plath: Critical Essays*, ed. Linda Wagner (Boston: G. K. Hall, 1984), Susan Van Dyne has discussed the ways in which Plath composed and revised on the reverse side of typescript pages containing texts by both Hughes and herself.

84 See Hughes, "The Thought Fox," in Ted Hughes, *New Selected Poems* (New York: Harper & Row, 1982), p. 1.

85 Hughes discusses his burning of Plath's last journal in his Foreword to Plath, *Journals*, p. xiii. To be sure, Hughes himself has explained that he burned the journal because it was so distressing that he did not want his children to see it.

Chapter 5

EPIGRAPHS: Thoreau, "Reading," in *Walden and Selected Essays* (1854; New York: Hendricks, 1973), p. 95; Emerson, *Emerson in His Journals*, ed. Joel Porte (Cambridge: Belknap Press of Harvard University Press, 1982), p. 271; H. D., *The Walls Do Not Fall* (1942) in *Trilogy* (1942–44), *H. D.: Collected Poems, 1912–1944*, ed. Martz, number 39, p. 540; LeGuin, "She Unnames Them," *The New Yorker*, 21 January 1985, p. 27.

1 Kristeva, "Women's Time," *Signs* 7:1 (Autumn 1981), 21.

2 See Lakoff, *Language and Woman's Place* (New York: Harper Colophon, 1975), and Spender, *Man Made Language* (London: Routledge, 1980); see also Casey Miller and Kate Swift, *Words and Women* (New York: Anchor, 1977), pp. 17–35; *Language and Sex: Difference and Dominance*, ed. Barrie Thorne and Nancy Henley (Rowley, Mass.: Newbury House, 1975); *Language, Gender and Society*, ed. Barrie Thorne, Cheris Kramerae, and Nancy Henley (Rowley, Mass.: Newbury House, 1983); a number of the essays in *Women and Language in Literature and Society*, ed. Sally McConnell-Ginet, Ruth Borker, and Nelly Furman (New York: Praeger, 1980); and Dennis Baron, *Grammar and Gender* (New Haven: Yale University Press, 1986). We have discussed these thinkers in more detail in "Sexual Linguistics," *New Literary History* 16 (1984–85):515–43.

3 "Invent the other history," and "only this space," Cixous, "Sorties," in *New French Feminisms*, ed. Elaine Marks and Isabelle de Courtivron (New York: Schocken, 1981), pp. 96–92; "constantly in the process," Irigaray, *This Sex Which Is Not One*, trans. Catherine Porter with Carolyn Burke (Ithaca: Cornell University Press, 1985), p. 29.

4 Kristeva, from "Oscillation du 'pouvoir' au 'refus' " [Oscillation between power and denial], an interview by Xavière Gauthier in *Tel Quel*, Summer 1974, trans. Marilyn A. August, in *New French Feminisms*, p. 166; to be sure, Kristeva is not talking here specifically about Woolf: her remark, in its entirety, is: "In women's writing, language seems to be seen from a foreign land; is it seen from the point of view of an asymbolic, spastic body? Virginia Woolf describes suspended states,

subtle sensations and, above all, colors—green, blue—, but she does not dissect language as Joyce does. Estranged from language, women are visionaries, dancers who suffer as they speak."

5 Joannes Ludovicus Vives, *A Very Frutefull and Pleasant Boke Called the Instruction of a Christen Woman,* trans. Richard Hyrd (London, 1540), is quoted in Diane Bornstein, "As Meek as a Maid: A Historical Perspective on Language for Women in Courtesy Books from the Middle Ages to *Seventeen Magazine,*" *Women's Language and Style,* ed. Douglas Butturff and Edmund L. Epstein, *Studies in Contemporary Language 1* (Akron, Ohio: University of Akron, 1978), pp. 135.

6 We have discussed Spenser's Errour and Swift's Goddess of Criticism in *The Madwoman in the Attic,* pp. 31–33; Pope, *The Rape of the Lock,* canto 4, 58–60 in *The Poems of Alexander Pope,* ed. John Butt (New Haven: Yale University Press, 1963), p. 234; Young, *Love of Fame, the Universal Passion* ("Satire VI: On Women") in *The Poetical Works of Edward Young,* Aldine ed., 2 vols (Westport, Conn.: Greenwood, 1970), p. 117.

7 Mrs. Slipslop and Mrs. Malaprop mangle the "King's" English in *Joseph Andrews* (1742) and *The Rivals* (1755) respectively.

8 Faulkner, *Mosquitoes* (New York: Liveright, 1927), p. 26. Also see the chapter on the twentieth century in Katharine Rogers, *The Troublesome Helpmate,* pp. 226–64.

9 James Joyce, *Finnegans Wake* (New York: Viking, 1939), p. 628.

10 Joyce, *Ulysses* (New York: Vintage, 1961), p. 284. Further references will be to this edition, and page numbers will appear in the text.

11 Joyce, *Selected Letters,* ed. Richard Ellmann (New York: Viking, 1975), p. 186.

12 de Feure, *The Voice of Evil,* in Patrick Bade, *Femme Fatale: Images of Evil and Fascinating Women* (New York: Mayflower Books, 1979), pl. 12, discussion on p. 122.

13 For a more detailed discussion of Eliot's attitude toward women, see Tony Pinkney, *Women in the Poetry of T. S. Eliot* (London: Macmillan, 1984).

14 See Aiken, *Ushant* (New York: Duell, Sloan & Pearce; Boston: Little, Brown, 1952), p. 233; on this quotation, see also Ronald Bush, *T. S. Eliot,* pp. 7–9.

15 Pound, "Hugh Selwyn Mauberley" and "Portrait d'une Femme" in *Selected Poems* (New York: New Directions, 1957), pp. 64 and 16–17. Interestingly, Pound's "Femme" is said to have been modeled on the actress-writer Florence Farr, one of whose novels seemed to Pound's wife Dorothy to be *"such a Sargasso Sea muddle":* see *Ezra Pound and Dorothy Shakespear: Their Letters: 1909–1914,* ed. Omar Pound and A. Walton Litz (New York: New Directions, 1984), pp. 130–33; we are grateful to A. Walton Litz for bringing this point to our attention.

16 In volume 2 we will discuss *The Waste Land* in connection with World War I and with hermaphroditism.

17 See, for example, Wittig in *Les Guérillères,* p. 112; Gagnon: "This language, although it is mine, is foreign to me," in "Body I," *New French Feminisms,* p. 179; Rich, "The Burning of Paper Instead of Children," in *Adrienne Rich's Poetry,*

selected and edited by Barbara Charlesworth Gelpi and Albert Gelpi (New York: W. W. Norton, 1975), p. 48; and Gallop: "The mother tongue, the language we learn at our mother's breast, is patriarchal language," in Gallop, "Reading the Mother Tongue: Psychoanalytic Feminist Criticism," *Critical Inquiry,* 13:2 (Winter 1987), 322.

18 Wittig, *Les Guérillères,* p. 112.

19 Lacan, "The Agency of the Letter in the Unconscious . . . ," *Ecrits,* p. 148.

20 Derrida, in *Of Grammatology,* trans. Gayatri Chakravorty Spivak (Baltimore: Johns Hopkins University Press, 1976), speculates that "the birth of writing . . . was nearly everywhere and most often linked to genealogical anxiety" (p. 124).

21 On this point, see, Claude Lévi-Strauss, *The Elementary Structures of Kinship,* trans. Richard Von Sturmer and Rodney Needham, ed. Rodney Needham, rev. ed. (Boston: Beacon, 1969), p. 496.

22 Stone, "Names," *Kentucky Poetry Review* 16:2/3 (Summer/Fall 1980): 14.

23 In her letters, Dickinson called herself variously "Emily, Emilie, Brother Emily, and Uncle Emily"; see, for instance, the letter of 1866 in which she observed that "Ned . . . inherits his Uncle Emily's ardor for the lie" (Thomas Johnson, ed., *The Letters of Emily Dickinson* (Cambridge: Belknap Press of Harvard University Press, 1971), p. 191.

24 See Edel, "Homage to Willa Cather," in *The Art of Willa Cather,* ed. Bernice Slote and Virginia Faulkner (Lincoln: University of Nebraska Press, 1974), p. 193.

25 For Dinesen's renamings of herself, see Judith Thurman, *Isak Dinesen* (New York: St. Martin's, 1982), passim.

26 On Riding's renamings of herself, see Jane Marcus, "Laura Riding Roughshod," *Iowa Review,* 12, 2 / 3 (Spring/Summer 1981), 295–99; Marcus quotes Riding's enigmatic verse about naming: "I am because I say / I say myself / I am my name / My name is not my name / It is the name of what I say. / My name is what is said. / I alone say. / I alone am not I. / I am my name. / My name is not my name, / My name is the name" (297).

27 Vivien, "Vivianne," *At the Sweet Hour of Hand in Hand,* trans. Sandia Belgrade (Tallahassee: The Naiad Press, 1979), pp. 47–49.

28 H. D. *Tribute to Freud* (New York: McGraw-Hill, 1974), p. 66.

29 Morris, "Reading H. D.'s 'Helios and Athene,' " in *The Iowa Review* 12:2 / 3 (Spring/Summer, 1981): 55.

30 For one of H. D.'s meditations on "D. H.," see *Tribute to Freud,* p. 141. Many of her most revealing meditations on Dowding are contained in as yet unpublished manuscripts, such as "Thorn Thicket" and "The Sword Went Out to Sea," which are held at the Beinecke Library, Yale University.

31 The phrase "daughters of educated men" is used continually by Virginia Woolf in *Three Guineas.* Ong's *Fighting for Life* (Ithaca: Cornell University Press, 1981) is crucial for an understanding of masculine competition and sexual anxiety in general and for a discussion of the mother tongue (as opposed to the *patrius sermo*) in particular: see especially pp. 36–37. Further references will appear in the text, preceded by the citation *Fighting.* Also important for an analysis of the

function of the classics in male education is Ong's *The Presence of the Word: Some Prolegomena for Cultural and Religious History* (New Haven: Yale University Press, 1967), pp. 249–50.

32 Eliot, *The Mill on the Floss*, ed. Gordon S. Haight (Boston: Houghton Mifflin, 1961), pp. 125, 131, 134, and 38. For an analysis of Eliot's revision of Wordsworth's language of nature, see Margaret Homans, "Eliot, Wordsworth, and the Scenes of the Sisters' Instruction," *Bearing the Word* (Chicago: University of Chicago Press, 1986), pp. 120–52.

33 Woolf, *The Voyage Out* (1915; New York: Harcourt, 1948), p. 171.

34 Stead, *The Man Who Loved Children* (1940; New York: Avon, 1966), p. 377. Further references will be to this edition, and page numbers will be included in the text.

35 Elgin, *Native Tongue* (New York: Daw Books, 1984), p. 215, and Elgin, *The Judas Rose* (New York: Daw Books, 1987). Further references will be to these editions, and page numbers will appear in the text preceded by *NT* or *JR*.

36 See Wharton, "Xingu," *Collected Short Stories*, 2:209–29.

37 Vivien's volumes include the novel *Une Femme m'apparut* (1904), discussed briefly in chap. 4, and two verse collections translated into English: *At the Sweet Hour of Hand in Hand*, and *The Muse of the Violets*, trans. Margaret Porter and Catherine Kroger (The Naiad Press, 1977). The original volumes have been collected in *Poems de Renée Vivien*, published by Alphonse Lemerre in 1923–24 and reprinted in facsimile by the Arno Press in 1975 in one volume.

38 See Lanser, "Speaking in Tongues: *The Ladies Almanack* and the Language of Celebration," *Frontiers* 4:3 (Fall 1979): 39–46; see also Carolyn Allen, " 'Dressing the Unknowable in the Garments of the Known': The Style of Djuna Barnes' *Nightwood*," in *Women's Language and Style*, pp. 106–18.

39 Stein, *Tender Buttons*, in *Selected Writings of Gertrude Stein*, p. 496.

40 "Know no English": Stein, *The Autobiography of Alice B. Toklas*, in *Selected Writings of Gertrude Stein*, p. 66; "sacred cows" and "sexual cows": Catharine Stimpson, "The Mind, the Body, and Gertrude Stein," *Critical Inquiry* 3:3 (Spring 1977): 489–506; and Elizabeth Fifer, "Is Flesh Advisable? The Interior Theater of Gertrude Stein," *Signs* 4:3 (Spring 1979): 472–83.

41 Williams, "The Work of Gertrude Stein," in *Selected Essays of William Carlos Williams* (New York: Random House, 1954), p. 116.

42 Duncan, "The H. D. Book, Part Two: Nights and Days, Chapter 9," *Chicago Review* 30:3 (Winter 1979): 88.

43 H. D. describes her vision of "the writing on the wall" in *Tribute to Freud*, pp. 44–56; her alchemical redefinition of words appears in *Tribute to the Angels*, the middle book of *Trilogy* (1944; *H. D.: Collected Poems, 1912–1944*, numbers 1, 8–9, 11–14).

44 Richardson, *Oberland* (1927), in *Pilgrimage*, vol. IV, p. 93; Hanscombe, *The Art of Life*, p. 75; Richardson, *The Tunnel* (1919), in *Pilgrimage*, vol. II, p. 210.

45 Richardson, *Dawn's Left Hand* (1931), in *Pilgrimage*, vol. IV, p. 230.

46 Richardson, Foreword to Vol. I, *Pilgrimage*, pp. 9, 12. To be sure, Richardson here identifies Charles Dickens and James Joyce as two writers who understand "Feminine prose."

47 See Woolf, "Dorothy Richardson," in *Women and Writing*, p. 191.

48 Further references to Woolf's novels—*Night and Day* (New York: Harcourt, 1919), *To the Lighthouse* (New York: Harcourt, 1927), *Orlando* (New York: Harcourt, 1928), *The Years* (New York: Harcourt, 1937) and *Between the Acts* (New York: Harcourt, 1941), as well as works cited earlier—will refer to these editions, and page numbers will appear in the text.

49 Rhoda's traumatic experience in trying to step over a puddle is recounted in *The Waves*, p. 219.

50 On the song sung by the "tube station crone," see J. Hillis Miller, "Virginia Woolf's All Soul's Day," in *The Shaken Realist: Essays in Modern Literature in Honor of F. J. Hoffman*, ed. O. B. Hardison, Jr., et al. (Baton Rouge: Louisiana State University Press, 1970).

51 Cather, *The Song of the Lark* (1915; Lincoln: University of Nebraska Press, 1978), p. 301.

52 Cather, *Death Comes for the Archbishop* (1927; New York: Alfred A. Knopf, 1971), pp. 125–28. For a comparable vision of linguistic horror, this time dramatized in a male-authored work, see the Marabar cave episode in E. M. Forster, *Passage to India* (1924; New York: Harcourt, 1952), pp. 124–25, 146–50.

53 Stevens, "The Idea of Order at Key West," in *The Collected Poems of Wallace Stevens*, p. 130. Further references to poems by Stevens will be to this edition, and page numbers will appear in the text preceded by the citation *CP*.

54 On the vernacular as opposed to the "Latin Middle Ages," see Ernst Robert Curtius, *European Literature and the Latin Middle Ages*, trans. Willard R. Trask (New York: Pantheon, 1953), passim.

55 Eliot, *Selected Prose*, ed. Frank Kermode (New York: Harcourt and Farrar, 1975), p. 206–07; further references to essays in this volume will be included in the text, with page numbers preceded by the citation *SP*.

56 Pound, *The ABC of Reading* (1934; New York: New Directions, 1960), p. 100–01 and 51; further references to essays in this volume will be included in the text, with page numbers preceded by the citation *ABC*.

57 See Ong, *The Presence of the Word*, pp. 250–55.

58 Whitman, "Song of the Exposition," and "Carol of Words," in *Leaves of Grass: A Norton Critical Edition*, ed. Sculley Bradley and Harold Blodgett (New York: W. W. Norton, 1973), pp. 441 and 220.

59 James McGowan, *66 Translations from Charles Baudelaire's LES FLEURS DU MAL* (Peoria, Illinois: Spoon River Poetry Press, 1985), p. 11; Rimbaud, "Voyelles," *Oeuvres Complets* (Paris, Gallimard, 1972), p. 53; Sartre, *The Winds*, trans. Bernard Frechtman (Greenwich, Conn.: 1964), p. 114.

60 Lawrence, "Cypresses," in *Complete Poems of D. H. Lawrence*, 1:296–97. Further references to Lawrence poems will be to this edition, and page numbers will be included in the text.

61 Williams, "The Trees," in the *Collected Earlier Poems of William Carlos Williams* (New York: New Directions, 1938), p. 66.

62 See Lawrence, "Poems from *The Plumed Serpent*," in *Complete Poems*, 2: 786–813, esp. "[First Song of Huitzilpochtli]," pp. 804–05.

63 See Beckett, *Waiting for Godot* (New York: Grove Press, 1954), pp. 28–29.

64 For "all the dead voices," see *Waiting for Godot*, p. 40.

65 Tennyson, "Merlin and Vivien," in *The Poetical Works of Tennyson*, ed. G. Robert Stange, pp. 672–81; on this text, see also, Elliot L. Gilbert, "The Female King" (ch. 1, note 60).

66 Mallarmé, "Un Coup de Dés," in Mallarmé, *The Poems*, trans. and introduced by Keith Bosley (New York: Penguin, 1977), pp. 254–97.

67 "Manifesto: The Revolution of the Word," in *transition workshop*, ed. Jolas (New York: Vanguard, 1949), p. 174. Further references to selections in this volume will appear in the text, with page numbers preceded by the citation *T*.

68 Cixous, "The Laugh of the Medusa," in *New French Feminisims*, p. 256.

69 In Carroll's *Through the Looking-Glass* (1871; New York: W. W. Norton, 1986) Humpty Dumpty justifies his interpretation of "Jabborwocky" by boasting that he can make words mean what he wants because he is "master" (chapter 6, p. 163).

70 See Joyce, *A Portrait of the Artist* (1916; New York: Viking, 1956), p. 215: "The artist, like the God of the creation, remains within or behind or beyond or above his handiwork, invisible, refined out of existence, indifferent, paring his fingernails."

71 Kristeva speaks of the semiotic *"chora"* in *Revolution in Poetic Language*, trans. Margaret Waller, with an intro. by Leon S. Roudiez (New York: Columbia University Press, 1984), pp. 25–30.

72 Hartman, *Saving the Text: Literature, Derrida, Philosophy* (Baltimore: Johns Hopkins University Press, 1981), pp. 9 and 24.

73 Stein may, of course, be a prominent exception here; see our discussion of her as a "Founding Father" of modernism in ch. 4. In addition, in our next volume we will discuss the ways in which Stein aligns linguistic experimentation with masculine mimicry.

74 Lawrence's famous remark that he loved his mother "like a lover" was first recorded in Jessie Chambers, *D. H. Lawrence: A Personal Record, by E. T.*, introduction by J. Middleton Murry (New York: Knight Publications, 1936; 1st English pub. 1935), p. 184; for Bly, see Bly, "I Came Out of the Mother Naked," in *Sleepers Joining Hands* (New York: Harper & Row, 1973), pp. 29–50; see also Hall, "Goatfoot, Milktongue, Twinbird: The Psychic Origins of Poetic Form," in *A Field Guide to Contemporary Poetry*, ed. Stuart Friebert and David Young (New York: Longman), pp. 26–36; and Simic, "Some Thoughts About the Line," in *A Field Guide*, p. 78.

75 Olivier, *Les Enfants de Jocaste* (Paris: Denoel, 1980), p. 142; translation by Elyse Blankley, to whom we are grateful for calling this passage to our attention.

76 Lacan, "God and the *Jouissance* of ~~the~~ Woman," *Feminine Sexuality*, ed. Rose and Mitchell, p. 144; Lacan famously adds: "it has to be said that if there is one thing they themselves are complaining about enough at the moment, it is well and truly that—only they don't know what they are saying, which is all the difference between them and me."

77 Lemaire, *Jacques Lacan*, p. 89.

78 Freud, *Beyond the Pleasure Principle*, trans. James Strachey (1920; New York: W. W. Norton, 1975), pp. 8–11.

79 Claude Lévi-Strauss, *The Elementary Structures of Kinship*, p. 496.

80 Bettelheim, *Symbolic Wounds* (Glencoe, Illinois: Free, 1954), p. 20.

81 Zilboorg, "Masculine and Feminine," *Psychiatry* 7 (1944): 257–96; quote on p. 294; Karen Horney, M. D., "The Dread of Woman: Observations on a Specific Difference in the Dread Felt by Men and by Women Respectively for the Opposite Sex" (1932) in *Feminine Psychology*, ed. and with an intro. by Harold Kelman, M. D. (New York: W. W. Norton, 1967), pp. 133–46; also see Ralph Greenson, "The Mother Tongue and the Mother," *International Journal of Psychoanalysis* 31 (1950): 22.

82 Lurie, "Pornography and the Dread of Women: The Male Sexual Dilemma," in *Take Back the Night*, ed. Laura Lederer (New York: William Morrow, 1980), pp. 159–78. Also see Lurie's "The Construction of the 'Castrated Woman' in Psychoanalysis and Cinema," *Discourse* 4 (Winter 1981–82), 53.

83 Neumann, *The Great Mother: Analysis of an Archetype*, trans. Ralph Manheim, Bollingen Series 67 (New York: Pantheon, 1955), p. 168.

84 Chodorow, *The Reproduction of Mothering: Psychoanalysis and the Sociology of Gender* (Berkeley: University of California Press, 1978), esp. pp. 159–70.

85 Griffin, "Thoughts on Writing," in *The Writer On Her Work*, ed. Janet Sternburg (New York: W. W. Norton, 1980), p. 110.

86 Thomas Wentworth Higginson, "Ought Women to Learn the Alphabet?", *Women and the Alphabet*, pp. 12 and 19.

87 Plath, *The Bell Jar* (New York: Bantam, 1972), pp. 101–02.

88 Owen, "The Devil," *Nursery Rhymes for the Dead* (Ithaca: Ithaca House, 1980), p. 41.

89 Stone, "Poetry," *The Iowa Review* 12:2/3 (Spring/Summer 1981): 322.

90 Atwood, *Lady Oracle* (New York: Simon & Schuster, 1976).

91 Atwood, "It is dangerous to read newspapers," *Selected Poems* (New York: Simon & Schuster, 1976), p. 60.

92 To be sure, as John Irwin demonstrates in *American Hieroglyphics* (New Haven: Yale University Press, 1980), writers of the American Renaissance were obsessed with the relationship between the hieroglyphs of nature and the hieratic graphs of culture. Also, from Rudyard Kipling (in two of the "Just So" stories) to Wallace Stevens (in "The Comedian as the Letter C" and "The Man with the Blue Guitar") to the contemporary American poet David Young (in "A Lowercase Alphabet"), men of letters meditate on the alphabet, as do such theorists as Roland Barthes (in *S/Z*) and Jacques Derrida (in *Glas*). Yet, unlike those of literary women, male-authored works often remake or reread the alphabet in order to appropriate the power of the precursor. For a discussion of this issue, see our essay, "Ceremonies of the Alphabet: Female Grandmatologies and the Female Authorgraph," *The Female Autograph*, ed. Domna C. Stanton, Guest Editor, and Jeanine Parisier Plottel, General Editor, *New York Literary Forum* 12–13 (New York: Hunter College and the Graduate Center, C.U.N.Y.): 23–52.

93 Plath uses the phrase "pristine alphabets" in "The Ghost's Leavetaking," *CP*, p. 91.

94 Wylie, "Dedication," *Collected Poems* (New York: Knopf, 1932), pp. 109–11; see also Nelly Sachs' description of the "alphabet womb" in *O the Chimneys*, trans. Michael Hamburger, Christopher Holme, Ruth and Matthew Mead, and Michael Roloff (New York: Farrar, Straus, 1967), p. 125.

95 On writing in "white ink," see Cixous, "The Laugh of the Medusa," in *New French Feminisms*, p. 251.

96 Wittig and Zweig, *Lesbian Peoples/Material for a Dictionary* (New York: Avon, 1979), pp. 4, 5, 100, 166.

97 Broumas, "Artemis," *Beginning with O* (New Haven: Yale University Press, 1979), p. 23.

98 Levertov, "Relearning the Alphabet," *Relearning the Alphabet* (New York: New Directions, 1966), pp. 110–20.

99 Cota-Cardena, "Spelling the Cosmos," in *The Third Woman*, ed. Dexter Fisher (Boston: Houghton Mifflin, 1980), p. 398; here, see also, Margaret Atwood, "Spelling," in which the speaker, teaching her young daughter to spell, asks "How do you learn to spell?" and answers "Blood, sky & the sun, / your own name first, / your first naming, your first name, / your first word" (Atwood, "Spelling," in the *Norton Anthology of Literature by Women*, ed. Gilbert and Gubar, p. 2298).

100 We are grateful to Elaine Showalter for bringing "She Unnames Them" to our attention; for a few other contemporary revisions of the (linguistic) story of Adam and Eve, see John Hollander, "Adam's Task," *The Night Mirror* (New York: Athenaeum, 1971), p. 63, and Judith Wright, "Eve to Her Daughters," *Collected Poems 1942–1970* (Sydney: Angus and Robertson, 1971), pp. 234–36. For a more recent meditation on language by LeGuin, see "Ursula LeGuin on the Mother Tongue at Convocation," *Bryn Mawr Alumnae Bulletin* (Summer 1986): 3–4.

Index

For complete information on authors and their works, refer to the title of the work as well as the author's name.

Beer, Thomas, 142
Beerbohm, Max, 133, 140, 141, 175, 177, 178, 194, 217, 220–23; consternation at women writers, 125–29, 131, 133–37, 145, 155, 228; women's response to, 165–66
Beginning with O (Broumas), 269–70
Beguiling of Merlin, The (Burne-Jones painting), 225, 242
Behn, Aphra, 129, 165, 208
Bell Jar (Plath), 113, 268
Benedict, Ruth, 34
Bennett, Arnold, 150
Berger, Thomas, 46, 59–60, 116
Bernays, Martha, 180
Berryman, John, 157–60
Besant, Annie, 34
Bettelheim, Bruno, 264
Between the Acts (Woolf), 193, 249
Bird, Isabella, 17
Birth control, 34–35, 59
Bishop, Elizabeth, 158, 159, 211–14, 216–17, 223
Black, William, 76, 93
Black literary tradition (male), 49–50, 53–55
Black literary tradition (female), 74, 95–96, 101, 102–04, 237–39
Blackmur, R. P., 155
Blackwell, Elizabeth, 13
Blake, William, 99, 256
Blast (magazine), 97
Blavatsky, Madame, 34
Bleak House (Dickens), 35
"Bleeding" (Swenson), 113
Blithedale Romance, The (Hawthorne), 23–26, 38, 142, 145–47
Bloodsmoor Romance, A (Oates), 215
Bloom, Harold, 195; his "anxiety of influence" theory, 130, 160, 167, 170, 171, 199, 200; concerns about male literary tradition, 131, 133, 254.
Bluest Eye, The (Morrison), 113
Bly, Robert, 3, 61, 220, 263
Bodichon, Barbara, 12, 13
Body as metaphor, 158, 227–51 passim; penis as weapon, 46, 48, 50–52, 56–57, 113–14; penis as pen, 158, 227; womb as mouth, 227, 232–33, 265. *See also* Sexuality
Bogan, Louise, 158, 205, 206
Bostonians, The (James), 80, 98, 215, 246; antifeminism in, 25–28, 31, 130, 235; battle of the sexes in, 38
Bowen, Elizabeth, 112–13
Boy in the Bush, The (Lawrence), 153

Braddon, Mary Elizabeth, 130, 142, 146, 241
Bradley, Marion Zimmer, 116, 117
Bradstreet, Anne, 158, 160
Bridge, The (Crane), 211
Brontë, Anne, 185, 197
Brontë, Charlotte, 70, 159, 192; as precursor, 68, 129, 130, 143, 147, 194–95, 197, 198, 200, 204, 211; precursors of, 169, 179; use of pseudonym, 185, 186, 240. *See also Jane Eyre*
Brontë, Emily, 159, 202; as precursor, 68, 69, 129, 143, 147, 197, 198; use of pseudonym, 185
Brooks, Van Wyck, 143
Broughton, Rhoda, 143, 146
Broumas, Olga, 66, 269
Brown Girl, Brown Stones (Marshall), 114
Browning, Elizabeth Barrett. *See* Barrett Browning, Elizabeth
Browning, Robert, 39
Brownson, Orestes, 173
Bryher (Winifred Ellerman), 147, 242
Buckley, Jerome, 10, 154
Burgess, Anthony, 157, 158
Burne-Jones, Edward, 225, 242
Burney, Fanny, 165, 206
"Burning the Letters" (Plath), 220–24
Burroughs, William, 52
Butler, Samuel, 21, 125, 131
Byron, Lord, 220

Cables to Rage (Lorde), 118
Canon formation, 131, 134, 153–56, 166, 174, 194–208 passim
Cantos, The (Pound), 156
Carlyle, Thomas, 11, 220
"Carol of Words" (Whitman), 254
Carpenter, Edward, 34
Carroll, Lewis, 251, 259
Carter, Angela, 116, 117–18
Cassatt, Mary, 16, 34
Cassidy, Neal, 52
Cat and Mouse Act, 78
Cather, Willa, 254; female autonomy in works by 94, 174–76, 181, 250–51; on women writers, 205, 208; use of pseudonym, 241
Chafe, William, 33, 47
Chambers, Jessie, 153
Chatterton, Thomas, 251
Chaucer, Geoffrey, 142, 252–53
Chicago, Judy, 210
"Child Who Favored Daughter, The" (Walker), 113
Chodorow, Nancy, 265

Cholmondeley, Mary, 176–78, 181, 220
Chopin, Kate, 81, 87, 166, 191–92; and
female aesthetic renunciation, 181–82
Christie, Agatha, 91
"Christmas Banquet, The" (Hawthorne),
23
Churchill, Caryl, 210
Cixous, Hélène, 230, 259
Cleaver, Eldridge, 59–60
Clothing, 14, 15, 99, 110, 117–18;
transvestism, 6, 8, 106, 138; codpieces,
58–59; and suffrage movement, 78
"Clouds" (Ball), 258
Cochran, Josephine, 16
Coleridge, Mary Elizabeth, 207
Coleridge, Samuel Taylor, 255, 256
"Colonel's Lady, The" (Maugham), 140–
41
"Coming, Aphrodite!" (Cather), 94
Common Cause (newspaper), 78
Common Reader, The (Woolf), 126, 201,
204
Common Reader, The, second series
(Woolf), 202, 203, 204
"Company of Wolves, The" (Carter), 117–
18
Comus (Milton), 249
Cooke, Nicholas Francis, 13
Cooper, James Fenimore, 145
Corelli, Marie, 146
"Correspondances" (Baudelaire), 254
Costello, Bonnie, 148
Cota-Cardena, Margarita, 270
Coup de dés, Un (Mallarmé), 258
"Cousin Nancy" (T. S. Eliot), 31
Crane, Hart, 211
Crèvecoeur, J. Hector, 145
"Crime, The" (Beerbohm), 126–29, 131,
165–66, 175, 177, 190, 194, 217, 220–
23
Crippen, Dr., 37
"Critical Fable, A" (Lowell), 205, 218–21
Crow (Hughes), 3
cummings, e. e., 154–55
Cummins, Maria Susanna, 146
"Curse for a Nation, A" (Barrett Brown-
ing), 73
"Cypresses" (Lawrence), 255–56

"Daddy," (Plath), 121
Dancing on the Grave of a Son of a Bitch
(Wakoski), 118
Daniel Deronda (G. Eliot), 72–73, 83, 143,
192
Dante, 156, 252–53, 257
Darwin, Charles, 14, 21, 22

Davies, Emily, 12
Davison, Emily Wilding, 80, 82
Death Comes to the Archbishop (Cather), 251
"Death of the Lion, The" (James), 134
de Beauvoir, Simone, 119, 160
de Feure, George, 233–35
"Demon Lover, The" (Bowen), 112–13
Derrida, Jacques, 237, 252, 258, 261, 270
Deutsch, Helene, 34, 180
Diana of the Crossways (Meredith), 20
"Dichtung and Diction" (S. Gilbert), 259
Dickens, Charles, 35, 47, 91, 112
Dickinson, Emily, 18; as precursor, 66,
177, 206, 208–09, 239–40; on battle of
the sexes, 67, 69, 74, 172; male views
of, 148, 155, 159; and male literary
tradition, 169, 179, 195–96; her fe-
male precursors, 211, 213, 243, 247,
262, 266–67
Diehl, Joanne Feit, 172
Dijkstra, Bram, 28
Dinesen, Isak, 242
Dinner Party (Chicago), 210
Discords (Egerton), 81, 83
Disraeli, Benjamin, 144
Diving into the Wreck (Rich), 118
Dollmaker, The (Arnow), 183
Dolphin, The (R. Lowell), 216
Donne, John, 198
Doolittle, Hilda. See H.D.
"Dorothy Wordsworth" (Woolf), 201–02
Dos Passos, John, 147
Douglas, Ann, 157
Dowding, Hugh, 243
Drabble, Margaret, 208
"Dream of Slaughter, A" (Jackson), 74
Dream Songs, The (Berryman), 159
Dryden, John, 154
"Duchess of Newcastle" (Woolf), 201, 204
Duncan, Isadora, 34
Duncan, Robert, 247
Dutchman (Baraka), 53–54, 158

Edel, Leon, 241
Edgeworth, Maria, 169, 179
Education and women: in Princess, 6–8;
campaign for, 12–13; mockery of, 13–
14, 16, 33; achievement of, 32–33; in
Tarkington, 41; Barrett Browning's interest in, 71–72; turn-of-the-century,
75; Woolf's portrayal of, 91–93; and
women's exclusion from study of the
classics, 243–45, 252–54
Egerton, George, 65, 81–82, 84–88, 241
Egoist, The (magazine), 162
Egoist, The (Meredith), 20